NATO AND THE RANGE
OF AMERICAN CHOICE

INSTITUTE OF WAR AND PEACE STUDIES
OF THE SCHOOL OF INTERNATIONAL AFFAIRS
OF COLUMBIA UNIVERSITY

NATO and the Range of American Choice is one of a series of studies sponsored by the Institute of War and Peace Studies of Columbia University. *Defense and Diplomacy* by Alfred Vagts; *Man, the State, and War* by Kenneth N. Waltz; *The Common Defense: Strategic Programs in National Politics* by Samuel P. Huntington; *Strategy, Politics, and Defense Budgets* by Warner R. Schilling, Paul Y. Hammond, and Glenn H. Snyder; *Political Unification* by Amitai Etzioni; *The Stockpiling of Strategic Materials* by Glenn H. Snyder; and *The Politics of Military Unification* by Demetrios Caraley are other volumes in the series. *Theoretical Aspects of International Relations,* edited by William T. R. Fox; *Inspection for Disarmament,* edited by Seymour Melman; and *Changing Patterns of Military Politics,* edited by Samuel P. Huntington are all volumes of essays planned and edited by Institute members. The Institute of War and Peace Studies and the Russian Institute of Columbia University jointly sponsored the publication of *Political Power: USA/USSR* by Zbigniew Brzezinski and Samuel P. Huntington.

NATO
AND THE RANGE OF
AMERICAN CHOICE

WILLIAM T. R. FOX

ANNETTE B. FOX

COLUMBIA UNIVERSITY PRESS

NEW YORK AND LONDON 1967

Mr. Fox is Professor of International Relations
and Director of the Institute of War and Peace
Studies at Columbia University. Mrs. Fox is Research Associate of the Institute of War and
Peace Studies.

Copyright © 1967 Columbia University Press
Library of Congress Catalog Card Number: 67-11560
Printed in the United States of America

To the memory of

MYRTLE PERRIGO FOX

AND

JOHN SHARPLESS FOX

PREFACE

THIS is a book about the United States government in NATO and not about NATO itself. *NATO and the Range of American Choice*, like a number of other Institute of War and Peace Studies publications, is much more a study of the policy process than an evaluation of past policies or a prescription for future United States action. Only by understanding how the United States has developed its policies for and in NATO can one discover how the policy process may be made more effective.

We were led to undertake this study by a request from Professor Max Beloff of Oxford University, on behalf of the North Atlantic Studies Committee, to write the United States volume in a series of studies of the impact on governmental institutions of NATO countries resulting from post-World War II commitments to participate in NATO-like organizations. Our study is the fifth of the series to be published.[1]

For help in preparing this study our debts are numerous, substantial, and varied. If they cannot be repaid, they can be acknowledged: to the Ford Foundation for financial support of the research program of the School of International Affairs, of which the Institute of War and Peace Studies is a part, while *NATO and the Range of American Choice* was

---

[1] The four studies previously published are Professor Beloff's British study, *New Dimensions in Foreign Policy* (London: George Allen and Unwin, 1961); Rudolf Wildenmann's German study, *Macht und Konsens als Problem der Innen- und Aussen-politik* (Frankfurt am Main: Athenäum Verlag, 1963); Einar Löchen's *Norway in European and Atlantic Co-operation* (Oslo: Universitetsforlaget, 1964); and a symposium volume prepared by an interuniversity study group of Belgium's Institut Royal des Relations Internationales, *Les conséquences d'ordre interne de la participation de la Belgique aux organisations internationales* (La Haye: M. Nijhoff, 1964).

being written; to the Rockefeller Foundation for support during 1962–
1963; to the unnamed persons in Washington, Paris, and elsewhere
whom we interviewed; to our colleagues in the Institute of War and
Peace Studies and fellow members of the University Seminar on the
Atlantic Community, whose discussions of our project clarified many
doubtful points; to the *Political Science Quarterly* for permission to re-
publish in revised form Mrs. Fox's article, "NATO and Congress," as
Chapter VIII of the present book; to Professor James L. McCamy of
the University of Wisconsin for some felicitous suggestions which we
gladly accepted; to Jane B. Schilling for painstaking and sensitive
editing while the authors were several thousand miles away; to Professor
Warner R. Schilling, in 1966 acting director of the Institute of War
and Peace Studies, as involuntary consultant on very many trouble-
some questions of detail; and to Anna K. Hohri, who assembled a
valuable clipping file on the United States and NATO and with her
staff produced typescripts of successive drafts of this study.

We also wish to acknowledge permission to quote passages from
Dean Acheson's *Sketches from Life of Men I Have Known,* published
by Harper & Row, Publishers, Inc., and from Alastair Buchan's *NATO
in the 1960's* (revised edition), published in the United States by
Frederick A. Praeger, Inc.

We do not believe that either the war in Vietnam or President de
Gaulle's announcement in March, 1966 that all French forces would
be withdrawn from NATO commands and French personnel from
NATO military planning activities have made it necessary to alter our
main conclusions. Illustrative details are another matter, and some of
these will inevitably be out of date before this book leaves the press.
The problem remains for the United States government and the American people to learn, not merely by trial and error but whatever possible
by retrospective analysis, how to use wisely the international institutions
which since 1945 have been growing in the wide North American–
West European zone of peace.

                                                                                    A. B. F.
                                                                                    W. T. R. F.

Columbia University
August 17, 1966

CONTENTS

ABBREVIATIONS
AND SHORT TITLES

ACDA	Arms Control and Disarmament Agency
ACE	Allied Command Europe
AEC	Atomic Energy Commission
AGARD	Advisory Group for Aeronautical Research and Development
AID	Agency for International Development
AIRCENT	Allied Air Forces Central Europe
ANZUS	Australia–New Zealand–United States alliance
BANK	International Bank for Reconstruction and Development
BMEWS	Ballistic Missiles Early Warning System
CENTO	Central Treaty Organization
CERN	European Center for Nuclear Research
CIA	Central Intelligence Agency
CINCEUR	Commander-in-Chief, Europe [United States]
COCOM	Coordinating Committee for the Control of the Export of Strategic Goods to the Soviet Bloc
DEW-line	Distant Early Warning line
ECOSOC	Economic and Social Council [of the United Nations]
EDC	European Defense Community
EEC	European Economic Community
EFTA	European Free Trade Association
ELDO	European Launcher Development Organization
ESRO	European Space Research Organization
Euratom	European Atomic Community
Fund	International Monetary Fund
FY	fiscal year
GATT	General Agreement on Tariffs and Trade
GNP	gross national product
IAEA	International Atomic Energy Agency

IBRD	International Bank for Reconstruction and Development
ICBM	intercontinental ballistic missile
IDA	International Development Association
IFC	International Finance Corporation
IMF	International Monetary Fund
IRBM	intermediate-range ballistic missile
ISA	Office of the Assistant Secretary of Defense for International Security Affairs
ITO	International Trade Organization
JCAE	Joint Committee on Atomic Energy
JCS	Joint Chiefs of Staff
MAAG	Military Assistance Advisory Group
MLF	Multilateral Force
MMRBM	mobile medium-range ballistic missile
MRBM	medium-range ballistic missile
NASA	National Aeronautics and Space Administration
NATO	North Atlantic Treaty Organization
NORAD	North American Air Defense Command
NSC	National Security Council
OAS	Organization of American States
OECD	Organization for Economic Cooperation and Development
OEEC	Organization for European Economic Cooperation
POLAD	Political Adviser [to certain United States military commanders]
SAC	Strategic Air Command
SACEUR	Supreme Allied Commander Europe
SACLANT	Supreme Allied Commander Atlantic
SAGE	Semi-automatic Ground Environment system
SEATO	Southeast Asia Treaty Organization
SHAEF	Supreme Headquarters, Allied Expeditionary Force
SHAPE	Supreme Headquarters Allied Power Europe
USIA	United States Information Agency
USRO	United States Mission to Regional Organizations [in Paris]
WEU	Western European Union

NATO AND THE RANGE
OF AMERICAN CHOICE

CHAPTER ONE

THE TREATY AND THE ORGANIZATION

THE CORE of the North Atlantic Treaty is the military guarantee in Article 5. Not long after the signing of the treaty in April, 1949, came the Soviet success in breaking the American atomic monopoly and the armed attack on South Korea. As a consequence of these radical changes in world politics, the Atlantic allies implemented their military commitment to each other by establishing a North Atlantic Treaty *Organization* for coalition military planning and diplomatic effort. To sign the treaty and to join in creating the organization were each unprecedented steps for the United States.

Not surprisingly, the habit and the obligation of taking part in NATO activities have brought changes in the United States' conduct of its foreign affairs. Americans commonly view NATO as an instrument, to be used or set aside as American convenience of the moment may dictate; but they often overlook NATO's reverse impact on American policy processes. It has altered American estimates of what can and ought to be done; it may have changed attitudes as to who the "we" are in whose name the United States may have to act and whose consent has first to be gained. As governments in a prosperous and revived Europe have become confident and articulate, as they have in the 1960s, that impact has taken on new significance.

With the United States the strongest of the non-Communist powers in a bipolar world, American ways of conducting foreign affairs would have changed greatly in any case. No one can say precisely how much these changes are to be explained by the new imperatives of world politics and how much by United States participation in such multilateral organizations as NATO. In spite of this difficulty, it is important, as pressures grow to modify NATO, to find out how the North Atlantic Treaty Organization of the 1950s and 1960s has affected United States methods of making and implementing its foreign policy and national security decisions.

Since World War II American policy towards the countries of Europe has less and less been developed one country at a time; relations with any one country inevitably have affected that country's relations with others. Whole sets of intra-European relationships are of the most immediate concern to Americans. Although most negotiations continue to be bilateral, they are by no means exclusively so. Not only NATO but also the European Communities and the Organization for Economic Co-operation and Development (until 1961 the Organization for European Economic Cooperation) are forums for multilateral negotiation. So are numerous United Nations agencies. United States foreign policy should be all of a piece; and American policy for Europe must take sufficient account of American concerns in other parts of the world; else it will not even be adequate for Europe. These other concerns have led the United States to join in additional regional organizations.

Like NATO, these other organizations, for which the United States has also been a major sponsor, cause Americans and the nationals of the member states to identify with each other in new ways. They create new sets of expectations regarding the actions of the members, and they permit the articulation of new demands by the United States and the others on each other. They also provide additional machinery—cumbersome almost to the point of uselessness in some cases—through which the United States can pursue particular objectives. Furthermore, they tend to take on a life of their own regardless of American action. Are such organizations, with the additional assents required, just so many more obstacles to effective policy? Or do they on balance provide genuine opportunities to accomplish more than the United States could achieve if acting by itself? If they do not, they only complicate the task of the foreign-policy makers by increasing the number of ways and the number of situations in which the United States must formally consider the views of others.

In practically any organization there are both centrifugal and centripetal forces. Each member weighs the gains from participation against the cost of reduced freedom of action and of additional responsibilities incurred; the United States is no exception. In NATO this means comparing the increased security derived from collective defense with the increased risk of having to make good on a guarantee to contribute to the safety of fellow members. Those who are convinced that the gains of combined action far outrun the risks may give a high priority to achieving an alliance-wide consensus, even at the expense of policies they might otherwise have preferred. In other regional organizations also, Americans become anxious about conflicts among members which in the absence of such a formal combination they might regard as insignificant. The history of the United Nations General Assembly clearly illustrates these same tendencies. Once the members agree on a policy, however, each may be additionally strengthened by consensus organized in advance of the need to use it. For NATO this means a more effective deterrent because armed forces of the coalition have been collected and made ready.

Organizing such consent is the very essence of the political process within the organization but a subject not widely studied. Even less attention has been paid to how common policy is implemented, which is also part of the political process. Most of the implementing part of the process takes place inside the nation-state, even in the case of the "supranational" European Communities.

Even serious students of this process often confuse action policy and declaratory policy.[1] In the United States as elsewhere, leaders may announce their intentions, but fail to arrange for their practical implementation. They elaborate myths of international cooperation, which seems to obviate the need for taking effective steps in the announced direction. Some myth-making is essential to organizations, but the propagation of myths is no substitute for action if the organization is to continue to be taken seriously by member governments. Scholars ought not to swallow the myths, no matter how advantageous it is for others to do so.

How wide is the gap between words and deeds, between pretension and accomplishment, in any given regional organization? One measure is the extent to which the members fail to observe the policy agreements they have made with each other or act contrary to the declarations of

---

[1] This distinction is made by Paul H. Nitze in "Atoms, Strategy and Policy," *Foreign Affairs,* January, 1956, pp. 187–98.

their leaders. To refuse to modify national policies after formally agreeing to do so is to render the organization ineffective.[2] It is not, however, unambiguous violation of or faithful observance of formal agreements which furnishes the bulk of the evidence regarding accomplishment. There are many instances in which American preaching and practice have failed to correspond. In 1962 Henry Kissinger complained that Americans "have tended to confuse our periodic expressions of reassurance with the creation of a true partnership, and the muffling of European expressions of concern with meeting the cause of concern." [3] On the other hand, there are also remarkable examples of effective American leadership in truly cooperative conduct.

If our concern were only to determine how collective is a particular international organization, a study of the record of American participation might be misleading. The United States would not be a typical member; and its very atypicality makes more difficult a genuinely collective development for NATO—or any other organization in which it participates. In any case, formal tests to gauge the degree of cooperation are likely to be too simple. In a pluralistic state there are many selves with many goals in the name of which the government acts. Some of these selves overlap with those in other pluralistic states; an international organization may provide opportunities for these "transnational selves" to move toward their specific goals. Where goals differ, there may be conflict, either within the state or internationally. Just as claims based on different value preferences have to be adjusted to each other in domestic politics, so similar adjustments can be looked for in an international organization. In both national and international arenas one task of the policy-maker is to accommodate as much as possible the many diverging claims which erode the common interest, or at least to reduce conflict enough to allow the collectivity to move ahead in promoting the interests which are shared.

Such a task is enormously difficult for American policy-makers. A serious restraint on the operations of the United States in international organizations is the American political system. Familiar to and often feared by many of its allies are the central features of its Constitution:

---

[2] See Ernst B. Haas, "Regional Integration and National Policy," *International Conciliation,* May, 1957, p. 384, for some indices of national resistance to collective action.

[3] "The Unsolved Problems of European Defense," *Foreign Affairs,* July, 1962, p. 541.

the tripartite separation of powers and the federal distribution of powers. The gargantuan size of the American government, its characteristic division into many contending quasi-sovereignties, and the publicity with which it operates further impede unified and decisive action. Raymond Aron speaks of it as "the most talkative and on surface the most incoherent political system in the world."[4]

There are external restraints, too. American interests are truly global, but they are not unlimited. The power of the United States is very great, but it too is limited. The policies of allies (forty-two of them in 1966) and of uncommitted countries whose good will Americans desire to maintain require the United States to adjust its own course of action to some extent. Their policies are, however, often incompatible with each other, and sometimes totally incompatible with those of the United States. Yet arguments in support of such policies are strongly put—and heard—in a large number of international organizations. The United States government's range of effective choice may also be limited by precedents it has already set and mistakes which cannot be completely undone.[5] The diversified challenge of the Communists calls for a wide variety of techniques to meet it; but some of those proposed are, at least publicly, out of bounds for Americans.

Whatever may be the case with allies in general in the 1960s the United States is no longer free to be inattentive to the views of its European allies, whether policy differences reflect divergent interests or different views as to how best to promote their common interests. The day of European dependence on American largesse is past, and the constraints which hope of further American financial aid might have imposed have disappeared. Furthermore, with the development of Soviet intercontinental ballistic missiles, Europeans look critically at American promises the fulfillment of which would expose American cities to thermonuclear attack. Dissuaded from launching thermonuclear attacks on each other, the two superpowers, they fear, may again find in Europe the critical zone of confrontation. So long as the United States is believed reluctant to protect its European allies by using atomic weapons if they become

[4] "Reflections on American Diplomacy," *Daedalus*, Fall, 1962, p. 719. Cf. Alastair Buchan: "Certainly no system of government is less suited to the leadership of an alliance than the American . . . ." [*NATO in the 1960's* (New York: Frederick A. Praeger, 1960), p. 44]. This quotation does not appear in the 1963 revised edition.

[5] Cf. Stanley Hoffman, "Restraints and Choices in American Foreign Policy," *Daedalus*, Fall, 1962, p. 678.

necessary to check non-atomic attacks, it cannot expect automatic acceptance of its proposals. To win cooperation of NATO allies in Europe, the United States must itself be ready to cooperate in such a way that European misgivings may be lessened. Does American behavior suggest that the "we" in whose name the free world is to be defended includes men and women on both sides of the Atlantic?

Admittedly, the United States remains the most free to take policy initiatives; but in the absence of agreed policies several other NATO members are quite capable of taking initiatives which can get all the rest into trouble, as the Suez debacle clearly demonstrated.[6] There can be no dictation, for the members remain free to act independently on matters deemed vital to their security. The controversy over a nuclear role for NATO and especially for some of its European members demonstrates the depth of misgivings over an American policy which does not command alliance-wide support and arouses criticisms even at home. It also demonstrates the American policy-maker's dilemma when he thinks he must choose between a more efficient policy and one that will gain wider acceptance in NATO.

Let us remind ourselves of some of NATO's relevant characteristics. It is extremely large for an alliance—fifteen members, counting France —and extremely diversified as to the kind of states which belong, even though all share in Western culture and all border on the North Atlantic or its Mediterranean and North Sea extensions. The members vary greatly in involvement when particular crises arise around the world. For Germany and for some of the smaller states NATO has represented the backbone of their security policy; but at least three of the largest members have on occasion found it convenient to ignore NATO. Each state also bears marks of its unique history and unique geographical situation, both of which inhibit complete cooperation. As the threat of Soviet-Western military conflict has come to seem less immediate, internal dissension has grown more marked, and NATO's future has more often been questioned. Moreover, NATO is unlike the United Nations; for if it were to wither, the public outcry in the United States might not be great. Over the years NATO's functions have been modified, but the attentive public tends to see it for what, strictly and formally speaking, it has been all along, a military alliance and a way to allocate more rationally the military effort of a coalition of states.

[6] See Geoffrey Crowther, "Reconstruction of an Alliance," *Foreign Affairs,* January, 1957, p. 174.

One can view NATO in several ways: as an international institution which formulates a program to deal with threats emanating from outside the NATO area; as a forum for bargaining among its members; and as an instrument of member governments to implement their respective policies. Choosing the third focus, we look for signs of the reciprocal influences of NATO and American government policy processes on each other. What role does membership in NATO and comparable organizations play in the definition and implementation of American foreign policy objectives? Ernest May has distinguished between "calculated" and "axiomatic" policies, the latter more often rooted in history, the former more volatile.[7] On the calculated level, NATO has helped the United States to protect itself against a specific serious threat in a specific time period, the expansionism of the Soviet Union in the decades after World War II. If this threat should cease to exist, NATO might also disappear, unless the organization had meanwhile developed functions related to other aspects of the members' foreign policy.[8] In contrast, the foreign policy reasons for United States membership in certain economic organizations might appear "axiomatic"; for the desire for increased prosperity is unlikely to disappear, and the underlying reasons for economic cooperation seem more durable. Some organizations, such as the Organization of American States, are believed to serve several different foreign policy objectives at once; and the deeply rooted Pan-

[7] "The Nature of Foreign Policy: The Calculated versus the Axiomatic," *Daedalus*, Fall, 1962, pp. 653–67.

[8] As Ernst B. Haas demonstrates in his *Beyond the Nation-State: Functionalism and International Organization* (Stanford, California: Stanford University Press, 1964), the International Labor Organization did survive after the conditions that prevailed at the time of its creation ceased to exist. The ILO successfully adapted to the post-World War II world and the era of disimperialism. The ILO and its secretariat, the International Labor Office, survived because they appeared to their new clients to be serving the purposes of these clients. To the extent that NATO is the victim of its own success and is no longer relied upon to serve the members' shared purpose of the early 1950s it too must adapt or wither. But, like the ILO, NATO's viability and potential importance must be assessed at any given time in terms of the identifications, expectations, and demands prevailing at that time. In the definition of new common tasks knowledge of success in performing the old tasks, the habit of collaboration, and the integrative sentiments fostered by this collaboration are all conditioning factors.

Note, however, the differing emphases of the Haas study and our own. He stresses the unintended integrative consequences of widespread participation in a limited-purpose international organization for the *international* system. We ask how NATO and the participation of the United States in NATO affect the range of *American* choice. Inevitably, both studies have had to deal with modifications of both international and national political systems induced by a state's participation in an international organization.

American tradition is likely to continue in some form so long as Latin-Americans live in the same hemisphere with the United States. Despite its apparently more "calculated" basis for existing, NATO has called forth in dollars and men a far greater commitment than any other regional or functional organization. The record may at times be spotty; but for the most part it upholds what Secretary of State Rusk said on August 13, 1962: "NATO is not a limited liability company. For us, and for our allies, the defense of NATO requires whatever means are necessary. . . . We consider that the safety of NATO as a whole is critical to our own security." [9]

NATO might be called a fourth step in a progression of organizational adaptations to twentieth-century security requirements. The first, early in this century, was the creation of the Army general staff; it reflected a recognition of the need for military policy. Then came a series of interservice planning devices culminating in the World War II establishment of the Joint Chiefs of Staff and the postwar creation of the Department of Defense. After a variety of experiments with interdepartmental planning devices, the third step was the formation of the National Security Council. The fourth step has been the formation of an institution for effective coalition planning arrangements. The wartime agencies which so greatly facilitated Anglo-American combined action were the precursors of NATO in this fourth organizational adaptation.

Viewed in this context, American participation in NATO appears to have been the logical next step. The initiative for an alliance came from some of its other members; but in its transformation into an organization for continuous, coalition defense planning American leaders quickly picked up and shaped the original idea to fit American security requirements. In doing so, they were also ensuring that the United States could implement its guarantee to the other members.

Because of the vastness of the United States bureaucratic machinery and the great range of Congress' legislative concerns a very small proportion of policy-making can be principally oriented toward NATO or any other international organization. Pressures generated in such an organization may pose issues which the United States cannot evade, but the response is unlikely to involve a radical change in American policy.

The problems of the American government in collaborating are in any case difficult; but collaboration in security matters apparently poses

[9] Dean Rusk, *The Winds of Freedom* (Boston: Beacon Press, 1963), p. 646.

unique problems. Exchanges of information may be sufficient to provide the basis for roughly parallel action in economic matters; but agreement has to be exact and complete for coalition defense, especially in what might be a very short war. The pressures for military cooperation, so long as the common threat is great, may be more potent than those for economic collaboration; but the collaborative activity may come closer to the heart of a state's sovereignty. With a reviving sense of security the cement holding a military organization together may be insufficient to maintain international military cooperation, whereas realization of the ever expanding promises of gain from economic cooperation may make for still more such cooperation. On the other hand, an economic organization may adversely affect interest groups powerful in domestic politics; these can thus impede a rational program of international collaboration.

Several difficulties confront the analyst who would assess the reciprocal impacts of an international organization and the United States government. For example, how far can we isolate changes in decision-making due to membership in the organization from those due to other new requirements faced by the government, internally and internationally? Also, one must be especially careful to observe *changes* in impact. We are not appraising states of affairs but patterns of evolution, which involve goals, environment, and instruments in interaction.[10] Both the international organization and the United States are evolving, and in addition there are major transformations taking place in world politics. By keeping an eye on simultaneous courses of evolution we may discover that NATO (as well as other comparable international organizations) is an outward symbol of other changes.

In this study we compare American expectations with the actual role played by the United States in NATO and also relate American claims on the organization to the techniques used to advance these claims. To pursue our inquiry we examine not only decisions involving national security and the Soviet military threat but also those involving arms control, "disimperialism," and international cooperation for an expanded economy and for assistance to underdeveloped countries. We investigate policies in which NATO instrumentalities might have been used but

[10] Cf. Max F. Millikan, "Inquiry and Policy: The Relation of Knowledge to Action," in Daniel Lerner (ed.), *The Human Meaning of the Social Sciences* (New York: Meridian Books, 1959), pp. 174–77.

were not, as well as those in which NATO played a major role. Our inquiry gives brief attention to certain other international agencies but only for purposes of comparison: the Organization of American States, the Southeast Asia Treaty Organization, the Organization for Economic Cooperation and Development, the International Bank for Reconstruction and Development, the International Monetary Fund, and the General Agreement on Tariffs and Trade. We point to instances where formal commitment has not eventuated in action at the national level, as well as where it has.

It is impossible to prove a close causal relationship between specific commitments to an international organization and specific choices in United States policy. Nevertheless, we can hope to learn something from an examination of trends in the frequency with which NATO seems to be considered in the making of important American decisions. Our study covers sixteen years of experience.

For evidence we depend upon Congressional hearings, official reports, interviews, written reminiscences, records of Americans who have been in and out of offices related to the above-mentioned international organizations, and monographs on particular aspects of these organizations and related topics.

The contribution to theoretical knowledge of either American government or international relations which a single case permits can only be modest and at a rather low level of generalization. Nevertheless, the effort seems justified: we are dealing with a relatively new framework for action in a rapidly changing field of politics and with a situation which calls for greater sophistication among policy-makers than in earlier periods. NATO and related international organizations are presumably something more than unself-consciously hypocritical expressions of illusory or transitory unity. If this be so, there are likely to be changes in the American way of making public policy which are the logical consequence of American participation in each of the organizations. Rational action to promote the interests which have led to American participation (and to promote interests which participation makes possible) depends upon an awareness of these changes, especially when the record suggests that such changes in the policy process have in fact not yet occurred. Where they have not, the gap between official hopes for a given policy and the gains subsequently achieved will be unnecessarily wide.

Our concern is to understand more clearly some aspects of the political process within NATO and only incidentally to assess its effectiveness in coping with substantive problems. Formal organization and policy product are significant to us here mainly as they relate to the way in which the giant member participates.

Within this rather restricted context a number of generalizations are possible. They pertain to the opportunities offered by and the constraints entailed by membership, to burden-sharing and gain-sharing in international organizations, to the complicated and multiple balance of power inside as well as outside the organization, to the way in which the organizations arouse public interest or become subject to the scrutiny of unofficial interest groups, to confidence levels and specialization of functions among the members, to the transcending of parochial perspectives by those who have participated in international organizations, to the rigidity of policy developed in international organizations, to improved accuracy of perceptions regarding other members' behavior and preferences. We may also cast light on the validity of others' observations, such as George Liska's statement that "modes of integration and commitment can help restrain both the adversary and the scope of conflict. And they can help allies restrain each other." [11]

Other kinds of generalizations can be made about how membership in international organizations affects the way in which the United States government operates. These generalizations deal with such subjects as coordinating procedures and methods of accountability. They also concern the distribution of power between the executive and the legislative branches and raise questions about the extent to which public officials are aware of the full implications of partnership. Those whose intellectual concerns with the NATO type of organizations are theoretical as well as practical may wish to refer to Appendix A, "One Model of an Organized Alliance."

Where is NATO to be located on a continuum between an old-fashioned alliance with a few modern trimmings and a supranational body which has assumed attributes formerly associated with sovereignty? Where along this continuum, and in which direction NATO is moving, may become clearer after an examination of its impact on the leading member. Is it approaching a point where the representatives of the members are legislating, rather than conducting a modern variation of traditional diplomacy? Are the common interests which run counter

[11] *Nations in Alliance* (Baltimore: Johns Hopkins Press, 1962), p. 138.

to specific members' interests promoted by appropriate national action? Can an organization ostensibly among equal sovereign states accommodate one which is a giant with respect to all the others and still maintain its international character? Is harmonization of national policies sufficient to meet the common problems? How feasible does it appear for the United States to pursue the publicly enunciated objective of some kind of Atlantic Community with or without an integrated Europe? Do the peculiarities of the United States government present insuperable obstacles to greater unity among the Western nations?

To answer these and similar questions certain aspects in the evolution of NATO need to be reviewed. Chapter II provides this background. Appendix B contains comparable information on other international organizations.

CHAPTER TWO

THE DEVELOPMENT OF NATO AND OTHER ORGANIZATIONS

OUR DISCUSSION in this chapter is focused on certain threads in NATO's evolution which pertain especially to our subject, namely, developments with respect to the overall power relationship, the kinds of problems dealt with, methods chosen to deal with them, the alliance relationship and problems outside the NATO area, and NATO's relationship to other international organizations. We also trace the evolution of the process by which the organization decides to take action. Finally, we compare NATO, as it has developed, with the Organization of American States, the Southeast Asia Treaty Organization, the Organization for Economic Cooperation and Development, and certain United Nations specialized agencies dealing with economic matters— all these being either regional security organizations or economic groupings with comparable features.[1] Details regarding these other organizations appear in Appendix B.

IMPLEMENTING THE COMMITMENT

The North Atlantic Treaty registered the determination of twelve European and North American states to prevent further expansion by Soviet Russia, whose hostile, imperialist drives had become overwhelmingly evident with the coup in Czechoslovakia and the Berlin Blockade. Clearly the United Nations was unable to cope with this kind of threat. Signed April 4, 1949, the Treaty was erected on foundations laid in the

[1] We have omitted ANZUS. Although it is a functioning alliance characterized by regular consultations and a rather high degree of informal coordination, it lacks formal institutions.

1948 Brussels Pact between England, France, and the Benelux countries, a pact which, like the earlier Anglo-French Dunkirk Treaty, had ostensibly been aimed at protecting the members against a resurgent Germany. The ink had hardly dried on the Treaty of Brussels when Secretary of State Marshall, Under Secretary Lovett, and Senator Vandenberg, strongly supported by President Truman, had begun to explore ways of so involving the United States as to link these tentative steps in a wider guarantee. The Canadian Prime Minister, Louis St. Laurent, had made an important contribution by his call, in April, 1948, for a comprehensive mutual defense system to include and supersede the Brussels arrangements. Other states had expressed an interest in joining an alliance. The Brussels Pact signatories, together with Canada and the United States, therefore invited Denmark, Norway, Iceland, Portugal, and Italy to participate in the negotiations out of which came the agreement to enter into a treaty of mutual guarantee. (Sweden and Ireland had already indicated their unwillingness to join.) Although the Soviet Union was not named in the treaty, there was no doubt against whom it was directed.[2]

The pact was originally, like most old-fashioned defensive alliances, simply a political commitment; its signatories contemplated no formal organization to implement it. Senator Vandenberg, in July, 1949, interpreted its meaning as follows: "Whoever is attacked will have dependable allies who will do their dependable part, by constitutional process, as swiftly as possible to defeat the aggressor by whatever means it deems necessary." [3] Then came the Communist attack on South Korea in June, 1950. The allies realized that something more concrete than the commitments of mutual guarantee were necessary to prevent similar

[2] Prior to the conclusion of the negotiations for the alliance, the Soviet Union had already set the pattern of trying to prevent it from being effective.

[3] For the origin, see Lord Ismay, *NATO: The First Five Years, 1949–1954* (Paris: NATO, n.d.); Ben T. Moore, *NATO and the Future of Europe* (New York: Harper and Brothers, 1958); M. Margaret Ball, *NATO and the European Movement* (London: Stevens and Sons, 1959); Harry S. Truman, *Memoirs*, vol. II (Garden City: Doubleday and Co., 1956); Arthur H. Vandenberg, Jr. (ed.), *The Private Papers of Senator Vandenberg* (Boston: Houghton Mifflin Co., 1952); NATO Information Service, *Facts about the North Atlantic Treaty Organization* (Paris: NATO, 1962); Walter Millis, Harvey C. Mansfield, and Harold Stein, *Arms and the State* (New York: Twentieth Century Fund, 1958), pp. 212–13, 221–23 and 237–38. See also Dirk U. Stikker, *Men of Responsibility* (New York: Harper and Row, 1966), for important details on NATO's origins. This valuable memoir appeared too late to be cited at several other points in our study for which it provides additional, confirming data.

aggression in Europe. In September, 1950 the allies agreed to establish an organization in Paris that would carry on joint military planning and to set up combined commands over armed forces assigned by most of the members to defend the continental European theater. The various commands were brought under the political supervision of a "North Atlantic Council" of the twelve nations. A "Supreme Headquarters Allied Powers Europe" (SHAPE) was established in a Paris suburb, under the command of a "Supreme Allied Commander Europe" (SACEUR). There was universal acclaim for President Truman's nomination of General Eisenhower for this post. The sense of urgency attending these arrangements is shown by the comment of a subsequent SACEUR, General Lauris Norstad, to the effect that the question asked in 1951 and 1952 was not whether war would come but "Which month of this year will it start?"

The new alignment in world politics to which the North Atlantic Treaty was a response was underscored by three subsequent events. In December, 1951, an exchange of notes among twenty-four interested states released Italy, for all practical purposes, from restraints imposed by the 1947 peace treaty. (The answer given to the protesting Soviet Union and Czechoslovakia was that the treaty had already been violated when Russia opposed Italy's entrance into the United Nations.)[4] In October, 1951 the "Atlantic" connotation in the treaty became further attenuated with the accession of Greece and Turkey. But the most dramatic and significant addition to the membership came late in 1954 when Germany was admitted. The previously proposed European Defense Community had been intended to solve the problem of obtaining needed German military forces and of making good on a NATO "forward strategy" which would include West Germany. After the French Parliament rejected the EDC, the objective of bringing Germany into the European defense scheme was instead achieved by expanding the Western European Union to seven members (the Brussels Pact members plus Italy and Germany) and by tying this organization to NATO for certain functions. In order to calm French fears of a rearmed Germany SACEUR's powers were expanded to ensure in effect, that all German armed forces would be under his command, and at the same time the

[4] Senate Committee on Appropriations, Subcommittee, *Hearings, Foreign Assistance Act for 1962,* 87th Cong., 1st sess. (1961), p. 160 [which refers to exchange of notes between Italy and 24 interested states, December 1951].

members declared that the North Atlantic Treaty was of "indefinite duration." [5] (The terms of the treaty itself permitted review of its provisions after ten years and withdrawal of a member after twenty.) Despite provisions which were intended to prevent the former enemy from again becoming a danger, such as that prohibiting Germany from manufacturing atomic weapons, German entrance into NATO clearly meant that the other allies were throwing down the gauntlet to the Soviet Union. The challenge was not really accepted until the Berlin ultimatum in 1958, a move that followed a number of dramatic improvements in the strategic power of the Soviet Union, the most significant being Russia's demonstration of missile and space technology leadership in 1957.

The West's management of the 1958 Berlin crisis illustrated a feature of NATO which could have been evident to all from the beginning: it contained a nucleus of the largest Western powers organized around an Anglo-American kernel which dated from an earlier period. It was an unstable nucleus, since it contained France, whose leader, President de Gaulle, began in 1963 to bring about the most serious crisis of confidence that the organization had suffered in its very long history of crises. (None of these crises was directly caused by the Soviet Union, against whom the alliance had been founded.)

Even before the NATO command was established, military plans had been made for three contingencies: war beginning almost immediately; war held off for a year or two, permitting that much build-up of the alliance's defenses; and a longer period for build-up. Plans for the second and third contingencies were further developed when the permanent military structure of NATO was established. Visualizing conditions like those that had characterized the later stages of World War II, the planners sought forces which would deter a Soviet attack, or failing that, would prevent a Russian occupation of Europe. These objectives posed the problems of developing a large force or combination of forces (in an early stage envisaged at about one hundred divisions) and of securing ample territory for defending Western Europe (which inevitably meant the inclusion of West Germany). Despite substantial agreement among the allies at the time of the Korean War on how to meet these problems, a gap developed between what the European members were

[5] *Department of State Bulletin,* October 11, 1954, p. 520; *ibid.,* November 8, 1954, pp. 852–55.

in fact willing to contribute and what the military planners thought was necessary.[6] Meanwhile, the European allies continued to rely on the United States Strategic Air Command to deter a Russian nuclear attack on Europe and on the very substantial United States ground forces stationed in Europe alongside the other members' troops. However, the security problem faced by NATO changed rapidly after the Russians began their astonishingly swift advances in nuclear technology and missilery. Not only Europe but also North America eventually became vulnerable. During this period a bewildering variety of choices was opened up to the Western allies by the development of different kinds of atomic weapons, especially tactical weapons, and the acquisition of some nuclear capability by Britain and later France. By 1963, unsettled strategic questions seriously threatened the solidarity of the alliance. Such problems had been chronic from almost the beginning, but they grew increasingly acute with the changing perspectives about the Russian threat and the internal rivalries among the larger members of the alliance.

Although the main problems which brought NATO into existence were military, others flowed from these; and several of them were faced at once by the founders of the alliance. Article 2, providing for economic and cultural cooperation, reflected a fear that the asserted common bonds might prove insufficient to hold the "Atlantic" countries together unless they were strengthened in ways not directly related to military cooperation.[7] Unlike the other organizations, notably the OEEC, that were being promoted on the economic front, NATO was not confined to Europe, but spanned the Atlantic, presenting greater difficulties in cohesion.[8] On numerous occasions up to 1956 questions were raised regarding NATO's role in dealing with economic problems; the report of the second group of "Three Wise Men" more or less ended this discussion. The allies agreed that most economic questions were better left to other, more appropriate agencies. But another problem, the coordination of the members' foreign policies, has been an increasingly pressing

---

[6] For the early strategy, see Roger Hilsman, "NATO: The Developing Strategic Context," in Klaus Knorr (ed.), *NATO and American Security* (Princeton: Princeton University Press, 1959), pp. 13–24.

[7] Moore, *op. cit.*, p. 10. It also softened the treaty for those who did not like old-fashioned alliances.

[8] *Ibid.*, p. 26.

one. (This whole question and the effort to deal with it by "political consultation" are examined later.)

Coordination, or at least consultation, came to seem increasingly important as the NATO members became aware that the region defined by the treaty (roughly Europe, North America, and Algeria) represented only part of the area in which the members could encounter the threat of Soviet expansion. No satisfactory way has yet been found for dealing within NATO with the broadening scope of the Communist threat, nor for enlarging the means by which the increasingly complicated non-military Communist instrumentalities can be countered. However, such problems are regularly discussed in the North Atlantic Council.

The growth in the membership of NATO halted at fifteen, but France announced its withdrawal from the organization in March 1966. Aside from the European neutrals, the only other serious candidate for membership, Spain, has been excluded because some of the European members do not wish to be allied with Generalissimo Franco. The United States, however, has close military ties with Spain, including permission to use air and naval bases on Spanish territory, and to some extent the other NATO members profit from an arrangement in which they do not have to have a part.

Similarly, the United States, France, and Great Britain each belong to non-European regional security organizations which might have been more closely associated with NATO but for the unwillingness of some NATO members to be bound to them in any way. In the case of the OAS, there was reluctance on both sides. A combination consisting solely of NATO-member states which is nevertheless only indirectly bound in with NATO procedures is the Canadian-American North American Air Defense Command, with its headquarters in Colorado.

Writing in 1959, Paul Nitze outlined five functions which NATO was performing: drawing a line to give the Communists clear notice of the United States commitment to intervene if this line were violated; keeping enough American forces on the continent to show the United States' determination to honor this commitment; providing collectively enough forces to restrain a probing attack of some dimensions, though not enough to halt a major invasion; providing ready and secure forces which would be in a position to deter a major attack; and constituting an organizational framework and political symbol capable of allowing the Western powers so to coordinate their economic and political power as to balance the Communist bloc.[9] This is a fair—if abbreviated—statement of what NATO does; how does it perform these functions?

The outstanding operating feature of the North Atlantic alliance is that it has an integrated force-in-being in peacetime. This is, however, confined to NATO's central front and has never reached the full size agreed upon a year after NATO's command structure and organization were established. In addition, all members except Iceland (whose contribution is in the form of an airbase) have agreed to maintain reserves which would be available to NATO if needed. Only one member, Germany, has all its forces committed to NATO; its contribution in manpower on NATO's central front is greater than any other member's. A country can withdraw committed forces, and this has been done by France and Britain.

The integrated commands are another distinctive feature of NATO, especially "Allied Command Europe" (ACE), which is by far the most important. Its Supreme Commander, SACEUR, through his headquarters organization, exercises operational control over all ground and tactical air forces "assigned" to his Command and is expected to ensure their proper organization, training and equipment. (Other forces, "earmarked" for his Command, come under his operational control in time of war or emergency mobilization, or under other specified conditions.) Under the general guidance of the North Atlantic Council's Military Committee he prepares plans to deter or defend against various possibilities of attack. In time of war he would be responsible for the conduct of all operations of forces coming under his command. As Jean Laloy has made clear, in time of peace the Supreme Command does not really "command"; it "monitors, surveys, recommends, coordinates." [10]

Although each member remains responsible for the logistic support of its own forces, SACEUR must see that logistical arrangements are coordinated. Since 1959 a unified air defense system for Europe has been coordinated by SACEUR in cooperation with the regional and Allied Tactical Air Force Commanders. One important part of this system, the AIRCENT command, under a British officer, comprised

---

[9] Paul H. Nitze, "Alternatives to NATO," in Knorr (ed.), *op. cit.*, pp. 263–67. See Chapter IV, *infra*, for a more detailed description of American views as to NATO's role.

[10] *Entre Guerres et Paix, 1945–1965* [Paris: Librairie Plon, 1966], p. 246. Among other writings on the integrated forces and the integrated command see Hanson W. Baldwin, "NATO's Uneven Steps toward Integration," *Reporter*, March 11, 1965, pp. 32–34.

over 2,000 aircraft of seven countries in 1964.[11] SACEUR must not only devise plans, but get them carried out; this has meant traveling around to work with top officials in the member governments. It is their decisions which ultimately determine whether or not his plans for deployment and priorities for mobilization will be implemented.

There are two other commands, the Atlantic Command and the Channel Command; the latter does not concern us here.[12] Unlike SHAPE, the Atlantic Command has no forces assigned in time of peace, but it makes plans for wartime coordination of the naval forces of the seven appropriate members, and frequent exercises are conducted under its auspices.

An operating procedure which has had great implications for the interpenetration of governments' decision processes is the "Annual Review." In practice this review is continuous. Visiting teams examine the defense preparations of each member with an eye on their economic capabilities for further exertions; elaborate questionnaires are filled out by the appropriate defense authorities; and NATO officials discuss recommendations and progress on previous recommendations. Each member's defense plans are justified in the presence of the high defense officials of the others, on the basis of reports prepared by SHAPE and by the committees in the NATO secretariat responsible for the data on financing problems. As a result of this procedure, plans, strengths and capabilities of each are known to all the others and are subjects for common discussion.

Still another noteworthy feature of NATO's operations is the "infrastructure," a system of fixed installations—principally communication networks, fuel-supply lines, and airfields—for the common use of NATO forces. For example, a communications network of more than

---

[11] For a description of AIRCENT, see *NATO Letter,* June, 1964, pp. 14–18.

[12] Strictly speaking, there are *four* command areas for the defense of which the Military Committee is the supreme military authority. The leading role of the United States in the European and Atlantic Commands is described in the text. The organization of the Channel Command—with United Kingdom commanders reporting to a Channel Committee composed of the four chiefs of naval staff of the four Channel powers—reflects Britain's unique interest in this small command. The Canada-United States Regional Planning Group, the lone survivor of NATO's original five regional planning groups, is not really a "command" at all. Its organization testifies to the lack of need for close NATO supervision of purely North American defense planning. NATO's command structure reflects the need for participation of its North American members in the defense of Europe much more than of the European members in the defense of North America.

8,000 miles extends from northern Norway to Turkey's eastern boundary.[13] Infrastructure projects are constructed by civilian contractors who have been selected by international competitive bidding and are paid for according to cost-sharing formulas agreed upon in the North Atlantic Council.[14]

Other cooperative endeavors include the NATO Defense College, the Mutual Weapons Development Program, the Maintenance Supply Services Agency, a scholarship and fellowship program, an Air Training Advisory Group, a Science Program, the La Spezia Anti-Submarine Warfare Research Center, the Advisory Group for Aeronautical Research and Development, and an Air Defense Technical Center which, inter alia, was responsible for establishing the early-warning communications system for European air defense. Some defense production activities are undertaken jointly by interested countries, working on common designs. Thus, at least some standardization has taken place regarding weapons, ammunition, airplanes, radar and sonar equipment, mine sweepers, mapmaking, and the like. A number of emergency planning agencies, such as the Planning Board for Ocean Shipping, have worked to coordinate members' preparations in case of war.

One critical portion of the allies' defense is not under the control of the organization; we refer, of course, to American control of the nuclear weapons upon which NATO heavily relies. This has increasingly serious implications for the cohesion of the alliance and brings us to consider the strategic expectations underlying existing cooperation.

Disregarding earlier, more ambitious manpower objectives for allied ground forces in Europe, let us begin with the setting of the famous Lisbon goals in February, 1952. These were adopted after intricate and exacting negotiations on a report by the Temporary Council Committee (the first "Three Wise Men"). This group had sought to reconcile the defense needs of the alliance with the economic and other capabilities of the individual members in order to determine how much more each could contribute in the immediate future and (less precisely) for longer periods. Getting acceptance of the general recommendations, including a goal of ninety-six divisions, thirty-five to forty of which were to be battle-

[13] For a description of the communications network, see *Military Review*, February, 1964, p. 104.
[14] *Facts about the North Atlantic Treaty Organization*, pp. 121–29; Ismay, *op. cit.*, pp. 114–24; Johnson Garrett, "An Alliance Goes into the Construction Business,"*NATO Letter*, February, 1965, pp. 3–10.

ready, proved to be more "a moral than a material achievement."[15] Almost at once the members began to scale down their intended future allocations, if not their actual contributions of the moment. Quite soon military commanders began speaking of the need to rely more heavily on nuclear weapons in order to make up the difference between what the members were willing to do and what the Soviet Union could do with its "armed hordes" plus its own supplies of nuclear weapons. This view coincided with the preferences of the political leaders in the various countries; for heavier reliance on nuclear weapons, especially American nuclear weapons, seemed to open the way to reallocating funds to their domestic budgets and reducing the military drain on their economies. Planning in this period was based on the expectation that a future war in Europe would inevitably be nuclear, with the peak of destruction in the first few days and the outcome determined by forces already in being.

Almost simultaneously with the admission of Germany, whose contribution was counted on to augment significantly the other members' forces committed to NATO, the North Atlantic Council authorized the military to base their plans on the use of nuclear weapons. Early in 1957, General Norstad, then SACEUR, called for a NATO force of thirty divisions (more than double the existing force). They would be armed with both conventional and nuclear weapons and would stand ready on the forward line at all times. Behind them would be other divisions equal to about one-quarter of those originally called for by the Lisbon agreement. The Military Committee plan, "MC-70," adopted that year, was said to provide that NATO troops be given training in the use of atomic weapons, while the custody and control of all the warheads remained in American hands. NATO forces, in General Norstad's view, were to contribute to deterring aggression; but if aggression occurred, at the minimum they could enforce a pause. The pause would identify the action as aggression in fact or intent and by emphasizing the cost and consequences of proceeding would force the aggressor to make a second decision as to whether to proceed. This important objective would not diminish NATO's responsibility for taking every necessary step to deny to the aggressor occupation of alliance territory and to defend it if required. NATO forces would also contribute to making more

[15] J. D. Warne, *NATO and its Prospects* (New York: Frederick A. Praeger, 1954), p. 38.

credible the strategic retaliatory forces by their ability to meet all requirements up to those of general war.[16]

General Norstad, while continually (and futilely) calling for thirty divisions, stressed the need for quality forces which were well equipped, especially with "modern" (mostly atomic) weapons. He also created in 1961, from already existing units, a small, highly mobile, multinational unit intended to act like a fire brigade in getting quickly to any threatened area. He and his successor, General Lemnitzer, who has strongly supported this brigade, have stressed its usefulness as a deterrent. Its multinational composition should inform a potential aggressor that an attack on a lonely outpost of one weak state could actually become an attack on many closely associated allies.[17]

General Norstad's concept of the "pause" helped to bridge the gap between the earlier ideas of all-or-nothing choices made necessary by heavy reliance on strategic nuclear weapons and the subsequent "flexible response" of the 1960s. It succeeded the idea of the "trip-wire" or "plate-glass window" function for NATO forces, an idea developed by distinguishing between the "Sword" (SAC) and the "Shield" (NATO conventional forces). The early 1960s saw an upheaval in NATO strategic planning, not only because the European members were reluctant to act according to new American concepts about conventional warfare capability, but also because many ideas were being offered to meet the political demands of some of the European allies for participation in controlling the strategic forces upon which they depended. Part of the convulsion in strategic doctrine arose from technological changes which made obsolete fixed liquid-fueled intermediate-range missiles based in Europe. The advent of the Polaris and Minuteman missiles called for new thinking on the use of strategic nuclear weapons to defend the NATO area; but it did not alter the situation with respect

[16] See General Lauris Norstad's speech to the NATO Parliamentarians in November, 1961, published as "SACEUR's Views" in *Survival,* January-February, 1962, pp. 13-14. General Norstad's views are emphasized since his tenure lasted over a lengthy period of SHAPE's history and were of decisive influence in NATO planning.

[17] See House of Representatives Committee on Foreign Affairs, *Hearings, Foreign Assistance Act of 1962,* 87th Cong., 2nd sess. (1962), p. 283; John Hodder, "NATO's Mobile Force in Action," *NATO Letter,* September, 1964, pp. 11-19; and "An Interview with Major General the Hon. Michael Fitzalan-Howard, Commander of the Land Component of the Allied Command Europe Mobile Forces," *NATO's Fifteen Nations,* June-July, 1965, pp. 77-84.

to the tactical nuclear weapons distributed among NATO forces (the warheads of which were in American custody).[18]

Another important feature of the alliance's operation was military aid. From the very beginning, American assistance was part and parcel of NATO ventures. The first mutual security legislation was in fact enacted almost immediately after the ratification of the treaty (August 1949 and October 1949), in response to a request from the Brussels Pact powers for material assistance, which, they maintained, was necessary to achieve an integrated, collective defense.[19]

The legislation envisaged a kind of division of labor, with the European members providing most of the manpower and the Americans providing the matériel. (Canada in these early days also made a substantial matériel contribution to the European members.) Unarmed European troops would be useless; the Americans had surplus arms. At the insistence of some leading Congressmen, who wrote the requirements into the mutual aid bill, money was not to be made available until after the President had approved recommendations for integrated defense of the North Atlantic area to be made by the North Atlantic Council and its Defense Committee. The Korean War adversely affected the rate of recovery of the war-torn economies of the European members. It further complicated the relationship between United States aid and NATO operations. The triple requirements of building adequate NATO forces, of sharing the resulting burden equitably, and of minimizing the adverse effects in Europe of the war in Korea led in 1951 to creation of the Temporary Council Committee (the first of NATO's "Three Wise Men"), which reported at the Lisbon meeting in February, 1952. This crisis in NATO affairs also brought about other forms of American aid, such as offshore procurement of military items. From that time onward, there was a tendency for the United States to make up any European material deficiencies which the administration regarded as unendurable if the alliance were to remain effective. The coming of nuclear weapons prolonged this tendency; otherwise, except for certain kinds of training, the prospering European states had no further need for economic aid for their military forces.

Although the basis for American aid was to be "balanced, collective

---

[18] For a recent extended discussion of the problems of NATO's strategy, see Henry A. Kissinger, *The Troubled Alliance* (New York: McGraw-Hill Book Co., 1965), chaps. v and vi.

[19] Ismay, *op. cit.*, pp. 23–24.

forces" in NATO, the aid was, for the most part, arranged for and provided bilaterally. Nevertheless, in recent years American aid has tended (in relatively small amounts) to go to NATO-wide or mutilateral projects under NATO auspices somewhat like seed-money, i.e., to start off a new operation, such as the science program, which is contributed to jointly by the members. Despite this rather modest development in support for multilateral projects, Lincoln Gordon's conclusion made in 1956 still holds true: the economic aspects of coalition diplomacy were never really put to a severe test. The great disparity between United States economic resources and those of other NATO members permitted the awkward question of how the burdens should be shared to be largely evaded in return for sympathetic consideration of proposals of great interest to the wealthiest member. If the disparity had been less, the United States might have been less able to assume so large a burden, and the others might have been less willing to acquiesce in American initiatives.[20]

The other main feature of NATO's operation is the "political consultation" which has taken place on the civilian side. The treaty itself called for such consultation only when a member's territorial integrity or security was threatened; but this has been interpreted very liberally, particularly after the Suez crisis and the report of the Committee on Non-Military Cooperation, the second committee of "Three Wise Men." From the beginning, however, questions only remotely related to the cold war have been raised. Full, frank, unpublicized discussion has taken place; and the practice has been praised enthusiastically by participants. One should note certain distinctions, however, regarding this practice. Although more than unilateral dissemination of information has occasionally taken place and there have often been genuine multilateral exchanges of views, intergovernmental coordination of national policies or the formulation of a NATO common policy has been confined to questions of immediate, alliance-wide interest. Consultation, of course, has not meant commitment to accept others' views.

THE POWER TO ACT

On only a limited number of subjects can NATO officials actually take a decision without depending upon the members for implementa-

[20] Lincoln Gordon, "Economic Aspects of Coalition Diplomacy—the NATO Experience," *International Organization,* November, 1956, pp. 542–43.

tion. Who has authority? As is frequently pointed out, NATO is an organization of sovereign states; and nowhere is this clearer than in its highest political body, the North Atlantic Council. Whether meeting in ministerial sessions, which occur two or three times a year, or in the weekly sessions of the Permanent Representatives (ambassadors sent to NATO by the member governments), decisions are taken unanimously; or more accurately, no decision is taken if there is a dissenting voice. Some of these decisions are simply statements of a general agreement on, for example, the legitimacy of the three Western powers' position in Berlin. Voting is unnecessary, since the questions are usually discussed informally and agreed upon prior to being offered for official approval. If an action is proposed from which only a small minority dissents, that minority may find itself under some pressure to conform; but there is no general rule except that all shall agree. (One of the most divisive issues, the admission of Germany, arose very early in the history of NATO. This issue was not directly faced and solved until four years later, after the chief opponent had, in the meantime, a chance to find another solution.) If the matter vitally concerns a small state, this member has both the legal and political ability to prevent an adverse course from being taken. The unanimity rule is of special importance to the small states, for it has prevented the adoption of many procedures which would have given more power to the leading or most interested states.

A very important function of the North Atlantic Council is the supervision and control of general policy to be followed by the military commands; the Council always has the last word on any proposal by the military personnel. On some military matters, indeed, the Council has had little choice, as when it has requested a nomination by the President of the United States of a general to be SACEUR and has then accepted his candidate. And in all important actions of the Council, each member will have been instructed by his own government.

The Secretary General's role in the discussions of the Council has grown since the days of the first holder of the office, Lord Ismay of Britain. The Secretary General now presides at meetings of the Council. He may initiate discussions; he is also responsible (through the Secretariat) for implementing Council decisions. He has direct access not only to all NATO agencies but also to member governments; his formal access to SACEUR, however, is only through the Military Committee. Just as SACEUR has always been an American, so the Secretary General has always come from the European side of the Atlantic. Messrs. Spaak, Stikker, and Brosio held high political office in Belgium, Holland, and Italy, respectively, prior to their appointment (and in M. Spaak's case, subsequently).

Under the Secretary General's direction is a civilian international secretariat numbering about one thousand, many of whom are seconded from their own governments. Some are nominated by their governments from private affairs. Relatively few Americans serve in the Secretariat. There is a publicly unacknowledged quota system, which operates flexibly; it is customary to name a successor in a particular post from the same state as his predecessor, if one is qualified and available.[21]

Another important feature of the civilian side of NATO is the Political Advisory Committee, a product of the report of the "Three Wise Men" in 1956. This committee can discuss political questions more informally than can the Council; because it functions at a lower official level, its deliberations have not the authoritative character which some Council discussions are likely to have. Here a distinction once made by Paul Nitze is apt: political consultation can be useful even when its object is not to reach binding commitments but only to clarify the problem and exchange views.[22] (The process of consultation leads to agreement on what the problem is, rather than to commitment; but it may still imply certain recommendations.)

On the military side, the senior officials have been those on the Military Committee (on which all members are represented except Iceland, which chose not to be included) and, until 1966, its executive committee, the Standing Group, composed of the United States Chairman of the Joint Chiefs of Staff and the equivalent officials from Britain and France. The Group sat in Washington, functioning through deputies, but was abolished after France's withdrawal. Although SHAPE formally operates under the direction of the Military Committee, SACEUR has gradually made SHAPE into the most influential center for military policy.

The growing weight of SHAPE, though formally headquarters for only one of three high commands, in part can be traced to its proximity to the political organs, to the fact that its composition is the most international, and to the circumstance that it operates within several countries. More

---

[21] Ball, *op. cit.*, p. 59.

[22] "Defining the Coalition and Coalition Diplomacy," speech at Conference on Coalition Diplomacy, Rutgers University, on May 18, 1956, p. 18. (Mimeographed.)

important, however, the forces of SHAPE directly confront the adversary in the core area of NATO concern and, still more important, the United States attributes to SHAPE the most prominent role among all the NATO organs. The visits to Europe in 1949 of General Gruenther and the United States Joint Chiefs of Staff were initial steps in the process leading to the appointment of an American general to an integrated European command. Even before General Eisenhower was formally selected for that command, the staff of SHAPE was beginning to be gathered together. Its mode of operations drew to some extent on the experience of SHAEF during World War II and on the preliminary work of the Western European Union (the Brussels Pact organization). Although the British would have preferred a looser form of organization based on committees, the compromise outcome was closer to the hierarchical American models, but with some extra divisions of staff responsibility added. The main appointments were divided among different members, and each chief of a staff division had a deputy of another nationality.[23] From the beginning, General Eisenhower insisted that each member was to regard himself as an international officer, ignoring the prior claims of his particular country or service.[24] A legal question about loyalty oaths for members of SHAPE was resolved by declaring that the organization was linked to the treaty, which was part of the law of the land for each country. A genuine international spirit has pervaded the headquarters.

Unlike some of the European organizations, NATO has no official quasi-representative assembly. There are two groups of legislators, however, which interest themselves in NATO and work to influence its decisions. One, an official body, is the Assembly of Western European Union, made up of parliamentarians from seven of the NATO members. The other, which has no official standing, is the NATO Parliamentarians' Conference, composed of legislators from all the NATO states. In contrast to the WEU Assembly, which confines its NATO concerns rather closely to military questions, the unofficial body ranges far and wide in its discussions.[25]

[23] For the beginnings of SHAPE, see Lt. Col. William A. Knowlton, "Early Stages in the Organization of SHAPE," *International Organization,* Winter, 1959, pp. 1–18.
[24] Field Marshal the Viscount Montgomery of Alamein, *Memoirs* (Cleveland: The World Publishing Co., 1958), p. 461.
[25] See Appendix B for brief descriptions of the OAS, SEATO, the OECD, the Fund, the Bank, and GATT.

NATO AND OTHER ORGANIZATIONS

How does NATO's development compare with that of other international organizations having some of NATO's characteristics? NATO and the others have all had to operate within the same configuration of power relationships and have had to adjust to the same changes in these relationships, but the aspects which have been significant have varied according to the role the organization has had to play in this general configuration. The United States has had more influence in each of them than any other single member. The growth in importance of the underdeveloped countries, including the ex-colonies, has not greatly affected the functioning of NATO; it has played an important part in the development of the Bank and the OECD. Alone among the organizations considered, NATO, by the very fact of its creation, altered the general power situation. In fact, NATO has held the fort, permitting the others to function. Therefore, NATO's role in the grand policy of the members could be expected to be far more important than that of the other organizations, and changes in the direction of NATO policy consequently more cumbersome and the gap between a member's declaratory and action policies probably much larger than in the cases of the other organizations.

Communist threats and the nuclear balance have been central preoccupations for NATO. For the economic organizations, the great-power relationships have not been of overwhelming importance; for the minor security organization, SEATO, and the multipurpose regional organization, OAS, they have been less significant than the power of the leading member has been. Since security touches the very core of sovereignty, it is hardly surprising that the whole orientation of a member's foreign policy may thus be affected by NATO affairs. With the exception of SEATO, NATO was the only organization with an adversary as its raison d'être.

NATO is held together not only by the formal treaty commitment but also by the widely shared belief within all the member states that they have much more in common than simply the threat of Soviet expansion, that similar political and cultural characteristics are evidence of shared values. The undemocratic character of Portugal's government has been conveniently ignored; and when the two states in the Eastern Mediterranean were added, the reality deviated still further from the belief.

However, the assumption of moral solidarity is by no means wholly specious. Like NATO, the OAS has a significant ideological aspect. For members of the inter-American system the sense of belonging to the New World and being separate from the wickedness of the Old not only colors OAS operations but often substitutes for real action. Since this vision of a New World, culturally differentiated from the Old and morally united—the Bolivar ideal—is greater among the Latin-American members than in the United States, certain problems are posed for the latter. But the prevalence of the myth has supported the principal OAS function: to keep peace among its members. This kind of moral justification is unnecessary in economic organizations, for they are supposed to focus on practical, business-like action. Again, in such economic groups a member state can more easily live up to its declared cooperative intentions.

From the United States' point of view the other members of the OAS are all "Latin" and "small powers" and may be perceived as very like each other, however much this may be untrue in fact. The United States is more like most of the other members of NATO than it is like most of the other members in the OAS. The gulf between the United States and its Asian partners in SEATO is even wider than that between it and its fellow members in the other two organizations. The OECD, with its highly industrialized, advanced countries of Europe and North America plus Japan is a leading organization in the North-versus-South political configuration; NATO, though less inclusive, represents one side of an East-West confrontation.

Security and prosperity both are values which may be enhanced by joint action among member states in an international organization. The material advantages which flow from cooperative action in an economic organization are, however, more easily and objectively demonstrable than are security advances in an organization like NATO. The lukewarm and the hostile can in this latter case much more readily find reasons for withholding their collaboration. When it is a question of assigning armed manpower to NATO, tendencies toward caution are especially strong. Thus, national sensitivity and the inherent subjectivity of security calculations together are a sizeable drag on proposals to strengthen NATO.

If there are special difficulties in evoking support for new or increased NATO activities, NATO is at least spared the determined opposition of economic interest groups articulate in the domestic politics of the member countries. The virtue of being able to demonstrate objectively a national advantage in participating in, for example, the OECD and GATT has its drawbacks; for disadvantaged interest groups can more easily detect potential deprivation. The goal of national security, on the other hand, does not tend to divide various interest groups, however wide differences of opinion may be as to correct policy. Furthermore, the very size of the NATO operation arouses the positive interest of NATO suppliers. (Only the Bank and the Fund, among the other organizations, have big operations of their own and possess property of significant magnitude.)

All the other organizations have produced numerous cooperative ventures, but nothing as elaborate as NATO's joint infrastructure. In common with all but the OAS, NATO has tended to confine cooperation to the function for which it was established.

All the organizations exchange some kinds of information among the members and make studies which require at least some standardized classifications, but the intimacy of communication varies greatly. NATO and the predecessor to OECD pioneered in the remarkable practice of "confrontation," which has continued in the OECD and was copied in the Alliance for Progress. The Annual Review, in particular, and the habit of confrontation, generally, remind member governments of their obligation to live up to their declarations. It is especially effective when a responsible minister hears from his counterparts in the other member countries their opinions of how his responsibilities are being carried out. That government officials are willing to reveal their future plans already suggests a relatively high level of mutual confidence. The officials participating in such procedures cannot ensure that their respective governments will act according to their preferences, but there is an undeniable psychological impact in a place which counts.

For reasons to be explained later, the United States government is less susceptible to pressures from the confrontation in NATO than to pressures in the OECD. Another method especially adaptable to NATO, namely, political consultation on large foreign policy questions, may to some extent take the place of confrontation in this organization as a means of emphasizing to the United States representatives considerations of importance to their colleagues.

Political consultation, if carried out conscientiously, can produce greater coordination in the members' policy on a particular issue, but a disposition to coordinate national policies has been more characteristic of participants in some of the organizations other than NATO. For NATO during much of its life has been primarily an operating agency, not one which recommends principles, rules, and standards for the members to observe. Operations once established usually leave the participating states less choice about their details, the large choices having been made in the beginning.

One way in which participants in some of the economic organizations have successfully dealt with the unequal concern of the members regarding particular questions is by acting through committees composed of only those members with the special interest in or ability to deal with the questions. In NATO, however, the smaller members have so intense a sense of legal equality and of the overriding importance of security issues that this method has seldom been formally used except in the case of the now defunct Standing Group. There are, however, committees on which individual members have chosen not to be represented. Moreover, prior consultation among the larger powers on the Berlin problem and similar "political" questions is a fact of life which the others accept.

Although the United States has been able occasionally to take an important initiative in the economic organizations, such as the Kennedy Round in GATT, Americans have been much less influential in these groups than in the security organizations. After the dollar gap disappeared, there was nothing comparable in the economic organizations to the unilateral United States nuclear guarantee to NATO, literally a life-and-death matter to the other members (despite President de Gaulle's preferences).

Although the organizations with security responsibilities—NATO, SEATO, and the OAS—have a number of stated goals in common, the members of each have been reluctant to be tied to either of the other security groups in any but the loosest form of information exchange. They prefer reciprocal isolation. The key member, the United States, has had to be the chief coordinator where any connections are made. The economic organizations have much more extensive liaison arrangements, but duplication of functions even between them and NATO exists, although not to a harmful degree.

In all the organizations under discussion the most authoritative organ is a council consisting of representatives from each member state.[26] In all cases, action by the councils depends in the last analysis on the actions of the governments of the members, which the councils may affect to a greater or lesser extent, depending on a number of complicated factors. The councils do serve a forum function (which does not differentiate them from the United Nations itself), which is usefully performed because their quiet private discussions have attracted little public attention. In all the organizations much of the work of the councils is routine and is carried on by deputies. Government instructions loom large, indeed, in the deliberations of the North Atlantic Council when it is the Permanent Representatives who are meeting.

In NATO and in the economic organizations the growing importance of the Secretary General has reflected rising confidence levels and mutual trust among the members. By contrast, in the United Nations it has been lack of consensus in the General Assembly and particularly in the Security Council which has created the need and the opportunity for the office of the Secretary General to become pivotal. On the other hand, in the OAS and in SEATO the Secretary General's political importance is slight, for neither consensus nor a power vacuum has given the office importance. NATO's Secretary General has a constituency sufficiently independent of the United States government that his views must be carefully weighed in American decisions. At least equally important is SACEUR's relative freedom from United States domination. Although he is an American general, he does command an international armed force and has been able to inspire great confidence among the other members. SHAPE has no counterpart in any of the other organizations compared here.[27]

Whatever their special characteristics all the organizations have one common feature: the predominant role of the United States in them. We next look more closely into American perspectives on the functions of NATO and the other organizations and the manner in which the United States should play its role in them.

[26] The Inter-American Conference, scheduled to meet once every five years, is moribund and has at no time during the OAS period been an influential policy-making body.

[27] For further discussion of organizational questions in NATO, see Chapter IX. See also Otto Pick, "The 'O' in NATO," *NATO Letter*, December, 1965, pp. 14–20.

CHAPTER THREE

AMERICAN PERSPECTIVES: THE ROLE OF NATO AND OTHER ORGANIZATIONS

TIME AND CIRCUMSTANCE may set objective limits to what an international organization can do; within these limits what it will do is largely conditioned by what its leading participants expect of it. We need to discover, for various stages in the development of NATO and the other organizations under discussion: (1) What contributions did United States policy-makers believe the organization could make to the realization of American goals? (2) What role did they believe the United States should play in the organization? Our analysis in this and the succeeding chapter is based, for the most part, on public expressions of views held by high officials. Views which high officials have not deemed suitable for public airing can only be deduced from an examination of actions inconsistent with these statements and of public statements inconsistent with each other.

NATO'S ROLE

The North Atlantic Treaty and the organization subsequently created to implement that treaty were intended in one way or another to frustrate presumed aggressive designs of the Soviet Union, preferably without firing a shot. The multilateral effort to influence the Russians took two forms: the treaty itself was a warning that the signatories could not be coerced individually, and the organization increased the capacity and intensified the will of the members to deal effectively with the Soviet Union.

Official statements over a fifteen-year period as to what NATO could or should do range from advocacy of only a narrowly limited, almost purely military action to advocacy of functions only very indirectly related to security. The expectations of American officials regarding NATO's role and the American interest which they hoped to advance through it fall into nine overlapping clusters. Seven have been clearly articulated; two may be reasonably deduced from official statements.

1. Proponents of the Atlantic alliance, if one is to judge by the Vandenberg Resolution and the accompanying Senate committee reports, stressed two interrelated themes; it was expected *to promote both "self-help" and "mutual aid."* [1] The European signatories were to defend themselves in cooperation with each other and with the United States, which would aid in European defense and thereby improve its own defense. Even while the alliance remained in the first stage, a political guarantee without organization, United States officials understood that "mutual aid" principally meant providing American matériel and training for European forces to bring them up to a higher level of effectiveness than they could attain by themselves. With the establishment of SHAPE went a United States commitment of ground troops to be stationed alongside European forces. To the chronic Congressional complaints regarding the inadequacy of the "self-help" European part of the bargain, administration spokesmen were wont to reply that the European allies contributed much that would have been lacking without the alliance, including access to essential territory, the majority of the ground forces, and their will to resist.

In developing NATO strategy in the first years the American capability of deterring "all-out" war through its nuclear power was assumed. How many divisions were needed to avoid defeat in any other kind of war, how essential was the rearmament of Germany, and how far east ground forces should attempt to hold a line against a Soviet attacking force—all had to be debated. The first answers were to rearm Germany, to call for one hundred divisions, and to agree to a "forward strategy."

[1] Senate Resolution 239, 80th Cong., 2nd sess. (1948); Senate Executive Report No. 8, 81st Cong., 1st sess. (1949). Fifteen years later, when asked by a Congressman to define "the nature and purpose of NATO," the Deputy Assistant Secretary for Atlantic Affairs, Department of State, replied offhand, "to contribute in the most material way to the security of the United States" [Joint Committee on Atomic Energy, Subcommittee on Agreements for Cooperation, *Hearings, Agreement for Cooperation with NATO for Mutual Defense Purposes*, 88th Cong., 2nd sess. (1964), p. 40].

In later years, the 100-division force goals were tacitly scaled down; the other allies were to provide a "shield"—ground forces and tactical aircraft—to complement the atomic "sword."

As the gap between American and Soviet nuclear weapons' capabilities narrowed, the sword-shield division of labor between the United States and its European allies became, in NATO's second decade, less appealing. Europeans tended to regard their non-atomic contributions to NATO forces as more symbolic than substantial, or at the most, as garrison forces. For many, doubts about the credibility of the American nuclear guarantee could not be assuaged by building up the European non-atomic contributions to the collective defense; Europeans too would have to have some control over the nuclear defense of their countries. Reversing the complementary appellations and calling the European conventional forces the "sword" and United States strategic air and missile power the "shield," as was done in the Nassau declaration, defined for the European allies a role which many policy-makers on the Continent were not prepared to accept. European conceptions of "self-help" and "mutual aid" differed more and more from those of the Americans, whose "mutual aid" had earlier tended to define NATO's strategy.

2. From the outset American policy-makers expected that the alliance would help to *raise the morale of the Europeans* and so increase their will to defend themselves.[2] The very genesis of the treaty, the United States' affirmative response to the initiative of the Brussels Treaty members, bore witness to this expectation. The transformation of American forces in Europe from occupation to defense forces and the sending of additional American ground troops to Europe also attested to the morale-raising intention of United States diplomacy; their presence has been continuously effective in doing so. Encouraging the Europeans by guarantee and participation was especially important and useful in keeping the smaller states in line. Otherwise, they might have relapsed into earlier habits of neutrality and perhaps become vulnerable to the "salami tactics" of the potential aggressor, with the result that their strategic location would have been lost to the defense against Communist expansion. NATO operated as a morale-booster for Americans, too,

---

[2] See Robert E. Osgood, *NATO: The Entangling Alliance* (Chicago: University of Chicago Press, 1962), chap. ii; Harry S. Truman, *Memoirs* (Garden City: Doubleday and Company, 1956), pp. 245 and 248; Arthur H. Vandenberg, Jr. (ed.), *The Private Papers of Senator Vandenberg* (Boston: Houghton Mifflin Company, 1952), pp. 419 and 495.

providing a symbol of continued interest in the defense of a major sector of the free world.

The effectiveness of NATO in raising European and American morale, however, was partly self-defeating. With morale improved and the evidence of NATO's success in deterring Soviet invasion, the allies slackened their efforts. More than one SACEUR found himself constantly warning against "dangerous relaxation." The communiqué following every ministerial meeting of the North Atlantic Council contained passages describing the continued seriousness of the Soviet threat; but the governments of most of the ministers did not seem to hear very well, if one is to judge by their actions. Their morale was high in the sense that they had gained the self-confidence which they lacked in the late 1940s, but it did not express itself noticeably in increased military expenditures except in the period of general alarm following the Korean aggression. Few of the allies acted as if they believed their own security would be affected by decisions to scale up or scale down their own defense expenditures, and one, France, demonstrated in 1966 a lack of further concern over Soviet aggression by deciding to withdraw from the organization.

3. A third way in which United States officials anticipated that NATO would serve American interests was *to provide an instrument for coordinated action*. The Vandenberg Resolution and accompanying explanation, as well as the Senate committee report accompanying the North Atlantic Treaty, register this belief. The hope and the anticipation were quickly converted into a requirement when Congress approved the mutual security legislation following ratification of the treaty. As mentioned earlier, implementation of the Act depended on the allies producing an integrated plan of operation under NATO auspices. Coordination was expected, inter alia, to reduce the costs of defense. The emphasis upon integration grew steadily stronger, its first great mark of acceptance being the organization of the joint commands and, most significantly, of SHAPE with its coalition forces. "Balanced force" became the watchword in the very early 1950s, and a common set of defense plans was developed. Up to a point cooperation grew with the cooperating. The allies accepted and largely met the need for joint maneuvers, joint training, and common infrastructure. The need for standardization was also self-evident, but this proved a more difficult nut to crack. Only modest progress could be noted, as in the adoption of common proce-

dure and nomenclature. Even more difficult to implement was the idea of coordinated weapons production. In the Eisenhower administration United States leaders began to talk about "harmonizing policy," but this often appeared to mean that the others should bring their policy into conformity with American views. (Secretary of State John Foster Dulles spoke frequently in this vein during the spring of 1956 prior to the Suez crisis, a crisis which marks the low point of NATO harmonizing.) Nevertheless, the habit of political consultation grew very markedly in the late 1950s under American leadership. Similarly, cooperative activities under Article 2, such as SHAPE medical conferences and seminars of scientists on subjects such as outer space, were initiated. But on the crucial question of how to cooperate on a common strategy to meet changing political and technological conditions, the Americans' reach was greater than their grasp.

4. From the time of the North Atlantic Treaty onward, American officials expected the alliance *to deter aggression by being prepared to meet it*; this required filling the power vacuum left in Europe after World War II. Until the outbreak of the Korean War, the Americans relied on giving the potential enemy advance notice that the allies would react militarily and together if one were attacked—what was early called "certainty of action." In the spring of 1949 neither the United States nor its allies had as yet envisioned any concerted action prior to attack, although all agreed that some kind of advance preparation was necessary (on a modest scale not involving increased defense expenditures). This view quickly altered; by mid-1950 the Americans began to press for a united and greatly strengthened force-in-being. They assumed that there was only one all-out war for which to prepare, and that this all-out war was the only kind for which it was necessary to be ready in Europe. They saw only one enemy to deter, the Soviet Union, even if the early American utterances and the treaty itself had not named that country. (In fact, the Senate Foreign Relations Committee reports emphasized that the treaty was aimed at no state, only at "aggression.") Joint exercises appeared to be useful not only as good practice but also to indicate to friend and foe that NATO was ready. At times the Eisenhower administration leaned particularly hard on the propaganda key, muting the known inadequacies of the preparations actually achieved. For example, they claimed at a time when all members were shrinking the forces which they planned to contribute to NATO that NATO had between

ninety and one hundred divisions, active *and reserve*. Still, deterrence continued to have a highly military connotation, especially when combined with the strategy of the American nuclear deterrent. Secretary Dulles spoke, for example, in 1954, of NATO's creating "considerable local defense power" and of its also helping to implement "our broad deterrent policies." [3]

Concentration on United States nuclear power as a means of foiling Communist thrusts tended in the mid-1950s to supplant the earlier efforts to build up the European allies' powers of resistance, economic and political as well as military, efforts which had been, at least in the first two spheres, remarkably successful. The massive retaliation doctrine gave way in the later years of the Eisenhower period to that of "graduated deterrence" and in the Kennedy administration to the somewhat similar doctrine of flexible response. The idea of a many-sided as well as a multileveled deterrence was called forth by the increasing diversity of the Soviet techniques evident in the mid-fifties. Preparation for a flexible response, however, had two aspects: in addition to deterring different kinds of Russian attacks, it also gradually became associated in American minds with preventing escalation of local violence into full-scale nuclear war and thus providing a foundation for negotiation with the Russians. The Kennedy administration's special stress on the flexible response began to look to some Europeans, especially Germans, more like preparation to fight the Russians on the ground than like an effort to prevent them from attacking at all. This interpretation of the new emphasis on building up conventional forces did not coincide with official views in Washington. The notions of deterrence earlier propagated by American officials had been learned too well by the European allies, for the time lag in strategic understanding between the American leaders and European officials persisted. Different meanings of the terms "deterrence" and "defense" made it seem even larger.[4]

5. A more vaguely defined but recurring theme in American pronouncements was that the Atlantic partnership would help *to build an Atlantic community*. From the outset Americans, both administration policy-makers and interested members of Congress, spoke of the North

[3] Testimony of Secretary John Foster Dulles, Senate Committee on Foreign Relations, *Hearings, Mutual Security Act of 1954*, 83th Cong., 2nd sess. (1954), p. 2.
[4] Sir John Slessor, "Control of Nuclear Strategy," *Foreign Affairs*, October, 1963, pp. 97–98.

Atlantic Treaty as not just an old-fashioned alliance, but as a combination of like-minded countries with a common heritage. In fact, members of the Senate Foreign Relations Committee were at pains to point out that although not geographically contiguous like the countries in the inter-American system, the North Atlantic countries could nevertheless constitute a community because of their ideological agreement. The same committee, however, in reporting out the treaty, described Article 2, which contains references to this community and to the desirability of cultural connections, as a "reaffirmation of faith" and an "encouragement for action" rather than an obligation requiring legislative implementation. The fuzziness of the community concept was evident whenever references in this vein were made to NATO. Thus, Secretary Dulles, a few months prior to Suez, when the military aspects of the alliance were not in the forefront of attention, spoke of the need for NATO to go beyond the "initial phase to the totality of its meaning." [5] Somewhat bolder in its launching, the Kennedy Grand Design was not much clearer in its definition of "community," although NATO was to play a prominent part in it. His fresh effort to build an overarching Atlantic association was still not clearly articulated.

One of the claims advanced in support of the Vandenberg Resolution was that the North Atlantic Treaty would forward *European* unity. Sometimes this unity was thought of in terms of reconciliation of old enemies, whose earlier quarrels had involved the United States, sometimes as a counterpart to the kind of federal union represented by the United States itself, and sometimes as a necessary prerequisite (rather than an obstacle) to a transatlantic community. On the other hand, while reconciliation and European union were seen as desirable, Americans did not want such close, exclusive friendship between some of the European states as to endanger the wider association in which the United States would be a leading member. Ambivalence regarding the European community was doubly marked because the United States, while maintaining in reality a "special relationship" with Britain, was occasionally seen trying to nudge a rather reluctant England to enter Europe.[6]

[5] "Developing NATO in Peace," *Department of State Bulletin,* April 30, 1956, p. 709.
[6] Cf. Livingston Merchant, "Evolving United States Relations with the Atlantic Community," in Francis O. Wilcox and H. Field Haviland, Jr. (eds.), *The Atlantic Community: Progress and Prospects* (New York: Frederick A. Praeger, 1963), pp. 92–109, and in *International Organization,* Summer, 1963, pp. 610–627.

6. Part of the confusion about the content of the community idea arose because of the desire of some Americans to use NATO *to serve economic purposes*. When proposed to the Senate, the treaty was said to be useful, inter alia, for assisting the economic recovery of war-torn Europe, already being aided under the Marshall Plan. By giving Europeans confidence in their future, it would help remove the fear of a Communist aggression that was holding back the will to greater rehabilitation efforts. At that time (1948), although economic recovery was to have first priority, with defense expenditures not to be changed greatly in size, the two efforts, economic recovery and defense cooperation, were expected to support each other. Later, with the Korean War raging, there was a genuine conflict between the two objectives, a conflict that the vast program of American military aid to Europe obscured.

Thus a constant strain developed between the Americans and their European allies over the economic sacrifices which the latter were to make in support of NATO. It was first signalled by the unwillingness of the Europeans to live up to the force goals to which they had committed themselves at Lisbon in February, 1952. For a period the Americans rationalized this failure, which was rooted in economic considerations, by pointing to the qualitative improvements in NATO forces. This enabled them to argue that NATO did not have to match the Soviet Union in quantity. Apparently, an increase in quality justified parsimony in the defense budget. (Secretary Dulles' use of adjectives to describe this stress on quality such as "more compact," "tougher," "more effective" helped to foster the impression that a modified NATO strategy dependent on tactical nuclear forces rendered the "economically unfeasible" Lisbon goals militarily obsolete.) As the continental European members became more affluent, Americans said less about NATO's contribution to their greater prosperity. On the other hand, the British seemed to find in NATO's costliness reason for trying to ease their balance of payments difficulties by cutting down on their commitments in Europe. Soon the Americans also began to link their own balance of payments problems with alliance commitments, but they did not go so far as the British.

In addition to its possible contribution to the prosperity of its members, NATO has at times been considered by Americans capable of performing two other economic functions. One, to serve as a vehicle for economic cooperation, was, as previously mentioned, resolutely rejected in 1956 when the question of expanding functions under Article 2 was investigated by the three-man committee on non-military cooperation.

At that time, the United States view was that other, more appropriate agencies were already available. However, Americans have sometimes included economic information during political consultations. They usually have done so in the process of using NATO for the second function, to coordinate economic pressures on the Soviet Union. Another, more informal grouping, the Coordinating Committee for the Control of the Export of Strategic Goods to the Soviet Bloc ("COCOM," the membership of which is not identical with that of NATO), has been the regular means by which the United States influenced other governments to limit the flow of particular goods to Russia. COCOM's recommendations have, however, sometimes come before NATO. The United States has overlooked few opportunities presented by ministerial meetings of the North Atlantic Council to call attention to the need for more economic aid to underdeveloped countries.

7. The practice of political consultation highlights another function of NATO in American eyes: *to provide a channel for communication and diplomatic pressure.* Although the three or four most powerful members were likely to confer separately from NATO, they also carried on part of their negotiations through this organization where other members could be recruited to a particular point of view. When Secretary Dulles referred to this function, he spoke of NATO as the "political framework for harmonizing allied policies and programs"; this suggests more than communication and an exchange of views. However, he also spoke of avoiding being "enmeshed" in a "procedural web" and stressed that the harmony to be sought was only on "fundamentals." Whether or not NATO has been effectively used as a means for concerting policy, the United States has found in it a convenient way to present American views and get quickly the reactions of others and a useful supplement to regular bilateral negotiations.

NATO has been a channel not only for communication between member governments but also, in various ways, between the United States and the Soviet Union. The deployment of NATO forces, as required by a succession of strategies evolved for the alliance, conveyed a succession of messages to the Soviet opponent. The forces were variously to be a trip-wire to sound the alarm for an American response, a shield to assure that Soviet forces attacking in Europe would have to concentrate and so become lucrative targets for bombing, and a means to enforce a pause before full-scale nuclear war had to be resorted to. They provided at all times a way to test Soviet intentions. The presence of allied forces in Germany permitted their augmentation during the 1961 Berlin crisis to serve as a kind of "military representation."

8. Another function for NATO, not always frankly acknowledged, is *to extend the area and resource base* to which the United States has access in promoting its national security and other foreign policy objectives.[7] Administration spokesmen have often referred to NATO's help in providing bases, other kinds of military facilities, and additions to American armed forces in the European area. What has not been spelled out is that the existence of NATO made it possible for the United States to continue to station forces in Europe after their occupation duties in Germany were completed. Similarly, NATO provided an opportunity for intermediate-range missiles and tactical nuclear weapons (under American control) to be situated in Europe. True, the Americans usually described the provision of missile bases as an opportunity for their European allies to contribute to their own defense rather than to that of the United States. NATO's role in justifying United States-controlled missile bases in Europe developed only in the late 1950s. Before that time, NATO's forces had provided a complement to American strategic air power, a complement which General Gruenther and others had described as indispensable, in answer to those who imagined that the latter type of power was sufficient for American security. In 1955 he drew attention to the usefulness of the "shield" in making an attacker concentrate his forces and thus become vulnerable to "our new [tactical] weapons." In General Norstad's view in 1961, NATO forces were, inter alia, necessary to make credible "the great strategic retaliatory forces."

In the non-military field NATO had long been perceived by American diplomats as a way of supporting United States policy beyond the European area. As early as 1952, Secretary Acheson was using NATO as part of his diplomatic armory in getting leading members to uphold the United States policy in Korea. Secretary Dulles frequently succeeded in getting similar assistance in the form of statements from the North Atlantic Council in support of American policy objectives outside of Europe.

The available record does not reveal that changes in diplomatic align-

---

[7] Such an extension was essential if the United States was to carry out its responsibilities as the leader of the non-Communist world.

ments in the United Nations can be traced to American pressure on its NATO members through NATO channels. Where voting on an issue showed solidarity among the allies, one need not posit undue American pressure. Solidarity can as well be due to a relatively spontaneous recognition of common interests. There is some evidence that members on occasion purposely avoided giving the impression that NATO formed a bloc in the United Nations.[8]

9. Conceivably the most important function of NATO, but one which was unstated in the earlier days, was *to help manage the problem of Germany.* Actually, it did not go quite unmentioned, for the Senate committee report accompanying the treaty noted in passing its potential for bringing Germany back into the fold. A solution to this problem seemed to become more urgent with the outbreak of the Korean War and the felt inadequacies of the ten European members of NATO to fend off the Russian "hordes," especially if these had already crossed German territory to the Rhine. The whole question of a "forward strategy," about which so many strategists talked, was bound up with German participation in NATO. When the first effort—to render reborn German forces harmless by incorporating them into a European Army through the abortive European Defense Community—failed, NATO was there to pick up the pieces. Through it another solution was found, one eventually accepted by the French, who had earlier, in 1950, balked at German rearmament. All during this period the Americans had felt that the sooner Germany participated in NATO the better; for it seemed to them to offer the best means of having German strength available but under control, and in a form least disturbing to the other indispensable allies.

In the performance of each of these functions anticipated by Americans there were *restraints* on NATO, most of them having been laid down by the United States itself. Many of the initial limitations which had been spelled out in the Senate committee reports accompanying the Vandenberg Resolution and the North Atlantic Treaty gradually disappeared, especially that on political consultation.[9] One is still continually emphasized by American officials, namely, that NATO is in no way a

[8] See testimony of Secretary of State Rusk, Senate Committee on Foreign Relations, *Hearings, Foreign Assistance Act of 1962,* 87th Cong., 2nd sess., (1962) pp. 45–46.
[9] Consultation was to occur *after* a specific threat of aggression.

supranational organization, but rather a cooperative agency of national sovereignties, equal juridically, each of which retains the right and responsibility to determine its own policy. However, remarks made about the limited nature of American guarantees during the Senate's consideration of the treaty seem to have been quickly forgotten. In later years the United States government insisted that its commitment in Article 5 to come to the aid of those attacked really meant what it said and took practical steps to demonstrate this.[10] The American leaders originally did not conceive of NATO as restricted in membership, retaining an open mind about future applicants. However, when the number reached fifteen, the Americans were ready to rest at that point and refrain from acting on a certain preference for having Spain admitted. Open-mindedness regarding new applicants was coupled with single-minded insensitivity to the implications for responsibility. The three later entrants were looked on as accretions to American (or NATO) strength without much notice in the United States that their admission also greatly extended the obligation of the others to defend them.

Another kind of limitation existed in the earlier days, however, one which suggested that while NATO was the keystone of America's *European* policy, it was no more than that. Secretary Dulles, for example, tended to regard NATO as just one among a number of almost equally important alliances which could be kept quite separate.[11] Thus the United States occasionally took initiatives in other parts of the world against the preferences (when discovered) of its NATO allies.[12] Secretary Dulles emphasized that NATO could not cover all of a country's vital interests; protection of some of them might require independent judgment and prompt decision.[13] (In an attenuated form this attitude has persisted.)

[10] The Senate report accompanying the treaty stated that "Article 5 is the heart of the treaty," establishing the principle that an armed attack against one member was to be considered an attack against all. It then proceeded to suggest that specific American measures to be taken would depend upon the location, scale, nature, and other characteristics of the attack.

[11] In contrast, Secretary McNamara told the Senate Committee on Foreign Relations in June, 1961 that "Western Europe is the absolute foundation of our series of alliances." [*Hearings, International Development and Security*, 87th Cong., 1st sess. (1961), p. 655.]

[12] For example, in the case of Quemoy and Matsu. The allies (except France in the mid-1960s) were careful not to make public their disagreement. Such caution reduced the possible disadvantage to the United States of becoming, through NATO, unwillingly aware of allied dissatisfaction.

[13] "Developing NATO in Peace," *loc. cit.*

Almost from the beginning Americans have assumed that the Atlantic alliance would last indefinitely. When the treaty was first contemplated, its proponents, partly to fend off criticism, had declared that collaborative action through the alliance was needed *until,* and by implication only until, the United Nations was able to handle the problem. Once the North Atlantic Treaty Organization had been built upon the foundation of the treaty commitment, little was heard from the American side about either the date 1959, when changes in the treaty could be proposed, or 1969, when a member could withdraw. In 1955, when Germany became a treaty signatory and was brought into the organization, the United States government declared that it regarded the treaty as "of indefinite duration." It did so in part to reassure France and other apprehensive allies. Whether or not the North Atlantic Treaty *Organization* is also "of indefinite duration" and a fundamentally unchanging institution is another point and, according to President de Gaulle, a separate one. He has in the mid-1960s, and particularly in March, 1966, dramatically challenged American assumptions both about the Organization's permanence and about the inseparability of treaty commitment and organization membership.

The initial response of the other fourteen members demonstrated that De Gaulle's government stood alone. Even though treaty commitment and participation in the Organization are legally separable, the United States and the other thirteen NATO members declared on March 18, 1966 that the commitment in the treaty can under present conditions only be met by accepting the principle of military integration. This, they said, meant that the system of bilateral agreements with which France proposed to replace the integrated NATO command structure was no substitute for participation in the Organization.[14]

Let us look briefly at American perspectives on the role of two other international regional security organizations in order to compare them with perspectives on NATO's role.

SEATO'S ROLE

The United States has stood almost alone in acting as though SEATO had permanency—or even much substance. Its very creation represented less the juncture of several states' initiatives than a final phase in the spate of military pacts which the United States concluded during the late

---

[14] For text of the fourteen-nation declaration, see *New York Times,* March 19, 1966.

1940s and the early 1950s. Neither in 1954, when it was founded, nor at any time since, has there been sufficient community of interest in this area among the signatories to permit SEATO to become much more than a shadowy organization.[15]

Some of the functions the United States government perceived as possible for SEATO resembled those performed by NATO, but with significant additions and omissions. Furthermore, time seems not to have altered American hopes and expectations for SEATO as noticeably as it has altered those for NATO.

The most obvious hoped for role of SEATO was as counterpart to that of NATO: to help prevent Communist expansion in Southeast Asia. Secretary Dulles, who was most responsible for the Manila Pact, which established SEATO, envisaged that it would be connected with other American alliance arrangements to supplement American nuclear power in the Pacific.[16] SEATO was a sign of United States commitment to the defense of Southeast Asia, but the treaty commitment was more limited than in the case of NATO: the parties merely agreed that if there were an armed attack against any signatory in the treaty area or in Laos, Cambodia, or Vietnam, they would act "to meet the common danger in accordance with" their own constitutional processes. The alliance was to serve as a sign reading "Thin Ice" to show Communist observers that the United States was serious in this particular area.[17] Secretary Rusk, in a joint statement with the Foreign Minister of Thailand on March 6, 1962, declared that the United States' obligation "does not depend upon the prior agreement of all other parties to the treaty, since this treaty obligation is individual as well as collective." [18]

---

[15] As Paul Nitze pointed out in 1956, its origin gave the appearance of being an expedient designed for a short-range situation ["Defining the Coalition and Coalition Diplomacy," speech at Conference on Coalition Diplomacy, Rutgers University, May 18, 1956, p. 8. (Mimeographed.)]. In 1964 Admiral Felt, Commander-in-Chief Pacific, testified that "SEATO is valuable. ANZUS can be useful. But the real binder is commitment by the United States in bilateral security treaties and military assistance agreements" [House of Representatives Committee on Foreign Affairs, *Hearings, Foreign Assistance Act of 1964,* 88th Cong., 2nd sess. (1964), p. 694].

[16] See Royal Institute of International Affairs, *Collective Defence in South East Asia* (London: Royal Institute of International Affairs, 1956), pp. 12 and 20–21; also C. P. Sulzberger, *New York Times,* April 8, 1963.

[17] See Myron Weiner, "United States Policy in South and Southeast Asia," in Stephen D. Kertesz (ed.), *American Diplomacy in a New Era* (Notre Dame: University of Notre Dame Press, 1961), pp. 177–82; and Coral Bell, *Negotiation from Strength* (New York: Alfred A. Knopf, 1963), p. 93.

[18] George Modelski (ed.), *SEATO: Six Studies* (Melbourne: F. W. Cheshire, 1962), p. 293.

SEATO was expected to help counter armed aggression, but not through a coalition force; such a force would have been almost impossible to construct. American forces, backed up with units earmarked by other members, were counted on to do the job. These American forces were not to be "committed" as in the NATO case but would merely be part of the regular defense forces of the United States in the Pacific. Secretary Dulles spoke of the "mobile striking power" of the United States, not ground forces, as the main reliance.[19] Through the ANZUS Pact the United States already had an effective alliance with the two leading powers in the Southwest Pacific; SEATO offered only a little additional scope for cooperation among these three of its signatories.

SEATO increasingly became an instrument through which the United States could bring about the coordination of the other members' armed forces with its own much more powerful forces in order to protect the treaty area in an emergency. Also, the SEATO relationship made easier the provision of military facilities useful for logistics and communications, even though there were no "SEATO bases." The United States had, through other arrangements, acquired its own bases in the Philippines, Taiwan, Korea, Japan, and Okinawa. The joint exercises held under SEATO auspices probably have been the most noteworthy feature of SEATO's functioning. On one or two occasions these exercises have served another purpose: as demonstrations in the vicinity of possible Communist aggression.[20]

The United States also regarded SEATO as useful in improving the quality of the armed forces belonging to the less developed members especially through intensive and standardized training. Since American efforts to improve the defense capabilities of Asian countries not in the alliance appear to have been at least as successful, a question arises about the necessity of an organization like SEATO for this purpose. Nor has SEATO always been needed to influence some of its members. Constant American pressure on Australia to increase its defense forces has not required SEATO as a lever; ANZUS could have served as well (or as poorly).[21]

---

[19] Weiner, *op. cit.*

[20] As in the spring of 1963 [*Washington Post,* April 10, 1963 and *New York Times,* September 8, 1963].

[21] Neither United States nor British pressure sufficed to bring about an improvement until the Malaysian-Indonesian conflict became threatening to the Australians [see Tillman Durdin in *New York Times,* January 10, 1965].

Within SEATO, information relating to the Communist threat has been regularly exchanged and evaluated, but it has not been an effective means for coordinating foreign policy in the treaty area. Not even the three SEATO members belonging to NATO—the United States, Britain, and France—have been able to agree on a joint policy for critical issues. On several occasions the United States has tried to gain the support of other members for its policy towards Communist China.[22] As the situation in Vietnam grew increasingly dangerous, the United States was successful in gaining some diplomatic support in the semiannual SEATO meeting of April, 1964 and stronger support in May, 1965 despite Pakistani reservations. In 1964 France, however, having already parted company with the United States because of its proposals as to how Communist China should be treated, only halfway endorsed the need to resist Communist aggression and abstained altogether from the statements about Vietnam.[23] In 1965 France again abstained. The French foreign minister did not even attend the ministerial meeting, and the French representative clearly enunciated his country's objections to the other allies' support of American policy in Vietnam. By 1966 abstention had changed to outright obstruction.

The United States has not shared the view of the Asian members that SEATO should be a funnel through which various types of aid, military and otherwise, might reach them. Nevertheless, membership in SEATO has helped them to get special consideration when such American aid was available generally.[24] By the end of the 1950s SEATO had become an instrument for some modest cooperative projects in cultural, scientific, and social fields. The United States has never, however, conceived of it as an economic aid agency; aid to countries of Southeast Asia has gone through bilateral channels or through specialized agencies of the United Nations.

Little has come of American expectations that SEATO would be an

[22] Cf. W. Macmahon Ball, "A Political Re-examination of SEATO," *International Organization*, Winter, 1958, pp. 17–25, esp. p. 21.

[23] *New York Times*, April 12 and 16, 1964. Further pressure was exerted at the Standing Group's meeting in October [*ibid.*, October 14, 1964].

[24] Secretary Dulles' statement at news conference held February 28, 1956, which appears in *Department of State Bulletin*, March 12, 1956, p. 409. He pointed out that other important Asian nations were not members. Secretary McNamara justified military aid to the Philippines partly because of its membership in SEATO [House of Representatives Committee on Foreign Affairs, *Hearings, Foreign Assistance Act of 1964*, 88th Cong., 2nd sess. (1964) p. 92].

effective instrument, of a kind not needed in Europe, for cooperation in preventing subversion. As with action taken in support of NATO commitments, action in support of SEATO commitments represented to the United States government a way acceptable to the Asian members to extend American military power to areas otherwise less susceptible to its influence. The tremendous disparities in power between the Asian members and the others made it impossible (or unnecessary) to adopt forms emphasizing the equality of the allies or even to speak of "self-help"; for the Asian members had not reached a stage of economic and social development comparable to even the least developed of the United States' allies in Europe. Too weak to express their displeasure with American policies in ways open to NATO members, the Asian states belonging to SEATO could assert their lack of dependence on the United States only by threatening to withdraw from the alliance, boycotting SEATO, or otherwise publicizing their lack of cohesion; they could not do it while declaring their unity with the leading partner, as all but De Gaulle's France have done in NATO.

THE ROLE OF THE OAS

United States hopes for the OAS, unlike those for SEATO, were rooted in a long tradition. Pan-American relations have been close for a century, and the OAS is closely interlaced with other portions of the inter-American system. Yet, from the point of view of the United States, the OAS is like SEATO in that it has been plagued by the problems of the great versus the small. There is only one great power in the OAS; although the twenty other members vary greatly in size and influence, not even Argentina, Brazil, and Mexico have a weight in the organization comparable to that of Britain, France, and West Germany in NATO. In any alliance the interests of each member are likely to be at some variance with those of the others; in the OAS, which is both more and less than an alliance, the main disharmonies have been all too obvious. As one official long associated with inter-American agencies remarked, at times the OAS has appeared to be an "Organization of Latin America vs. the United States" rather than the organization which its name implies.[25]

In 1947, when the United States was considering the Treaty of Rio de

---

[25] William Manger, *Pan America in Crisis: The Future of the OAS* (Washington: Public Affairs Press, 1961), p. 57.

Janeiro, no fear was expressed of an armed attack by any American republic upon any other, but only of a threat from a non-American power.[26] Not until the Cuban crisis of October, 1962 did this danger seem very real to the other OAS members; they were much more concerned about intervention in Cuba by the United States, ostensibly to keep out some non-American power. Indeed, in the 1950s the usefulness of the OAS in deterring a possible attack from an outsider also seemed remote to United States officials.

For many years North American leaders saw the OAS as one instrument for maintaining stability in Latin America. The United States government put tranquillity above other policy objectives.[27] President Eisenhower described the OAS in 1958 as "the most successful sustained adventure in international community living that the world has seen." [28] Two years earlier, Secretary Dulles had held it up as a model organization which "takes account of external perils but . . . concentrates primarily upon its own positive accomplishments." [29] The employment of the OAS for keeping the peace among its members has no counterpart in the other regional organizations in which the United States participates. Americans have, however, recognized the value of NATO as an agency for reconciling divergent national policies.

By the late 1950s the United States had begun to look upon the OAS as useful also to prevent Communist subversion of recognized governments, a danger which was affecting not only peaceful relations among the Latin-American states but also between one of them and the United States. The Americans have been faced in Latin America as in Southeast Asia with a dilemma: protection against Communist subversion has seemed to involve protection of unrepresentative governments or governments insensitive to the need for social reforms and has often seemed to range the United States against indigenous demands for change which have been increasingly difficult to resist. The United States has been

[26] For the Senate's expectations, see Senate Committee on Foreign Relations, Executive Report, No. 11, *Report on the Inter-American Treaty of Reciprocal Assistance* (Rio Pact), 80th Cong., 1st sess. (1947).

[27] John C. Dreier, *The Organization of American States and the Hemisphere Crisis* (New York: Harper and Row, 1962), pp. 75–76, and Edwin Lieuwen, *Arms and Politics in Latin America* (rev. ed., New York: Frederick A. Praeger, 1961), pp. 2 and 11.

[28] Quoted by Assistant Secretary of State Roy R. Rubottom, "United States Relations with Latin America," *Department of State Bulletin,* March 31, 1958, p. 519.

[29] "Developing NATO in Peace," *loc. cit.*

both prompt and vigorous in demanding OAS approval of its own actions to prevent Communist-inspired coups.[30]

The United States might have, but has not consistently and vigorously, used the OAS to mount a hemisphere-wide campaign for human
rights; neither has the United States consistently responded to Latin-
American pressure to use the organs of the inter-American system for
promoting economic development. The formation of the Inter-American
Development Bank in 1960 and the launching of the Alliance for
Progress in 1961 suggest a new willingness to act through multilateral
organizations; but as with its alliance partners in NATO and SEATO, in
matters of foreign aid the United States has customarily preferred to
deal with each directly and individually. Even the Alliance for Progress
connections with the OAS were at first rather tenuous. However, the
Alliance's roots were multilateral; and the OAS has become more and
more involved in the Alliance for Progress.[31] As for trade matters, the
United States has preferred to act through other organizations, ones
which also have European members, especially because of the triangular
North American–European–Latin-American trade relationship.[32]

As an organ for military coordination the OAS has not appeared useful either to the United States or to its Latin-American fellow members.
For most of the latter, a joint armed force against aggression from outside the Western Hemisphere, or even OAS bases, seems to be a cover
for United States armed force or United States bases and so runs counter to the emotion-laden principle of non-intervention. The United States
has not been much tempted to use the OAS in these ways; for in the
atomic age even the Caribbean countries have had little of military importance to offer, and that little is already available through bilateral

---

[30] M. Margaret Ball, "Issues for the Americas: Intervention vs. Human Rights
and the Preservation of Democratic Institutions," *International Organization,*
Winter, 1961, pp. 25–26 and Dreier, *op. cit.,* pp. 94–115.

[31] For the United States response on Latin-American economic questions, see
Dreier, *op. cit.,* pp. 83–84 and 108–10; Milton Eisenhower, "The Alliance for
Progress: Historic Roots," in John C. Dreier (ed.), *The Alliance for Progress*
(Baltimore: Johns Hopkins Press, 1962), pp. 11 ff.; Adolf A. Berle, *Latin America:
Diplomacy and Reality* (New York: Harper and Row, 1962), p. 47; and A. Lleras
Camargo, "The Alliance for Progress," *Foreign Affairs,* October, 1963, pp. 25,
27–29, 31, 35–36.

[32] Dreier, *The Organization of American States and the Hemisphere Crisis,* pp. 76–
78; Manger, *op. cit.,* p. 72; Arthur P. Whitaker, "United States Policy in the
Western Hemisphere," in Kertesz (ed.), *op. cit.,* pp. 154–55.

arrangements.[33] Military assistance to Latin-American countries, compared with that to other parts of the world, has remained small; and its distribution has been governed largely by non-military considerations.

The use of the word "*cooperation*" to describe a giver-taker relationship is as semantically confusing as another phrase much more often used regarding the OAS: "hemispheric solidarity." This concept is the OAS counterpart to "Atlantic Community." In the OAS case, however, the United States does not have to contend with allies as powerful as other leading countries in NATO. The cultural differences between the United States and the other members of the OAS are greater than those between the United States and almost all other NATO members. These conditions plus the traditional Latin-American distrust of the giant partner have meant that necessity more than sentiment has been the rock on which the lender and the others have built their inter-American system. One should add, however, that the United States and the Latin-American countries have dealt with each other in the framework of a "special relationship" much longer than the United States has done so with any other group of states.

The United States has managed to avoid certain undertakings which reflect the Latin-Americans' preference for a "juridical" approach to problems in their relations with their great Northern neighbor. Yet the Americans too have formed the habit of making declarations stand for deeds. The United States has tried repeatedly, and with little practical effect, to persuade OAS members to declare against Communism and all its likely adherents.[34]

NATO and SEATO, from their inception, have permitted American power to be applied in support of American policy objectives in ways and places not otherwise possible; a similar function is hard to discern in the OAS. The power was already there, and the problem has been how

[33] The United States proposal in the spring of 1965 to create an inter-American peace force may seem to reflect a shift in policy; in reality, it does not. What was proposed was not a NATO-like military coalition against an external aggressor, but an institution to do collectively what was denounced as "unilateral intervention" in the Dominican crisis at that time. It proved possible to establish under OAS auspices only an ad hoc force for the Dominican Republic disorders, a force to which only a few OAS members contributed.

[34] The United States has attempted to use the OAS to cope with the Cuban problem and NATO to cope with the German problem. However, the effort in the OAS was to isolate Castro's Cuba and in NATO to bring Germany back into effective collaboration with the other Western powers.

to maintain it in the face of changing conditions. Thus the OAS has been useful to make the realities palatable by accenting both the giant member's special obligations and the other members' equal rights. It has also served to obtain diplomatic support for United States policy which might not be forthcoming otherwise and to legitimate and make more respectable the dominant position of the United States in the western hemisphere. For such purposes the OAS has provided a convenient channel of communication to the whole of Latin America. In these respects, what American officials expected of the OAS resembles what they came to expect of NATO in the 1960s. As a means of political consultation, however, the OAS does not in range and detail compare in importance with NATO.

THE ROLES OF THE ECONOMIC ORGANIZATIONS

Although the Bank, the Fund, GATT, and OECD differ in important ways, some of which are touched on in Appendix B they can be discussed together for purposes of comparing American perspectives on their usefulness to the United States. Despite obvious differences from the regional security organizations, they have served American interests in somewhat similar fashion. The Bank, Fund, GATT, and OECD were intended to aid in promoting world trade and thereby American trade. The economic functions of one or another have included providing conditions for full employment, promoting economic stability, widening markets, easing the gold drain from the United States, and sharing the financial burdens of the leadership which the United States had assumed for non-Communist countries. The last two functions suggest how the role of these organizations has changed as America's position in the world economy has changed. Although the Communist-bloc countries belonged to none of these organizations, the activities of the Bank, the Fund, GATT, and OECD have been carried on without reference to cold war objectives.

This observation suggests a difference from and a similarity to American perspectives on the regional alliances. From the point of view of the United States, each of the economic organizations was intended to prevent a number of undesired events: trade clashes, discrimination against United States commerce, predatory manipulation of exchange and trade controls, spread of economic recessions, pressure for changes in the price of gold, and the like. But the actors some of whose possible actions were to be deterred were already in the organization; they were not outsiders against whom the organization was formed. The United States nonetheless did not lose sight of the fact that if such deterrence succeeded, the "free world" would be stronger in its competition with the Communist bloc.[35]

Like NATO, SEATO, and the OAS in the diplomatic field, the economic organizations have been looked upon as useful instruments for coordinating policy in areas where non-coordination would be injurious to the American economy. They also have been means for working together on joint projects in which each participant helps the others while helping itself. In none of these organizations have the members been divided up into a few patrons and many clients; all are assumed to be capable of contributing. (As the Bank's and the Fund's membership has expanded to include over one hundred states and the number of GATT's participants has risen to more than seventy, this assumption has become hard to demonstrate in practice.)

The OECD has been regarded by many Americans as the economic counterpart to NATO in building an Atlantic community, despite the fact that the OECD's membership is broader, even including Japan. The United States had pressed for the change from the OEEC, in which it was not a member, to the OECD in order to broaden what might have grown into a European community into one in which the United States and Canada also are members.

Although it was not mentioned publicly, the economic organizations also were means, as were SEATO, NATO, and the OAS, of extending American influence into areas otherwise closed to the United States. We have already noted that the Americans thought of the OECD as a useful channel of communication and pressure in getting other members to help in assisting underdeveloped countries. In the case of the Bank and the Fund, American methods of influencing the others have been more subtle; through these agencies economic practices in foreign countries which the United States could not change unilaterally have been altered to accord with American preferences. Members of an international or-

---

[35] Thus Secretary of the Treasury Dillon declared in an ECOSOC meeting regarding GATT, that the "United States could not consider as a step forward any proposal to bring about universal membership in GATT, if admitting the centrally-directed countries entailed the sacrifice of the principles of liberal multilateral trade" [Summary of ECOSOC activities, *International Organization*, Winter, 1961, p. 173].

ganization have sometimes taken advice from the experts in that organization which would have been unacceptable if given directly by United States experts. How GATT has promoted American objectives in otherwise unavailable ways is not so easy to see. Like other negotiations, tariff bargaining is based on give-and-take, but presumably in any agreement each participant believes his "take" has exceeded his "give." GATT has reinforced the most-favored-nation principle, a rule long enshrined, although not strictly observed, in American foreign economic policy.[36]

Americans have sometimes sought to use international organizations for incompatible purposes. Within NATO, there is much evidence to suggest that the goal of building morale stood in the way of the goal of a more balanced program of collective force. Efforts to improve the European allies' military standards through American efforts in NATO did not always induce a spirit of, or a capability for, self-help; the improvement brought greater dependence in some instances. On the other hand, as some of the larger allies have become stronger, they have felt less compelled to join in cooperative ventures. So long as NATO's main task is to give strength and unity to a military alliance to deter the Soviet Union from expansion, NATO cannot be useful as an organ for accommodation with Russia; nor can it be the institution for rapidly developing an Atlantic Community.

Americans have sometimes seen NATO as an organization for promoting United States foreign policy objectives in certain geographic areas more effectively than would otherwise have been possible. Not so often have they been willing to see it as an organization for promoting our allies' foreign policy objectives in North America. Influence gained in one direction is at least partially offset by the constraints imposed by participation in multilateral organizations.

On the other hand, success in cooperative undertakings has enhanced the growth of community sense and has heightened the morale of the smaller allies. The United States could reasonably expect to maintain its leadership status by taking advantage of NATO's consultative function, by granting aid to its NATO allies, and by profiting from NATO's ability to deter the Soviet Union. NATO's help in managing the German

---

[33] One reason for promoting the Kennedy Round was fear in the United States that an "inward-looking" Common Market would injure American interests—as well as those of other non-members of the EEC.

problem reinforced the alliance's deterrence function despite frequent Soviet allegations that Germany's position in NATO was provocative.

The incompatibility of functions which OAS and SEATO have been expected to perform is more apparent than in the case of NATO. Also, in the former organizations the other members' views about who is the enemy have often diverged from American perspectives. In regions where the rulers are reactionary or dictatorial the American view of the organization as a deterrent to the spread of Communist power has often been implemented in such a way as to run counter to the American desire to promote domestic reform in the less developed member countries. The two policy goals, stability and dynamic change, are in conflict. This was especially true before the United States recognized the need to respond to their poorer allies' economic demands. The question, "Who are *we?*" arises in much more acute a form in the OAS and SEATO than in NATO.

This question of "we-ness" becomes even more complicated when the unity of the United States with its NATO partners is jeopardized by its unity with non-NATO allies. Inconsistencies in American perspectives regarding these alliances are intimately related to the worldwide responsibilities of the United States.[37] Until it became a leader in World War II, the United States could follow divergent policies in different parts of the world without suffering the disadvantages of inconsistency. Now the "seamless web" sometimes has holes.

Within the economic organizations incompatibilities are less numerous. Since they serve more limited functions, these agencies do not have to carry the sentimental load borne by NATO and the OAS. A security organization demands sacrifice to limit damage from the foe; it thus tempts members to try to shift the burden to other allies. When military strength is built up at the expense of economic development, the alliances will operate at cross-purposes to GATT, the Bank, the Fund, and the OECD. However, success in using the alliances to deter attacks can provide favorable conditions for the success of the economic agencies

---

[37] Cf. Arnold Wolfers' comment that if an alliance system is envisaged as a wheel, "one could say that the friends and allies of the United States are spread out along its rim, each occupying the end of a spoke, while the United States is located at the hub of the wheel" [Arnold Wolfers (ed.), *Alliance Policy in the Cold War* (Baltimore: Johns Hopkins Press, 1959), p. 7]. On the problem of priorities, note Dean Acheson's quotation from Plautus about the difficulty of blowing and swallowing at the same time [*Power and Diplomacy* (Cambridge: Harvard University Press, 1958), p. 105].

while the latter are promoting interests which make it worthwhile for allies to band together in their defense.

This cursory comparison of the roles which Americans have expected NATO and the other selected international organizations to play suggests how much more rigorous are the tests by which NATO is judged. Because Americans have looked to NATO to perform more different functions more effectively, its burden is far heavier. Like NATO, however, the others are expected to be instruments for mutual aid, for improved coordination of member governments' actions, and for an extension both geographically and functionally of American influence.

For every function and in each organization, the United States is in the most influential position to see that actions in each are compatible with those in all the rest. What other roles has the United States been expected to play? We examine these in the following chapter.

CHAPTER FOUR

AMERICAN PERSPECTIVES: THE ROLE OF THE UNITED STATES IN NATO

JUST AS the net advantages of international organization for different members vary, so do the members' perspectives regarding the roles they intend to play in the common enterprise differ. Americans think of the United States as a full member of NATO with all the benefits and responsibilities suggested in the previous chapter. But they do not think of the United States as just another member. Policy-makers have at one time or another envisaged at least seven distinctive roles for the United States in furthering the objectives sought through NATO. Each of these seven somewhat overlapping roles has been performed mainly, and a few entirely, by the United States. Each is also without precedent in American peacetime experience.

1. From the beginning, American officials have expected their country *to make good the deficiencies of the alliance as a whole;* this is the first United States role we shall discuss. What other allies could not or would not provide, the United States would have to contribute, directly in the form of land, sea and air forces or indirectly in the form of military assistance—giving, loaning money for, or selling materials and supplying training and technical help.

Leaders among all the allies expected some form of American military assistance to implement the United States commitment in the North Atlantic Treaty; but at the insistence of Senator Vandenberg and some of his Congressional colleagues, the offer of military aid was conditioned on allied preparation of an integrated plan for mutual defense. Some would have preferred that the aid then be channeled through an alliance organ. Most of it in the first years, however, was granted bilaterally, though in line with multilaterally approved plans. When the various commands were organized and SHAPE was established at the end of 1950, and especially after joint enterprises were started, some of the military "assistance" was actually the American share (the giant one to be sure) in the cost of common undertakings. The United States government expected that American military aid would enable the European allies to increase their contributions of troops and, later, of other essentials. In the earlier years Canada also provided assistance.[1]

At first, aid consisted largely of World War II stocks of equipment given to European allies which were rebuilding their armed forces almost from scratch. Thus Britain, which by 1951 had ceased to need economic assistance under the Marshall Plan, could still receive spare parts for its rearmament effort; similar aid helped to boost the military capacity of the other allies. This was the period when, in the light of the first Soviet atomic bomb test and the heat of the Korean War, American officials were giving budget-making instruction to European allies as to what their defense budget allocations must be if they wished to continue receiving aid.[2] During this period of intense American defense mobilization effort, the United States inaugurated the program of "offshore procurement" which, inter alia, helped the Europeans set up their own productive facilities for military equipment. Purchasing under this program also gave the United States unusual powers in determining allies' foreign economic undertakings, just as the counterpart fund system had provided unprecedented opportunities for participating in other countries' "domestic" affairs.[3] Secretary Dulles denied that aid was ever used as a lever to alter the foreign policy of a recipient.[4] NATO's Annual Review procedure, however, permitted the United States to maintain

---

[1] See Appendix C for figures on military aid.

[2] See testimony of American aid officials (Milton Katz and Richard Bissell) on efforts to influence European defense budgets [Senate Committee on Foreign Relations, *Hearings, Mutual Assistance Act of 1951*, 82nd Cong., 1st sess. (1951), pp. 61, 63–65, and 180].

[3] As Herman M. Somers said, "Procurement is not merely buying" ["Civil-Military Relations in Mutual Security", *Annals* of the American Academy of Political and Social Science, July, 1953, p. 30]. Cf. also Michael M. Cardozo, *Diplomats in International Cooperation* (Ithaca: Cornell University Press, 1962), pp. 74–75.

[4] It was only for specific purposes sought by the United States [House of Representatives Committee on Foreign Affairs, *Hearings, Mutual Security Act of 1957*, 85th Cong., 1st sess. (1957), p. 535].

rather constant pressure on its allies to improve their defense forces in directions which would support strategies and policy objectives approved by the United States while shifting some of the onus for this pressure to an organization in which the allies might come to understand their own needs and commit themselves to defense programs consonant with those needs.

From the start, American officials insisted in their Congressional appearances that the object of the military aid program was joint protection and that it had no "give-away" aspect whatever. It was, they said, not "foreign," but truly mutual, combined defense. Expenditures for aid to allies' forces gave the United States more defense for the dollar than comparable expenditures for American forces. Secretary Dulles spoke of military assistance as the "foreign component of our own defense structure." Defense officials pointed out that since the security of the United States depended upon allied forces as well as upon its own, the allied forces had to be brought up to American standards, and for this aid was necessary.

The growth of European prosperity and the increasingly variegated threat of the Soviet Union caused changes in the type of aid given to the NATO allies. Economic assistance to them had tapered off by 1955. After 1954 military aid funds were for maintenance, "modern" (nuclear and non-nuclear) weapons available only in the United States and "critical" types of equipment, and training in the use of such weapons and equipment. Eventually, what had at all times been a selective program for individual countries changed from gifts to sales of equipment; only training remained in the "aid" category. Greece and Turkey alone continued to be important recipients of military assistance grants. Methods became more supple. The United States tried pump-priming by cost-sharing projects; it sought to induce European allies to embark on new types of programs and to make a greater contribution to them as American aid diminished. Such projects included the Maintenance and Supply Service, the Anti-Submarine Warfare Research Center, and the Air Defense Technical Center. These, and most especially the Mutual Weapons Development Program, were intended also to bring about the best use of scientific and technical resources in the alliance and to produce compatibility in tactics, weapons systems, and military doctrine. This last objective became increasingly important as the opportunities for standardization afforded in the earlier period by the United States position as the sole supplier of (surplus World War II) equipment lessened. The

Mutual Weapons Development Program disappeared from the military aid category in 1964. Its place was taken by aid to allies in jointly financed research and development, but only when the United States was interested in the end product or when another United States program would be helped. The United States also promoted the licensing of American weapons systems and equipment for joint production by a number of manufacturers in the NATO countries. By the 1960s the inflow of payments for military equipment had come to exceed the flow outward in military aid to the NATO allies.[5] The United States had also changed the emphasis from direct training of allied military personnel to the instruction of allied teachers for allied trainees.

Although military aid to NATO allies, even on this diminished scale, has continued to be the target of determined critics, each administration has found it indispensable. Government officials have variously argued that there was danger, without the remaining projects, of the allies' withdrawing into themselves, that the military aid has encouraged the allies to do things they would not otherwise do, or that United States defense plans depended upon aid. There were few who in their public testimony also pointed out that if an ally knew the United States military really wanted it to have a particular weapon, it could depend on American aid to provide the weapon, with no need for that ally's budget to suffer the cost of supply.[6]

Whatever may have been the case with respect to equipment and training, military leaders in the early 1950s declared and apparently believed that the need for stationing United States military forces in Europe would be temporary. Although these forces were numerically only a minor portion of the total allied forces assigned to NATO, they were much the strongest and were almost literally the backbone of the allied

[5] For the stages in which the United States phased out aid, see David Bendall, "Burden Sharing in NATO," *NATO Letter*, September, 1963, p. 13. He pointed out that the most equitable sharing would still leave the United States the giant contributor. See also House of Representatives Committee on Foreign Affairs, *Hearings, Foreign Assistance Act of 1964*, 88th Cong., 2nd sess. (1964), p. 652; and E. Vandevanter, *Coordinated Weapons Production in NATO* (Santa Monica: Rand Corporation, 1964), p. 76.

[6] But a RAND member did: Malcolm Hoag in "The Economics of Military Alliance" in Charles J. Hitch and Roland G. McKean *et al.*, *The Economics of Defense in a Nuclear Age* (Cambridge: Harvard University Press, 1960), p. 295. In the 1960s, when the balance of payments problem was being met in several ways, the United States often simply facilitated the recipient ally's obtaining credit assistance commercially.

command. As years went by, they continued to be the best-trained and best-equipped forces in Europe and the readiest for any military confrontation.[7]

The United States has filled the breach at sea as well as on land. The United States Sixth Fleet is the major element of NATO's naval strength in the Mediterranean, but it is only to be "assigned" to SACEUR in case of war. Naval units belonging to a number of other NATO countries have as a principal task the protection of this fleet.[8] The main portion of NATO's naval strength in the Atlantic, too, is provided by the United States, although here also ships are not permanently assigned to the Supreme Allied Commander Atlantic (SACLANT) in peacetime, but only during joint exercises.

2. The second role Americans have envisaged for the United States in NATO has been *to act as pilot in the strategic planning of the alliance.* He who pays the piper is usually in a position to call the tune (some might say that since the United States has been calling the tune it should pay the piper, or at least the largest share), but there have been other reasons for expecting that this role would be played.[9] In the first years of the alliance American military officers did not want to be committed in advance to any responsibilities which they thought they could not meet.[10] Nor did they consider the possibility that the creation of NATO would alter their planning for American security by requiring them to

[7] General Earl Wheeler, Chief of Staff of the Army, described them in February, 1963 as "the finest Army probably that the United States has ever had in peacetime." The only comparable allied force was the Canadian, but it was just one brigade, about a third of a division [House of Representatives Committee on Armed Services, *Hearings, Military Posture and H.R. 2440,* 88th Cong., Ist sess. (1963), p. 767]. What has been said for the provision of United States ground forces in the Central European area can also be said for the American contribution to the Allied Tactical Air Force. For the United States contribution to allied defense, see the annual estimates of the Institute for Strategic Studies, London, *The Military Balance.* For another comment from a European source, on the American contribution, see Forschungsinstitut der Deutschen Gesellschaft für Auswärtige Politik, *Der Stand der europäischen Sicherheit* (Frankfurt am Main: Alfred Metzner Verlag, 1962), pp. 100–01.

[8] F. W. Mulley, *The Politics of Western Defense* (New York: Frederick A. Praeger, 1962), p. 168.

[9] See, for example, Secretary of Defense McNamara's testimony before the House of Representatives Committee on Armed Services, in January, 1963, for an illustration of American reasoning on the responsibilities of the member carrying the giant share [*Hearings, Military Posture and H.R. 2440,* 88th Cong., 1st sess. (1963), p. 297].

[10] See President Truman's description of the view of the Joint Chiefs of Staff, *Memoirs,* vol. II (Garden City: Doubleday and Company, 1956), p. 245.

share responsibility for that planning with others. Whatever the American military views, there were, apart from the British, scarcely any alliance partners capable of significantly sharing in this task at the time. With the increasing importance, after 1954, of the nuclear deterrent in NATO strategy the gap widened between the Americans, who more than ever believed themselves capable of solo piloting of the alliance's strategy, and the others in the alliance. Technological developments were not the only explanation. From the beginning there had been a gap due to the tremendous disparity between American and allied resources and to the Americans' tendency to think of themselves as almost exclusively gifted in knowledge of appropriate strategy because they were "ahead" in some phases.[11] Steps taken to implement American-induced strategy for NATO, particularly those which put main reliance on the strategic deterrent, increased United States dominance in this field. Subsequently, in the 1960s, the United States' stress on mobility increased the likelihood that the country most capable of developing a mobile force would conduct the alliance's strategy. With the new emphasis on the interrelatedness of the several facets of alliance strategy, the United States pressed its European allies for contributions the latter had earlier been taught to discount in importance, urging these at a time when the allies could no longer be brought by financial inducements to do what they did not believe in. The more the Americans stressed the flexible response, the less credible to their allies appeared United States guarantees regarding the strategic deterrent. During this same period the diversification of the Communist challenge increased the difficulty of maintaining United States dominance in planning NATO's strategy.[12]

3. Closely linked with the first two roles for the United States is the third: *to guide the general policies of NATO.* American initiatives were crucially important both in the adoption of the principle of collective, balanced forces and in the creation of the posts of SACEUR and SACLANT. Influential European officials participated, but the initiative and the insistent pressure came from the United States. Americans also took the lead in persuading the alliance to admit the three new members, the most important of which was Germany, whose rearmament had been an objective of American policy from 1950 onward. When thwarted momentarily by France's setting-up and tearing-down of the EDC, the

[11] See Bernard Brodie, "What Price Conventional Capabilities in Europe?" *Reporter*, May 23, 1963, p. 27.
[12] Cf. Alastair Buchan, *NATO in the 1960's* (New York: Frederick A. Praeger, 1960), p. 17.

Americans utilized a device for securing German rearmament that was not of their designing. The British had learned that the way to influence the alliance's policies was to influence the United States, and it was their formula that resolved the impasse created by French rejection of the EDC.[13]

Once a policy was accepted in general by the alliance, bilateral arrangements could be made with the more eager members. Where the United States was not eager and determined, other members' suggestions did not get very far, as in some of the more ambitious proposals to flesh out Article 2 by developing non-military tasks for NATO. For some purposes the other allies have been able to exert counterpressure, however; and the United States has found them more and more recalcitrant as they have regained confidence in their ability to evaluate American initiatives or withstand the consequences of American displeasure. Seldom, however, have all fourteen joined in active and decisive opposition; many of the smaller members at least have found good reasons for siding with the United States against more powerful states in their immediate vicinity. Highly attractive inducements continue to make American guidance palatable, particularly to the poorer countries of the Mediterranean. In recent years United States officials have talked a great deal about listening to their allies' views, but when they fail to hear a united voice from the other side of the Atlantic, they do not wait long before filling the aching void with their own proposals—to the satisfaction of most of the allies, it should be added.[14] When Americans have suggested that NATO extend the scope of foreign policy coordination to

[13] Cf. Raymond Aron, *Paix et Guerre* (Paris: Calmann-Lévy, 1962), pp. 438–41, who contrasts the British methods with the French tendency to demonstrate France's power by opposition.

On the admission of Germany see Sir Anthony Eden, *Full Circle* (Boston: Houghton Mifflin, 1960), esp. pp. 182–83; Laurence W. Martin, "The American Decision to Rearm Germany," in Harold Stein (ed.), *American Civil-Military Decisions* (Birmingham: University of Alabama Press, 1963), pp. 643–65; Truman, *op. cit.*, pp. 253–55; Dean Acheson, *Sketches from Life* (New York: Harper and Brothers, 1959), pp. 25–27; Secretary Dulles' testimony before Senate Committee on Foreign Relations, *Hearings, Mutual Security Act of 1954*, 83rd Cong., 2nd sess. (1954), pp. 3–4; Robert E. Osgood, *NATO: The Entangling Alliance* (Chicago: University of Chicago Press, 1962), pp. 84–87 and 91–98. Recognizing implacable opposition among some allies towards admitting Spain, the United States indirectly coordinated American defense forces in Spain with NATO activities, and American officials regularly visited Spain to brief General Franco after ministerial meetings of the North Atlantic Council.

[14] See, for example, McGeorge Bundy's speech in Copenhagen before the Atlantic Treaty Association, September 27, 1962, quoted in Senate Committee on Foreign Relations, *Problems and Trends in Atlantic Partnership I*, Senate Doc. No. 132, 87th Cong., 2nd sess. (1962), p. 40. Also see Mulley, *op. cit.*, p. 235.

areas outside Europe, however, their guidance has not been accepted.

4. Many important decisions, even within the NATO area, are not for the United States to make; a fourth role for the United States in NATO has been *to induce, energize, and stimulate actions which its allies can only undertake by themselves.* What kinds of actions? First, and foremost, and always, measures to increase the number and improve the quality of the forces the allies devote to collective defense. Quality, because it can be raised by American contributions, has been easier to improve than quantity, which is closely related to the ticklish question of length of military service, a domestic matter in which the Americans can hardly interfere. (Most of the allies have reduced their period of training far below what Americans believe to be the minimum necessary to produce a qualified soldier.) Through NATO the United States has induced research, development, and production programs for military purposes—first in individual countries and later across national boundaries in cooperative undertakings—and has promoted other kinds of cooperative programs, including certain service functions for NATO forces.

Occasionally the United States has sought diplomatic support from its NATO allies for a stand which it was going to take anyway, such as non-recognition of Red China and the barring of its entrance into the United Nations. Sometimes the United States, instead of trying to stimulate action by its allies, has tried to discourage it, as when Secretary Dulles damped down some of the allies' pressure on the United States to agree to an East-West summit meeting in 1958. Or the government has chosen not to incite action because it wished to avoid similar action itself, as when the architects of the New Look refrained from pressing for increases in either allied or United States conventional forces. On the other hand, the Americans displayed fresh energy in the post-Sputnik era in stimulating cooperative NATO programs, if only to invigorate the lagging European confidence in American technological leadership. Political conditions within NATO countries as well as changes in technology have altered the pressure Americans have exerted for particular programs. Thus they offered strong inducements to gain permission to implant IRBMs on European soil in 1958 but withdrew these same missiles rather quietly in 1963.

What are the means by which the United States has sought to stimulate actions which it wishes its allies to take? For many years the United

States could rely on manipulating the military aid program, called by General Norstad the "catalyst." However, the only publicly declared threat to reduce military aid in order to get desired action was the one made when the ratification of the EDC hung in the balance in 1954.

Offers to facilitate the acquisition of desired military equipment, to contribute capital for joint enterprises in military items, and to provide training in the use of "modern" equipment have proved effective incentives to action. Putting up a large share of the necessary funds made possible the installation of the NATO Air Defense Ground Environment System, which helped to unify several national air defense systems under allied command.[15] Training and exchange programs have the special advantage that by reaching key people or individuals who will become leaders, they spread the American viewpoint like ripples on a pond. The heavily subsidized Mutual Weapons Development Program, while useful in other respects did not insure that the end product would be purchased by the member countries, even though a weapon had been designed to meet NATO requirements.

In the American (and also British and Canadian) experience, cost-sharing in the form of a conditional grant-in-aid from a wealthier to a needy government is a familiar voluntary device for getting others to participate. The United States used this method for certain NATO allies in the early 1960s. To achieve the American desire for improved logistics in NATO and at the same time diminish the balance of payments deficit, the United States ceased to subsidize the NATO Maintenance and Supply Organization and persuaded the other members to accept a pro-rata cost-sharing of future programs as well as a greater responsibility for management. It also extended credits for increased purchases of American-made military equipment.[16]

Such methods appear to be more effective than the pep talks by leading American officials which have become almost a ritual since the appointment of General Eisenhower as SACEUR. One limitation to the

---

[15] House of Representatives Committee on Appropriations, *Hearings, Mutual Security Act of 1961,* 86th Cong., 2nd sess. (1961), p. 2564; Vandevanter, *op. cit.,* p. 71; and C. L. Sulzberger in *New York Times,* April 10, 1963. The SHAPE Air Technical Center at first was completely financed by the United States, but after some years was transferred to NATO funding [H. George Franks, "International Team Solving Many Defence Problems," *NATO's Fifteen Nations,* August–September, 1964, p. 84].

[16] House of Representatives Committee on Foreign Affairs, *Hearings, Foreign Assistance Act of 1964,* 88th Cong., 2nd sess. (1964), pp. 93, 508, 510, 638.

effectiveness of these lectures in recent years is the loss by most of the European allies of that general sense of urgency in preparing for Soviet aggression which is chronic (or chronically stimulated) in Washington.[17] Warnings have often fallen on deaf ears, especially when the listener targets were France and Portugal, which had other concerns. Since outright criticism would be counterproductive, quiet appeals to reason made by American officials to their opposite numbers either in NATO bodies or their national capitals had to be utilized; such appeals could hope to be only moderately successful. More effective were promises such as that given by President Eisenhower in 1954 during negotiations for Germany's admission into NATO. He assured the allies that the United States would continue to maintain appropriate units of American military forces on the Continent and, in addition, would share information authorized by Congress regarding the military use of the new tactical nuclear weapons.[18]

5. A fifth role for the United States has been *to fill the principal military commands in the alliance.* This does not mean that the NATO commanders who are American take orders from the United States government in their NATO capacity, although several, including SACEUR, also hold American commands. All but the first SACEUR, General Eisenhower, have also been Commander-in-Chief of the United States Forces in Europe. (Their deputies in this latter command seem to have borne the main burdens of it.)

The North Atlantic Council appoints the Supreme Commanders and has always appointed Americans to the SHAPE and Atlantic commands. In anticipation of a vacancy the United States informally sounds out its allies as to a particular officer's acceptability. With foreknowledge of the President's intended nominee, the Council then formally asks him to make a nomination, which it accepts. In addition to SACEUR and SACLANT, the Commander-in-Chief Mediterranean (who is, however, subordinate to SACEUR) has always been an American. In most of the NATO military command structure a commander and his deputy are of different nationalities. Americans have held high positions even

[17] For one among many commentaries on such differences in the evaluation of the Soviet danger, see Louis Halle "The Cracked Alliance," *New Republic,* February 23, 1963, pp. 17–20.

[18] "Agreement on Restoration of German Sovereignty and German Association with Western Defense, *"Department of State Bulletin,* October 11, 1954, pp. 519–20; "United States Policy Declaration on Western European Union," *ibid.,* March 21, 1955, pp. 464–65.

where there are no American forces, as in the case of the air commander for Allied Forces Northern Europe, an American serving under a British commander.[19]

Subordinate commands occasionally change as to nationality of the occupant and jurisdiction of the command; but the pattern of nationalities participating in the main commands was set rather early, although not without struggle among the Americans, British, and French and not without considerable scaling down by the Americans of their original demands.[20] American officials were nevertheless able to put an enduring print on the military organization, having already begun developing an international staff before SHAPE was established and having then had the dominant voice because there were so few others to oppose them. (Part of the command structure did, however, stem from the work of the Western European Union prior to the organization of NATO.) [21] Successive SHAPE commanders have publicly expressed their sense of double responsibility, to NATO and to the United States government for carrying out their NATO duties. By 1960 some Europeans had become unhappy about the dominating position of SACEUR. On the other hand, Senator Taft's prediction that making an American SACEUR would greatly increase the United States responsibility toward NATO has been borne out.[22] Since NATO is above all a military alliance, the fact that few Americans are in the civilian secretariat of NATO and that the Secretary General has always been a European does not detract from the importance of Americans in the military command posts.[23]

6. A sixth role assumed by the United States on NATO's behalf has been *to manage the nuclear deterrent for the alliance*. This role, like that of making good NATO's military deficiencies according to the American image of what is essential, is the product less of agreement among the members than of American capabilities and wishes. In the first year this

[19] Testimony of General Norstad, House of Representatives Committee on Foreign Affairs, *Hearings, Mutual Security Act of 1957*, 85th Cong., 1st sess. (1957), p. 540.

[20] Matthew B. Ridgway, *Soldier* (New York: Harper and Brothers, 1956), p. 239; J. D. Warne, *NATO and Its Prospects* (New York: Frederick A. Praeger, 1954), pp. 13–16; Osgood, *op. cit.,* p. 168; William A. Knowlton, "Early Stages in the Organization of SHAPE," *International Organization*, Winter, 1959, pp. 1–18.

[21] Lord Ismay, *NATO: The First Five Years, 1949–1954* (Paris: NATO, n.d.), p. 38.

[22] Senate Committee on Foreign Relations and Committee on Armed Services, *Hearings, Assignment of Ground Forces to Europe*, 82nd Cong., 1st sess. (1951), pp. 623–34.

[23] There are also few Americans in the OAS and SEATO secretariats.

role was natural and one in which the other members concurred; it emerged from the United States' having sole possession of atomic bombs. Even after the Soviet Union had broken the American monopoly, the other members continued to accept American dominance, until the development of missiles. Nor was the United States in the mid-fifties adamant about its monopoly in the alliance. The British having demonstrated their ability to develop and produce nuclear weapons, the Americans were at that time quite ready to acquiesce in their having a minor role in providing NATO's strategic nuclear deterrent.

So long as the European allies did not have to acknowledge how slight was their role in the management of the nuclear deterrent, they could accept the fact and feel safe in leaving control with the President of the United States, especially since SACEUR's plans already were very closely coordinated with those of SAC.[24] Yet they could not avoid the fact that an indispensable part of NATO strategy lay outside NATO control, in the hands of American officials. In 1957–58 discontent grew rapidly; it reached major proportions by the 1960s. In the late 1950s the fear that the Americans might be trigger-happy—demonstrated in mutterings about "no annihilation without representation"—began to be replaced (in part) by the opposite fear. With a growing Soviet missile force capable of delivering thermonuclear bombs to the United States, would the Americans fail to live up to their pledge to use strategic weapons if an attack came in Europe? The Americans, on the other hand, were worrying increasingly about proliferation. An arms control agreement with the Soviet Union, for example, appeared less and less possible the more widespread the proliferation. For this and other reasons the United States did not welcome any further expansion of "the nuclear club" even among their NATO allies.

The United States had already made a solution to the problem of nuclear weapons management more difficult by a course of action, from 1954 to 1958, which had promised short-range benefits to its allies; it succeeded in getting NATO approval for strategy based on the deployment in Europe of tactical nuclear weapons and IRBMs. By such actions and by bilateral agreements for "sharing" technical information on the use of certain nuclear weapons, the Americans had temporarily evaded the critical question of who could "press the button." But the

---

[24] Gardner Patterson and Edgar S. Furniss, Jr., *NATO: A Critical Appraisal* (Princeton: Princeton University Press, 1957), p. 38.

"genie" about which President Kennedy warned in 1963 had already come part of the way out of the bottle some years earlier. Rather suddenly in December, 1960 a lame-duck United States delegation to the NATO ministerial conference responded to European dissatisfactions by offering to earmark Polaris-armed submarines for NATO. The Kennedy administration went further, proposing in 1963 a "mixed-manned" multilateral nuclear force. Since the missiles of the proposed force could not be fired without United States consent, this device did not significantly allay European "credibility anxieties." [25] By 1963 the American government was ready to accept the *principle* that allies should participate in the nuclear strategic planning of NATO. Also, in the same year American officials had begun to provide more technical information to aid allied military strategists in understanding the strategic situation. These moves did not radically change national positions. If others did not wish to be involved in a nuclear war without their consent, neither did the Americans. The Kennedy administration, in fact, tightened up control over some nuclear weapons.[26]

7. With respect to "conventional" defense, the United States has assumed a seventh role: *to demonstrate by example what other allies might also profitably do.* Its most important demonstration has been the deployment of approximately six divisions on the central front in Europe, including the best-trained and best-equipped American forces anywhere in the world. From the very beginning of NATO these divisions have had a great psychological impact; they have shown the Europeans that the Americans were with them physically as well as in spirit. Early suggestions from some Congressmen that American numbers should be based on the numbers contributed by the other allies have at no time been accepted by the executive branch. Later temptations to reduce significantly the United States forces in Europe were put aside because American officials feared that this step, instead of inducing the allies to fill the gap, would cause them to lessen their own efforts and have other bad political effects. During and after the Berlin crisis of 1961, the

[25] For further discussion, see Chapters V and VI.

[26] President Kennedy said to the NATO Military Committee, April 11, 1961, that "we propose to see . . . that our military forces operate at all times under continuous, responsible command and control from the highest authorities all the way downward—and we mean to see that this control is exercised before, during, and after an initiation of hostilities against our forces, and at any level of escalation." In the 1964 presidential campaign a minority view, favoring loosening of American control, was occasionally expressed. Its appearance suggested a difficulty for the United States in managing some of its security problems through NATO.

United States expanded its own forces in Germany, partly in the hope of stirring the European allies to follow the American lead. (The allies did expand their forces, but to far less striking a degree.)

The United States has set an example for others to follow in certain aspects of the Mutual Weapons Development Program, in pilot projects such as the NATO Science Program, and in additions to the infrastructure, in this case by financing a new communications system for an early-warning radar network. It has led in expanding the frequency and scope of political consultation in the North Atlantic Council.[27] The greater size of the United States has made the material contribution of all the others in NATO look small, even when all mitigating circumstances are weighed in. (Of course, the United States defense budget, except as a percentage of the American gross national product, could hardly be cited as a model; its level has not been set in order to influence European allies.) The allies were not disposed to follow the American example in embargoing the sale of particular products to various Communist countries. Too frequent exercises in preceding may sometimes be self-defeating because they can stifle important initiatives from the potential emulators.

PROBLEMS OF LEADERSHIP

Gradually the Americans have been learning new attitudes regarding the need for reciprocity and compromise; but the pace is slow because the United States is so powerful a member of the alliance and so energetic a leader. Yet, as Geoffrey Crowther pointed out some years ago,

[27] For example, see General Robert J. Wood's explanation to Representative Morgan that "we have to set the example in saying that we definitely will underwrite our percentage of the cost [of a proposal]" [House of Representatives Committee on Foreign Affairs, *Hearings, Foreign Assistance Act of 1964*, 88th Cong., 2nd sess. (1964), pp. 631–32]. The retiring Deputy Secretary General of NATO said in 1964, ". . . the United States had given in NATO a good example of behavior in arguing their case with their allies, listening to the counter-arguments, coming back with more evidence, their obvious purpose being to be able to persuade or to be persuaded, without ever allowing the discussions to become a dispute" [Guido Colonna di Paliano, "The State of the Alliance," *Atlantic Community Quarterly*, Fall, 1964, p. 405]. See also Secretary General Spaak's speech to the Atlantic Treaty Association September 27, 1958, quoted in Carol E. Baumann, *Political Co-operation in NATO* (Madison: University of Wisconsin, 1960), p. 14. Secretary Rusk stated in April, 1964 that in the previous year the United States "initiated consultation or exchange of information in NATO on approximately thirty issues of importance" ["Mr. Dean Rusk and the Atlantic Alliance," *NATO Letter*, June, 1964, p. 20].

even the leader cannot simply give a lead whenever he feels like it.[28] The United States has been even less willing than other countries to agree to specialize in certain kinds of defense force and to depend more heavily on its allies for certain other kinds; probably this is impossible. As a world leader it cannot leave itself disarmed in any essential component, which rules out some kinds of force specialization which may rationally be expected of other allies. Matériel specialization is another matter; strong economic interests in the United States prevent a more rational distribution of the work load throughout the alliance.[29] We would have a better test of the willingness of the Americans to cooperate if there were more initiatives from the other allies for collective enterprises which include the United States; such initiatives are not often revealed, if they exist. Observers and participants acknowledge that seldom are even a few of the allied governments united in favoring a policy not desired by the Americans.[30] Multilateral undertakings are especially hard to promote where allies prefer their own special arrangements with the leader. It is in the nature of the superpower that it has more to offer each of the others than they have to offer to each other.[31]

Two or three patterns in the United States treatment of its NATO allies recur whoever the responsible American officials and whichever the party in power. There are many splendid sermons on how the United States should behave as a genuine partner.[32] Sometimes in the same

[28] "Reconstruction of an Alliance," *Foreign Affairs*, January, 1957, p. 181. Note relief of allied governments when the new President devoted important speeches to NATO early in February, 1961, after having failed to refer to it specifically in his Inaugural Address [Hanson Baldwin in the *New York Times*, February 5, 1961, and C. L. Sulzberger, *ibid.*, April 17, 1961].

[29] Hoag, *op. cit.*, p. 289.

[30] See C. M. Woodhouse, "Attitudes of NATO Countries Toward the United States," *World Politics*, January, 1958, p. 212. Although this article was written when NATO was less than ten years old, the situation has not since changed so far as unity of European members versus the United States is concerned.

[31] If the other allies were united, their bargaining position vis-à-vis the United States would be much stronger.

[32] For example, on retiring from his post as Secretary of State, Dean Acheson said, "We are aware in this country that our European allies are in a true sense of the word partners and that we must work with them and treat them as partners. . . . [O]n their side they see the nature of the effort which they must make to maintain their part of the partnership" [*Department of State Bulletin*, January 26, 1953, p. 130]. Later that year General Gruenther, as SACEUR, had this to say: "Our problem is essentially a task of being the strongest element in the North Atlantic community and still being sufficiently modest and understanding to work well within it. We must be able to work effectively on a partnership basis with a pro-

speech, but more often when caught off guard, the same or officials of equivalent standing reveal an attitude which appears to equate "NATO" alternately with "they" or "American," depending upon the context.

John Foster Dulles, prior to becoming Secretary of State, wrote in January, 1952 that "treaties of alliance and of mutual aid mean little except as they spell out what the people concerned would do anyway." [33] Later he learned to spell out more completely the treaties already in force and the new ones negotiated. On a television program with President Eisenhower in May, 1955, in which the two officials discussed his recent appearance at the North Atlantic Council, Secretary Dulles related how he had explained to the NATO allies that the United States' Asian policy was the same as its policy in Europe and that "the reason we are acting this way in Europe is because we really believe in these things and if we believe in them we are going to act the same way in Asia." "That is a wonderful way to tell them," responded the President.[34] As the United States became deeply involved in Vietnam, President Johnson and Secretary Rusk began to talk in similar vein.

Some oscillations in American style have come with changing events

---

found respect for views and interests other than our own. The one thing that the European resents—and naturally so—is dictation" ["The Defense of Europe," *ibid.,* November 9, 1953, p. 636]. In presenting the "military posture" of the United States to the House of Representatives Committee on Armed Services in early 1962, Secretary McNamara stated that "if for no other reason than our own self-interest, we must maintain within the NATO alliance the closest kind of co-operation at all levels and in all spheres; we must concert our efforts no matter how great the difficulties. And, indeed, the difficulties or existence of difficulties should not dismay us. After all, we are dealing with sovereign nations whose history extends back far beyond our own, nations with their own particular devotion to . . . freedom. They clearly are entitled to their own views and their views are entitled to the most careful consideration by us [*Hearings, Military Posture,* 87th Cong., 2nd sess. (1962), p. 3166]. Senator Fulbright wrote in 1963: "We must find a way to bring our allies into meaningful participation in the vital decisions relating to war and peace. The crux of the problem is the development of a solid strategic consensus among NATO allies. The development of such a consensus can be approached through a system of allied participation in the planning and shaping of strategic policy, in determining the *conditions* under which the American deterrent will be brought to bear" ["A Community of Free Nations," *Atlantic Community Quarterly,* Summer, 1963, p. 118].

[33] Quoted by Coral Bell, *Negotiation From Strength* (New York: Alfred A. Knopf, 1963), p. 91.

[34] *Department of State Bulletin,* May 30, 1955, p. 872. American perspectives on the role of the United States in SEATO (or in the OAS and the international economic organizations) do not, however, seem to us at all comparable with American perspectives on the American role in NATO. This chapter, unlike earlier ones, does not, therefore, have a concluding section comparing NATO and other organizations.

or complications in the general environment. Thus President Kennedy stated in May, 1962 that "we cannot and do not take any European ally for granted and I hope no one in Europe would take us for granted, either." When such hints failed of their purpose, he was reported on December 31 of that year to have instructed his subordinates that the United States should proceed with what it regarded as the correct course and pay less attention to whether or not that course of action displeased allies.[35] Utterances of national leaders gain widespread public attention; but there can also be pervading, often unconscious, attitudes among lesser officials which do not improve the community spirit within the alliance.[36]

Depending upon one's point of view, one can classify American official manners as "confusing, dictatorial, ruthless, insensitive" or "courteous, tactful, diplomatic." [37] Whichever appellation is given to them, the manners do reveal some special problems of leadership. First, they may spring from the need to appeal to many different groups, both inside and outside the United States, in order to gain consensus for particular policies. Second, they sometimes arise from the mixture of functions of NATO, the symbolic representation of close association and the attention to the hard military realities. Third, and politically most important, they are instances of the dual vocabularies of law and politics, of the difference between the "sovereign equality" of each member of the alliance and the very unequal distribution of power among them. "Partnership," "sharing," "consultation," "balanced," "mutual," and "cooperation" help to make endurable those relationships which are not wholly symmetrical or reciprocal and which are better not publicly described by American officials in the harsher language of power differentials if the alliance is to hold together. The important questions are: do such statements mislead the leaders as to their political functions? At what point do they lead the other allies to brand the Americans as insincere or unworthy of trust?

Lest we assume that the inconsistencies in utterance have been blown up by overzealous journalists, let us note that there have been numerous

[35] James Reston, *New York Times,* February 7, 1963.

[36] Laurence I. Radway, "Military Behavior in International Organization: NATO's Defense College," in Samuel P. Huntington (ed.), *Changing Patterns of Military Politics* (New York: The Free Press of Glencoe, 1962), p. 106, an essay which examines an early stage in that joint undertaking.

[37] For a more detailed discussion of style see Chapter VI.

instances where it was not statements but deeds which revealed heed-
lessness of the alliance association. Unilateral American actions on matters concerning the whole alliance will be examined in Chapter VI. But
first we should observe the ways in which the United States has taken
account of its NATO affiliation in numerous policies and on many occasions. Chapter V examines some of these occasions.

CHAPTER FIVE

UNITED STATES POLICY AND INTERNATIONAL ORGANIZATION MEMBERSHIP

HOW IS ONE to describe and assess the impact of participation in an international organization on a member state? Presumably, policies adopted by that state which relate to the functions of the organization reflect that impact more accurately than do official declarations divorced from immediate action. As in the United Nations, so in NATO there is often a sharp contrast between the "extravagant quality of public pronouncements" and the pragmatic expedients adopted at the moment of action.[1] United States officials say publicly and privately that defense and foreign policies are affected by membership in NATO and also, if less strikingly, by membership in the other regional and functional organizations. Sometimes they claim too much, but even modest and apparently justified claims are difficult to document.

A major policy decision grows by often undetectable increments and by the actions of many persons having some authority. For any particular "decision," anything less than a book-length case study may be insufficient. Thus in the present inquiry we can only pick out a few threads to follow, threads of inquiry which may provide at least partial answers (in the case of NATO) to the following questions: Was NATO heeded by the decision-makers when they were working out alternatives? Formally or informally, jointly or severally, or both severally and jointly, were the NATO allies consulted? If so, were American policy-

---

[1] See Lincoln P. Bloomfield, "United States Participation in the United Nations," in Stephen D. Kertesz (ed.), *American Diplomacy In a New Era* (Notre Dame: University of Notre Dame Press, 1961), pp. 474–75.

makers prepared to alter their objectives or strategies? (We can only judge this by actual changes, a crude index which does not tell what changes might have taken place or failed to take place in the absence of consultation.)

In the past decade or so, important United States decisions have been taken in at least five areas of policy that could have been affected by membership in NATO or the other organizations under consideration: defense, disarmament and arms control, economic aid to underdeveloped countries, foreign trade, and decolonization. Participation in NATO may also have affected the handling of specific diplomatic issues such as those related to Berlin, the Indo-China inheritance, and Cuba. Can any impact be detected? Where?

DEFENSE POLICY

Although NATO's functions, as pointed out earlier, are not purely military, it is the defense policies of the members that show the most striking effects of the alliance. Much of NATO's policy bears the American imprint, but what about NATO's influence on America's own defense policies? We may take it for granted that many other considerations—military requirements in other parts of the world, financial and morale problems, and others of a global nature, such as the Communist threat—influence recommendations on defense policy. "Practically every military decision from this time on [when the United States began forming its alliances] was affected to some degree by collective security," we are told. "It had an impact upon the size of the forces, their deployment, and even their organization, training, and equipment." [2] To what degree and exactly how American participation in NATO had such an impact is very difficult to ascertain, however. [3] There is a constant mixing of the words "our allies" and "the alliance" when United States defense authorities describe their calculations.

Officials have repeatedly told Congressional committees that their

[2] Charles H. Donnelly, *United States Defense Policies Since World War II*, House Doc. No. 100, 85th Cong., 1st sess. (1957), p. 13. William W. Kaufmann pointed out that with Europe's revival a need developed for coordinating United States defense plans with the others in NATO, involving "the hammering out of agreed strategic concepts, force levels for their support, and the division of costs among the allies" [*The McNamara Strategy* (New York: Harper and Brothers, 1964), p. 8].

[3] It is still more difficult to assess the impact when we try to imagine what the other members would have done without an alliance of which the United States was a part. Also, what reliance does the United States put on the potential support of "unallied" but not unfriendly states like Sweden?

estimates of United States defense requirements take account of the allies' strengths and weaknesses and American commitments to them.[4] As Admiral Burke in the spring of 1961 told the Senate Committee on Appropriations, "if there were not naval forces of NATO members available for guarding the approaches to Europe, the United States would have to furnish anti-submarine warfare protection up to their coasts in time of war." [5]

In the command structure of the United States defense forces, which consist of seven "unified" (i.e., interservice) commands, as well as the various "specified" (i.e., single-service) commands, two of the unified and two of the specified commands operate in the land and sea areas for which coalition defense arrangements have been made in NATO.[6] These are the European Command, the Atlantic Command, the Strategic Air Command, and Naval Forces Eastern Atlantic and Mediterranean. One source of confusion over the impact of the alliance on United States defense planning has been that the American command structure involves no single "super-command" for the whole area of NATO defense arrangements.

Another source of confusion stems from the fact that very often NATO commanders have been Americans who concurrently held commands over United States forces. In this latter capacity they were in the purely American chain of command. Like any other head of a unified command, the United States Commander-in-Chief Europe (CINCEUR), who was also SACEUR, was assigned target lists for the American tactical air forces under his command and was responsible for preparing, under United States Joint Chiefs of Staff direction, contingency plans for their use.[7] A similarly ambiguous situation is illustrated

[4] For a typical statement, see testimony of Secretary McNamara on February 2, 1963 before House of Representatives Committee on Armed Services, *Hearings on Military Posture,* 88th Cong., 1st sess. (1963), p. 428, and his reference to the combined allied strength as a major feature in his assessment of Western defense, *New York Times,* November 19, 1963. In his statement to the House of Representatives Committee on Armed Services on January 27, 1964, he went into detail on NATO forces while presenting the United States "military posture." On the other hand, President Johnson, in his exposition of America's armed strength given to the Coast Guard Academy in June, 1964, mentioned NATO only in passing while describing one facet: the ability to fight less than an all-out war [*New York Times,* June 4, 1964].

[5] Senate Committee on Appropriations, *Hearings, Department of Defense Appropriations for 1962,* 87th Cong., 1st sess. (1961), p. 155.

[6] Charles H. Donnelly, *United States Defense Policies in 1961,* House Doc. No. 502, 87th Cong., 2nd sess. (1962), p. 39.

[7] House of Representatives Committee on Armed Services, *Hearings, Military Posture Briefings* (87th Cong., 1st sess. (1961), p. 1209.

by General Norstad's call for augmented American contingents during the early stages of the Berlin crisis. It was not clear whether his request was considered as coming from SACEUR or CINCEUR; it was probably the latter.[8] The administration was not responsive to his requests; but it could not therefore be interpreted as being unresponsive to the requirements of NATO.[9]

One should also distinguish between United States defense planning *for* the NATO area, *in the light of* NATO capabilities and commitments, and its defense planning as a "loyal" member of NATO. United States defense officials were deeply involved in planning for NATO even before President Truman approved the early plans for NATO defenses.[10] At Lisbon in 1952 much more detailed agreements on forces and force goals were reached among the twelve states then members of the alliance. "The whole operation," wrote Secretary Acheson, "was like one of those games where a dozen little shots have to be maneuvered into holes in a cardboard field: the slightest jar in trying to get the last one in shakes all the others out." [11] Such coordination is far harder to accomplish than that required when only two states are involved, as in the arrangements for American-Spanish cooperation.

Planning of each individual member's defense program in the light of the programs of the other allies should be more efficient because of the exchange of information. Even here, however, the United States has not always been completely aware of what major allies, such as Great Britain, have planned to do; American officials did not anticipate the deep budget cuts made by the British in 1955. Nor did the Administration adjust its 1958 defense budget to the radical British changes in 1957.[12] Other members besides the United States have sometimes followed de-

[8] Testimony before Senate Committee on Armed Services, Preparedness Investigating Subcommittee, *Hearings, Major Defense Matters,* 86th Cong., 1st sess. (1959), p. 13. See also *ibid.,* pp. 41–42, and House of Representatives Committee on Armed Services, *Hearings, Military Posture Briefings,* 87th Cong., 1st sess. (1961), p. 1206.

[9] At the time of the Berlin crisis Hanson Baldwin described the United States Seventh Army, "the largest field army ever maintained by the United States in peacetime," and the Seventeenth United States Air Force as practically the backbone of NATO's defenses on the Central European front [*New York Times,* October 6 and 11, 1961].

[10] Harry S. Truman, *Memoirs,* Vol. II (Garden City: Doubleday and Company, 1956), p. 252.

[11] *Sketches from Life* (New York: Harper and Brothers, 1959), p. 47.

[12] Charles H. Donnelly, *United States Defense Policies in 1957,* House Doc. No. 436, 85th Cong., 2nd sess. (1958), pp. 42–44; and House of Representatives Committee on Appropriations, *Hearings, Department of Defense Appropriations for 1957,* 84th Cong., 2nd sess. (1956), p. 59.

fense policies not in accord with their general understandings reached in NATO. Such individual actions occasionally affected United States defense policy. But the effects did not flow *from* NATO membership except insofar as the United States was relying on allied forces under NATO auspices. On the other hand, when the French started their drive for an independent nuclear deterrent, the United States looked *to* NATO in the hope of devising some alliance arrangement to discourage such proliferation. Since any of the sovereign states in the alliance may have reasons other than adherence to NATO plans for deciding upon a particular defense policy, it is not surprising that even the United States, which has the strongest influence over planning by SHAPE, on occasion chooses not to act in accord with a SHAPE "requirement." [13]

Occasionally a NATO-sponsored policy has served as rationalization for an American defense policy which was going to be adopted anyway. Defense Secretary Wilson justified cutbacks in American force levels by anticipating a German contribution to the alliance's forces.[14] Similarly, but at a later date, the NATO-approved MC-70 plan, worked out under General Norstad's leadership at SHAPE, was one support for Defense Secretary McNamara's changes in the opposite direction during the build-up of American armed forces in 1961–62. In general, however, the size of American forces in Europe from the early 1950s onward has numbered between 300,000 and 400,000.[15] The figure does not seem to have been affected one way or the other by the extent to which the other NATO members were meeting their respective commitments.

Since military assistance was indispensable to NATO's functioning in the early years, American defense officials were obliged, in planning amounts and objectives, to take careful note of the capabilities of the other members of the alliance. At the same time, they had to gear their military aid proposals to the technical and domestic political limitations on American capabilities.[16] Stemming from the organization of NATO were other effects on American defense activities less far-reaching than

[13] Cf. Senate Committee on Foreign Relations, *Hearings, International Development and Security*, 87th Cong., 1st sess. (1961), p. 737.

[14] Testimony of General Ridgway, House of Representatives Committee on Appropriations, *Hearings, Department of Defense Appropriations for 1957*, 84th Cong., 2nd sess. (1956), pp. 566–67 and 624; also Samuel P. Huntington, *The Common Defense* (New York: Columbia University Press, 1961), p. 61.

[15] *See* House of Representatives Committee on Armed Services, *Hearings on Military Posture*, 88th Cong., 1st sess. (1963), pp. 582–83.

[16] Testifying in support of the proposed Foreign Assistance Act of 1963, General Taylor, then Chairman of the Joint Chiefs of Staff, said, "We use the same strategic planning aids to establish the requirements for United States forces world

the stationing of several divisions of American ground forces in Europe. For example, Admiral Burke told a Congressional committee in 1956 that the Navy had changed the way it participated in joint exercises: rather than trying out highly sophisticated new maneuvers, it practiced more elementary procedures in which the naval personnel of the European allies needed training.[17]

Let us look at NATO's role with respect to a few other specific defense policies. American military officials took the lead in urging the rearmament of Germany—first upon their civilian colleagues—and then through them, upon the other allies. It was, however, a meeting of the North Atlantic Council in September, 1950 that provided the occasion to bring the American proposal to a head.[18] This policy was ultimately accepted by NATO late in 1954, after President Eisenhower promised that the United States would keep troops in Europe, and specifically in Germany, as long as they were required. His successors have continued to honor the commitment. This promise was part of a package agreement which included French consent to German membership in NATO. (The 1954 event was the second package deal in which German rearmament was involved. The first was the American proposal in September, 1950 to permit German rearmament, to establish for European defense a Supreme Commander, and to develop an integrated force.)

A not dissimilar proposal was made in 1960 when the French, again recalcitrant, objected to an integrated air defense system for Europe

---

wide and for the military establishments in friendly countries which we need to support our national strategy. Thus we examine concurrently our own forces and those which we would like to see maintained by our friends . . . [Regarding NATO and SEATO] we are interested in assisting primarily those forces committed to specific contingency plans. Consideration of these coalition requirements is a constant reminder to the JCS of the interlocking relationships existing between our national military program and those of military assistance" [House of Representatives Committee on Foreign Affairs, *Hearings, Foreign Assistance Act of 1963,* 88th Cong., 1st sess. (1963), p. 68.] The recommendations of the President's Committee to Study the United States Military Assistance Program (the Draper Committee) for military aid to European countries were based on a program General Norstad presented to the House of Representatives Committee on Appropriations.

[17] House of Representatives Committee on Appropriations, *Hearings, Department of Defense Appropriations for 1957,* 84th Cong., 2nd sess. (1956), pp. 704–05.

[18] See Laurence W. Martin, "The American Decision to Rearm Germany," in Harold Stein (ed.), *American Civil-Military Decisions* (Birmingham: University of Alabama Press, 1963), p. 655. Field Marshal Montgomery gave them valuable support in his vigorous espousal of the notion [*ibid.,* p. 647].

which would be based on a joint air warning system. The arrangement was finally made acceptable when among other arrangements, the United States agreed to put all its own air forces in Germany directly under NATO command.[19]

Coordinated production of armaments and equipment, under NATO auspices for purchase by the participating governments, fitted into United States defense plans. Joint manufacture of the F-104 and G-91 aircraft and of the Hawk missile would, it was expected, make other NATO forces into more effective co-fighters by significantly promoting standardization. Meanwhile, many of the licensing arrangements had the effect of bringing the users to the United States to buy spare parts and replacements; in so doing they made substantial contributions towards righting the United States balance of payments. To help the payments problem the Pentagon also actively promoted the sale of United States equipment to NATO allies in the 1960s, offering heavy inducements.[20]

With respect to procurement policies, United States military officials have purchased small arms which are NATO standard, citing advantages in training, logistics, and operations.[21] When new weapons are introduced, the Seventh Army apparently has had first priority.[22] As for Canada, the United States defense officials have made special efforts outside NATO channels to mesh the two countries' productive capabilities; they have occasionally given a production contract or a research and development contract to a Canadian organization.[23]

Cooperation in research and development has been closer with

[19] Richard P. Stebbins, *The United States in World Affairs,* 1960 (New York: Random House, 1961), pp. 146–47; see also the summaries of current activities in NATO in *International Organization,* Spring, 1960, p. 356; and *ibid.,* Autumn, 1960, p. 684.

[20] House of Representatives Committee on Appropriations, *Hearings, Mutual Security Appropriations for 1961 and Related Agencies,* 86th Cong., 2nd sess. (1960), pp. 2378–80; Senate Committee on Foreign Relations, *Hearings, International Development and Security,* 87th Cong., 1st sess. (1961), p. 707; Department of Defense, *Annual Report,* July 1958–June, 1959 (1959), pp. 86 and 277; E. Vandevanter, *Coordinated Weapons Production in NATO* (Santa Monica: Rand Corporation, 1964), esp. pp. 62–63, 65, 70–89, and 91.

[21] Testimony of Secretary McNamara, House of Representatives Committee on Armed Services, *Hearings, Military Posture,* 87th Cong., 2nd sess. (1962), p. 3255.

[22] House of Representatives Committee on Armed Services, *Hearings, Military Posture,* 87th Cong., 2nd sess. (1962), p. 3204.

[23] House of Representatives Committee on Armed Services, *Hearings, Military Posture,* 87th Cong., 1st sess. (1961), p. 848, and Department of Defense, *op. cit.,* p. 94.

Canada and the United Kingdom than with other NATO partners, although Germany began to figure prominently in joint ventures in 1964.[24] Among the joint projects in which the United States is engaged with the British is a search for an acceptable V/STOL aircraft. All the relationships have been bilateral, even if "within a NATO framework." [25] The United States does, however, have experts working with almost every NATO research and development group. The Mutual Weapons Development Program was the most important of these, but the armed services have sponsored other research programs in Europe, mostly in educational institutions.[26]

Defense policy for North America, when it has not been unilateral, has been bilateral; there have been close arrangements with Canada since 1940. Canada voluntarily sent a planning staff to the United States in 1954 when the United States Joint Chiefs unified the command for air defense. NORAD was set up informally in the fall of 1957, following the orbiting of Sputnik, and was formally approved in May, 1958. Its Commander-in-Chief is responsible to the United States and Canadian Chiefs of Staff, whose representatives comprise the Canadian-United States Regional Planning Group. (Four other Regional Planning Groups had been created by the North Atlantic Council in September, 1949, but were replaced by Allied Military Commands in 1950.) The North American group provided plans for and relevant information about the defense of North America to the Standing Group; it is expected to co-

[24] For examples, see House of Representatives Committee on Armed Services, *Hearings, Military Posture,* 88th Cong., 1st sess. (1963), p. 385, and "Statement of the Secretary of Defense Robert S. McNamara before a Joint Session of the Senate Armed Services Committee and the Senate Subcommittee on Department of Defense Appropriations for the Fiscal Year 1966–70 Defense Program and 1966 Defense Budget" (Mimeographed, 1965), pp. 150–51, 156, and 159.

[25] For examples, see House of Representatives Committee on Appropriations, *Hearings, Mutual Security Appropriations for 1961 and Related Agencies,* 86th Cong., 2nd sess. (1960), p. 2567; House of Representatives Committee on Foreign Affairs, *Hearings, Foreign Assistance Act,* 87th Cong., 2nd sess. (1962), pp. 148–50. A NATO Committee of National Defense Research Directors to promote the application of scientific discoveries to armaments was created in 1964 [*Report of Tenth NATO Parliamentarians' Conference,* Senate Committee on Foreign Relations Committee Print, 89th Cong., 1st sess. (1965), p. 31].

[26] Study on pooling military research and development information for the President's Committee to Study the United States Military Assistance Program, *Composite Report,* vol. II (Washington, 1959), p. 170. The Chief of Research and Development of the United States Army stated in 1962 that benefits from scientific and technical cooperation accrued to the United States along with the other members [Arthur S. Trudeau, "From Idea to Hardware," *NATO's Fifteen Nations,* April–May, 1962, p. 29].

operate with other NATO military agencies and to eliminate conflicts in plans.[27] The same year that NORAD was approved, the two governments sought to improve Canadian-American relations in the defense field and to provide civilian guidance in continental defense by organizing a special cabinet committee, the Canadian-United States Committee on Joint Defense. It consists of the United States Secretaries of State, Defense, and the Treasury and their Canadian counterparts.[28] The obsolescent DEW-line and SAGE, joint Canadian-American warning systems for continental defense against manned bombers, are being phased out as missiles become the more credible threats. In their place the Ballistic Missiles Early Warning System guards against missile attack across the Arctic. It relies on three stations—Clear, Alaska; Thule, Greenland; and Fylingdales Moor, England. None of these is in Canada, although they are linked electronically to the Canadian headquarters for NORAD. On an occasion when Secretary McNamara was asked by a Congressman whether the Department of Defense considered NATO in its planning, he replied: "Our forces in Western Europe of course are part of SACEUR's command, and we discuss through the Joint Chiefs problems of military operations between the United States forces and the other forces of SACEUR," but when pressed about whether this procedure extended to the North American continent, he replied, "No." [29]

The subject of missiles brings us to nuclear strategy and American defense policy, areas in which the United States could operate quite independently during the early days of NATO. With the end of the American nuclear monopoly and with increasing sophistication in the types of nuclear weapons and methods of delivery, each twist and turn in American defense planning has involved NATO, although not always explicitly. Early in the Eisenhower administration the United States government began to rely upon "tactical" planes carrying nuclear weapons and later upon tactical nuclear weapons as the main means to defend Europe rather than as merely a supplement to conventional methods of

[27] L. S. Kuter, "The North American Air Defense Command," *NATO's Fifteen Nations,* April–May, 1962, p. 48. See also John S. Hodder, "NORAD's Underground Brain," *NATO Letter,* September, 1963, pp. 15–19, and *Report of Eighth NATO Parliamentarians' Conference,* Senate Committee on Foreign Relations Print, 88th Cong., 1st sess. (1963), pp. 22–23.
[28] Richard P. Stebbins, *The United States in World Affairs, 1958* (New York: Random House, 1959), pp. 376–77.
[29] House of Representatives Committee on Armed Services, *Hearings on Military Posture,* 88th Cong., 1st sess. (1963), p. 381.

warfare or as a deterrent to Soviet use of non-conventional weapons.[30] Hand in hand with this new role for nuclear weapons went the "long haul" concept and the gradual reduction of conventional forces, both a response to a number of factors but, especially, the budgetary concern to reduce sharply defense expenditures. This set of policies, "the New Look," was not a prescription merely for the United States. It was urged upon the allies as appropriate for NATO as a whole, and the allies were not loathe to accept the proffered opportunity to cut back on their own defense expenditures. By 1954 the American military planners were concentrating on a single strategy: reliance on nuclear weapons for both strategic and tactical purposes, although the strategic deterrent would be "reinforced" by *local* defense forces. This was the year of Secretary Dulles' massive retaliation speech, intended as a warning to aggressors in the Far East, but the implications of which for Europe and specifically for NATO were not overlooked by the NATO allies. It was also the year in which the North Atlantic Council made its major decision that NATO strategy henceforth would be based on the expectation that nuclear weapons might be used from the outset of hostilities, a decision that required arming the NATO forces in Europe with tactical nuclear weapons.[31]

A number of responsible officials, especially in the Army, had grave reservations about the changes in American defense policy. Generals Ridgway and Taylor, as their memoirs make clear, were outspoken opponents of drastic reduction in American ground forces, believing that such a reduction would, among other things, cause a decrease in the credibility of United States commitments to its allies. But Secretary Wil-

---

[30] This policy accorded with advice given by Sir John Slessor, who had been sent by Prime Minister Churchill to discuss the question with American officials.

[31] Glenn H. Snyder, "The 'New Look' of 1953" in Warner R. Schilling, Paul Y. Hammond, and Glenn H. Snyder, *Strategy, Politics, and Defense Budgets* (New York: Columbia University Press, 1962), pp. 379–524, esp. pp. 406, 453, 468 ff., 496, and 519; Donnelly, *United States Defense Policies Since World War II*, p. 35; Roger Hilsman, "NATO: The Developing Strategic Context," in Klaus Knorr (ed.), *Nato and American Security* (Princeton: Princeton University Press, 1959), pp. 26–27; John Foster Dulles, "The Evolution of Foreign Policy," *Department of State Bulletin,* January 25, 1954, pp. 108–09; *idem,* "Policy for Security and Peace," *ibid.,* March 29, 1954, p. 461; James E. King, Jr., "Collective Defense: the Military Commitment," in Arnold Wolfers (ed.), *Alliance Policy in the Cold War* (Baltimore: Johns Hopkins Press, 1959), pp. 219–20; Huntington, *op. cit.,* pp. 63 and 80; and Paul Y. Hammond, *Organizing for Defense* (Princeton: Princeton University Press, 1960), pp. 332–35.

son, Admiral Radford (then Chairman of the Joint Chiefs), and some Air Force officials had defined such commitments narrowly, arguing that the United States had merely agreed to send a number of military units to defend the allies. General Gavin, another dissident, reported later that "when the Army's dwindling divisional strength made it apparent that it would have difficulty meeting the nation's commitments to NATO, Secretary Wilson said that we had no commitment to NATO. This was a thunderbolt, but by juggling words, and finally by a change in NATO's standards of readiness, he made it stick." [32] Clearly, the United States was not, during this period, restrained by its membership in NATO from depleting its ground forces. One has no way, however, of knowing how much greater would have been the reduction in American ground forces had there been no NATO commitment, no SHAPE, and no NATO habit of coalition peacetime military planning.

As some members of NATO became concerned over the drastic reductions in American forces, Admiral Radford assured the NATO Military Committee in July, 1956 that the United States intended to honor its commitments. The government, he said in a prepared statement, would make no significant changes without following the regular NATO procedures, including the concurrence of the other members.[33] They were not completely reassured; for the German, French, and Norwegian foreign ministers warned at the April, 1957 North Atlantic Council meeting against reduction of conventional forces based on increased reliance on atomic weapons.[34] Part of the allies' fear stemmed from an independent move by Britain (culminating in the Defence White Paper

[32] James M. Gavin, *War and Peace in the Space Age* (New York: Harper and Brothers, 1958), p. 156. See also Snyder, *op. cit.,* esp. pp. 428–40; Matthew B. Ridgway, *Soldier* (New York: Harper and Brothers, 1956), pp. 244 and 303–4; Maxwell D. Taylor, *The Uncertain Trumpet* (New York: Harper and Brothers, 1960), pp. 50, 51, and 61–63, and his testimony before the Senate Committee on Armed Services, Preparedness Investigating Subcommittee, *Hearings, Major Defense Matters,* pp. 41–42. See also Secretary Dulles' justifications in House of Representatives Committee on Appropriations, *Hearings, Departments of State and Justice, the Judiciary and Related Agencies: Appropriations for 1957,* 84th Cong., 2nd sess. (1956), p. 19; and Admiral Radford's views of the impact on NATO of reductions in United States ground forces in House of Representatives Committee on Appropriations, *Hearings, Department of Defense Appropriations for 1957,* 84th Cong., 2nd sess. (1956), p. 295.

[33] "United States Position Regarding NATO Commitments," *Department of State Bulletin,* August 13, 1956, p. 263.

[34] M. Margaret Ball, *NATO and the European Movement* (London: Stevens and Sons Ltd., 1959), pp. 100–101.

of 1957) radically to reduce its own forces in Europe and to rely instead on nuclear weapons.[35] The year 1957 saw particularly sweeping reductions by the Department of Defense. These continued even after evidence of startling Russian progress in missile and space technology began to accumulate; this information (confirmed shortly thereafter) might have been expected to raise questions about American superiority in science and military technology and the West's inability to match Russian forces man for man. Congress, however, was as insensitive to the military implications of the probable Soviet advances as was the administration, if one is to judge by its cuts in defense appropriations that year.[36] If the likelihood that the Russians would overtake the United States in missile and space techniques did not jolt the American planners of defense, how could the doubts and questions of some relatively weak NATO members?

During the years in which war in Europe was almost by definition regarded as a general war, the planners assumed that nuclear weapons would play a major role almost from the start. At whatever stage they became operative, however, these weapons were the backbone of NATO's defense. General Norstad stated in 1959 that "all of our plans in Allied Command Europe . . . are based on the assumption that the long-range strategic retaliatory forces will continue to be adequate to their task." [37] Moreover, President Eisenhower still was reluctant the following year to accept the full budgetary implications of the increased Soviet threat, although he authorized the speeding-up of the missile program.[38]

Reliance on nuclear retaliatory forces for NATO had long before 1960 come to be based upon the doctrine of the "Sword and Shield." Inter alia, such reliance meant that the Sword was to be wielded by the United States without the other members of NATO having much to say about it at the moment of crisis. In the early stages of nuclear development this raised no problems which the other members were unwilling to accept. The only other nuclear member was Britain. It had joint target-

---

[35] See F. W. Mulley, *The Politics of Western Defense* (New York: Frederick A. Praeger, 1962), p. 124; and Robert E. Osgood, NATO: *The Entangling Alliance* (Chicago: University of Chicago Press, 1962), pp. 88–89 and 118–20.

[36] Richard P. Stebbins, *United States in World Affairs, 1957* (New York: Random House, 1958), pp. 19 and 55–58.

[37] House of Representatives Committee on Foreign Affairs, *Hearings, Mutual Security Act of 1959,* 86th Cong., 1st sess. (1959), p. 440.

[38] Richard P. Stebbins, *United States in World Affairs, 1960,* p. 35.

ing arrangements with the United States, with which SHAPE also co-ordinated its plans.[39] There were even SAC forces in some European countries, including Britain; an important SAC base was in Spain, which was not a member of NATO. Prior to the development of ICBMs, the European bases were essential; even after missiles began to replace manned bombers as the significant delivery vehicles of the strategic retaliatory force, they had too short a range to serve as deterrents if based in the United States.[40] Arguments waged hotly among the United States armed services regarding the responsibility for and the size, composition, and deployment of the strategic weapons; for a year or two these debates were more in the limelight than were questions raised by the other members of NATO. Nevertheless, from the mid-fifties onward, military planners in Europe were unhappy about their respective governments' lack of control over the deterrent upon which NATO was depending.

Further discussion is devoted to this problem in Chapter VI; at this point it is worth noting that United States defense-policy makers still do not envisage fundamentally relaxing the American hold on the nuclear striking force. This was the implication of Secretary McNamara's 1963 statement regarding the importance of a "single, integrated strategic nuclear force, responsive to a single chain of command, to be employed in a fully integrated manner against what is truly an indivisible target." He continued, "As long as we do carry so great a share of the total burden, we cannot escape carrying a proportionately large share of the responsibility for leadership and direction." [41] The United States, in effect, wished to be master of the decision to embark on a nuclear war with the Soviet Union.

Most of the public controversy has raged around the strategic retaliatory weapons, yet some interested Europeans have also called attention to the less dramatic issue of the tactical nuclear weapons on which the NATO forces have more and more relied. (Although the French refused

[39] Mulley, *op. cit.*, p. 64; Richard C. Lindsay, "The Military Potential of NATO," *Annals* of the American Academy of Political and Social Science, July, 1957, p. 92.

[40] Regardless of the missiles, air bases in Europe continued to be very useful to the United States for such purposes as back-up points and support bases in case of limited war and as sites for tactical aircraft [Hanson Baldwin, *New York Times*, November 7, 1962].

[41] Testimony in January before House of Representatives Committee on Armed Services, *Hearings on Military Posture,* 88th Cong., 1st sess. (1963), p. 297. This was also stressed in his famous address at Ann Arbor in June of the same year.

to permit nuclear warheads to be stockpiled on French soil, even their airplanes in Germany were eventually equipped with them as were those of several other members. The United States announced on April 12, 1966 its intention of withdrawing the warheads provided to the French air force in Germany, because of President de Gaulle's decision to retire that force from NATO.[42]) The use of these tactical weapons is to come under the control of SACEUR and the European commanders responsible to him whose forces are so equipped, but this will occur only after the President of the United States has authorized employment of the warheads. General Norstad described these arrangements as simply a kind of supply system, "a program by which we give to the countries, regardless of nationality or location, the delivery means and train them in the use of delivery means" and "which is run by the United States in order to avoid any dangerous proliferation of control." [43] Despite the arrangements for control, many American officials at first regarded tactical nuclear weapons as not very different from conventional weapons, even going so far as to use the latter term to cover the new weapons.[44]

For a few years a doctrine of "limited" war in which tactical weapons might be used found favor not only in the United States but also among officials of other NATO governments, including notably Lester Pearson, then Minister of External Affairs of Canada.[45] Some Europeans welcomed the idea also because a defense based on tactical nuclear weapons seemed politically more feasible than one based on conventionally armed troops, which they themselves would have been expected to supply and which would, it was said, have been necessary for matching the "Russian hordes." [46] Since "NATO-required" modern weapons for European forces—apart from the nuclear warheads which were in any case to remain under American control—were for some time to be sup-

[42] See James Reston, *New York Times,* March 25, 1966.

[43] Senate Committee on Government Operations, Subcommittee on National Security Staffing and Operations, *Hearings, Administration of National Security,* 88th Cong., 1st sess. (1963) [hereafter cited as Jackson Committee, II], Part 5, pp. 22–23.

[44] See, for example, Secretary Dulles' statement that they were "merely weapons which have greater destructive capacities than the former weapons" ["Strategic Concept," *Department of State Bulletin,* January 3, 1955, p. 14]. See also Donnelly, *United States Defense Policies in 1957,* pp. 3–5.

[45] Lester Pearson, "A Measured Defense for the West," *Orbis,* Winter, 1958, pp. 431–33 and 434.

[46] Cf. comment by Osgood, *op. cit.,* p. 217.

plied through mutual assistance by the United States, the recipients were not worried about the cost of being so equipped.[47]

Gradually, however, doubts were raised on both sides of the Atlantic regarding how well these weapons could be controlled, as well as doubts as to who would and should control them. Such doubts increased with a diversification in the family of atomic weapons which made the distinction between "tactical" weapons and "strategic" weapons less meaningful.[48] On the other hand, the development of reliable central controls over the use of ground-to-ground atomic weapons of limited range and fractional kilotonnage has made it *more* possible to authorize the battlefield use of atomic weapons incapable of strategic use by decisions quite separate from those relating to the atomic weapons of greater range and destructive power. Along with an emphasis starting in 1961 on the importance of building up conventional warfare capabilities as a way of meeting the escalation danger, the Kennedy administration began to tighten up the methods of control over the tactical nuclear weapons already distributed.[49] The British raised the whole question of control at the North Atlantic Council meeting of May, 1962, but the American proposals for dealing with the control of strategic nuclear weapons overshadowed (as usual) this other nuclear problem.[50] As Joseph Alsop pointed out on March 4, 1963:

In the four "Honest John" battalions in the Italian army, the total kilotonnage of the warheads is certainly several times as great as the kilotonnage of the warheads as yet available to President Charles de Gaulle's embryo nuclear striking force. The total kilotonnage of the warheads integrated into the German armed forces is not less than 20 times and perhaps as much as 30 times the current French total.

Each of these warheads now in German and Italian hands, of course, has its attendant American sergeant or corporal; and all of them are equipped with the electronic lock, to which Washington holds the key. But the fact

[47] Note the Draper Committee report's recommendation for increases in mutual aid for this purpose and the eventual follow-through by the Eisenhower administration and Congress [President's Committee to Study the United States Military Assistance Program, *op. cit.,* vol. I, pp. 10 and 176, and Stebbins, *United States in World Affairs, 1960,* pp. 40 and 64–65].

[48] See Mulley, *op. cit.,* p. 73, who also points out (p. 52) the importance of distinguishing between the missiles, which many members, including Germany, have and the nuclear warheads with which they might be equipped.

[49] See, in addition to President Kennedy's speech to the NATO Military Committee, April 11, 1961, Kaufmann, *op. cit.,* pp. 143–44; and Jack Raymond, "How Bomb Control Works," *New York Times,* October 18, 1964. See E, p. 7.

[50] *New York Times,* May 4, 1962.

remains that the Germans can use their nuclear arms if only two men, President Kennedy and Chancellor Konrad Adenauer, agree on the need, and the Italians can do the same. . . .[51]

This aspect has not been stressed by those Europeans who are vocal about the American veto over the use of the strategic deterrent. Yet the likelihood of the latter being called upon is far less than that tactical nuclear weapons might be brought into play if conventional defenses proved inadequate to stop aggression.[52]

Accompanying the earlier American move to base NATO strategy on the use of nuclear weapons for tactical purposes was another action, an almost inevitable consequence of the first: the sharing of some kinds of classified information. This occurred, however, only after pressure had been brought by allied commanders, including Marshal Juin (then Commander-in-Chief, Allied Forces Central Europe).[53] Knowledge to be shared did not include how to make weapons, but only how they might be used and the techniques for using them. Beginning in 1954, the administration sought a loosening of restrictions imposed by the Atomic Energy Act to permit such sharing for purposes of military planning. It sought a further change four years later; it asked for approval by the Joint Atomic Energy Committee of the bilateral agreements with recipient countries to make possible training in the use of the weapons. Agreements with seven countries were involved, but the kinds of information to be supplied the Canadians and the British differed from the others; the French were to get only the right to purchase enriched uranium for a prototype nuclear submarine propulsion unit.[54]

[51] *Washington Post,* March 4, 1963.

[52] In 1964 the longest range of such weapons was a little more than 400 miles (the Pershing), and there was a gap of large dimensions between this and the Polaris A–3, which had a range of 2,500 miles. On this subject, see House of Representatives Committee on Armed Services, *Hearings on Military Posture,* 88th Cong., 1st sess. (1963), p. 425. There was still no decision to proceed with the development of an MMRBM in 1965.

[53] Osgood, *op. cit.,* p. 107, citing *New York Times,* September 2, 1953, pp. 1 and 16.

[54] Secretary of Defense, *Annual Report,* July 1958–June, 1959, p. 85; Stebbins, *United States in World Affairs, 1959* (New York: Random House, 1960), pp. 65–66; *idem, United States in World Affairs, 1960,* p. 126; Charles H. Donnelly, *United States Defense Policies in 1958,* House Doc. No. 227, 86th Cong., 1st sess. (1959), p. 40; North Atlantic Council Holds Twelfth Session," *Department of State Bulletin,* January 4, 1954, p. 8; "Program for Building National and International Security," *ibid.,* February 1, 1954, p. 144; "Agreement for NATO Cooperation on Atomic Information," *ibid.,* April 25, 1955, pp. 686–89; Joint Committee on Atomic

The decision to differentiate the British from the others, based on the argument that they already "had the bomb," had important consequences for the NATO alliance. Two principles were in conflict: mutual support in the alliance and the need to prevent proliferation. At the time that the bilateral agreements were being discussed in Congress the French had already proved themselves recalcitrant partners by such actions as withdrawing their Mediterranean fleet from assignment to NATO. The discrimination in favor of a state already possessing nuclear weapons could only be expected to spur some ambitious states without such a capability to acquire it as quickly as possible.[55]

Several problems which later threatened the cohesion of NATO can be traced to this period when the policy of sharing information on a carefully discriminating basis was being implemented. At the time, administration spokesmen for the 1959 agreement with Britain argued that the United States would profit from the arrangement. The proposed sharing of components for a nuclear submarine plant and military nuclear reactors would enhance the British nuclear weapons capability and thereby allow increased participation in NATO's defense and military strength. The United States would obtain additional plutonium. Solidarity would be promoted. Finally, greater standardization of weapons and greater flexibility in the use of these weapons could be expected, thus promoting the best use of the collective resources of the two countries.[56] Not articulated publicly was the desire to bind the British effort inseparably to the American effort.

Another kind of "sharing" was involved in the American determination to have intermediate-range ballistic missiles based on the territory of certain European members of NATO, partly as a means of counteracting the startling and demoralizing events connected with Sputnik. The deployment of missiles in one of the member countries had to be approved by SACEUR and United States defense officials, as well as by its own government, so that the deployment was tied in to NATO's strategy. Eventually American missiles appeared in only three countries: the

Energy, *Hearings, Amending the Atomic Energy Act of 1954: Exchange of Military Information and Material with Allies*, 85th Cong., 2nd sess. (1958); and *idem, Hearings, Agreements for Cooperation for Mutual Defense Purposes*, 86th Cong., 1st sess. (1959) [cited hereafter as JCAE, *Hearings*, 86–1].

[55] See Osgood, *op. cit.*, chap. viii, "The Problem of Nuclear Diffusion," esp. p. 218.

[56] JCAE, *Hearings*, 86–1, p. 62.

Thors in England, where they were under dual control of the United States and Britain, and the Jupiters in Italy and Turkey.[57] Thought of as a kind of stop gap until less vulnerable or more mobile missiles could be produced, they appeared to form an important part of the strategic deterrent to offset the apparent Russian lead in long-range missiles. Since neither the Thor nor the Jupiter was yet ready for emplacement in 1957, the proposal was, for the moment, only a gesture to show that the United States was not being left behind by Soviet advances.[58]

Some American officials thought the potential recipients would regard having missile bases as a matter of prestige, since the bases would be manned by their own armed forces, and thus each recipient government could have a veto on their use. The range of the missiles was sufficient to permit coverage of targets from a wide choice of sites. The Americans also regarded the bases as reassurance to countries distant from that part of Europe protected by nuclear-armed American forces.[59] Members of NATO did not rush forward to offer their territory, however; and the very thought, casually mentioned by Secretary of the Army Brucker, of furnishing some missiles to Germany roused great anxiety in many quarters.[60] The type of missile involved was so vulnerable that its emplacement soon appeared to be a risky arrangement for the host country, expecially since its most feasible use seemed to be as a first-strike weapon.[61]

These disadvantages loomed larger with the rapid development of more attractive alternatives, the Atlas intercontinental ballistic missile, the Minuteman, and the Polaris. After arguing that the United States was simply pursuing an agreed-upon policy of "modernization," Ameri-

[57] The Jupiters were completely supported by American military assistance while the Thors in England were owned and operated by the United Kingdom and only partly maintained with America assistance funds [House of Representatives Committee on Foreign Affairs, *Hearings, Foreign Assistance Act of 1962*, 87th Cong., 2nd sess. (1962), p. 102].

[58] Donnelly, *United States Defense Policies in 1958*, pp. 22–23.

[59] Donnelly, *United States Defense Policies in 1957*, p. 45. See forthcoming study by Michael Armacost on "The Thor-Jupiter Controversy in the United States Government," based on unpublished Ph.D. thesis, Columbia University, 1965.

[60] In a talk on July 4, 1960. See Charles H. Donnelly, *United States Defense Policies in 1960*, House Doc. No. 207, 87th Cong., 1st sess. (1961), pp. 48–49; also Stebbins, *United States in World Affairs, 1957*, pp. 364–66.

[61] Bernard Brodie, *Strategy in the Missile Age* (Princeton: Princeton University Press, 1959), pp. 342–45; Taylor, *op. cit.*, p. 141; General Paul Stehlin, "The Evolution of Western Defense," *Foreign Affairs*, October 1963, pp. 73, 74, and 76; Albert Wohlstetter, "The Delicate Balance of Terror," *ibid.*, January, 1959, pp. 223–24.

can defense officials removed the Jupiters from Italy and Turkey in 1963, bringing to an end two years' negotiations with the two countries' governments. Their removal was also discussed in the North Atlantic Council, and to all interested parties the United States explained that they would be replaced by a far more effective type of protection. Their removal came at a time and with a kind of unsolicited publicity which confused the pertinent issues (the action took place when the Russians were removing their missiles from Cuba). What was not often stressed was that the substituted Polaris submarines were completely under United States control and were only "made available and assigned to NATO" for support. They would, however, be targeted by SACEUR.[62] Not only had the Italian and Turkish governments exchanged a modicum of control over some intermediate-range ballistic missiles for better protection and less vulnerability, but NATO's role also appeared to have been diminished.[63] Secretary McNamara testified that the British government itself had decided to eliminate the Thors, by a decision in which the Polaris submarine substitute was not involved, and affirmed that by the end of the year 1963 the only nuclear missiles in the alliance would be possessed by the United States.[64]

Public discussion about the Jupiters' removal did not stress the consequent reduction in the NATO allies' influence, but when other aspects of American defense policy appeared also to be developing somewhat independently of NATO, the pressure built up among Europeans for a larger role in decisions involving the strategic deterrent. General Norstad proposed to meet the European demand by giving NATO its own land-based nuclear force of medium-range ballistic missiles and thus letting NATO become "a fourth nuclear power." The United States government was not completely deaf to the discontent expressed by its European allies and was in any case concerned about the direction of French and German policy; accordingly, American officials made a number of suggestions to satisfy NATO members. Just before the Eisenhower ad-

<hr>

[62] Testimony of Secretary McNamara, House of Representatives Committee on Armed Services, *Hearings on Military Posture,* 88th Cong., 1st sess. (1963), p. 281.

[63] According to Secretary McNamara, the discussions with the Turkish Government began before the Jupiters were actually installed, although after the agreement with the Turks had been concluded, and in spite of American determination to take them out, the program went forward until 1963 before the Turks could be persuaded that there would be no "psychological loss" from their removal [*ibid.,* p. 283].

[64] *Ibid.,* p. 279.

ministration left office, Secretary of State Herter offered to the North Atlantic Council the "concept" of committing five Polaris submarines with eighty missiles to some form of NATO control. The other members showed no outstanding enthusiasm for this idea, especially as it was associated with a further Herter suggestion that these members purchase from the United States one hundred additional medium-range ballistic nuclear missiles.[65]

The Kennedy administration renewed the offer in May, 1961, but without reference to the 100-missile purchase. This offer served to pose the problem of multilateral NATO control, but offered no solution. Nor did any of these offers answer the need which led General Norstad to advance his proposal. The Norstad proposal was indifferently received in Washington.[66] The submarines—three have since been "assigned" and "committed" to NATO—are completely manned by Americans and financed solely by the United States. (Thus, in respect to both manning and financing, what was done differed from the later proposal involving mixed-manned surface ships, the much discussed MLF.) [67]

General Norstad has described the dissatisfaction of NATO's European members as follows: "If the Europeans base their defense on atomic weapons . . . should there not be some firm guarantee that those weapons will be available to that defense in case of necessity rather than subject to the unilateral decision without consultation of one party? . . . Should we [the Europeans] not have some influence, some degree of influence over how, when, and where, and under what circumstances these weapons will be used?" [68] Such questions have posed for United States officials a series of dilemmas. One has been how to maintain the indivisibility of control so often stressed by Secretary McNamara while giving a sense of participation to the other allies in the basic

[65] Osgood, *op. cit.,* p. 233, and Alastair Buchan, *The Multilateral Force: An Historical Perspective,* Adelphi Papers No. 13 (London: Institute for Strategic Studies, 1964), p. 5. The purchase proposal reflected the growing American concern over the effect of United States forces in Europe on the United States deficit in its balance of payments.

[66] See Osgood, *op. cit.,* pp. 229–34.

[67] Those substituted for the Jupiter missiles in the Mediterranean became operational in 1963 [Donnelly, *United States Defense Policies in 1961,* pp. 21–22; Stebbins, *The United States in World Affairs, 1960,* p. 149; Senate Committee on Foreign Relations, *Hearings, International Development and Security,* 87th Cong., 1st sess. (1961), p. 709; House of Representatives Committee on Armed Services, *Hearings on Military Posture,* 88th Cong., 1st sess. (1963), pp. 412 and 427–28].

[68] Jackson Committee II, *Hearings,* Part I, p. 23.

decisions of the alliance. Another has been how to reconcile any kind of sharing with the American objective of preventing proliferation of nuclear weapons. A third has been how to head off French threats to disrupt the alliance through an independent nuclear force without jettisoning the special Anglo-American relationship. Still another has been how to keep the Germans, the most important bulwark of conventional NATO forces on the Continent, happy in a non-nuclear role. A further dilemma, less often in the forefront of the responsible officials' thoughts, has been how to reconcile the smaller, less ambitious members' preference for a system putting a major part of the responsibility on the United States with the larger members' demands for greater power in the alliance. Then there has been the persisting balance of payments problem, which has posed the dilemma of how to get other relatively wealthy partners to bear a larger share of the alliance's costs without the United States' having to give up the overriding decision on how the costs are to be incurred. For our study, a dilemma posed for each administration by Congress' role has been particularly pertinent: how to alter the decision-making process within the NATO alliance regarding nuclear weapons without first securing a change in United States law, a process likely to be at least as difficult as conciliating the other allies. When compared with the political problems, the military difficulties have seemed easy to handle.

The Kennedy administration first tried waiting for a European proposal which might, perhaps, have called for a joint European deterrent integrated under NATO direction with the United States deterrent force.[69] But the European members lacked the technical information needed to make such a proposal, even if they could have come to agreement with each other. Meanwhile, the French proceeded with their *force de frappe;* this and the Skybolt affair at the end of 1962 hastened the pace of events. By the first months of 1963 the outlines of the American proposal were clear.

To offset British disappointment over the abandonment of efforts to develop the Skybolt missile, upon which the British had based their hopes of keeping their strategic V-bomber force effective into the 1970s,

[69] See speech by McGeorge Bundy at Copenhagen, September 27, 1962, in Senate Committee on Foreign Relations, *Problems and Trends in Atlantic Partnership I,* Senate Doc. No. 132, 87th Cong., 2nd sess. (1962); "Secretary Rusk's News Conference of December 10," *Department of State Bulletin,* December 31, 1962, pp. 994–95.

President Kennedy offered a number of alternatives to Prime Minister Macmillan at Nassau in December, 1962. (It is ironical that the meeting at Nassau, which was to have such wide repercussions throughout the alliance, should have taken place only a few days after a ministerial-level meeting of the North Atlantic Council.)

The least unsatisfactory of the proffered alternatives in Macmillan's view was one by which the United States would sell Polaris missiles to Britain, and the two countries would at the same time enter into "new and closer arrangements for the organization and control of strategy in Western defense." At Macmillan's suggestion the two governments agreed to make an immediate start "by subscribing to NATO some part" of the United States strategic forces (presumably some Polaris type of submarines), as well as the whole of the British V-bomber force. These, together with the tactical nuclear forces in Europe, "would be assigned as part of a NATO nuclear force and targeted in accordance with NATO plans" (Article 6 of the Nassau Statement).

To meet American preferences, a different formula was evolved in Article 7 according to which the United States would supply Polaris missiles, namely, "the development of a *multilateral* [our italics] NATO nuclear force in the closest consultation with other NATO allies." The United States would "make available on a continuing basis Polaris missiles (less warheads) for British submarines." These British submarines would be assigned to NATO and targeted in accordance with the provisions of Article 6. The United States on its part agreed to make at least equal American nuclear forces available to NATO. Then came a provision in the Nassau "agreement" which was soon to cause trouble: "The Prime Minister made it clear that except where Her Majesty's Government may decide that supreme national interests are at stake, these British forces will be used for the purpose of international defense of the Western alliance in all circumstances."[70] (By April, 1963 the two governments had signed a technical agreement for the sale to Britain of an as yet undeveloped Polaris type of submarine missile.[71])

It should be noted that there was no specific reference in the declaration of Nassau to a "mixed-manned" aspect of the projected multilateral force. It was this aspect which was to give the word "multilateral" the

[70] Reprinted in Senate Foreign Relations Committee, *Problems and Trends in Atlantic Partnership II*, Senate Doc. No. 21, 88th Cong., 1st sess. (1963), pp. 54–56.
[71] *Ibid.*, p. 17; and *New York Times*, April 7, 1963.

connotation which clearly differentiated it from "multinational" and "interallied" when the American government decided in 1963 to press for an "MLF."

At Nassau the British accepted the American offer of an advanced-design delivery vehicle for a sea-based strategic striking force in lieu of Skybolt. But if the purpose of having Skybolt had been to maintain an independent British striking force, the language of Nassau, whatever interpretation be put upon some ambiguous phraseology, undermined that purpose. The new British strategic force would be both more dependent on the United States and more committed to NATO than the old one had been.

This was not, however, the way it looked in France. Where before there had been only one NATO partner "more equal than the others," it now appeared to the French that there were two. The "Anglo-Saxons" had made another bargain behind De Gaulle's back. The fat was in the fire, even though the United States quickly made a similar (though vague) offer to France. President de Gaulle soon had his revenge. He may have had several other reasons for decisively vetoing the long-pending and apparently almost successful entrance of Britain into the Common Market, but the events at Nassau provided a fine excuse.

Reactions and counterreactions continued at a dizzy pace, with the Americans improvising new features as they went along. The most noteworthy shift came with the announcement in February, 1963 that the proposed multilateral nuclear force should consist of surface ships armed with Polaris missiles, contrary to what most people had earlier thought was involved, namely, nuclear-powered, Polaris-armed submarines. American officials traveled extensively in Europe to persuade their counterparts that such a force was not only militarily feasible but politically desirable. At first, only the Germans seemed interested; to achieve their objectives American advocates of the MLF had to have a much wider alliance participation. The British were balky, and the French would have nothing whatever to do with the plan. However, at its May meeting in Ottawa, the North Atlantic Council approved steps being taken to organize nuclear forces assigned to SACEUR and to give the other members more information and participation in the nuclear activities guarding the alliance.[72]

[72] *New York Times,* May 23 and 24, 1963. See also *Washington Post,* February 19, March 8, 11 and 14, 1963; and *New York Times* summary of events during New York City newspaper strike, April 1, 1963.

What the American advocates were trying to win was the support of different members of the alliance for a mixed-manned force of twenty-five surface ships armed with Polaris missiles, jointly financed and operated, but with each member having a veto on the use of the force. Apart from questions as to military feasibility or utility, about which the American defense officials were very persuasive, there were objections of a different kind. Control over when the missiles might be fired continued to be subject to American veto, the fleet's missile power would be very small in relation to the American strategic deterrent, the cost to the participants would be substantial, the proposal would distract attention from a pressing need for larger European contributions to NATO's conventional capabilities, and it would especially expose the participants to Soviet countermeasures. Even President Kennedy himself acknowledged that there was, from the point of view of defending the United States, no *military* need for the fleet, that it was an effort to promote cohesion in the alliance.[73]

The most impressive American argument in its favor was that it might promote sophistication among the participants regarding nuclear weapons and thus make them understand American strategic views more easily. Such an effect could, at least in some measure, be achieved in other ways, particularly by the agreement reached in 1963 to involve NATO officers from other countries in the coordination of operational planning at the SAC headquarters. A liaison team from SAC had long been at SHAPE, and for many years the NATO regional commanders worked together with the staff at SHAPE in developing their nuclear strike program.[74] Receiving European NATO officers at Omaha had the advantage of giving responsibility to the learners which had been absent in an otherwise very welcome move made earlier by United States defense officials. At the Athens meeting of the North Atlantic Council in May, 1962, Secretary McNamara had won acclaim from his allied colleagues by a frank disclosure of the nuclear facts of life and the Ameri-

[73] March 6, 1963. For some of the political arguments, see editorials in the *New York Times,* such as that of October 21, 1963. Illustrative in their exposition and arguments about the MLF are *Problems and Trends in Atlantic Partnership II,* pp. 12–21; and Institute for Strategic Studies, *The Control of Western Strategy,* Adelphi Papers No. 3 (London, 1963).

[74] General James E. Moore, "The Military Effectiveness of NATO," in Karl H. Cerny and Henry W. Briefs (eds.), *NATO in Quest of Cohesion* (New York: Frederick A. Praeger, 1965), p. 167.

can strategy based on them.[75] He promised more to come. After some impatient waiting the allies finally did get eagerly desired information when United States defense officials traveled in Europe during early 1963, giving further intensified, highly classified briefings. New cooperative agreements for additional information sharing were concluded with NATO (and some allies) in 1964, with the approval of the Joint Committee on Atomic Energy.[76] In September of 1964 President Johnson took Manlio Brosio, the new Secretary General of NATO, to SAC headquarters, where Signor Brosio received information about targets and missile emplacement no foreign official of comparable rank had ever before obtained.[77]

A much more restrained allied reception met the continued American appeals associated with a related aspect of the "McNamara defense policy": improved conventional warfare capability for a more flexible response to a potential Soviet attack.[78] Here it was the Americans who were dissatisfied, not the other NATO members. As in the case of nuclear sharing, however, the United States reacted within the NATO framework.[79] Too long inured to earlier American doctrine regarding

[75] *New York Times,* May 8, 1962; *Problems and Trends in Atlantic Partnership I,* p. 43.

[76] See Joint Committee on Atomic Energy, Subcommittee on Agreements for Cooperation, *Hearings, Agreement for Cooperation with NATO for Mutual Defense Purposes,* 88th Cong., 2nd sess. (1964), esp. pp. 4–5, where Under Secretary of State Ball explained the reasons for the government's more expansive policy.

[77] *New York Times,* September 30, 1964.

[78] In presenting his first defense budget President Kennedy stated that "any potential aggressor contemplating an attack . . . must know that our response will be suitable, selective, swift and effective. . . . Our weapons must be usable in a manner permitting deliberation and discrimination as to timing, scope and targets in response to civilian authority" [quoted in Mulley, *op. cit.,* p. 99]. For a full exploration of this policy see Kaufmann, *op. cit., esp.* pp. 65–68, 84–88, 309–11. President Kennedy had already foretold it during his presidential election campaign [*ibid.,* p. 43].

[79] Secretary McNamara testified in February, 1963 that "the presently programmed United States forces, together with the present forces of other NATO countries, would not be able to contain an all-out conventional Soviet attack without invoking the use of nuclear weapons. . . . Today NATO forces can deal with a much greater range of Soviet actions without resort to nuclear weapons, including a major incursion or probe. Continued efforts would be required to deal with even larger attacks [House of Representatives Committee on Armed Services, *Hearings on Military Posture,* 88th Cong., 1st sess. (1963), pp. 430–31]. The following year he reported no significant change except a heightened ability to deal with conventional attacks on Europe over earlier estimates, which he regarded as unduly pessimistic. Further, the chief problems were readiness, equipment shortages, and deployment capability rather than overall manpower levels or budgets for defense

nuclear reliance, the European members of NATO seemed indifferent to the emphasis the Kennedy administration put on conventional capabilities for NATO forces. Some Europeans, particularly some Germans, felt that the new United States views went too far in the opposite direction from the earlier variations on massive retaliation, which had tended to downgrade the importance of the "Shield." [80] They feared that Germany, in particular, might be overrun before the Americans would permit the use of nuclear weapons. But there were others, in the Institute for Strategic Studies in England, and in the WEU Defense Committee, for example, who were thinking along the same lines as the Americans.[81]

In any case, the Department of Defense, through such leaders as Under Secretary Gilpatric, reiterated that if NATO forces were on the point of being overwhelmed by non-nuclear attacks, NATO would use nuclear weapons.[82] The Americans nevertheless continued to prod the NATO countries individually and through the NATO Council to meet their earlier commitments and to improve the equipment, quality, and mobility of the forces they had assigned to NATO, as well as their reserves. In this exhortation they were solidly supporting SACEUR. They encouraged a NATO study of the members' resources in relation to strategy and force requirements which was to prepare the way for bringing about a "satisfactory" balance between nuclear and conventional arms.[83]

Meanwhile, the Americans stimulated a modest build-up of European forces during the Berlin crisis in the latter half of 1961 by their own far

---

[*ibid.*, 88th Cong., 2nd sess. (1964), pp. 6912–14 and 7020–23]. In 1965 he declared that although the United States was still not satisfied, the "NATO forces deployed in Western Europe are at a higher peak of effectiveness today than has ever been the case in the past" [*ibid.*, 89th Cong., 1st sess., p. 155].

[80] See Richard P. Stebbins, *The United States in World Affairs, 1961* (New York: Random House, 1962), p. 133; *New York Times,* May 14, 1961; Brodie, "What Price Conventional Capabilities in Europe?", *Reporter,* May 23, 1963, pp. 25–33; House of Representatives Committee on Armed Services, *Hearings on Military Posture,* 87th Cong., 1st sess. (1961), p. 67.

[81] Nevertheless, Secretary McNamara had difficulty in his attempts "to justify his views to fourteen other nations with distinctive and often irreconcilable ideas about strategy. He found, in doing so at the periodic ministerial meetings of NATO, that achievement of a consensus on strategy, forces, and budgets was a slow and laborious process" [Kaufmann, *op. cit.,* p. 103].

[82] *New York Times,* June 7, 1961. General Wheeler, Chief of Staff of the Army, testified in February, 1963, "The NATO defensive concept rests upon early use of nuclear weapons, not only tactically but strategically." He said that "thin" NATO ground forces endangered the tactical nuclear defenses [House of Representatives Committee on Armed Services, *Hearings on Military Posture,* 88th Cong., 1st sess. (1963), pp. 780–81].

[83] See Article 9 of communiqué of NATO ministerial meeting at Ottawa, *New York Times,* May 20, 1963.

more dramatic expansion. At the same time, the United States government set about greatly enhancing its own conventional war capability.
The President issued a directive in May, 1961 for a reorganization and
modernization of the Army's divisional structure which would also increase non-nuclear firepower, ensure flexibility in meeting any kind of
threat, improve tactical mobility, provide modern mechanized divisions
in Europe, and "facilitate its coordination with our major Allies." [84]

To build up the forces available to NATO in Europe has required cooperation from a number of allies, with the United States leading the
way. Has the United States, on the other hand, been able unilaterally to
retrench or diminish its own forces without affecting its commitment to
NATO? The answer seems to be no, or at least not without the courtesy
of quiet "consultation" in the North Atlantic Council nor without an
outcry from the member most immediately concerned, Germany.[85]
(Since only Germany was coming close to fulfilling its earlier commitments, the others could not so easily protest.) The Eisenhower administration had been obliged to make its retrenchments inconspicuously, by
altering the characteristics rather than reducing the number of American
divisions in Europe. In the Kennedy administration arguments which
had been used earlier were heard again, such as that the total strength of
the United States commitment was actually being increased through
"modernization." Under Secretary McNamara there has indeed been a
tremendous increase in the effectiveness of the defense forces generally,
and in categories of particular interest to the NATO allies, such as air
lift capacity, weapons efficiency (shifting to solid-fueled rather than the
older, bulkier liquid-fueled tactical nuclear weapons), and readiness
level of "general purpose forces." [86] These advances have been very
costly. In the early 1960's there were quantitative improvements, too;
but in the mid-1960s force levels were back down to those of the late
1950s. The number of American troops increased from 226,000 in 1959
to a peak at the height of the Berlin build-up of at least 268,000 and
dropped by 1966 to a "normal" 225,000. (In the summer of 1966 the
actual figure was 211,000 because 15,000 specialized troops had been
withdrawn for the Vietnam war, but Secretary McNamara testified that

[84] See Mulley, *op. cit.*, p. 143; also Donnelly, *United States Defense Policies in
1961*, pp. 26–29; *Time*, February 15, 1963; and Kaufmann, *op. cit., passim.*
[85] See, for example, *New York Times*, October 1 and 22, 1963.
[86] See Secretary McNamara's testimony before House of Representatives Committee on Armed Services, *Hearings on Military Posture*, 88th Cong., 1st sess.
(1963), pp. 430–31.

they would be replaced by the end of 1966.) [87] With the military budget increasing by about 25 percent during the Kennedy administration to a total of over $51 billion, with defense spending rising further in the Johnson administration to a rate exceeding $55 billion in 1966, and with a large part of the balance of payments problem attributable to spending for overseas troops, defense officials had a good argument for reducing the number of the latter where possible without weakening Western strength.[88]

When Under Secretary Gilpatric described the reduction program in late 1963, he said such adjustments would be based on consultation with the United States' allies and "so far as possible" in accordance with NATO policies.[89] This reduction, along with Operation Big Lift in the fall of 1963, aroused much public concern in Germany.

What about the case in which an ally may want the United States to withdraw? The Icelandic discontent which boiled up in 1956–57 was eventually cooled down by the Americans, following some economic adjustments and the shock of the Russian behavior in Hungary.[90] The Portuguese objective in the protracted negotiations over renewing the Azores base agreement was not to get rid of the Americans, but to get better terms. In both cases, although the bases were important to NATO's strategy, the negotiations were handled by the United States alone, since the original agreements were also bilateral. (It would be tempting to compare the success of the United States negotiations with Spain over bases in this non-NATO country with the outcome in the Portuguese case, but too many factors in addition to membership in NATO must be considered.[91] Whether it is the Americans or the host

[87] Senate Committee on Armed Services, Preparedness Investigating Subcommittee, *op. cit.*, pp. 18–19; *Christian Science Monitor,* February 15, 1963; *New York Herald Tribune* (Paris ed.), June 26, 1963; *New York Times,* October 1 and 22, 1963. A map appearing in the "Week in Review," *New York Times,* November 8, 1964 showed 35,000 United States troops in England, 50,000 in France, 10,000 in Italy, 6,000 in West Berlin, and 260,000 in West Germany, but these figures were probably too high. C. L. Sulzberger, in *New York Times,* August 13, 1966, reported that American forces in Germany were at a peak strength of 291,000 in December, 1961. Secretary McNamara said on August 1, 1966 that "the Army's strength in Europe [*sic*] was then 211,000 [*ibid.,* August 13, 1966].

[88] However, from 1961 onward, the dollar cost of United States troops in Germany was balanced by German military purchases in the United States.

[89] *New York Times,* October 20, 1963.

[90] *Department of State Bulletin,* August 20, 1956, pp. 306–08; Donnelly, *United States Defense Policies in 1957,* pp. 32–33.

[91] For the Portuguese case, see Senate Committee on Foreign Relations, *Hearings, International Development and Security,* 87th Cong., 1st sess. (1961), p. 709.

country who desire withdrawal, however, the evidence illustrates Oskar Morgenstern's observation: "Although our strength supports our allies, our bases also put us in their hands." [92] Bases acquired for NATO purposes, however, apparently weaken the power of both the United States and the host country over each other.

Having forces abroad has required adjustments in the legal procedures for handling controversies arising from servicemen's personal behavior which violated local law. At the request of General Eisenhower when he was SACEUR, the United States negotiated precedent shattering "Status of Forces Agreements" to cover the jurisdictional problems involved.[93]

In all these aspects of United States defense policy the process of decision has often been circular: American officials took an initiative, sometimes independently, but often with individual NATO allies or (less frequently) with NATO; on the basis of reactions to such an initiative the calculations of American officials were modified, with some effects on policy. To what extent and specifically by whom, even the policymakers might have difficulty in saying. (Sometimes, but less often, a NATO ally took the initiative.) American officials have often urged their allies in NATO to take cognizance of the world-wide problems of the United States, but they have been accustomed nevertheless to make much defense policy for non-European areas without reference to NATO, despite the high priority given Europe in American planning. Domestic influences on defense policy seem usually to have been greater than those emanating from NATO or from specific NATO allies, especially when there has been a change of administration. Although planning may have been done in the NATO context, the implementation has almost always been through bilateral arrangements with individual members. Especially in nuclear matters, the Americans have tended to use NATO to achieve some objective, such as the prevention of diffusion, while not including the United States completely in the "integrated" measure. Something was held out.[94]

[92] Oskar Morgenstern, *The Question of National Defense* (New York: Random House, 1959), pp. 98–99.

[93] See George Stambuk, *American Military Forces Abroad: Their Impact on the Western State System* (Columbus: Ohio State University Press, 1963). The status-of-forces agreement with NATO was the first multilateral agreement.

[94] That either the OAS or SEATO would be likely to alter United States defense policy markedly would be an unrealistic assumption. However, in three respects United States membership in these organizations did affect American military

ARMS CONTROL POLICY

Theoretically, armament and disarmament policies are two sides of the same coin; the objective in either case is greater security. For a long period, however, this relationship was rarely explicitly recognized either in United States policy or in NATO decisions. The *formal* connections were often noted, beginning with Article 5 of the Vandenberg Resolution which precipitated the North Atlantic Treaty, an article which called for intensive efforts to secure "universal regulation and reduction of armaments." Communiqués of the North Atlantic Council have regularly included a paragraph deploring the Soviet Union's unwillingness to go along with the NATO members' ideas about general disarmament.[95]

Neither in the United States nor in the North Atlantic alliance during the early 1950s does arms control appear to have been taken as seriously as rearmament efforts. As Samuel Huntington described it, arms control was only a "country cousin" of American strategy and, therefore, of NATO defense policy as well.[96] This was due in part to the belief that safety from Soviet aggression depended upon the West maintaining a lead over the Communists by concentrating on advances in nu-

---

planning. In each case the treaty was a formal commitment to defend the region covered, thus requiring United States defense officials to deploy American forces with these commitments in mind. So far as the other members were concerned, such disposition of American strength took account of not only the dangers to the area but also the contributions which the other allies could make. This in turn required military assistance to make such contributions more effective. Thus General Twining declared to the House of Representatives Committee on Foreign Affairs March 18, 1959: "The Joint Chiefs of Staff decide what they feel the different countries of Latin America should contribute to fit into the world-wide— our world-wide planning of strategic forces. Naturally in Latin America you don't have the same problems you would have in NATO" [*Hearings, Mutual Security Act of 1959*, 86th Cong., 1st sess. (1959), p. 97]. General Lemnitzer told the same committee on March 15, 1962: "When we develop a contingency plan for operations in any area, particularly where there is a collective security arrangement, such as SEATO, planning representatives develop a force requirement. Then there is a canvassing of all the member nations to determine how much they are willing and able to contribute to this over-all force" [House of Representatives, Committee on Foreign Affairs, *Hearings, Foreign Assistance Act of 1962*, 87th Cong., 2d sess. (1962), p. 121].

[95] A typical expression was the following from the May, 1963 communiqué: "The ministers reaffirmed the importance, in building a peaceful world, of progress toward general and complete disarmament by stages and under effective international control. . . . They expressed the hope that the Soviet Union's attitude would evolve sufficiently to permit genuine progress to be made on the key disarmament questions."

[96] *Op. cit.*, p. 353.

clear weaponry.[97] Later in the 1950s a widespread concern appeared among officials regarding the "exponential" technological development in the nuclear field, and arms control began to interest defense officials more intensely.[98]

In the 1960s NATO has played a part in American disarmament discussions, but not as a major instrument. It has been less important than the United Nations and the International Atomic Energy Agency and has never been a direct participant in bargaining with the Soviet Union. Yet the alliance has inevitably become more and more involved in arms control proposals, because United States nuclear weapons (and to a much smaller extent those belonging to Britain) figure so importantly in NATO defense.

The long and seemingly promising negotiations in the five-nation subcommittee of the United Nations Disarmament Committee, which went on from May to September, 1957, provided the first occasion for NATO to play a significant advisory role.[99] An unfortunate contretemps occurred when the chief American negotiator, Harold Stassen, aroused the fear and anger of some of the allies by discussing in a preliminary way a possible step with his Russian opposite number without first notifying them. Immediately afterward, the United States made a very strong effort to align its policy with NATO's views.[100] When Secretary Dulles presented the United States proposals at London in early August, he had already consulted at length with the allies, especially about the most important issue, inspection.[101] In the end, the Soviet Union, perhaps flushed with the twin technological successes of an ICBM test-firing in August and the orbiting of Sputnik in October, torpedoed the discus-

[97] Cf. General Gruenther, "The Defense of Europe," *Department of State Bulletin,* October 18, 1954, p. 564.

[98] See testimony of Secretary of the Air Force Eugene M. Zuckert, House of Representatives Committee on Armed Services, *Hearings, Military Briefings,* 87th Cong., 1st sess. (1961), p. 1080. The stress on multiple options was linked to arms control in the McNamara defense regime [Kaufmann, *op. cit.,* pp. 144–47 and 167].

[99] The five were the United States, Britain, Canada, France, and the Soviet Union.

[100] Bernard G. Bechhoefer, *Postwar Negotiations for Arms Control* (Washington: Brookings Institution, 1961), pp. 403–08.

[101] President Eisenhower said on July 3, 1957: "You don't want to go to the Soviets or to any other nation . . . and make a proposal that affects a third country, without that third country's approval. . . . So you do have . . . the problem after you make out a program that seems logical and decent to us as a country, to go and take up the problem with Germany, with France, with NATO, the whole NATO group, with Britain, with Canada, everybody that is affected by that proposal, in order that you don't just destroy the whole effort by sudden re-

sions, after making counterproposals which if accepted would have seriously undermined, if not destroyed, NATO.[102]

At the heads of government meeting of NATO the following December (1957) the leaders declared they were ready to examine *any* proposal for general or partial disarmament. This readiness meant that President Eisenhower was prepared to go beyond the package presented in August. The leaders were also willing to support a foreign ministers' meeting to resolve the deadlock that would be created if the Soviet Union refused to participate in a new Disarmament Commission.[103] When the inspection proposals failed, another kind of step began to be discussed, principally by the Communists, namely disengagement in Central Europe. President Eisenhower replied in January, 1958, to one of the stream of Bulganin notes, that the NATO countries would study the question of denuclearizing an area in Europe. This general idea was anathema to General Norstad as SACEUR; he favored instead establishing a wide zone reciprocally controlled by ground and air inspection.[104] Secretary Dulles said of Polish Foreign Minister Rapacki's denuclearization proposal: "The military people—not only our own, but those of NATO—have considered the Rapacki plan and have advised us that in their opinion the plan as it stands is militarily very disadvantageous to the West." [105] One reason among many others for United States and NATO opposition to this kind of disengagement was the lack of depth of the NATO defenses in Europe; the whole forward strategy would have been ruined if it had gone into effect.

The United States kept in close contact with NATO in subsequent arms control negotiations. Along with the other members it agreed in the

---

calcitrance because someone believes their own sovereignty or their own rights have been ignored" [quoted in *ibid.*, pp. 347–48]. See also Senate Committee on Foreign Relations, Subcommittee on Disarmament, *Control and Reduction of Armaments,* Senate Report No. 1167, 85th Cong., 1st sess. (1957), p. 15.

[102] Summary of NATO activities, *International Organization,* Spring, 1958, p. 241, and Bechhoefer, *op. cit.,* pp. 245, 259–62, 269, 333, 341, 347–48, 365–66, and 386–91. As one among many reasons for the Soviet action at the end of this promising series of negotiations Bechhoefer listed the determination of Secretary Dulles to put the highest priority on securing agreement among the Western powers themselves [pp. 412–426, 427, 431–32].

[103] Bechhoefer, *op. cit.,* pp. 446–49. The Soviet Union declined, preferring a summit meeting.

[104] See his testimony, House of Representatives Committee on Foreign Affairs, *Hearings, Mutual Security Act of 1959,* 86th Cong., 1st sess. (1959), pp. 458–59; Stebbins, *The United States in World Affairs,* 1958, p. 155.

[105] House of Representatives Committee on Foreign Affairs, *Hearings, Briefing on World Situation,* 86th Cong., 1st sess. (1959), p. 19.

December, 1959 ministerial meeting of the North Atlantic Council to Italy's proposal that the five in NATO who were to participate in a new ten-country disarmament committee begin preparatory talks in Washington before the whole committee met in Geneva in 1960. Secretary Rusk stated in 1964 that a senior representative from the four Western Powers at the Geneva disarmament conference was reporting to the North Atlantic Council on developments.[106]

During the test ban treaty negotiations of 1963 between the Soviet Union, and the United States and Britain, the American and British leaders communicated frequently with NATO. Just prior to the formal negotiations, the former Secretary General of NATO, Belgian Foreign Minister Spaak, made a special trip to sound out Khrushchev's views and returned with an optimistic report for the North Atlantic Council.[107] The first successful effort to get an agreement with the Soviet Union on one aspect of arms control involved two issues on which important members of NATO felt strongly involved: proliferation and safeguards against surprise attack. France recognized itself as one of the objects of the antiproliferation measure and would have nothing whatever to do with it.[108] The West Germans dragged their heels briefly before signing the test ban treaty, for fear it would legitimize the status of the East German regime.[109] The same fear caused their determined opposition to discussion of a non-aggression agreement between NATO and the Warsaw Treaty alliance, acceptance of which appeared for a while to be Khrushchev's price for the test ban treaty.[110] It also lay behind their hasty move to get NATO support for caution in dealing with the proposed safeguards against surprise attack through the exchange of observers.[111]

NATO was, of course, in the very center of the controversy over the United States proposals for a multilateral nuclear force. The Americans pictured this plan to the Russians as a means of preventing proliferation of nuclear weapons; but the Russians declared it to be a way of spread-

[106] He added, "And before any major United States initiative in the disarmament field is put forward at Geneva it is subjected to close consultation with our allies to ensure that it does not adversely affect their interests" ["Mr. Dean Rusk and the Atlantic Alliance," *NATO Letter,* June, 1964, p. 20].

[107] *New York Times,* July 13, 1963.

[108] See De Gaulle's statement in previous day's press conference, *New York Times,* July 30, 1963.

[109] *New York Times,* August 20, 1963.

[110] *New York Times,* July 25 and 28, 1963.

[111] *New York Times,* August 20 and 22, 1963.

ing such weapons further. The United States has interpreted the Soviet Union position as just another example of Russian objections to any strengthening of the alliance.

FOREIGN ECONOMIC AND SOCIAL AID

The regional security organizations have had little effect on United States policy regarding aid to underdeveloped countries, especially when compared to United Nations agencies or to economic groupings. Major changes in the American foreign economic assistance program have in any case had other origins, mostly domestic. Such policy changes have included shifts in the emphasis as between private and public financing, in the balance between military and economic aid, and in the extent to which aid funds had to be used for purchases within the United States.

We have already noted that the United States effectively opposed using NATO for major types of economic activity and that special treatment accorded Greece and Turkey constituted an exception. Because of their relative poverty, their proximity to Communist borders, and their obvious need for help if they were to be depended upon to guard these borders, their pleas for exceptional consideration in NATO were successful. NATO itself did not organize aid to these two countries; individual NATO members extended assistance, while the problem of coordinating the aid was left to the OECD. The other relatively poor member, Portugal, was for the most part indifferent to outside aid. In the 1960s United States "defense support" to Greece and Turkey (as distinguished from outright military aid) was being phased out, while through the stimulus of NATO other forms of aid were being developed. These utilized the EEC, the International Bank, and consortia of private investors.[112]

We have also noted that the three Asian members of SEATO received some special consideration because their SEATO membership made them allies of the United States. But they did not receive as large amounts of strictly economic aid (as opposed to military assistance) as did important non-aligned recipients such as India. And the effectiveness

[112] Senate Committee on Appropriations, *Hearings, Foreign Assistance and Related Agencies Appropriations for 1962,* 87th Cong., 1st sess. (1961), pp. 285–86. A curious passage in President Kennedy's foreign aid message to Congress, April 2, 1963, stated that the United States was urging its *allies* to increase their assistance efforts, but did not identify which ones or suggest why they were singled out among the developed countries.

of the help may be questioned; all the American aid sent to Pakistan did not prevent this ally from accepting assistance from Communist China.

The Bank, and more particularly its affiliates which were designed to aid underdeveloped areas, have been of growing importance to United States policy. Not only do they offer appropriate multilateral instruments, but they also represent reliable media in which the American voice is strong. The very establishment of the International Finance Corporation has been cited as an example of the influence of one international organization, the Bank, on American policy.[113]

While the OECD is not itself an aid-granting institution, one reason for United States sponsorship of this organization was to stimulate a wider sharing of burdens in this field. The important Development Assistance Committee helps to coordinate the members' aid policies and, through confrontation procedures, to put organized, international pressures on members to provide more help to underdeveloped countries. One of the richest members, West Germany, has met the OECD-suggested standard of providing foreign aid equal to 1 percent of its GNP. To the extent that the OECD succeeds in these two functions, encouraging expanded aid and coordinating programs, the foreign aid activities of the United States are also affected. The United States went to the Development Assistance Committee to arouse interest in an international development bank for Southeast Asia which President Johnson's administration sought to organize in the summer of 1965. Meanwhile OECD's statistical work and publication of relevant information has already proved very helpful to the American AID in drawing up its own programs.[114]

A major foreign aid instrument is the Alliance for Progress, in the drafting of the agreement for which the Organization of American States played an important part.[115] Preceding its establishment came that of the Inter-American Development Bank, which the Latin-American

---

[113] B. E. Matecki, *Establishment of the International Finance Corporation and United States Policy* (New York: Frederick A. Praeger, 1957). The introduction by Richard Van Wagenen points out the "vast area of relationships" under the surface of the formal organization which helps to explain interacting influences [p. ix].

[114] House of Representatives Committee on Foreign Affairs, *Hearings, Foreign Assistance Act of 1962*, 87th Cong., 2nd sess. (1962), p. 314.

[115] Testimony of Secretary Dillon, Senate Committee on Appropriations, *Hearings, Foreign Assistance and Related Agencies Appropriations for 1962*, 87th Cong., 1st sess. (1961), pp. 228; John C. Dreier, *The Organization of American States and the Hemisphere Crisis* (New York: Harper and Row, 1962), p. 85.

countries had long urged, within and outside the OAS, upon the United States, and to which, according to Under Secretary of State Dillon, the United States finally acquiesced on political as much as on economic grounds.[116] This bank, in addition to its lending function, participates in implementing programs of the Alliance for Progress.[117] It has fostered a growing interest within the European Common Market for European investments in development projects in Latin America; such cooperation between inter-American and European organizations is a new phenomenon.[118] The greatly expanded funds made available by the United States for Latin-American development under the Alliance for Progress meant that the Americans were now putting dollars behind their support for the general principles they had agreed to earlier in OAS meetings regarding the need for land reform, tax reform, housing, and similar economic and social wants.

Some observers, in Latin America and elsewhere, have attributed the increased American interest in foreign aid to Latin America to a general anti-Castro campaign. Whether true or not, the United States has not been able to buy anti-Castro actions through its foreign aid activities. Two further trends are now vaguely evident. As a result of the practical experience gained, the United States is growing readier to leave to the inter-American organs some of the advisory responsibility for reviewing or recommending projects for Alliance for Progress financing, while it still retains the final decision regarding their acceptance.[119] And the Latin-American countries themselves are taking more responsibility for their own improvement by using these institutions, which is another kind of burden-sharing heartily desired in the United States.[120] It is too early

[116] House of Representatives Committee on Foreign Affairs, *Hearings, Mutual Security Act of 1959*, 86th Cong., 1st sess. (1959), p. 41. Cf. also Dreier, *op. cit.*, pp. 83–84.

[117] House of Representatives Committee on Foreign Affairs, *Hearings, Foreign Assistance Act of 1962*, 87th Cong., 2nd sess. (1962), p. 6; and Senate Committee on Appropriations, *Hearings, Foreign Assistance and Related Agencies Appropriations for 1962*, 87th Cong., 1st sess. (1961), pp. 48–49 and 56.

[118] *New York Times*, April 9, 1963. Originally sponsored by a NATO Parliamentarians committee under Senator Jacob Javits' leadership, a private Atlantic Community Development Group for Latin America has begun investment in that area [*Atlantic Community News*, May, 1965, p. 2].

[119] Summary of OAS activities, *International Organization*, Summer, 1962, pp. 657–58; A. Lleras Camargo, "The Alliance for Progress," *Foreign Affairs*, October, 1963, p. 35; *New York Times*, Jan. 30, 1964.

[120] See House of Representatives Committee on Foreign Affairs, *Hearings. Foreign Assistance Act of 1962*, 87th Cong., 2nd sess. (1962), pp. 442–43.

to make judgments regarding whether those conflicting economic interests of the United States and the other members of the OAS which relate to their different roles as buyer and seller and borrower and lender can be reconciled through international organizations in which they all participate because of a common concern with economic and social development in Latin America. The differing economic interests which distinguish the members of the OAS from those in NATO, where the conflicts are not so marked, help to explain the differential effects upon United States policy resulting from membership in these two organizations.

FOREIGN TRADE

Trade policy and defense policy for the NATO area (or for any other area) ought to be complementary. Ideally they should reinforce each other in promoting economic welfare and national security; at the least, they should not work at cross-purposes. How has membership in NATO affected the United States' pursuit of its trade objectives and the coordination of its trade and defense policies?

Given American devotion to the most-favored-nation principle, systematically discriminatory trade arrangements in favor of NATO allies have not been feasible, even assuming they were desirable. Thus, one instrument of national policy which might have evoked allied support for American security policies was not available.[121] NATO membership has therefore not constrained the United States in its trade policy with respect either to its allies or to the rest of the world.[122]

On the other hand, when the United States has wanted to use trade policy as an instrument of the cold war, NATO has been of only limited utility. For example, the United States pressed its Atlantic allies to support rules of COCOM discriminating against Communist countries; but it was unable to hold its allies in line and unwilling to follow them when they relaxed the harsh restrictions which the United States had urged

---

[121] Removing special barriers to trade in products of particular importance to one or more allies—for example, import restrictions on lead and wool and regulations to promote shipping in American bottoms—is another matter and will be considered in the next chapter.

[122] Coordination of the allies' defense plans through NATO machinery has led to some routine planning of emergency industrial and economic resource mobilization, a task in which the NATO staff participated [Senate Committee on Appropriations, *Hearings, Department of State . . . Appropriations for 1958,* 85th Cong., 1st sess. (1957), p. 316].

and had itself adopted vis-à-vis the Chinese People's Republic.[123] Here again we can discern a gap between what many Americans expected of the alliance and what is possible. This gap was implicit in the explanation Secretary of State Rusk felt obliged to offer as to why the United States had been unwilling to take retaliatory measures against allies who refused to conform to its own more restrictive trading practice with the Communists:

Our interests and the interests of our allies are so much intertwined in so many ways in NATO as part of the entire Western community, in the growing help they are giving underdeveloped countries, in support which we get from the rest of our NATO partners that it is very difficult for us to press a matter of this sort in effect to the breaking point.

He also argued that without a modicum of trade with the Soviet Union there would be no chance to show allied solidarity when punitive economic measures were to be taken.[124]

In the case of the OAS, we find even less evidence that the United States has altered its trade policy as a result of membership, except for one or two types of situations. After long years of Latin-American pressure inside and outside the OAS for some kind of commodity stabilization agreements, the United States began in 1959 to look more favorably upon such schemes, though not upon a hemisphere organization for their execution. The Americans have also pushed the case for more attention to Latin-American interests in other international organizations, notably GATT.

GATT and the OECD have both helped the United States to avoid having to deal directly with certain inconvenient trade requests. These have come from both Latin America and Japan and have included claims for special treatment and for market regulations not desired by the United States government. Granting them would have tended, American officials asserted, to make these countries unduly dependent on the United States. The United States' ability to direct the claimants to GATT or to the OECD for an alternative solution to some of their problems has helped maintain its trade policies.

In his message to GATT in November, 1962, Under Secretary of

---

[123] Cf. Stebbins, *The United States in World Affairs, 1957,* pp. 61–62; also Senate Committee on Foreign Relations, *Hearings, East–West Trade,* 83rd Cong., 2nd sess. (1954), p. 32.
[124] *The Winds of Freedom* (Boston: Beacon Press, 1963), p. 254.

State Ball listed as among the eternal verities of trade liberalization "the primacy of GATT in the reaching of arrangements for the expansion of trade through the negotiating process." Since the United States had worked through GATT in trying to remove the discriminations against American goods which had been imposed earlier because of dollar shortages, it was obliged at least formally to comply with these same rules. It did give formal (but not substantial) satisfaction to Denmark and Holland when they objected to a restriction in the 1950 Defense Production Act on certain cheeses. The United States agreed to repeal the provision, but then imposed similar restrictions under an amendment to the 1938 Agricultural Adjustment Act which permits import restrictions related to farm price support programs. GATT then authorized the Dutch to retaliate, which permitted them to cut flour imports from the United States. When Italy protested an American export subsidy on oranges, the United States modified the subsidies before Italy sought GATT authority to retaliate.[125] However, the United States remained remarkably hard of hearing when Canada sought through GATT and elsewhere to register protests against "unorthodox" methods of disposing of certain surplus agricultural products.[126]

Membership in an international organization implies multilateral negotiations, which in turn may imply changes in the methods a country formerly followed in trade bargaining. In the Kennedy Round of GATT negotiations the United States had to agree to a new technique: instead of item-by-item consideration of offers the United States accepted "across the board" consideration of broad categories of goods. This change in bargaining methods has special implications for the United States; unlike the tariffs of European members, duties on goods imported into the United States range from very high to very low; they do not cluster in a fairly narrow range.[127]

Some observers have called the OECD an "ante-room" to GATT. This is probably correct in the sense that OECD members, prior to GATT negotiations, do discuss frankly and intimately some questions to

[125] Cf. Peter B. Kenen, *Giant Among Nations* (New York: Harcourt, Brace, 1960), p. 48; also Richard N. Gardner, "GATT and the United Nations Conference on Trade and Development," *International Organization,* Autumn, 1964, pp. 685–704, esp. pp. 692 and 694, for how the United States used and itself felt the application of GATT's rules.

[126] See Stebbins, *The United States in World Affairs, 1957,* p. 290.

[127] Pierre Uri, *Partnership for Progress* (New York: Harper and Row, 1963), pp. 15–16.

be handled there. For the Americans it has been a chastening experience to lay their own problems before a critical audience, but they have readily played the game. They have done so not in the interests of any exclusive trading relations with the Atlantic nations but to further a more fundamental interest in expanded trade generally. The procedures are so quietly followed by the responsible officials of each government that it would not be easy to point out a direct relationship between discussion and altered policy, but American participants agree that they have been influenced by the discussion.[128]

The United States has also looked to the International Monetary Fund in its efforts to solve the balance of payments problem. In July, 1963 the government readily secured a stand-by authorization of $500 million, which it could borrow in other convertible currencies.[129] The United States Treasury Department's many-sided efforts to halt the dollar drain employ a number of other kinds of organizations as well as more informal groupings of fiscal officers and central banks in those countries important in the world's money market who are ready to cooperate because of their common interest in greater liquidity.[130]

Despite the intricate web of economic relationships between the United States and other countries operating inside and outside the organizations considered here, a very important move in the 1960s, the Trade Expansion Act, was not directly related to any of these organizations. Instead it reflected a desire to influence the actions of an organization in which the United States was not a member and did not wish to be, namely, the Common Market. (It was also an organization in which Great Britain was not a member, but the United States did wish it to be.) However, there was an indirect relationship: implementation of the

---

[128] However, the effect may not always have been what was intended. Early in the 1960s Europeans expressed through OECD their concern over the failure of the American economy to expand and to right the balance of payments. When President Kennedy and his advisers settled on a cut in taxes as a stimulant, this was in line with discussion in previous OECD Council meetings [cf. *New York Times,* November 7 and 29, 1962]. His proposal to Congress in the summer of 1963 for a tax on American purchases of long-term foreign securities as one means to deal with the balance of payments problem was not favorably received except as a sign that some action was being taken [*New York Times,* July 19, 1963].

[129] Robert V. Roosa, "Forming the International Monetary System," *Foreign Affairs,* October 1963, p. 120.

[130] *Ibid.;* also William Diebold, Jr., "Economic Aspects of an Atlantic Community," *International Organization,* Summer, 1963, pp. 672–73.

Act depends largely on GATT, an organization which is not confined to countries in the Atlantic world.

As we shall note in greater detail in Chapter VI, the United States has kept its trade policy and defense policy separate in many ways, one of which has been by using quite different international organizations for promoting these policies.

DECOLONIZATION

A majority of the original signatories to the North Atlantic Treaty possessed overseas dependencies. (These were the United States, Britain, France, Belgium, the Netherlands, Denmark, and Portugal; Italy obtained a United Nations trusteeship in 1950.) The well-known aversion of Americans to "colonialism" produced frictions in their relations with some of the European metropolitan governments in spite of the fact that the United States was itself a colonial power and, perhaps, because of the fact that the Americans' self-image was that of a "model" governor of other peoples. Upon the two most important colonial powers, Britain and France, however, the United States only privately and circumspectly exerted pressure towards dissolution of their empires. Its devotion to the principle of decolonization was far from absolute; after the colonial issues had become inextricably bound up with Communist expansion, it helped the French to try to hold Indo-China. Only during the Suez crisis of 1956 did the United States dramatically oppose its two large allies, and then the grounds for doing so were only partially related to the desire to take a strong anti-imperialist stand. Other reasons were much more compelling.

These same states have been allies of the United States in SEATO, along with other "white" countries which have administered United Nations trusteeships, Australia and New Zealand. Among South and Southeast Asian states only Thailand, the Philippines, and Pakistan would join with such a combination to form a Pacific regional security organization. On the ideological grounds of anticolonialism all the others have stayed out.

In the OAS, on the other hand, the United States is the only colonial power, although whatever reputation Americans still have as dangerous imperialists is not connected with outright possession of colonies then or now. In fact, the whole thrust of the American effort in the OAS and the

Alliance for Progress might be described as an effort to mitigate the harsh realities flowing from the inevitably very strong influence of a wealthy and powerful giant nation dwelling in the midst of weak and needy countries. In the early days of the OAS some Latin-American members tried but failed to organize a movement to eliminate dependencies of European states from the Caribbean; other members and the inhabitants of these dependencies were not interested.[131] However important the OAS may be in promoting regional security and economic development, its role has been slight either in facilitating or hindering decolonization in the Americas with respect to the colonies either of Europe or the United States.

When we come to specific colonial conflicts we find no clear evidence that United States behavior has been affected by its alliance associations. Most of its actions were taken in the context of United Nations consideration of colonial questions, for this organization became a major participant in promoting the evolution of colonies to independent states. Many observers saw a dilemma for the United States posed by conflicting loyalties to its allies and to the charter-prescribed goal of self-determination of peoples. Since the allies with colonies were also members of the United Nations and therefore committed to the same goal, the issue between them and the United States usually boiled down to one of means and timing for decolonization of particular countries. Whether or not the dilemma was a real one, on most of these specific conflicts the United States found itself blamed by both sides, whether it voted affirmatively or negatively, and even when it merely abstained on particular resolutions.

During both the independence and post-independence crises in relations between an emerging nation and a European power, whenever the United States tried to straddle an issue by urging both sides not to take "irrevocable" steps, the effect was to favor the insistent disturbers of the status quo and was similar to that often noted by Americans when Asian countries took a "non-aligned" stand on a Western-bloc vs. Soviet-bloc issue. In the Dutch New Guinea (West Irian) case, for example, "half-acquiescence" in Sukarno's demands did not really mean that the Americans were also offering the other half of their support to the Nether-

---

[131] Northwestern University, "The Organization of American States," a study for the Senate Committee on Foreign Relations, Subcommittee on American Republics Affairs, *United States-Latin American Relations,* Senate Doc. No. 125, 86th Cong., 2nd sess. (1960), p. 220.

lands; the position inevitably favored the more militant, which was Indonesia. This example also shows that factors other than loyalty to an ally or devotion to the principle of self-determination may be dominant in the American decision. The Americans knew that they could continue to count on the loyalty to NATO of the Dutch, whose good sense showed them where their priorities in security lay.

In the Dutch New Guinea case the United Nations acted, with the concurrence of the United States, virtually as a transfer agent to hand over the territory to Indonesia. In the preceding case of Goa, involving another NATO ally, the Americans in the United Nations were helpless, despite an anguished cry from the United States delegate about the consequences for the United Nations itself. The Portuguese had a good legal claim to Goa, as did the Dutch to West Irian; but the weight of influence of the ex-colonial countries in the United Nations prevented effective action against the Indian conquerors.

Another small NATO country, Belgium, was a principal party in a third case, the Congo. Here the United States, in the interest of keeping the cold war out of Africa, strongly supported a number of United Nations actions which insured that the Belgians would get out and stay out of what had been one of the few remaining really valuable colonial possessions.

Perhaps the chaos which developed in the Congo once it became "self-governing" has caused a little more circumspection in American actions in the United Nations regarding a fourth case, Portugal's African possessions. In this case the United States tried quiet diplomacy through the North Atlantic Council to persuade Portugal to modify its intransigeance when confronted by independence pressures emanating from the United Nations.[132] There is a greater risk here than in the Dutch and Belgian cases that the aggrieved ally will lose its devotion to NATO; but Portugal's position is less central to the alliance than that of the Netherlands and Belgium.[133]

[132] The Americans also quickly checked minor leakages from military aid given Portugal as a NATO ally; it had been flowing to Portuguese forces in Angola. This resembled an earlier leakage of aid to France which reached French forces in Algeria. However, unlike Angola, Algeria was a territory protected by the North Atlantic Treaty. See House of Representatives Committee on Foreign Affairs, *Hearings, Foreign Assistance Act of 1962*, 87th Cong., 2nd sess. (1962), pp. 145–46.

[133] For one thing, Portugal is not in "Allied Command Europe" but in the Atlantic Ocean Command.

Another colonial conflict, that out of which emerged an independent Cyprus, also gave rise to mediatory actions both in the United Nations and in NATO. Here was a dispute among three members of the alliance, and one in which the Asiatic and African countries took little interest at the time. The United States thus could find it easier to watch its allies settle the conflict among themselves; at least that is what the actions of the United States government seem to indicate. (The strife in Cyprus that arose in 1963 was not clearly a "colonial" issue.)

All these cases involved "minor" NATO allies who appeared even less important without their colonial possessions. (The Cyprus case belongs here only because of the Greek interest in it; the British were ready to concede *some* form of autonomy.) One incident involving three major NATO allies should also be cited to indicate how indistinct the pattern of American behavior appears. While the war for Algerian independence was still going on, Tunisia, already independent, sought some small arms. When the Tunisians could not obtain them from France, they turned to the United States and Britain, who obliged the Tunisians in November, 1957, in order to prevent the moderate leader of this North African country from being tempted to turn to the Communist bloc.[134] When the Tunisians and French came to blows over a French incursion into Tunisian territory in 1958, the United States and Great Britain together offered their good offices, for they hoped to avoid a public debate in the Security Council, where they would have had to take sides publicly.[135] So far as Algeria itself was concerned, the United States carefully abstained from United Nations resolutions. This caused French resentment, since Algeria was specifically mentioned in the North Atlantic Treaty as part of the area to be protected.[136] These cases involving the French in North Africa should be recalled in obtaining a perspective on the French discontent with NATO, not all of which stems from the nuclear dispute.[137]

Except possibly for Cyprus (where the Secretary General of NATO

[134] See Stebbins, *United States in World Affairs, 1957*, pp. 339–40; Donnelly, *United States Defense Policies in 1957*, p. 40; Senate Committee on Foreign Relations, *Hearings, Mutual Security Act of 1960*, 86th Cong., 2nd sess. (1960), p. 252.

[135] See Stebbins, *United States in World Affairs, 1958*, pp. 244–46.

[136] See Secretary Dillon's reply to Senator Fulbright in Senate Committee on Foreign Relations, *Hearings, Review of Foreign Policy*, 85th Cong., 2nd sess. (1958), pp. 323–24.

[137] See Edmond Taylor, "NATO after Spaak: A Loss and a Warning," *Reporter*, April 13, 1961, p. 18, citing Raymond Aron in *Figaro*.

tried "quiet diplomacy"), none of the cases mentioned involved NATO directly, only some of its members. A few members, notably Norway and Denmark, have been as resolutely anti-colonial as the United States, if not more so. (Norway and Denmark, as well as the United States, voted for a United Nations General Assembly resolution in 1961 declaring Angola's right to independence.) The Americans recognized that the independence aspects of the colonial problem were too divisive for NATO to handle. The economic aspects of the problem of the newly independent states, however, appeared to the United States government to be suitable for the OECD to consider.

American officials, in promoting the OECD, have hoped that to the extent that it is successful in increasing productivity within the member countries and in stimulating greater aid to the former colonial countries, it will improve relations between OECD's powerful, rich members and the poor, underdeveloped new countries. However, emotion and stereotyped thinking among the ex-colonies have hindered recognition of either the fact or the validity of American hopes. Communist-bloc countries have lost no time in describing such aid, especially from the United States, as "neo-imperialism."

SPECIFIC DIPLOMATIC CONFLICTS

Let us turn for a moment to some diplomatic conflicts of vital interest to the United States, the most vital of which during NATO's lifetime involved Berlin, Cuba, and Vietnam. Middle Eastern and African issues have been omitted, as being outside the range of the alliances examined in this study.

Only on the Berlin question is there evidence that "consultation" with America's allies has meant much more than the United States' informing its partners of its own views and intentions. Since at least 1955 (on the occasion of the Geneva summit meeting) the countries most involved in the Berlin problem have deliberated not only with each other but also with their NATO colleagues and have even produced draft proposals for their allies' comment before undertaking formal discussions with the Soviet Union.[138] This practice has continued and has become more frequent and more habitual as Russian threats to the Western allies' position in Berlin have persisted. A four-power "Ambassadorial Group" in

---

[138] Carol E. Baumann, *Political Co-operation in NATO* (Madison: University of Wisconsin, 1960), p. 30; Guido Colonna di Paliano, "The State of the Alliance," *Atlantic Community Quarterly,* Fall, 1964, p. 405.

Washington, composed of the United States, France, Britain, and Germany, has for some years worked out common policies vis-à-vis the Soviet Union; but they have regularly consulted also with the rest of the NATO members.[139] To pinpoint the origin of specific ideas in this complex of United States–NATO–"Ambassadorial Group" discussions would be impossible, even for the participants. Secretary Dulles testified that United States policy after Khrushchev's sudden ultimatum in the fall of 1958 regarding access to Berlin had not hardened prior to deliberations with the other allies.[140] He insisted that no exclusively American negotiations with the visiting Mikoyan would take place regarding Berlin, about which the United States intended always to negotiate only "in cooperation and partnership with" the allies.[141] Whatever may have been the case before, following the ultimatum the connection between NATO and United States policy regarding Berlin became and remained much more than "multilateral communication." [142]

During the early 1960s, and especially after the Wall went up, some critics (for the most part non-official) complained that the United States was being held back from a bolder course by allies who were less eager to take "tough" and perhaps provocative measures in Berlin.[143] Since military action would eventually involve NATO forces if violence be-

[139] Richard P. Stebbins, *The United States in World Affairs, 1959*, p. 211; Assistant Secretary of State Kohler in Senate Committee on Foreign Relations, *Hearings, Mutual Security Act of 1960*, 86th Cong., 2nd sess. (1960), p. 222; *New York Times*, September 17, 1961; Declaration on Berlin of the NATO Council on December 16, 1958, which is regularly reaffirmed at the ministerial meetings [NATO Information Service, *Facts about the North Atlantic Treaty Organization* (Paris, NATO, 1962), p. 36].

[140] House of Representatives Committee on Foreign Affairs, *Hearings, Briefing on Current World Situation*, 86th Cong., 1st sess. (1959), pp. 7–8.

[141] Senate Committee on Foreign Relations, *Hearings, United States Foreign Policy*, 86th Cong., 1st sess. (1959), pp. 10–11.

[142] This phrase is taken from Ruth Lawson, "Concerting Policies in the North Atlantic Community," *International Organization*, Spring, 1958, p. 170; see also Stebbins, *United States in World Affairs, 1958*, pp. 48 and 165–66; *ibid., 1959*, pp. 189–90; *ibid., 1960*, p. 132; Summary of NATO activities, *International Organization*, Spring, 1959, p. 342; *ibid.*, Autumn, 1960, pp. 682–83; "NATO Members Examine Problems Confronting the Alliance," *Department of State Bulletin*, January 8, 1962, pp. 51–52; Paul Henri Spaak, "New Tests for NATO," *Foreign Affairs*, April, 1961, p. 359; General Norstad at House of Representatives Committee on Foreign Affairs, *Hearings, Foreign Assistance Act of 1962*, 87th Cong., 2nd sess. (1962), p. 292; *New York Times*, December 16, 1961.

[143] See Stebbins, *United States in World Affairs, 1959*, p. 188; *ibid., 1961*, p. 86; *New York Times*, November 6, 1961; George Bailey, "The Gentle Erosion of Berlin," *Reporter*, April 26, 1962, p. 17. Here again there is a fallacy in equating "allies" with "alliance." See *New York Herald Tribune*, May 6, 1962, Sec. 2, p. 4; *New York Times*, September 6, 1963, for other examples.

came widespread in the area, it is not surprising that General Norstad, SACEUR at the time of the Wall's construction, was not among those who pressed for bolder steps.[144] Yet he had been among the first to acclaim the strong and unified reaction of the alliance as a whole when Khrushchev's ultimatum was first issued. The North Atlantic Council continued to show, at least publicly, an "impressive" unity. Berlin is perhaps unique in showing how the alliance could mold and keep within bounds the policy of the individual members, even the United States.

After Cuba became Communist, neither NATO nor the OAS were involved in any direct action to restrain or destroy the unwanted regime. The United States failed to interest its NATO partners in joint action to hem the Cubans in, until the missile crisis in October, 1962.[145] Then the others stood firm with the United States by accepting its quarantine move. They recognized that unilateral American action rather than lengthy explanation and deliberation was necessary at the moment.

From the OAS, the United States had previously obtained little more than simple declarations about the threat of Communism. The first such affirmation came many years before Castro's ascent to power, in 1948 at Bogotá. As the Communist tendencies in Castro's government became increasingly unmistakable, the United States secured more and more specific expressions hostile to the regime, but only meager implementation of their sense. Privately, OAS members would agree that the Cuban regime was dangerous to their security, but they could not agree to take public action to restrain or isolate it.[146] Not only did traditional Latin-American views on non-intervention prevent such action, but so also did their fear of domestic political repercussions.[147] Since Castro's regime posed no economic threat and United States armed forces in the Caribbean kept it from launching an armed attack against any other Latin-

---

[144] Testimony, House of Representatives Committee on Foreign Affairs, *Hearings, Foreign Assistance Act of 1962,* 87th Cong., 2nd sess. (1962), pp. 288–89.

[145] *New York Times,* February 19, 1962; November 3, 1962; October 23 and 24, 1962. For further discussion of NATO and Cuba, see Chapter VI.

[146] The furthest the majority would go at Punta del Este, January 22, 1962, was to exclude Cuba from inter-American meetings and to recommend suspension of arms shipments. At this conference they also agreed to study other kinds of embargoes and methods of Communist subversion [John C. Dreier, "The Organization of American States and United States Policy," *International Organization,* Winter, 1963, pp. 51–52; *New York Times,* February 1, 1962].

[147] See Dreier, "The Organization of American States and United States Policy," *loc. cit.,* pp. 47, and *idem, The Organization of American States and the Hemisphere Crisis,* pp. 91–93 and 111; Adolf A. Berle, *Latin America: Diplomacy and Reality* (New York: Harper and Row, 1962), pp. 102–03.

American country, "domestic political repercussions" that might enhance Castro's opportunities for subversive activity, were a genuine concern to the Latin-American governments.

In the refinement and execution of American policy towards Castro's Cuba, the OAS was a blunt instrument. We cannot say what the Kennedy administration would have done had the OAS not responded quickly and affirmatively to the quarantine policy invoked to meet the missile crisis; we do know that the United States put intense effort into securing this response.[148] Similarly, it has striven since the Cuban crisis for implementation of the resolutions achieved at the time, especially for steps against Communist subversion and for the isolation of Cuba. A majority of the OAS Council gave the Americans some satisfaction in July, 1963.[149] Further satisfaction arose from the Council's resolution of July, 1964, calling for economic sanctions after condemning Cuba as an aggressor, a charge brought by Venezuela.[150] The United States is, however, still dependent upon its Latin-American neighbors to give both support and substance to these approved policies. Perhaps we can conclude that while neither NATO nor the OAS had a positive or direct influence on United States policy regarding Cuba, both the solidarity which had been induced in both organizations prior to the crisis and the American desire for approval played a part in shaping the American actions.

Turning to Southeast Asia, we find that SEATO has had little influence on the formulation of United States policy in Laos and South Vietnam. Thailand and, to a lesser extent, the Philippines occasionally bemoaned the lack of an active role for SEATO in Laos. Even more than in other areas, the effect of French and British membership in this alliance was to curb action through SEATO by the United States.[151] Yet

---

[148] *New York Times,* October 24, 25, and 27, and November 3, 1962. The OAS action authorizing use of armed forces according to the Rio Treaty was unprecedented [Dreier, "The Organization of American States and United States Policy," *loc. cit.,* p. 53].

[149] *New York Times,* July 4, 1963; July 26, 1964; also *Christian Science Monitor,* February 26, 1963.

[150] *New York Times,* July 26, 1964. The Dominican crisis of 1965 gave rise to new United States efforts to use the OAS, some of which were partially fruitful. But the Americans were unable to interest enough other members to institute a regular procedure for collective intervention involving the use of armed forces under OAS auspices in possible future cases.

[151] See George Modelski (ed.), *Seato: Six Studies:* Melbourne: F. W. Cheshire, 1962), pp. 4–5.

the determination of the Americans to proceed by independent action if it seemed necessary has made such curbs relatively unimportant.[152] By 1963 the United States began actively employing SEATO to persuade the Australians and New Zealanders to participate more visibly in the Vietnam conflict; by 1965 it had succeeded.

In all three areas the United States' membership in the relevant alliance has somewhat inhibited its policy from diverging radically from that of its partners, especially when their support was sought for American-defined purposes. At the same time American participation in the respective regional organizations gave the other members some sense that the Americans would not "make a deal behind their backs."

Let us summarize our discussion by referring again to the main categories of foreign policy which could have been affected by United States membership in an international organization. American military policy has been most clearly affected by United States participation in NATO. This is hardly surprising, since the alliance is a security organization above all. Nevertheless, with respect to another means for protecting security, namely, arms control, NATO does not seem to have had much influence, in spite of frequent consultation within the alliance in recent years. Some European members' views differed so much from American views on arms control that the organization's impact on American policy could only have been negative in those cases in which it had any measurable influence.

Domestic considerations in the United States have continued to dominate the choice and implementation of measures to aid underdeveloped countries, in spite of increasingly important international programs in which the United States has participated. Nor has United States trade policy been greatly changed by membership in international organizations. The main effects have been certain tariff adjustments and, in the 1960s, a serious beginning in coordinated monetary policy, neither of which involved NATO directly. In its policies regarding decolonization and "disimperialism" the United States has been less influenced than in the other types of policies discussed here by participation in any of the organizations under consideration, and more by its participation in the United Nations.

The influence of NATO membership on United States policy—so far

---

[152] See House of Representatives Committee on Foreign Affairs, *Hearings, Foreign Assistance Act of 1962*, 87th Cong., 2nd sess. (1962), pp. 96–97.

as it has existed—has flowed in part from the heavy load of expectations which American decision-makers have placed on this organization. Furthermore the variety and number of ways in which NATO has operated are not only far greater than those characterizing the other organizations under consideration. NATO operations have also required more intensive participation, as in the cases of the integrated commands, the common infrastructure, and the systematic interchange of diplomatic views. Involvement has therefore gone beyond even that required by the procedures followed in the other organizations as well as NATO, such as confrontation, standardization, and coordinated strategies.

For all five types of policy there have been at least some signs that the need to develop policies which could be advocated and debated and perhaps implemented by these various organizations had entered into American decision making. The following chapter suggests ways in which the United States might make more effective use of the organizations.

CHAPTER SIX

NATO POTENTIALITIES AND UNITED STATES CHOICES

THE PRECEDING CHAPTER investigated the actual influence of NATO and other international organizations on United States foreign policy and inquired into whether they were an aid or obstacle to particular American objectives. In this chapter we compare actual with possible uses of NATO in support of relevant American policies and seek to identify missed opportunities for the United States to benefit from membership in NATO. In the course of this comparison we may also observe the costs of overuse or misuse.

In pointing to American foreign policy conduct which apparently did not make full use of the international organization, we must remember the danger of judging such behavior out of its total context and of overestimating the capacity of one nation, even the most powerful, to produce unity in a group of sovereign states. Thus we cannot simply use the model behavior of a member of some model integrated international organization as a yardstick for measuring the shortcomings of actual United States behavior in a particular organization, NATO or any other.

American declaratory policy concerning an organization presumably reflects what American policy-makers believed could and should have been done through the organization. The gap between declared policy and concrete action thus may be evidence of "missed opportunities." Policy declarations provide no direct basis for judging the essential feasibility or desirability for the United States of a particular course of action (or inaction).[1] Any such judgment of "NATO potentialities" rests on the observer's own estimate of what is desirable and possible. Note, however, that by speaking of the uses of NATO, we imply that NATO is not an end in itself; it is useful as it serves the interests of its members. The proclaimed policy preferences of responsible officials are important evidence of those interests. In asking how effectively American foreign policy actions have helped the organization to operate in accordance with these stated preferences, we cannot avoid speaking in terms more congenial to the organizational technocrat than to the politician; we can only note that the following observations are all subject to modification because politics is "the art of the possible."

BALANCED, COLLECTIVE DEFENSE

The United States has sought through NATO a more efficient allocation of tasks among the member states in the realization of the security interest which the members share and a more efficient mechanism for the pooled effort, in other words, "balanced, collective defense." Achieving this kind of defense implies some specialization according to capacity, i.e., more specialization than would be likely if each state tried to protect itself and more than would be likely if the implicit or explicit sharing of common objectives was not accompanied by the sharing of plans to realize those objectives.[2] Since the United States was for some years the only member with nuclear weapons and since these had to be carried by bombers many of which would require European bases, the principle was almost inevitably observed. The United States Strategic Air Command, by providing nuclear protection to the alliance, was supposed to give the European members reason for providing complementary bases and ground forces. The general principle of specialization

[1] There might be a number of reasons for the gap to remain, such as considerations of psychological strategy, the need to preserve certain decencies, the undesirability of trumpeting certain objectives, or their presumed impracticability. Or the policy-declarers might simply not know what they would want later. See Frederick S. Dunn, *Peacemaking and the Settlement with Japan* (Princeton: Princeton University Press, 1963), p. xiii, for a discussion of the perplexities facing the decision-maker, including "the difficulties of reaching accord with others sharing the decision-making power."

[2] NATO officials, such as Field Marshal Montgomery, also promoted this aim; see his *Memoirs* (Cleveland: World Publishing Co., 1958), p. 468, and North Atlantic Council communiqué of May 15–18, 1950, quoted in Lord Ismay, *NATO: The First Five Years, 1949–1954* (Paris: NATO, n.d.), p. 183.

continued to be observed when the British developed a hydrogen bomb deliverable by its own V-bombers; the United States could acquiesce in a British nuclear contribution to defense of the North Atlantic area because the targeting of the new force was "integrated" with American targeting. Yet the "special relationship" between Britain and America once again exemplified by this arrangement posed numerous dilemmas already noted in Chapter V. (For other aspects of this relationship, see below.)

The faith that the United States would indeed make good on its guarantee, a faith which is the prerequisite of balanced, collective forces, was at first unquestioned. The American nuclear umbrella over Europe did not in the early years of NATO expose American cities to any risk of nuclear destruction, and the armed forces of Western Europe were too weak for the beneficiaries of the guarantee to afford the luxury of questioning it. As Soviet nuclear strength grew, as missile technology developed, as thinking about nuclear strategy became more sophisticated, and as Western Europe's economic strength and political confidence revived, that faith began to erode.

On the American side, the sense of dependence on bases in the territories of NATO's European members for the application of United States strategic air and missile power declined. On the European side, the glamour and prestige which officials attached to possession of nuclear weapons soon caused some members to resent the "lowly" role they were to play, sometimes called "supplying the hoplites." Furthermore, some impolitic words and actions of American officials alarmed the Europeans. In any case, the question of control over strategic air and missile power was bound to arise sooner or later.

Like the earlier bombers, the first missiles capable of delivering strategic nuclear weapons required European bases. Although the warheads remained under American control, the countries in which they were put played a "balancing," specialized role by supplying territory and accepting a specific vulnerability to retaliation unshared by other members. (Each country also acquired a veto over the use of missiles to be fired from its territory.) Their removal in 1963 took place not for reasons related to "balanced, collective forces" but because more desirable types of missiles were developed, ones that were more invulnerable and much greater in range but, incidentally, more completely under unshared

American control. The reluctance with which Italy and Turkey gave up the intermediate-range missiles suggests that these countries did in fact feel there was both prestige and power-sharing in their location.

Two kinds of nuclear missiles (aside from the essentially "tactical" nuclear weapons) have been proposed for a *collective* force to protect the European allies from Russian medium-range ballistic missiles (MRBMs) known to be targeted on their territory. The first, a mobile medium-range ballistic missile (MMRBM), to be placed in Europe under NATO itself, was suggested by both General Norstad, as SACEUR, and his successor, General Lemnitzer; their recommendations apparently had little influence on the United States government. The non-existent MMRBM would have had to be developed; in 1964 the Pentagon gave up all but token research and development for such a weapon.[3] The second kind, Polaris missiles on mixed-manned ships at sea, was vigorously promoted by the American government in 1963 and again in 1964, partly as an answer to the first proposal. (The earlier offers to "assign" United States Polaris submarines to NATO involved no genuine collective ownership or operational control, nor did most of the various British proposals for similar "assignment.")

How did this proposal for a mixed-manned surface fleet armed with Polaris missiles, this "multilateral force," conform to the principle of "balanced, collective forces"? [4] The fleet was to be collective with respect to cost, manpower, and ships and also with respect to the tech-

[3] House of Representatives Committee on Armed Services, *Hearings on Military Posture*, 88th Cong., 2nd sess. (1964), pp. 6955 and 7618, and *ibid.*, 89th Cong., 1st sess. (1965), pp. 578–79; also Charles H. Donnelly, *United States Defense Policies in 1964*, House Doc. No. 285, 89th Cong., 1st sess. (1965), p. 70. The most common strategic argument against the proposal for an MMRBM under NATO auspices was the danger of land-based missiles in "crowded" Europe. Usually unexplicated was the objection that they would be difficult for the United States to control, a difficulty which Robert E. Osgood did explain in his pamphlet, *The Case for the MLF* (Washington: Washington Center of Foreign Policy Research, 1964), pp. 16–17. For an argument in their favor see General James Moore, "The Military Effectiveness of NATO," in Karl H. Cerny and Henry W. Briefs (eds.), *NATO in Quest of Cohesion* (New York: Frederick A. Praeger, 1963), p. 169. On this subject see also Alastair Buchan, *The Multilateral Force: An Historical Perspective*, Adelphi Papers, No. 13 (London: Institute for Strategic Studies, 1964), pp. 4 and 7.

[4] General Lemnitzer, as SACEUR, pointed out that from SHAPE's point of view a *mixture* of configurations, including land vehicles, would best meet NATO's requirements and that the proposal would therefore meet only part of the needs envisioned by his command ["General Lemnitzer's Address at WEU Assembly," *NATO Letter*, July–August 1963, pp. 20–21.]

niques for operating the ships and missiles once the foreigners in the fleet had been trained. But it would be collective only for those who contributed, although its use was supposed to be coordinated with NATO's plans. The great bulk of NATO's strategic nuclear deterrent would remain in American hands, and thus the principle of specialization would be breached only in a minor way. A major American motive for promoting the scheme was to prevent unwanted proliferation. Any further development of independent deterrents among the NATO members could be very detrimental to the idea of balanced, collective forces. At the same time, the United States did not wish to leave Germany dissatisfied. One criticism has been that instead of inoculating participants against the virus of independent deterrents, the MLF may have exposed them to the disease. Indeed, mere discussion of the MLF appeared, by 1965, to have had that effect.

American proponents also hoped that the MLF would help cement the alliance more firmly. A more cohesive NATO would facilitate acceptance of balanced forces. Yet controversy aroused by the scheme suggests that it would have substituted one kind of divisiveness for another and that if it were totally abandoned a third cause of interallied conflict would ensue.[5] (In any case, it would divide the MLF participants from others in NATO.) Hints by some American officials that at some undetermined future date their government would be "not averse" to discussing the formulation of some principle of majority rule to govern the fleet's action showed the disruptive implications for the alliance of the MLF proposal, even though the conditions were unlikely to occur soon which would make it possible for the United States to abandon its veto.[6] Britain would have regarded the plan as a fraud if it believed the United States would ultimately surrender its veto, and Germany would have regarded it as such if it believed the United States would maintain its veto.

Perhaps the most serious practical effect of proposals such as the

[5] It seems likely that "shared" manufacture, or ownership, or custody would tend in the opposite direction from cohesion. Cf. Robert E. Osgood, *Nuclear Control in NATO* (Washington: Washington Center of Foreign Policy Research, 1962), who thought this was not true, however, of shared information and consultation. Clearly the offer made late in the Eisenhower administration to sell Polaris missiles to members for committing to NATO would have run counter to the collective principle.

[6] For a few examples see Buchan, *The Multilateral Force*, p. 12. Several others could be cited.

MLF and similar forms of nuclear "sharing" was to divert attention away from other aspects of balanced, collective forces. The major way in which NATO has successfully exemplified the balanced, collective forces concept has been in the pooling of members' ground forces on the central European front.[7] The inclusion there of United States troops might at first seem to be hardly in accordance with the idea of specialization. However, as earlier described, the American contribution was intended to be an earnest of United States concern for *collective* defense, to give credibility to NATO's preparations, and to be a stimulus to contributions from the other members. The European forces have always lagged, in numbers, training, and equipment. Experts, both European and American, have often claimed that it was easily within the reach of the European members to live up to the goals they had set for themselves in NATO. What was lacking was motivation.

A fixation on specific numbers of troops was properly to be avoided.[8] No one, however, could seriously claim (except occasionally for diplomatic purposes) that the European members had come close to meeting their NATO commitments either quantitatively or, more important, qualitatively. (In 1965 Germany did fill its quota by fielding the twelfth division.) American statements and actions in the New Look period of the 1950s had helped to sap European governments' will to do what would in any case have been awkward in terms of domestic politics.[9] Threats of "massive retaliation" by nuclear weapons, reduced support for the United States' own ground forces, inadequate attention to reserves, periodic American hints at withdrawals, emphasis on potential savings through tactical nuclear weapons, lessened stress on the importance of non-nuclear military cooperation, all these eroded European

[7] Seven nations also contribute to AIRCENT, NATO's tactical air force for Central Europe.

[8] During the mid-1950s, for example, United States defense officials were inclined to justify their own reductions in strength by reference to numbers of allied troops; but General Ridgway pointed out how unrealistic such an appraisal was in view of differences in combat effectiveness [House of Representatives Committee on Appropriations, *Hearings, Department of Defense Appropriations for 1957*, 84th Cong., 2nd sess. (1956), pp. 566–67].

[9] For example, as late as March, 1959, General White, Chief of Staff of the Air Force, stated: "You cannot defend Europe with conventional weapons" [Senate Committee on Armed Services, Preparedness Investigating Subcommittee, *Hearings, Major Defense Matters*, 86th Cong., 1st sess. [1959, p. 92]. For a possible adverse effect on deterrence when declared goal and achievement were as widely separated as was the case with NATO ground-troop strength in the 1950s, see Glenn H. Snyder, *Deterrence and Defense* (Princeton: Princeton University Press, 1961), p. 137.

governments' concern and were occasion for constant worry among NATO military leaders. The statements and actions continued despite years of warning from Americans inside and outside the government, until the Kennedy administration attempted to undo some of the damage.

Its doctrine of the "flexible response" required much more of the allies than the earlier doctrine which presupposed that any war in Europe would have to be general and that the sole and ever present choice was between nuclear superiority and capitulation. Americans pressing for an MLF asked of their European partners the least important form of cooperation, what was in effect a financial contribution to a force Americans did not think was militarily required, plus provision of a relatively small number of men for the crews. Paradoxically, the vigor of the United States defense of Europe seemed to diminish the European members' interest in cooperating to defend each other; each was looking toward the United States. Paradoxically also, the greater strengthening of American defense forces (such as that resulting from improvements in air-lift capacity), the less was the *apparent* dependence of the alliance upon European contributions to Europe's defenses.

The great swings in United States military doctrine were constantly out of phase with the slower European changes in view, expecially with those pertaining to the role of tactical nuclear weapons. The United States urged tactical nuclear weapons for NATO forces in the 1950s not so much to accord with an internally consistent strategic concept as to compensate for the lack of conventionally armed troops.[10] This compensation set up a vicious circle, for once equipped with the American-supplied weapons, European members saw little reason to incur additional expense and political trouble in order to build up conventionally armed forces.[11] Once tactical nuclear weapons had been distributed to the armed forces of the European states and training of British and German armies had been based on the assumption that such weapons would be available, their military leaders were reluctant to accept the necessity

[10] See Robert E. Osgood, *NATO: The Entangling Alliance* (Chicago: University of Chicago Press, 1962), pp. 105–10, 116–46; Glenn H. Snyder, "The 'New Look' of 1953," in Warner R. Schilling, Paul Y. Hammond, and Glenn H. Snyder, *Strategy, Politics, and Defense Budgets* (New York: Columbia University Press, 1962), pp. 385, 446–47, 496 and 510; and James M. Gavin, *War and Peace in the Space Age* (New York: Harper and Brothers, 1958), pp. 132–34.

[11] See Alastair Buchan, *NATO in the 1960's* (New York: Frederick A. Praeger, 1960), pp. 105 ff.

for rigorous control over their use. Furthermore, as the weapons' usefulness as a "penultimate" deterrent gradually became evident, so did the political utility of such central control.[12] There have been suggestions that some kind of tactical nuclear force under a special command within NATO would be militarily more useful than the small strategic force envisaged in the proposal for an MLF.[13] The tactical force would pose a number of problems for the Americans, who have been generally less eager than some Europeans to rely on tactical nuclear weapons at the outset in the event of a Russian aggression. Are these Europeans so behind the times in their analyses that they fail to understand the logical implications of accepting the principle of balanced, collective forces? Does the inadequacy of their conventional artillery lead them to depend prematurely and possibly unnecessarily on nuclear support? Do they have such basically different interests from the Americans that they are led to prefer a collective defense effort balanced in a way different from that desired by the Americans? Inevitably we are led back, as in the case of the strategic deterrent, to the reluctance of the Americans to accept the others' genuine participation in the making of NATO strategy and the reluctance of the Europeans to accept a strategy in whose formulation they have played no significant part.

Once balanced, collective defense is accepted as essential for the alliance, all NATO capabilities must be treated as interrelated. Weaknesses in one area weaken other areas. Inadequate coordination of one force with the others lessens the gains in defense efficiency which specialization and balanced, collective forces make possible. Critics have asserted, for example, that reliance on the nuclear weapons of the tactical air force or on the nuclear warheads of the somewhat longer-range missiles, such as the Pershing, for interdicting enemy-force movements far behind the battle zone, formerly advocated by many American tacticians, could lead to actions which the enemy might misinterpret as strategic action and thus could initiate a general war.[14] Not much attention has been

[12] *Ibid.*, pp. 109–11; also Alastair Buchan and Philip Windsor, *Arms and Stability in Europe* (New York: Frederick A. Praeger, 1963), pp. 95 and 195.

[13] Henry Kissinger, "The Unsolved Problems of European Defense," *Foreign Affairs*, July, 1962, p. 40; T. C. Schelling, "Nuclear Strategy in Europe," *World Politics*, April, 1962, p. 426; Buchan and Windsor, *op. cit.*, p. 166; Buchan, *The Multilateral Force*, p. 9.

[14] Buchan and Windsor, *op. cit.*, pp. 167–68. If the range of the Pershing were to be increased from 400 to 750 miles, which some have contemplated, would this

paid to suggestions that militia-type forces be established for local defense, especially in Germany, although they could be helpful in preventing the low-level probings Communists often favor.[15] They would constitute a kind of national specialization which contributes to rather than detracts from the collective purpose. Similarly, current and potential contributors to the Allied Command Europe Mobile Force underrate it, if one is to judge by the support that has been given to this integrated effort to cover possible trouble spots quickly.

What has the United States done to exploit the potential advantages of balanced, collective naval forces for NATO? These advantages may be meager, especially since the tasks of the earmarked naval forces have been peripheral to the main job of securing Western Europe from Communist aggression.[16] If all forces, on land, in the air, and on the sea, which might be available for NATO purposes are considered together, there already exists a noteworthy "balance" in the naval arrangements for NATO. The disparity in size between the United States Navy and those of its allies, the lack of public attention to the Atlantic Command and its commander, SACLANT, and to the naval aspects of NATO, and quite possibly the more conservative traditions of navies have militated against American initiatives for developing further an allied naval contribution to the overall balance. As the Polaris type of sea-based missiles becomes increasingly important to the defense of both Europe and North America, allied pressures to participate more fully in the forces available to NATO at sea may increase. The American MLF proposal and the successive British proposals for an Allied Nuclear Force perhaps anticipated these pressures.

Provision for the defense of North America is a task the European

---

missile be transformed into a "strategic" weapon, based in Europe? (See, for example, Atomic Energy Commissioner John Palfrey's speech reported in *New York Times*, November 17, 1965. See also *ibid.*, November 22, 1964).

[15] B. H. Liddell Hart, *Deterrent or Defense* (New York: Frederick A. Praeger, 1960), pp. 65 and 172; James Moore, *op. cit.*, p. 175. For some reasons why these have been neglected, see Malcolm W. Hoag, "Rationalizing NATO Strategy," *World Politics*, October, 1964, pp. 130–31.

[16] See F. W. Mulley, *The Politics of Western Defense* (Frederick A. Praeger, 1962), pp. 153, 169–73; Timothy W. Stanley, *NATO in Transition* (New York: Frederick A. Praeger, 1965), pp. 303–05.

However, in 1965 the United States, Britain, Canada, and the Netherlands each contributed one destroyer to a squadron under NATO command to practice antisubmarine-warfare maneuvers, the first such force to be organized for an extended period at sea. [*Atlantic Community News*, February, 1965, p. 4].

members have been willing to leave to the Americans and their northern ally.[17] It requires cooperation only between Canada and the United States. This is consistent with the "balanced forces" concept, for specialization may be by region as well as by type of weapon system. There is only a tenuous connection between NORAD and NATO; but since successful collective defense requires the protection of North American installations upon which NATO's strategic deterrent depends, the other members have an interest.[18] This interest was officially recognized by the United States only in 1963, when the Americans invited NATO to assign officers from European members' countries to SAC headquarters. Some non-governmental American leaders have recommended going much further in this direction.[19] To what extent the other allies could help to keep the whole strategic retaliatory and continental air defense systems in a high pitch of efficiency or would even wish to try is beyond the scope of this inquiry. We can be more explicit about Canadian-American cooperation. Even Prime Minister Lester Pearson, when out of office in 1960 and speaking as a former Minister of External Affairs and as a Canadian leader not unfriendly to the United States, declared that there was nothing really "collective" about the Canadian-American air defense relationship.[20] Meanwhile, the Diefenbaker government then in power in Canada only reluctantly agreed to the "cooperation" the United States did seek in North American defense. Only after a political crisis in 1963 had overturned this government and brought the Liberals under Pearson's leadership into office were even these agreements fully implemented.[21] Neither the Conservative nor the Liberal governments were keenly interested in the deployment of ground-to-air

[17] NATO's defense arrangements might be thought of as a massive grid that permits defense energies to flow to points of need, regardless of where power is generated. Thus the European allies would not be expected to deliver energy into the North American region.

[18] Note also Bernard Brodie's comment that ". . . defense of a retaliatory force capability is defense of a *system,* one which comprises not only the bombardment vehicles, but also the relevant decision-making authority . . ." [*Strategy in the Missile Age* (Princeton: Princeton University Press, 1959), p. 222].

[19] For example, Dean Acheson, "The Practice of Partnership," *Foreign Affairs,* January, 1963, p. 260; *New York Times* editorial, December 7, 1964.

[20] "After the Paris Debacle," *Foreign Affairs,* July, 1960, p. 540.

[21] When these unpopular measures were finally carried out, it was apparently because Prime Minister Pearson felt Canada's word of honor was at stake [James Eayrs, "Sharing a Continent: The Hard Issues," in the American Assembly, *The United States and Canada* (Englewood Cliffs; Prentice-Hall, 1964), pp. 62–65].

nuclear missiles in Canada, but a large part of the responsibility for the friction between the two countries regarding this issue properly fell on the Americans. Not only were they tactless, but also they pressed on the Canadians the Bomarc weapons which they themselves thought obsolete.[22] Some spokesmen for Canada would like to see aspects of the Canadian-American joint defense more closely integrated with other NATO defense arrangements, thereby easing for both the United States and Canada the political difficulties of a relatively weak country inseparably bound up with a giant.[23] The NATO Parliamentarians' military committee reported without comment the conclusions of the Canada-United States Regional Planning Group that "as the . . . Group is not a military command, the development and implementation of detailed emergency defense plans remains a function of national commanders designated by Canada and the United States." [24]

Although United States defense probably depends more upon close coordination with Canada than upon relations with any other ally, it is the more powerful European members of NATO who raise especially difficult problems when Americans are concerned with balanced, collective forces. Particularly awkward to conserve are the enduring advantages for the security of both that the "special relationship" between the United States and Britain affords; to undermine it for slight or momentary gain is exceptionally shortsighted. This consideration has not deterred some American leaders and their advisers from an ambivalent course of action in matters affecting balanced, collective forces, which did in fact jeopardize that relationship. In a half-hearted, niggling way, the United States had taken steps during the 1950s that helped its wartime nuclear collaborator continue with the development of an inde-

---

[22] See *Greenwich* (Conn.) *Time,* January 31, 1963; *Christian Science Monitor,* February 2, 1963; *Washington Post,* February 5, 1963; William Hessler, "Washington Gives Canada an Election—and an Issue," *The Reporter,* February 28, 1963, pp. 29–31.

[23] See, for example, John W. Holmes, "The Relationship in Alliance and in World Affairs," in American Assembly, *op. cit.,* pp. 95–131. He stressed the fact that the alliance between the two countries was *multilateral* [p. 97]. See also testimony of Percy Corbett in Senate Committee on Foreign Relations, *Hearings, Review of Foreign Policy, 1958,* 85th Cong., 2nd sess. (1958), p. 707.

[24] *Report of Eighth NATO Parliamentarians' Conference,* Senate Committee on Foreign Relations, Committee Print, 88th Cong., 1st sess. (1963), p. 23. John Holmes pointed out that Canadian military leaders, unlike many political officials, tended to minimize the connection of NORAD with NATO in order to escape any possible interference from overseas [*op. cit.,* p. 97].

pendent nuclear deterrent (through special exceptions permitted by the Atomic Energy Control Act.).[25] Other United States steps such as downgrading the importance of conventional forces had in effect encouraged Britain to do so. The coming of the Kennedy administration brought efforts to reconcile almost diametrically opposed views. Thus when Secretary McNamara inveighed against other countries' attempts to develop an unintegrated, independent deterrent, the United States government had to add quickly that the British were not included in the denunciation, because their deterrent was "integrated" with that of the Americans.[26]

At Nassau in December, 1962 the United States offered the British the possibility of continuing to have some kind of strategic deterrent in exchange for an apparent agreement that the two countries should work towards an integrated, multilateral deterrent. The statement in the communiqué which proved most damaging to allied unity was that the British contribution to such a force could be withdrawn if that government decided "supreme national interests" were involved. This was followed by the statement that the nuclear defense of the Western alliance was "indivisible."

A belated suggestion that the Polaris offer also be made to France (which lacked both submarines and thermonuclear warheads for the missiles) also hardly conformed to earlier ideas about either a European nuclear force (perhaps conditional on Britain's entry into the Common Market) or a Franco-British *entente nucléaire*.[27] The bilateral action —some would say unilateral action by the United States—at Nassau produced a chain reaction. President de Gaulle found in the action a plausible basis for reaffirming his own plans for an independent nuclear deterrent and thereby dealt a further blow to the idea of balanced, collective forces. The French action raised the question of how long before the Germans would want to follow suit. To deal with these developments, some American officials began to push more vigorously a specific plan for a multilateral force. Since in the spring of 1963 only the Ger-

[25] See Thomas Field, "Britain's Deterrent and the Decision to Abandon the Blue Streak Missile," *NATO's Fifteen Nations*, February–March, 1962, pp. 26–42; Richard P. Stebbins, *The United States in World Affairs, 1957* (New York: Random House, 1958), pp. 97–98.

[26] This amendment was made after the famous Ann Arbor Commencement Address in June, 1962.

[27] See Senate Committee on Foreign Relations, *Problems and Trends in Atlantic Partnership II*, Senate Doc. No. 21, 88th Cong., 1st sess. (1963), pp. 22 and 23.

mans were showing much interest, the scheme's American promoters had to find other NATO members to join them. By the fall of 1963 the United States had managed to acquire four incongruous prospective partners: Greece, Turkey, Italy, and Germany. The American diplomats then used the interest demonstrated by the four to try to bring the British around to the American point of view. Belgium and the Netherlands were expected to follow the lead of Britain, the second most important member of NATO. They eventually agreed to discuss the project and even to join in the "pilot project," the experimental ship offered by the United States to test out mixed-manning.

British opinion on the MLF was even more divided than American opinion; leaders of the Labour Party, then out of office, opposed the MLF with varying degrees of hostility and skepticism. Important leaders of the Conservative Party, the party forming the government with which the United States had to deal, were also opposed. Meanwhile, the British Army on the Rhine was notoriously weak, and there were glaring gaps in British naval forces east of Suez, forces in which the United States had a strong interest for global security reasons and which contributed to the reality of balanced, collective forces. United States policy had fallen between two stools, and until December, 1964 there was little evidence that the Americans were searching for indirect ways to fold the British in.[28] When Labour came to power in October, 1964, it made proposals for altering very radically the MLF scheme (elaborating on the previous government's suggestion shortly before its demise); it then successfully postponed the "ultimatum" for a final decision which the United States had imposed. Meanwhile, the Wilson government retained the Polaris submarine projects begun after Nassau, arguing, inter alia, that they indirectly prevented further proliferation in Asia by providing a nuclear safeguard for the non-nuclear countries.

While the quest for defense forces collectively balanced according to American specifications made difficulties for the celebrated Anglo-American "special relationship," it led to an impasse in United States relations with France, America's uneasy partner since early in World

[28] C. L. Sulzberger reported that Defense Minister von Hassell had suggested in the summer of 1963 that an Anglo-American atomic-submarine contingent be attached to a multilateral force, but the Americans appeared not to be interested. They (McGeorge Bundy) claimed it would accent a "special relationship," which was not desired [*New York Times,* August 12, 1963]. The United States took a second look in December, 1964, after it had become more committed to placating both the Germans and the British.

War II. During the first years of NATO French leaders had appeared to favor a more collective approach than did the United States.[29] Whether or not changes in the internal economic and political situation in France would in any case have altered French views of the desirability of balanced, collective forces, the United States' continued practice of making bilateral arrangements for many aspects of its NATO policy did not encourage the French in their earlier interest. For whatever reason, after having received far more aid from the United States than their British rival and having emerged again as a thriving power, the French became eager to throw off all obligations to help create balanced, collective forces. French troops withdrawn from the NATO command to fight in the Algerian war were not returned to NATO but demobilized at that war's end. Naval forces were withdrawn from the integrated NATO-force structure without the French even bothering to assert that they were temporarily needed elsewhere.[30] Until 1966, United States officials, at least in their public statements, often minimized the importance to NATO of these partial withdrawals and maintained that in a crisis these French forces too would be available to the alliance.[31] Like the partial withdrawals, half-acquiescing American statements somewhat undermined NATO's collective character; the complete withdrawal announced in March, 1966 is another matter, whose significance Americans have not been tempted to minimize.

Whatever the meaning for Franco-American relations of the earlier partial withdrawals of French forces, the American campaign to "sell" the MLF greatly widened the gap opening between the two "indispensable" allies. American pressure for and French disdain of the MLF threatened the foundations of the alliance. France's harsh rejection acted

---

[29] See Dean Acheson, *Sketches from Life* (New York: Harper and Brothers, 1959), p. 25, for the French suggestion that NATO have a common defense budget; J. D. Warne, *NATO and Its Prospects* (New York: Frederick A. Praeger, 1954), p. 43, for a French proposal regarding aid on multilateral basis; and *ibid.,* p. 47, for a proposal for a common arms program.

[30] The French continued to maintain important forces in Germany, and until 1966 to participate in NATO's Fourth Allied Tactical Air Force, which is nuclear-armed and was composed of contributions from the United States, Canada, and Germany, as well as France. [Ambassade de France, Service de Presse et d'Information, *France and Its Armed Forces* (New York, December, 1964), pp. 10–12.]

[31] See Secretary Rusk's comments reported in *New York Herald-Tribune* (Paris ed.), June 22, 1963. As Supreme Commander, General Lemnitzer, however, diplomatically explained to the House of Representatives Committee on Foreign Affairs how difficult it was to plan, when French forces were unavailable before a crisis [*Hearings, Foreign Assistance Act of 1964,* 88th Cong., 2nd sess. (1964), p. 733].

not as a brake but as an accelerator on the United States. Eventually, and in part because of allied pressure, the United States, like Britain, began to modify policies which were isolating France; but the French leader himself preferred isolation, which he called "independence." American errors in handling President de Gaulle were probably no more important—perhaps less—in deciding the French course than were internal political requirements.

It is in the case of Germany that we find best observed the principle that "duplication and overlapping were to be avoided." [32] The admission of Germany to NATO was conditioned in part on the commitment of its entire defense force to the alliance and on its agreement not to produce nuclear weapons and long-range or guided missiles.[33] There were reasons other than economy of effort to recommend this course. The United States' leadership in urging German rearmament was initially somewhat divisive; eventually the other allies adjusted themselves to the logic of such rearmament and to the arrangements which lock Germany into the Western defense system.

As the NATO allies came to rely upon a large number of German divisions to make good the deficiencies in NATO forces, the Americans became less prone to put heavy pressure on other states which were not meeting their agreed-upon goals in conventional forces. Meanwhile, Britain and France sought to compensate for their conventional force deficiencies by developing the nuclear weapons capability which Germany had renounced. Their strong emphasis on nuclear arms and the emphasis which was implicit in the American pressure for the MLF as a device for deterring the development of independent deterrents among the allies helped generate in Germany precisely that concern for atomic status which MLF and "European deterrent" schemes were supposed to forestall. Many close observers believe that fears about German nuclear aspirations were initially exaggerated, and that it was American zeal in behalf of the MLF which finally aroused German interest. The Germans then clung to the offer, if only to gain some political advantage in return for continued German acceptance of the treaty ban on the production of, and the self-imposed prohibition against the acquiring of atomic

[32] Lord Ismay's expression, *op. cit.*, p. 29.
[33] Protocol III, Part I, Art. 1 and Annexes II and III of Protocol III, Brussels Treaty of October 23, 1954 [reproduced in NATO Information Service, *Facts About the North Atlantic Treaty Organization* (Paris: NATO, 1962), pp. 243–46 and in Ismay, *op. cit.*, Supplementary Appendix I, pp. 235–39].

weapons.[34] In the meantime, the United States failed to stress defense arrangements more in keeping with the idea of balanced, collective forces, arrangements which might help to satisfy Germany. For example, the United States could have more strongly urged that ACE's Mobile Force be expanded and better supported.[35] Or it might have proposed a much more integrated "tactical" air force equipped with nuclear weapons for the interdiction of mass movements of Soviet forces into Central and Western Europe.[36]

United States relations with the larger European members of NATO have been hard to manage partly because these powers cannot be related to United States security policy primarily through an organization.[37] But even where relations are amenable to negotiation in the NATO context they raise two acute questions related to balanced, collective forces, questions which face the small members also. How should the burdens of common defense be shared and how should the common strategy be determined?

An acceptable division of the burdens inherent in the collective defense of a region is complicated when some members claim global responsibilities while others recognize only more limited defense burdens more immediately related to the region covered by the alliance. Acknowledging that the United States shares Britain's concerns in some non-European areas, American officials have often excused the weaknesses of the British Army on the Rhine by referring to Britain's contributions elsewhere. Americans have been less ready to credit France with a contribution to the common defense when the French upheld their non-European interests, especially when these interests were opposed by local inhabitants.

---

[34] The price of Germany's adhesion to a non-proliferation treaty was reportedly some kind of allied nuclear force to assure a nuclear defense of West Germany and Soviet consent to "irrevocable" steps toward the reunification of Germany. See *New York Times,* July 13, 1965 for a report of statements by Foreign Minister Gerhard Schröder and the Federal Republic's press chief, Karl von Hase, following rumors that the United States might abandon the idea of an allied nuclear fleet as a price for Soviet agreement to a non-prolifration treaty.

[35] John S. Hodder, "NATO's Mobile Force in Action," *NATO Letter,* September, 1964, p. 19; *Report of Tenth NATO Parliamentarians' Conference,* Senate Committee on Foreign Relations Print, 89th Cong., 1st sess. (1965), pp. 17 and 30.

[36] See Mulley, *op. cit.,* pp. 147 and 151; Buchan and Windsor, *op. cit.,* pp. 169–73.

[37] For an elaboration of this problem of satisfying the three major NATO allies, see André Fontaine, "The ABC of MLF," *Reporter,* December 31, 1964, pp. 10–14.

For all the members, large and small, the Annual Review was intended to facilitate an equitable and efficient distribution of shares in the common task of Western defense. American officials have felt that since all members except the United States have backslid in one way or another from earlier commitments to NATO, each is unwilling to be very critical of any other—at least publicly. The periodical confrontation has become less and less effective in ensuring balance and overall adequacy of sacrifice, as the general lines of the strategy for which the Annual Review was geared have come into question. In part because the Americans thought a fundamental reappraisal would make the Europeans more aware of their own responsibilities for the defense of the West, the United States supported the "Stikker Exercise," begun in 1963, to match budgets, resources, and strategy.

Sharing burdens and sharing decisions are two sides of the same coin. As critics of American policy have reiterated, many members of NATO do not now have a genuine sense of participation in making the alliance's strategy, a subject to be discussed later in this chapter. Without this sense, America's major allies tend to turn toward national solutions of their defense problems; and all her NATO allies tend to be slack in their NATO commitments. On the other hand, a sure way to "earn" a share in the decisions which assertedly the United States is now making in the alliance's behalf is to provide forces which the United States would desperately not want to see withdrawn. Apparently, more sharing in NATO decisions will lead to more sharing of its burdens; but the opposite is also true, that shared burdens lead to shared decisions. The United States is in a better position to take the initiative on the first of these two positions; it must wait for its allies to act on the second.

If Americans are concerned about the cohesion of the alliance and the high price the United States has paid in an only partly successful effort to achieve a collective NATO defense balanced on an alliance-wide basis, the answer may well be that of the price so far paid, not all has been in the right currency. If the Europeans are to make military contributions to the common Western European–North American defense in a form and in an amount that seems adequate to Americans, they must have, before American policy has hardened, adequate information and opportunity for free discussion. Only then will they feel that it has been their own decision as to what and how they will contribute; and only then, if at all, will they choose to make the sacrifices for which the United States calls.[38]

A balanced, collective defense makes for a more efficient division of military labor, so long as there is unity of goals and agreement on arrangements for command and control. More than ever, in the 1960s, the United States must be concerned about the resultant savings, even as its economically revived and less fearful major European allies turn back to national solutions which they can now more easily afford and more confidently risk. Inducing the smaller members of NATO to sacrifice adequately for the common NATO defense poses a further dilemma: the more an effort is pooled, the less incentive among some to put in their share.[39]

FORMS OF COMBINED ACTION

INTEGRATION. Aside from those military forces to a greater or lesser extent integrated in the various NATO commands, the record of integrated NATO activity, especially in the supporting services, is meager; the United States has done little to realize the advantages it might gain from such integration.[40] There is, for example, no integration of the logistical support for the forces committed to NATO; each country has maintained its own, with the result that eight separate supply lines have been set up for the forces of the eight NATO allies in West Germany.[41] The United States and Germany tried in 1963 to remedy some of the most dangerous consequences of this situation by creating a common system between their two forces.[42] This step once again illustrated the dilemma involved in realizing short-run efficiencies to be secured through bilateral arrangements among the readiest participants at the cost, possibly, of

[38] Such participation could conceivably also cause such dissension as to reduce confidence, but could this be worse than the situation prevailing in the 1960's?

[39] Malcolm W. Hoag, "On NATO Pooling," *World Politics,* April, 1958, p. 483.

[40] See General Pierre M. Gallois, who in 1960 was deploring the lack of attention in NATO to the "strategy of means" ["New Teeth for NATO," *Foreign Affairs,* October, 1960, p. 79].

[41] See Mulley, *op. cit.,* pp. 191–92. A WEU committee rapporteur likened the situation to armies in feudal times, which were simple gatherings of vassals serving together for a short time, armed with their own equipment [Forschungsinstitut der Deutschen Gesellschaft für Auswärtige Politik, *Der Stand der europäischen Sicherheit* (Frankfurt am Main: Alfred Metzner Verlag, 1962), p. 150].

[42] Earlier the Americans, like the British and the French, opposed suggestions for integration of supply systems desired by the smaller members [Alastair Buchan, "Should NATO Become a Nuclear Power?" *Reporter,* April 14, 1960, p. 22].

the loss of the longer-run advantages that could be achieved through a more rationally integrated supply system for the European forces in NATO.[43]

NATO's infrastructure has been hailed as a noteworthy step in the direction of integration. Yet the cumbersome methods by which the common installations were planned and constructed have led the United States to prefer bilateral arrangements with the host country or *ad hoc* group arrangements with the countries directly involved.[44] Alastair Buchan has suggested that since more and more members of the alliance have a common interest in mobile as well as fixed defense arrangements, some kind of central bank for the alliance might be organized to permit common financing of commonly held NATO facilities or common services.[45] How this would appeal to the potentially largest contributor is hard to predict; the fact that no *aid* would be involved should make it more palatable politically. Yet the United States early set a bilateral pattern; it chose to make its financial contributions directly to *members* of the alliance. It may not have wanted the recipients to sit in judgment on each other's requests. Although the alliance is no longer between one patron and fourteen supplicants, the persistence of established habits makes attempts at an integrated approach more difficult.[46]

COOPERATION. To integrate supporting services is difficult, and not even the leading country can by itself bring about integration of a particu-

[43] See Buchan and Windsor, *op. cit.,* pp. 162 and 231–32. A subcommittee of the House of Representatives Committee on Foreign Affairs in 1963 severely criticized European allies for failing to integrate more completely the supply services upon which NATO forces depend; it suggested that continued United States aid kept them from feeling the need to assume more responsibility in NATO. The committee was particularly critical of the failure of recipient countries to keep United States-supplied equipment in good operating order [*Report of the Subcommittee for Review of the Mutual Security Programs in Military Aid to Western Europe, 86th Cong., 1st sess. (1963), pp. 9–11*].

[44] Cf. Buchan, *NATO in the 1960's*, p. 113.

[45] *Ibid.*, rev. ed., pp. 140–43. See also Mulley, *op. cit.,* p. 199. A not dissimilar proposal, the "Green Book," was proposed in the early days of the Mutual Security program [Warne, *op. cit.,* p. 45].

[46] In 1957 a study prepared for a Senate Special Committee to Study the Foreign Aid Program, gave, inter alia, the following reasons for individual aid in preference to collective programs: if an individual country did not live up to its obligations the whole group would not be penalized; countries dealing directly with the United States felt more "equal" than as parts of a regional group; and in particular cases the United States had wider latitude in pursuing mutually agreed-upon objectives when only one partner was involved ["Military Aid Program" by Systems Analysis Corporation, in *Two Studies and a Report,* Committee Print, 85th Cong., 1st sess. (1957), pp. 140–41].

lar alliance activity. But the opportunities for cooperation, as distinguished from integration, are many, especially as they usually involve fewer than all the allies. Ever since the Sputnik shock in 1957, United States officials have been talking about allied cooperation in research, development, and production of the armaments needed by NATO forces.[47] Private groups (such as the Committee for Economic Development) and officially appointed advisory bodies have strongly supported the idea, as have members of Congress, notably the late Senator Theodore Green and Senator Henry Jackson. Agreements in principle have been reported; and a number of modest programs have been undertaken with American initiative, such as the Mutual Weapons Development Program and the NATO Science Fellowships. Nevertheless, there has been a huge gap between aspirations and accomplishments. This lack of progress in scientific cooperation under NATO auspices is scarcely the fault of the United States; it has offered to cooperate in a number of programs, such as saline-water conversion and meteorological analysis.[48]

There are inherent obstacles to scientific cooperation. Narrow national prejudices are likely to affect cooperation less in basic research than at later stages of scientific development. Yet it is in the basic research stage that central planning is most difficult and least effective because many approaches may be desirable and communication among the researchers more important than agreement on a single research design.

NATO may offer a convenient framework for some kinds of scientific cooperation—especially, although not exclusively, those where the end product is for military use—and an almost necessary one for the kinds of rather scientific operational research concerned with special aspects of coalition military planning. It is by no means the only available framework. A large number of cooperative scientific activities in which the United States is officially engaged are taking place in other groupings, of which some are ad hoc, and some are formal international or-

[47] Prior to that time a typical attitude was that expressed by a Department of Defense official in a reply to a Congressman's inquiry as to why it would not be cheaper for European countries to manufacture for their own use such defense items as jet planes. He declared that "these countries don't want to build up, if they can help it, a very substantial munitions industry" [House of Representatives Committee on Foreign Affairs, *Hearings, Mutual Security Act of 1957,* 85th Cong., 1st sess. (1957), p. 612].

[48] See *Report of Seventh NATO Parliamentarians' Conference,* Senate Committee on Foreign Relations Print, 87th Cong., 2nd sess. (1962); and *Report of Eighth Parliamentarians' Conference,* pp. 12–18.

ganizations, and some are combinations with non-governmental partners. One example is a NATO Joint Satellite Studies Group, which is part of a network of organizations participating in the United States space program.[49]

Theoretically, greater economies and advances in the development of weapons and other products could result from Allied cooperation at the applied science stage and even greater ones at the production stage; but inertia among responsible defense personnel below the policy-making level still works against (and sometimes prevents) cooperative undertakings in military research and development. In their testimony before Congressional committees on research and development needs, officers have described contracts with agencies in other countries for some types of development in terms of the needs of a particular United States agency (Army, Navy, Air Force) or of specifically American interests.[50] The contracts are not particularly related to NATO, and the amounts involved are very small compared to the roughly $6 billion the Department of Defense requested for research and development in, for example, 1964.

In production for military use strong nationalistic tendencies are discernible.[51] A special study on military information pooling lamented the lack of regular means for making sure that products of the Mutual Weapons Development Program were actually used in the United States services.[52] Through 1964 the United States had not purchased for its

[49] "The NATO Joint Satellite Studies Group," *NATO Letter,* September, 1963, pp. 24–25.

[50] General Arthur S. Trudeau, head of United States Army Research and Development, told a House of Representatives Committee on Appropriations subcommittee in April, 1961 that one motive in extending research cooperation to Latin America was "to get acceptability of American science on university campuses" [*Hearings, Department of Defense Appropriations, 1962,* 87th Cong., 1st sess. (1961), p. 172]. General Hester, Deputy Director of Operations, USAF, quizzed by Representatives who were concerned that the "British are ahead of us" on the VTOL aircraft development, described one project started by Britain but which later became a NATO development, with each interested state contributing money; he added that "time wise" the British "are ahead," but then criticized the usefulness of their developments for meeting the Air Force's needs regarding range and weight-carrying capacity.

[51] An illuminating case was Canada's abortive effort to develop the CF105 airplane. In general, however, the United States and Canada have cooperated more closely in weapons procurement than has the United States with other allies. For the agreements on defense production-sharing, see Eayrs, *op. cit.,* pp. 65–69.

[52] Report of study group on military research and development to the President's Committee to study the United States Military Assistance Program, *Composite Report,* vol. II (Washington, 1959), p. 172.

own use any product of coordinated production, although it had purchased such products for distribution to other allies.[53] It is not only the
preferences of American military personnel for American products
which stand in the way of sharing development and production efforts;
there are also influential private economic enterprises working against
cooperative specialization by pushing effectively for their own products.
As European NATO members have regained their economic strength
and become more and more confident of their technological capabilities,
they have become increasingly critical of the American tendency to
dominate military production in the alliance generally, not only in the
nuclear field.[54] British and French critics have been particularly outspoken.[55]

In the procurement sphere the United States has evidently not acted
very often in accordance with its declared intentions to promote interallied cooperation in research, development, and production, but the
fact that European members themselves are frequently poor cooperators
with each other is a partial, even if not the main, explanation. Their failure to cooperate has at times been a drag on American efforts to initiate
cooperative development programs.[56]

[53] E. Vandevanter, *Coordinated Weapons Production in NATO* (Santa Monica:
Rand Corporation, 1964), p. 29, n. 31.

[54] For example, Lockheed tried in the fall of 1963 to go over the heads of the
Ministry of Defense to members of the Bundestag in an attempt to get Germany
to purchase its military transport in place of one being developed jointly by
France and Germany. Lockheed's chief sales representative was a retired United
States Air Force major general who had headed the MAAG in Bonn at the
time Lockheed's Starfighter was chosen over some foreign competitors for the
much heralded consortium building this United States plane in Europe [*New
York Times*, September 23, 1963 and November 1, 1963]. See Buchan, *NATO
in the 1960's*, rev. ed., pp. 145–46; also Vandevanter, *op. cit.*, pp. 61–72.

[55] Thus Sir John Slessor complained that "in theory Washington favors inter-
dependence in weapon production for NATO; in practice it is virtually non-
existent. . . . It is broadly true to say that when it comes to finding hard
currency to maintain our forces in Germany by selling aircraft or weapons in
Europe we virtually have not got a hope against American competition" ["Cuba,
Skybolt and the Congo," *Atlantic Community Quarterly*, Summer, 1963, p. 274].
See also Alastair Buchan, "NATO Divided: Nuclear Weapons, Europe and the
United States," *New Republic*, December 29, 1962, p. 16, and *idem*, "Partners
and Allies," *Foreign Affairs*, July, 1963, pp. 630–31, where he writes: "Every
advanced country in Europe has had an unhappy experience in trying to reach
interdependent arrangements on research and production with the United
States. . . ." [p. 31]. For the other side, see Vandevanter, *op. cit.*, pp. 35–47.

[56] See Jean Planchais, "France and Germany: Military Collaboration," from
Le Monde, August 17, 1963, reprinted in *Survival*, November–December 1963, p.
249; Vandevanter, *op. cit.*, esp. pp. 40 and 55–60.

One area in which substantial economies could be effected if the political obstacles could be overcome is that of ship-building. Some European members are especially well placed to contribute in this field, but the influence of the American maritime industry in the United States government is so great as to rule out the possibility of cooperation in this field. Since the other maritime countries show similar tendencies and the United States merchant marine is struggling against economic odds, the picture looks bleak for this type of rationalization on an alliance level.

Even where the political weight of a particular vested interest does not inhibit cooperation, the ever present balance of payments problem exerts a strong pull away from an efficient allocation of functions. Thus the vigorous efforts in the 1960s to sell United States military products to the allies has helped meet one difficulty by creating another, namely, the overwhelming of potential European competitors in the drive to supply the allies.[57]

One type of cooperation among NATO members, joint or "pooled" production of a complicated weapon meeting a NATO "requirement" by firms in several countries, under license from an American company, has given rise to second thoughts. As Malcolm Hoag has pointed out, many economies, especially those related to large-scale manufacture, are achieved by concentrating production, not by spreading it.[58] Despite high hopes for pooling, less than 5 percent of the allies' weapon purchases have been collaboratively manufactured under NATO auspices. The prospects for further joint projects are severely limited, partly because future weapons are likely to be technically too intricate and politically too sensitive. Most of the relatively few joint projects licensed by an American enterprise have been financially supported by the United States government.[59] European competitors of the American companies

[57] For the United States government efforts, see House of Representatives Committee on Foreign Affairs, *Hearings, Foreign Assistance Act of 1964,* 88th Cong., 2nd sess. (1964), pp. 508–12. On a lesser scale, these efforts continued, in effect, military aid, by subsidizing allied *purchases* in the United States.

[58] "On NATO Pooling," *loc. cit.,* p. 478. He mentioned the danger that matériel pooling could distract attention from the more elusive but more important gains to be secured by forces specialization. Experience with some coordinated weapons production suggests that whatever advantages may accrue, this system costs more [Vandevanter, *op. cit.,* pp. 49–54].

[59] *Ibid.,* pp. 2, 8, 60, and 70; House of Representatives Committee on Foreign Affairs, *Hearings, Foreign Assistance Act of 1964,* 88th Cong., 2nd sess. (1964), p. 488.

feel closed out by these licensing arrangements; their governments may rue the loss of the "spin-off" gains of development, especially in the nuclear field.[60] Interallied controversy over the most notable of these licensing ventures, the (F-104G) Starfighter, in some ways reminds one of disputes within the United States about choices of airplanes, such as that involving the TFX.[61] In the TFX case, however, Secretary of Defense McNamara had the power of decision. There is no such final arbiter in the NATO joint production effort, and some competing countries have simply refused to participate in arrangements determined through the international arms market, a market in which the United States has predominated.

STANDARDIZATION. Much of what has been said about cooperation in research, development, and especially production can also be said about the slow progress in standardizing items in common use in NATO. The United States presents a special problem: in that most affluent of the member countries the military are inclined to insist upon so technically refined a product that it exceeds the requirements of their opposite numbers elsewhere. Interservice controversies among the American military have further complicated decisions on standardization. In any case, since the great variety of its defense tasks makes the United States' military requirements much more complex, standardization is likely to be sought mainly on American terms.

Earlier in NATO's history the problem of standardization did not loom large, because the other members were mainly supplied with American armaments. Increases in the prosperity and efficiency of European enterprise brought increasing determination not to be closed out of the competition for armament orders by American-imposed standards.[62] Many allied governments have been as unready as the Americans to implement fine words about the desirability of standardized

---

[60] See Fritz Erler, "The Basis of Partnership," *Foreign Affairs,* October 1963, p. 92. However, some Americans reply that such gains come just as much from nuclear developments for peaceful uses and that those which might come from missile development also would be available through space activities not related to military use [*Report of Tenth NATO Parliamentarians' Conference,* p. 10].

[61] See Buchan, "NATO Divided," *loc. cit.;* Planchais, *op. cit.,* Vandevanter, *op. cit.,* p. 45.

[62] See Buchan, *NATO in the 1960's,* rev. ed., pp. 144–45. On the other hand, France broke with the other allies in 1964 by adopting a rifle using ammunition of a size different from that which had been standardized in NATO.

equipment when doing so meant modifying their own standards; pressing reasons of national pride as well as pressures from their own arms industries have shaped their attitudes.

Military services and manufacturers of military equipment in the United States are becoming readier to accept European ideas and designs, and a few Congressmen have acknowledged some specific European contributions to be desirable for American forces.[63] However, up to 1966 the United States had not bought a European military airplane or any missiles except short-range types such as an antitank weapon.[64]

At a certain point the problems of standardization merge with those dealing with cooperative research and development. Standardization of existing equipment is not likely, nor is standardization of equipment that is going through the generational stages of defining operational requirements, research and development to create the design, and production. It is only the third generation of a particular kind of weapon that can be standardized. The United States may find that uncompromising insistence on American views during the development process will result in standardization on a European basis. The sticking point comes usually in reaching agreement on the operational requirements for the item to be standardized, and this brings us back to the need for more integrated alliance-wide defense planning. Similarly, to integrate logistical systems requires more standardization than has yet occurred. Even in such areas as ammunition progress has so far been rather modest.

FUNCTIONAL COORDINATION

COMMAND AND CONTROL OVER NUCLEAR WEAPONS. For an alliance to be effective a number of functions must be coordinated, among them command and control; the problems raised by the need for such

[63] See House of Representatives Committee on Armed Services, *Hearings, Military Posture Briefings,* 87th Cong., 1st sess. (1961), p. 962, for a record of Navy and Marine Corps foreign procurement. In FY 1960 the United States spent $14,000,000 for ships in England, Norway, Denmark, and Portugal. It has also purchased the Canadian "Caribou" plane for transport purposes.

[64] See Buchan, "Partners and Allies," *loc. cit.,* p. 634; also House of Representatives Committee on Armed Services, *Hearings, Military Posture,* 87th Cong., 2nd sess. (1962), p. 877. Secretary McNamara's explanation to the Senate Committee on Armed Services concerning the purchase of a German-produced machine gun seemed almost apologetic ["Statement of Secretary of Defense Robert S. McNamara Before a Joint Session of the Senate Armed Services Committee and the Committee on Appropriations, Subcommittee on Department of Defense Appropriations on Fiscal Year 1966–70 Defense Program and 1966 Defense Budget,"

coordination in NATO have been only partially faced by the United States. By command and control we mean here responsibility and authority for giving such orders to fire nuclear weapons as will ensure that the weapons are not used unless the orders are given and that they will be used whenever the orders are given.[65] In a model integrated security organization this responsibility would rest completely in the hands of a jointly selected, "non-national" official or officials. In the real political and technological world of the 1960s, command and control can be *unified* only if the major elements are in the hands of the power possessing most of the nuclear weapons on which the alliance depends. As Secretary McNamara has pointed out, one ally's decision to use nuclear weapons would involve all the members signatory to the North Atlantic Treaty.[66] We are discussing here situations other than the rather unlikely "bolt out of the blue" massive attack, where little controversy exists about the American reaction.

Has the United States missed opportunities to perfect its system of control and to make this system palatable to its allies? The first has been easier to accomplish than the second.

Only belatedly, after the Kennedy administration came into office, did the United States recognize in practice the full complexities of the problem, which extends from control over the largest megaton bombs to that over the smallest "tactical" weapons.[67] Advocates of the MLF sometimes overlooked the fact that SACEUR already commanded an allied force equipped with nuclear weapons, in the joint planning for which German as well as other allied officers shared important responsibilities.[68] Under President Kennedy, organizational and mechanical reforms were

---

February 18, 1965 (hereafter referred to as "Statement of Secretary McNamara, Senate Armed Services"), mimeographed, pp. 86–87].

[65] Others have defined the terms more broadly to include decision-making. See JCS definition in Charles H. Donnelly, *A Compilation of Material Relating to United States Defense Policies in 1962,* House Doc. No. 155, 88th Cong., 1st sess. (1963), p. 41.

[66] "Statement of Secretary McNamara, Senate Armed Services," p. 27. For some of the reasons why unity and simplicity are essential, see Sir Solly Zuckerman, "Judgment and Control in Modern Warfare," *Foreign Affairs,* January, 1962, pp. 203–05. For some of the reasons why the practical measures remain complex, see Hanson Baldwin, *New York Times,* September 27, 1964, "Week in Review" section, p. 4E.

[67] It did accept the principle that nuclear means nuclear and differs qualitatively from conventional weapons. See Chapter V.

[68] James Moore, *op. cit.,* p. 167; "SACEUR's First Nuclear Deputy," *NATO Letter,* June, 1964, pp. 9–12.

instituted in the early 1960s to make certain that these tactical nuclear weapons in Europe would not be used without the approval of the highest American authorities.[69]

For the control of the more complicated nuclear weapons systems, and particularly of those which the United States may want to use either for NATO defense or to meet its defense commitments in other regions, it has been difficult to satisfy both the United States and its allies. A "two keys" solution appropriate to tactical nuclear weapons under SACEUR is inappropriate where the concern is to make sure that no one else holds a key which might at the moment of need *prevent* the weapons from being used. Special technical and political difficulties emerged with the development of the Polaris-armed nuclear submarine; this is one reason why the advocates of the MLF quickly turned to surface ships. Even then, the existence of a truly separate force raised extremely difficult problems about certainty of control. On the other hand, if the MLF proposal had been only a subterfuge for continued concentration of responsibility in American hands—which many people here and abroad believed—it would have solved few if any of the existing problems for which its advocates purported to offer a solution. The United States would have had a veto over the "multilateral" force and unrestrained nuclear freedom of action over the incomparably larger wholly American nuclear force. Either way, the campaign in behalf of the MLF distracted American attention from the basic conflicts of interest which bedevil the alliance's command and control problem.

The United States, with declining enthusiasm, has continued to accept an "independent" British nuclear capability, which in logic defies the principle of undivided control. In practice, American officials with nuclear responsibilities have appeared relatively unconcerned, because they seemed satisfied that an informal Anglo-American unity did exist.[70] Yet the Kennedy administration was unwilling to go further in assenting to "independent" deterrents by considering seriously the Brit-

[69] See Buchan and Windsor, *op. cit.*, pp. 94 and 164–65; *New York Times*, May 3, 1962 and November 21, 1965; President Johnson's exposition of the safeguards, *ibid.*, September 17, 1964; Charles H. Donnelly, *A Compilation of Material Relating to United States Defense Policies in 1962*, p. 42. Certain technical problems remain difficult to solve, for information capacity rarely keeps pace with advances in firepower and maneuver.

[70] See Malcolm W. Hoag, "Nuclear Strategic Options and European Force Participation," in Richard N. Rosecrance (ed.), *The Dispersion of Nuclear Weapons: Strategy and Politics* (New York: Columbia University Press, 1964), p. 231; and Buchan and Windsor, *op. cit.*, p. 190.

ish concept of a "multinational" nuclear force rather than its own scheme for MLF. Late in 1964, as the MLF appeared increasingly unattractive, the Johnson administration took a second look at a new British version, the proposed Allied Nuclear Force.

How could the United States promote in the rest of the alliance a level of confidence similar to that existing between it and Britain? Not, surely, by eroding the Anglo-American relationship, especially since the uniqueness of that relationship is accepted by most of the smaller members of the alliance. These smaller members accept it in the 1960s in part because they have come to recognize that the United States has the same concern for a safety-catch on nuclear weapons as they and the British have long had.[71] They have also accepted extension of the special relationship to nuclear matters because they feel a compulsion neither to prove that they can produce nuclear weapons nor to possess their own; they are accustomed perforce to depend for their security in good part on the larger powers. Where they do resemble the larger European members of NATO is in their desire to participate in some aspects of the decision to use nuclear weapons in defense of the alliance. But they have been far less interested in the independent use of these weapons than have been a number of officials in France and a few defense officials in Germany (the latter being concerned with tactical nuclear weapons). By 1963 the French had become more interested in their own *force de frappe* than in a NATO nuclear force; having rejected integration, the French could compel the United States to consider how the two national deterrents might be coordinated.

Americans are well accustomed to the relationship of a responsible executive advised by a group of counselors and guided in general terms by a body of representatives who are without authority to make specific applications of the principles in which their concurrence is required. It is a similar opportunity, i.e., to advise and to share in defining general principles governing the use of nuclear weapons, that many in Britain and on the Continent have been asking of the United States.[72] "Dele-

---

[71] Note earlier domestic attacks on the British government for providing facilities for American nuclear forces. Serious questions about British control were answered in terms of preventing action by potentially over-hasty Americans. For an example, see the interchange between Prime Minister Macmillan and opponents regarding the Holy Loch arrangements [Charles H. Donnelly, *United States Defense Policies in 1960*, House Doc. No. 207, 87th Cong., 1st sess. (1961), pp. 144–45].

[72] For example, Buchan, *NATO in the 1960's*, rev. ed., pp. 93 ff.; Mulley, *op. cit.*, pp. 101–02; *idem*, "Nuclear Weapons: Challenge to National Sovereignty," *Orbis*, Spring, 1963, pp. 39–40; and Erler, *op. cit.*, pp. 91–92.

gated authority" and "trusteeship" suggest an agreed purpose, with continuous and thorough discussion of the alternative measures available to achieve the purpose and with indication of preferred choices, plus the opportunity for verification. Credibility of a potential allied response to a common threat depends as much on these conditions as upon unified control. Having a "voice" in these matters and having "control" are not synonymous. In the acute crises there may be no time for alliance-wide discussion, and in a relaxed period all are entitled to be consulted; but for situations which are neither one nor the other special arrangements may have to be elaborated.[73]

The United States began trying to satisfy these allied desires for greater participation only in 1962. Secretary Rusk recognized the need to do so in his statement on the eve of the NATO Council meeting December 19, 1962: "The basic way in which American nuclear power is coordinated in the alliance is through consultation on policy and strategy, on the discussion of guidelines, on the determination of what has to be done where, and by whom, under what circumstances." He then said that if the other members wanted a more specific and operational role *one* (our emphasis) way would be through a multilateral nuclear force; the feasibility of establishing this force would depend upon examination of a great many complicated questions such as command and control.[74] Presumably some responsibility for strategic deliberations falls on the Nuclear Committee of NATO, which was authorized at the April, 1962 ministerial meeting, and on the new Deputy for Nuclear Affairs at SHAPE, whose position was created at the spring, 1963 meeting.[75] Nevertheless, the obstacles to any useful consultation were great so long as American officials in NATO were precluded from discussing details regarding nuclear plans with any of their colleagues except the British.[76] It was only in 1964 that the administration obtained Congres-

[73] Hoag, "Nuclear Strategic Options and European Force Participation," *loc. cit.,* pp. 240–51.

[74] *Department of State Bulletin,* December 31, 1962, p. 99.

[75] See "SACEUR's First Nuclear Deputy," *loc. cit.*

[76] "In effect, every NATO staff has an American wing in which a number of highly important papers circulate which may be seen only by American eyes. . . . The upshot of this has been that other governments have had only a very cloudy impression of American dispositions in Europe in so far as nuclear weapons are concerned, of the purpose they are designed to serve, or of the action the United States would take in an emergency [Buchan, *NATO in the 1960's,* rev. ed., p. 126]. Some of the ignorance was dispelled by information given at the Athens ministerial meeting of the North Atlantic Council in 1962. It was only in that year that German officials learned how many nuclear weapons were on their soil [Buchan, *NATO in the 1960's,* rev. ed., p. 67].

sional permission for the sharing of information necessary for planning within NATO and in the lower echelons of allied defense ministries.

The step taken to open SAC headquarters to selected NATO officers takes care principally of the question of targeting. Similarly, the more than 1,000 officers under SACEUR who were qualified to deal with nuclear information were concerned with weapons not labelled "strategic." [77] Bolder steps would seem necessary to erase the suspicion in the minds of the other allies that American determination to maintain unified control is dictated not so much by fears of an unstable nuclear environment as by the desire to maintain American domination in all aspects of nuclear policy. We have come a long way in strategic conception from the time when Americans thought the purpose of NATO forces was simply to provide a trip-wire to set off American strategic weapons and when Europeans were more afraid that the Americans would use nuclear weapons unnecessarily than that they might not use them when the Europeans thought they were needed. But more imaginative American thinking will be necessary if the European allies are to remain satisfied with American control, as well as more imaginative European thinking if the United States is to be satisfied that control may safely be shared. The complexity of "phased response" puts an extra burden on the allies' trust and makes pre-crisis consultation all the more necessary.

The United States would make one important political advance if it could somehow demonstrate that states without an independent nuclear deterrent have real weight in American (or NATO) councils.[78] Perhaps power assertedly based on possession of such a deterrent is already a myth. British influence on American decision-makers has not depended primarily on nuclear weapons; its foundations were laid long before these existed. Unfortunately, the old special relationship became entangled with a new nuclear-secrets special relationship, with the result

[77] See James Moore, *op. cit.*, p. 167.

[78] Dean Acheson has vividly outlined how the contrary belief was engendered, beginning with the "massive retaliation" doctrine and the constant American emphasis on "our" strategy, which resulted in the belief that "control and use of nuclear weapons was synonymous with the determination of political policy, military strategy, and the ultimate decision of war or peace . . ." [Institute for Strategic Studies, *The Evolution of NATO,* Adelphi Papers, No. 5 (London, 1963), pp. 8 and 12]. But as late as October, 1964, Secretary Rusk, in hailing the MLF experiment on the *Admiral Ricketts,* stated that the participating members could have an "enhanced position in disarmament negotiations because of their active and responsible role in nuclear deterrence" [*New York Times,* October 21, 1964].

that those here and abroad who sought to meet French or German dissatisfactions on the nuclear front felt they had to start by leveling down special relationships instead of leveling them up.

It is not difficult to show that Germany's influence on the course of American policy has grown steadily; it has not depended upon the Germans first acquiring nuclear weapons. German desires for prestige and a sense of full participation in a NATO that Germany has vigorously supported have been partly met by a revision of the NATO command structure to reflect Germany's very large contribution of non-nuclear forces.[79] (Even before 1966, these revisions had reached a point such that any further enhancement of Germany's role could only have been at France's expense.) Total French withdrawal from NATO must lead to a very great new strengthening of Germany's weight in the alliance.

To inspire trust requires acts of trustworthiness, such as that which the United States took in 1961 to bolster its forces in Berlin and that in 1964 to consider, at the request of the British, helping to keep order in Cyprus; in both cases NATO was clearly concerned. German confidence in the United States, in particular, can be advanced by the United States' actions to see that Communist accusations in the various bodies of the United Nations, where the Federal Republic is not represented, regarding alleged German "revanchism" and "militarism" are promptly and forthrightly repudiated.[80] This would accord with the statement following the Johnson-Erhard meeting of December 21, 1965 in which the two leaders "reject malicious allegations designed to cast doubt on the peaceful intentions of the Federal Republic of Germany." So far as France was concerned, given the increasing intransigeance of President de Gaulle, American officials came to believe by 1964 that for the time being the best they could hope for was target coordination between the

---

[79] *New York Times* (International ed.), May 13, 1963. The German interest in having a German director of the Standing Group's planning staff seemed quite reasonable, especially as a recognition of the importance of non-nuclear contributions. In July, 1964, this post was authorized and a German officer was appointed to it. In SHAPE the Supreme Commander has done what he could to bring in as many senior German officers as possible. See General Lemnitzer's comments on the problem to the House of Representatives Committee on Foreign Affairs, *Hearings, Foreign Assistance Act of 1964*, 88th Cong., 2nd sess. (1964), p. 750. On this general subject, see also *New York Times*, March 1 and April 15, 1964 and *NATO Letter*, July–August, 1964, p. 26.

[80] Admiral Friedrich Ruge, "The Need for a Common Nuclear Strategy," in Karl H. Cerny and Henry W. Briefs (eds.), *NATO in Quest of Cohesion* (New York: Frederick A. Praeger, 1965), 206.

French deterrent and other nuclear forces at NATO's disposal. As it turned out, even that hope has been frustrated.

STRATEGY. With respect to the formulation of strategy, each major European ally will pose special problems, but in the long run the sure way for the United States to gain and hold the confidence of all of them is habitually to make sure that each has a sense of participation in all main decisions taken on behalf of the alliance. There is no need to make them believe that such decisions are necessarily different from the ones the United States would have made without them; what is critical is that their participation take place *before* American strategic policy has congealed. Assuming that it is the latter rather than the former which Alastair Buchan and Philip Windsor mean by "influence," we can only agree that

> Europe's preoccupation with a nuclear strategy and the control of nuclear weapons, and their unreadiness to contemplate strengthening a more flexible form of defense, cannot be allayed until the European governments, individually or collectively, have a greater influence upon the strategic policy of the alliance, which means primarily influence upon the policy of the United States.[81]

American initiatives regarding nuclear weapons have regularly failed to get to the heart of the matter.[82] General Norstad put it this way: ". . . we sometimes confuse ourselves talking about hardware . . . the real crux of this problem is, is a guarantee going to be provided to [the other] NATO countries . . . Then give to NATO in some way the responsibility for making decisions in the NATO area." [83] For a long time the United States government apparently ignored British desires to have discussion of the MLF proposal placed in the larger framework of NATO strategy.[84] Such suggestions seemed to the American enthusiasts to be diversionary tactics. For a number of years the United States had been equally hard of hearing when other countries' leaders and private

---

[81] In a report on a three-nation study group's views, Buchan and Windsor, *op. cit.*, p. 188.

[82] This was true at least up to May 31, 1965, when Secretary McNamara made an important proposal to be considered later in this chapter.

[83] Testifying before the Jackson Committee, March 11, 1963 [Senate Committee on Government Operations, Subcommittee on National Security Staffing and Operations, 88th Cong., 1st sess. (1963), p. 24.] For a criticism of General Norstad's strategic conception and his plea for MRBMs, see William W. Kaufmann, *The McNamara Strategy* (New York: Harper and Row, 1964), pp. 36–37.

[84] For example, Lord Home's comments, *The Times* (London), June 26, 1963.

commentators here and abroad had pointed to the central dissatisfaction. Three years after the United States made its initial offer to assign some Polaris-armed submarines to NATO, the NATO Parliamentarians' Conference, in November 1963, recommended, in part, "that there be developed within NATO under the NATO Council a unified strategic planning system aimed at the development of a full strategic consensus among the members . . . in order to establish an effective basis for discussions regarding the use of both nuclear and non-nuclear forces," and that the Ottawa decisions regarding nuclear planning "be further developed to enable all member nations to have a real participation in the full strategy of the Alliance, covering both nuclear and conventional forces." [85]

For some years the United States, in the name of political cohesion, had been making to its resisting or indifferent allies proposals for nuclear "sharing" which, however otherwise meritorious, were somewhat irrelevant to the participation issue. For example, President Kennedy told the Canadian Parliament on May 17, 1961 that the United States looked to the possible establishment of a "NATO sea-borne missile force, which would be truly multilateral in ownership and control, if this should be desired and found feasible by our allies *once* NATO's non-nuclear goals have been achieved." [86] Meanwhile others, such as British Labour Party leaders, were asking for a way to share in determining the strategy "of the entire weapon, not some little section of the weapon." [87]

From the President down, and at several levels of authority, came statements that the United States was open to suggestion and unwilling to force an idea on uninterested allies. Yet in practice these avowals seem—at least to the outsider—to have been forgotten, especially in the case of American pressure on the British to accept the MLF proposal. For a long time counterproposals made by both the British and Germans were in effect brushed aside as being too vague or otherwise lacking merit, leaving the suspicion that to be meritorious they had to be of

[85] *Report of Ninth NATO Parliamentarians' Conference,* House Report No. 1478, 88th Cong., 2nd sess. (1964), pp. 42 and 48. One reason for American reluctance was that the dependability of the allies varied so far as their "security" capacity was concerned.

[86] Our italics.

[87] For example, remarks of Patrick Gordon-Walker, reprinted in *Survival,* January–February, 1964, p. 24.

American origin. The NATO allies were not in fact in a position to respond effectively to the American invitation to submit alternative proposals. It was never quite clear which of the many voices speaking for the United States was authoritative; the battle of Washington quasi-sovereignties had spilled over into Europe. The outlines of the MLF itself remained unclear and were constantly changing; there was no completed design for which refinements could be suggested. Even more important, there was no jointly determined strategy by which the American or any alternative proposals could be tested. President Johnson in December, 1964 finally called a halt to the pressure on the allies to accept the MLF, pressure which had been markedly stepped up in the preceding spring.[88]

The United States has acted in other ways as if the development of a joint strategy was a superficial or unimportant part of alliance policy. It has deployed and redeployed its NATO-assigned forces without much reference to alliance plans; often it has merely informed its allies, through the organization, that the deployment would occur.[89] The size and position of United States forces in Europe have on occasion been determined by such considerations as their leverage power on members' contributions rather than their utility in a jointly determined overall plan. Such actions often upset some of the allies simply because they had no part in making the altered strategy upon which the new deployment of American men and matériel was based. It is significant that the North Atlantic Council at its ministerial meeting at Athens in May, 1962 reported that "ministers *noted* with satisfaction the United States commitment of Polaris submarines to NATO" (our italics); they did not *accept* them in the context of a commonly worked-out military plan. The commitment was in effect a fait accompli. The relationship between the French and American governments later cooled in part because one

[88] See James Reston in *New York Times,* December 21, 1964, and Crosby S. Noyes in *Washington Star,* January 11, 1965.

[89] For example, in the American landing in Lebanon in 1958 [Henry A. Kissinger, *The Necessity for Choice* (New York: Harper and Brothers, 1961) p. 115] and the removal of the Jupiter missiles in 1963. The allies were all the more sensitive because American leaders such as ex-President Eisenhower in September, 1963 were calling reductions desirable in the European-based forces, and also because officials sometimes denied withdrawals would take place which eventually did occur (*New York Times,* August 1, 1962; October 23, 1963; October 27, 1963; November 1, 1963; and November 19, 1963).

ally no longer cared to dance to the tune chosen by the piper's payer.[90]

What have been some of the costs of the United States' failure to share with its allies determination of strategy for nuclear weapons? [91] A principal one has been continuing lack of interest among the European governments in improving conventional war capability.[92] This lack of interest was caused, to a considerable extent, by actions taken by the United States in the 1950s mainly for domestic political and budgetary reasons and not at all for the purpose of implementing a common strategy. These actions involved the United States, first, in relying heavily on nuclear weapons; later, in reducing its conventional armed forces and not maintaining their effectiveness; and finally, in suggesting that limited war in Europe was inconceivable. Since the Americans did not want the Europeans to follow suit, their guiding precept seemed to be "Do as I say, not as I do." [93] All of these actions tended to detract from the credibility of NATO as a joint enterprise with a common strategy.[94] What was the potential enemy to think when at the December 1958 NATO Council meeting Secretary Dulles was telling the other allies that NATO's military preparations were in good shape while the Supreme Allied Commander for Europe, General Norstad, was calling attention to their serious inadequacies? [95] Even the occasional American concern with a serious civil defense program unnerved the others in

[90] This, of course, begs the question of whether General de Gaulle would in any case have approved of any jointly determined strategy. When belated offers of "cooperation" were made by the United States in the summer of 1963 to obtain French acquiescence in the test ban treaty, President de Gaulle rejected them. Aside from the issue of this treaty, he did express the frustrations of other allies, who had also been constantly exposed to hortatory strategic doctrine enunciated by American officials.

[91] We are not here trying to strike a balance in which the gains from failing to share would be weighed against the costs.

[92] Numerous respected British and Continental defense specialists were, however, increasingly concerned. For one example, see Rear Admiral Sir Anthony Buzzard, *The Possibilities of Conventional Defence,* Adelphi Papers No. 6 (London: Institute for Strategic Studies, 1963), also Helmut Schmidt, *Defense or Retaliation: A German View* (New York: Frederick A. Praeger, 1962), esp. pp. 106 and 211 ff.

[93] See Arnold Wolfers, "Europe and the NATO Shield," *International Organization,* Autumn, 1958, p. 427.

[94] This assumes that a joint enterprise and common strategy were feasible, which may not have been so in the very early period. Even in December, 1957, however, the United States rather suddenly thrust the Jupiter and Thor proposals on its allies without preliminary discussion of their place in NATO's strategy.

[95] See Richard P. Stebbins, *The United States in World Affairs, 1958* (New York: Random House, 1959), p. 168.

the alliance because it did not seem to be related to shared planning.[96]

The costs of unilateral strategy-making in the 1960s are harder to estimate. That there is malaise in the alliance over nuclear control is generally recognized.[97] And American efforts to cope with technological change and an adverse balance of payments, if they had been shared with the other allies, might have produced more imaginative solutions. Under the Kennedy administration, as under its predecessors, the Americans shared their certainties much more often than their doubts. How many eventualities did they fail to calculate, how many assumptions did they make unwisely, without constructive criticism from those located in a different area? On both sides of the Atlantic the strategists working together might compensate for the tendency, noted by Bernard Brodie, for military planning to lack "freshness of outlook." [98]

Free and frank strategic discussion and planning would have minimized the opportunities for suspicions to focus on falsely attributed motives. It is one thing for an ally to have a function allocated to it, another thing for it to participate in deciding on the functions.[99] Willing allies make an alliance credible to the outsider. Moreover, if, as Glenn Snyder, for example, has pointed out, an effective strategy must include a conscious choice between the relative stress to be put on "punishment capacity" (deterrence) and that put on "denial capacity" (defense), the allies' voluntary agreement on the balance should contribute to the value of the strategy. The slow progress on the rather belated long-range re-

[96] Preparations for civil defense might alternatively have seemed to be evidence that the United States was getting ready to withstand nuclear blackmail either in North America or in Europe. But many Europeans regarded such preparations as the forerunner of a more independent nuclear policy.

[97] Dean Acheson, in arguing for more European participation in strategy and a greater European contribution, put it this way: ". . . the basic problem before the Atlantic Alliance is not how to control a particular weapon, but what ends the Alliance proposes to accomplish, how it proposes to accomplish them, and how to make the decisions to use force against force . . ." ("The Practice of Partnership," *loc. cit.*, p. 256).

[98] *Strategy in the Missile Age,* p. 260. He ascribes this to "constraints imposed by habit, tradition, service and personal interest, and hierarchy of authority within a corporate structure." See also *ibid.*, pp. 165–72, regarding one-sided calculations.

[99] See Buchan and Windsor, *op. cit.*, p. 188, regarding the Europeans' unwillingness to implement the doctrine of the flexible response. Dean Acheson went further, in his pleas for joint planning of concrete programs, by expressing the hope that eventually the planners would lose their national or service biases in a "professional absorption in their problems," viewing debates over the control, development, and use of nuclear weapons no longer as "thinly disguised national encounters for prestige and status" [Institute for Strategic Studies, *The Evolution of NATO,* p. 17]. Such attitudes are said to have prevailed within SHAPE.

examination of NATO's strategic plans and resources, begun in 1963, the so-called Stikker Exercise, indicates some of the alliance's inherent difficulties.[100]

In accordance with Secretary McNamara's promise to NATO in 1962 the United States has been providing the alliance partners with military information essential to a genuine transatlantic dialogue on ways of providing for the common defense. It is difficult, and perhaps impossible, for private scholars to judge the extent to which strategic decisions about the collective use of NATO forces in SHAPE are now shared; but so long as the alliance's strategic, air and missile force is unilaterally managed, the Europeans' sense of participating in basic choices in Western defense policy will be limited. Some students of NATO problems would meet this problem by having selected European military personnel brought into both the planning and operational parts of the American defense establishment.[101] If these Europeans were then free to communicate to their own governments' defense planners what they had learned, there might be an all-round disposition for each ally to contribute to fulfilling plans which appeared equitable and adequate to each.

We can only speculate about the consequences which would flow from the United States' acceptance of the full implications of determining strategy jointly. Such unified planning and execution of strategy has become the stated objective under President Johnson, which is not the same as being effectively observed throughout the administration.[102] Changes in NATO strategy would surely be slowed down; there would be fewer occasions on which the appetite for action which goads some

[100] Agreed upon in May, 1963, the study at first appeared bogged down by French unwillingness to have it carried on except directly under the North Atlantic Council. Reports on procedural difficulties appear in *New York Times,* July 26, 1963, and the *Economist,* November 9, 1963, p. 543. The study picked up again late in the year. See *Atlantic Community News,* November 1963, p. 6 and "Statement of Secretary McNamara, Senate Armed Services," pp. 28–29.

[101] For example, Acheson, "The Practice of Partnership," *loc. cit.,* p. 260; Hoag, "Nuclear Strategic Options and European Force Participation," *loc. cit.,* pp. 233–34; and Alastair Buchan, "The Changed Setting of the Atlantic Debate," *Foreign Affairs,* July, 1965, p. 586. Admittedly, a serious security problem would be one obstacle.

[102] In his Defense Message to Congress, January 18, 1965, President Johnson continued: "We invite our NATO allies to work with us in developing better methods for mutual consultations and joint strategic study. We shall continue to seek ways to bind the alliance even more strongly together by sharing the tasks of defense through collective action."

Americans would lead them into goading their European opposite numbers. Some kinds of policy changes which in retrospect seem to have been oscillations or random movements might thereby be avoided altogether. Evening out the waves of strategic development might help solve the problem of "gaps" between current preparedness and what is suddenly proclaimed to be necessary, gaps which make the existing forces look dangerously obsolete. (This is one reason some Europeans are afraid to abandon immediate reliance on nuclear weapons.) With strategy evolving more steadily and on the basis of a more stable alliance-wide consensus, NATO planners would be less concerned with "crash" programs to fill possibly artificial gaps and more with long-range planning; but in this direction they can move no more rapidly than the most powerful participant. The impression of hand-to-mouth planning operations, however, is probably inevitable in any large organization, national or international, which must cope with swiftly moving events. Internal bargaining within the United States government on aspects of the joint international strategy might increase in intensity because the bargainers could more often look for supporters within some of the allied governments. Such interallied bargaining bonds might, however, increase the cohesiveness of the alliance as a whole.[103]

American defense officials have undoubtedly often shied away from wholehearted acceptance of the principle of joint determination of strategy for all weapons because they fear that it is not really strategies but goals which are at issue. They recognize certain ineluctable differences in interest between the European members, with their very confined defense area very close to the potential enemy, and the two transatlantic partners with their vast spaces seemingly distant from that enemy. Only in the case of a conflict confined to Europe does the option for NATO of large-scale non-atomic war exist; many Frenchmen and Germans do not believe it exists there even in that case. And only in an atomic war would the United States be "in the bull's eye." Would seeming differences in interest, especially as they apply to the use of nuclear weapons, disappear on closer inspection of information held in common by participants? Or would the differences stubbornly persist and thus require political bargaining for their resolution before a joint strategy could be

---

[103] We do not consider here the effects which an earlier adoption of the habit of joint strategy-making might have had upon the lack of congruence between United States strategy and United States world commitments, often asserted by American critics of that strategy during the mid-1950s.

arrived at? Does such bargaining necessarily tend to *disintegrate* an organization? At the least, genuine participation by all the major allies in NATO's overall strategy-making would reveal upon how large a rock of common interest the alliance rests.[104]

Another consideration seems to have kept American officials from welcoming full European participation in nuclear strategy. They have seen little reason to share responsibility for decisions about the disposition of a force to which the petitioners have made no material contribution. (The same objection could be made by the French, if not the British, to integrating or at least coordinating their independent deterrents with the major nuclear deterrent for NATO.) One wonders if an augmented contribution to the conventional forces available to NATO could not be equated with participation in a joint NATO nuclear effort to provide a ticket of admission to strategic councils. Still another reason inhibiting American officials is fear of immobility, especially since Americans tend to be more activist than their European—or Canadian —counterparts.

Secretary McNamara's proposal on May 31, 1965 to form a "select committee of four or five North Atlantic allies empowered to improve strategic nuclear planning and consultation on the use of nuclear weapons" was an important American initiative to meet the European need for a sense of genuine participation. Its immediate impact was to isolate France; France was unwilling to do more than agree to the establishment of a committee to discuss the proposal, a committee in which it did not participate. So many other members were anxious to join the discussion that the "select" character ceased to exist except as a subject for negotiation, but the proposal was an earnest of United States intentions to get to the heart of the nuclear discontent.

In 1965 and 1966 ten of the defense ministers in the Atlantic alliance —all but those from France, Iceland, Luxembourg, Norway and Portugal —were meeting "to develop close, continuing consultation on nuclear targeting and planning, military intelligence and emergency communications." Five of them—from the United States, Britain, West Germany,

[104] See Malcolm Hoag's observation that even without consensus developing, participation would clarify issues and give some satisfaction to the allies. He also thought that the more Europeans debated the conditions which should govern the use of nuclear weapons the more attractive would become the non-nuclear alternatives ["Nuclear Strategic Options and European Force Participation," *loc. cit.*, pp. 234, 236 and 249–50].

Italy, and Turkey—constituted a working group on nuclear planning, the so-called Inner Committee, with Secretary McNamara as chairman, "to permit a greater degree of participation in nuclear planning by non-nuclear nations . . . and to make possible appropriate consultation in the event their use is considered." [105] Evidently, progress was being made toward the creation of a permanent new organ of NATO to satisfy, by interallied consultation and participation in nuclear planning, goals which had earlier been sought by proposals to create an allied nuclear force. Despite the uncertainties regarding the powers, composition, and complete acceptability of some kind of steering committee for strategy, the proposal could lead to a major change in American policy and in the organization of the alliance.

SHARING KNOWLEDGE. Joint strategy implies joint access to relevant knowledge, with no unilateral or narrow determination of what is relevant. United States officials—and others—have sometimes declared that states must possess nuclear weapons to know fully their implications and to enter into agreements about them that have substantive meaning. Although both the British and the French have eaten of the forbidden fruit, they do not share the official American views on the subject.[106]

Development of an atomic bomb during World War II was a collaborative effort engaged in by scientists of various nationalities, an effort in which the British and Canadian governments were participating before the American government became the dominant partner.[107] These wartime ties were broken, and the McMahon Act of 1946 imposed a regime of secrecy in atomic research since breached in only a few places. Legislation intended to prevent the Soviet Union from catching up with the United States became largely irrelevant to its original purpose once the Soviet Union had become in the mid-1950s a significant nuclear

[105] *New York Times,* June 1, 1965; November 26 and 28, 1965; December 15, 1965; April 30, 1966 (for an account of the work and objectives of the "Inner Committee"); June 22, 1966 (for Secretary McNamara's testimony on the subject before the Jackson Committee); and July 27, 1966.

[106] It is one of the fictions of the post-World War II period that states "know" things, as if they were individuals. The result is a variety of governmental regulations which open and close avenues of cooperation among individuals with common scientific and technical skills but of different nationalities.

[107] See A. J. R. Groom, "United States-Allied Relations and the Atomic Bomb in in the Second World War," *World Politics,* October, 1962, pp. 123–37. The British already had some cooperative agreements with French scientists prior to the United States-Canada-United Kingdom agreement of 1943, which conflicted with the latter [*ibid.,* pp. 130–31].

power. Worse still, it had also become highly productive of friction within the NATO alliance. Ever new reasons for continuing to withhold research and design information from America's allies were advanced. One reason was fear that their "security" systems were inadequate to prevent information leaking to the Russians; a later reason was implied in a high Eisenhower Administration official's arguments against "Operation Candor": he feared that some of the information might unduly (or dangerously) alarm the Americans' allies because it would reveal certain weaknesses in United States defenses.[108] Still later came the fear of proliferation of atomic weapons. The reasons were so varied and, to some Europeans, so specious that some of the allies began to suspect that unwillingness to share some information was related to American desires to maintain a commercial monopoly on certain products of nuclear technology.

The United States appeared to its allies to have failed to behave as a genuine partner (albeit one with special responsibilities in the Atlantic alliance); and this reinforced their desires to be "independent" of the United States. As a former Secretary General of NATO, Paul Henri Spaak, wrote in 1963: "Is it really essential to European pride that Europe discover again what was long ago discovered in the United States? And on the other hand, would the security of the United States be jeopardized if it told its friends secrets which are already known to its enemies?" [109] Ten years earlier a similar view had been expressed by J. Robert Oppenheimer.[110] He pointed out that technical collaboration with the NATO governments was "surely a pre-condition for effective planning, and for the successful defense of Europe" and concluded that . . . "we cannot operate wisely if a large half of the problem we have in common is not discussed in common. This does not mean that we should tie our hands. It means that we should inform and consult. This could make a healthy and perhaps very great change in our relations with Europe." [111]

[108] See quotation from Robert Cutler, "The Seamless Web," in W. W. Rostow et al., *United States in the World Arena* (New York: Harper & Brothers, 1960), pp. 318–19.

[109] "Hold Fast," *Foreign Affairs*, July, 1963, p. 617. This was a question he said he used to ask while Secretary General.

[110] Allegedly mirroring the attitude of the "Acheson Committee" appointed to look into such questions, but whose recommendations were rejected by the Eisenhower Administration [Rostow et al., *op. cit.*, pp. 316–18]. One should note that President Truman from the start shared the preferences of others in his government for keeping atomic "secrets" even from the British [*Memoirs* (Garden City: Doubleday & Company, 1956), Vol. I, pp. 523–44 and Vol. II, pp. 11–15, 298, and 301–06].

[111] "Atomic Weapons and American Policy," *Foreign Affairs*, July, 1953, p. 533.

He could have added that the mutual confidence of allies has to rest, like the visible tip of an iceberg, on a much larger unseen mass of transnational contact, at scholarly, informal, and lower governmental levels.

It was only after Sputnik had flashed across the skies in 1957 that President Eisenhower sponsored legislative action which would, in part, meet what he called "the tragic failure to secure the great benefits that would flow from mutual sharing of appropriate scientific information and effort among friendly countries." [112] Cooperative agreements with seven of the NATO members took place in 1959, but only the agreement with Britain covered information on design of weapons or nuclear propulsion. (See Chapter V.) The agreement with the British prohibited passing on information to third parties lacking comparable knowledge, a provision which later formed one of the obstacles to French-British collaboration on a European nuclear deterrent and, in any case, was a psychological irritant in the alliance. All these agreements were bilateral, although they were rationalized in terms of being "first steps" in NATO collective defense planning for nuclear weapons.[113] Their actual framing was unilateral; consultation with the other allies was only in the most general terms. Since the agreements were means to enhance the "cooperating" ally's ability to arm with nuclear weapons, they provided no leverage for inducing members to work harder to reach the conventional force goals set by SACEUR.[114] In all of them the United States grasped (somewhat feebly) one horn of a dilemma presented by nuclear weapons; it preferred trying to prevent proliferation at the cost of trying to strengthen the defense alliance through some kind of multilateral arrangements. Even the concessions to the British were in part aimed at getting their compliance with a United States view that was being advanced at the concurrent arms control negotiations.[115] But devotion to

[112] President's Committee to Study the United States Military Assistance Program, *op. cit.*, Supplement, Annex F, p. 165. Secretary Dulles had already hinted that the secret of making an atomic submarine might be shared [Osgood, *NATO: The Entangling Alliance*, pp. 221 and 403].

[113] Joint Committee on Atomic Energy, Subcommittee on Agreements for Cooperation, *Hearings, Agreements for Cooperation for Mutual Defense Purposes*, 86th Cong., 1st sess. (1959) (hereafter referred to as JCAE, *Hearings*, 86–1), esp. pp. 26, 38–39, 41, 44, 46–47, 53–55, 60 and 67.

[114] Note Committee member Chet Holifield's inquiry at the 1958 hearings, Joint Committee on Atomic Energy, *Hearings, Amending the Atomic Energy Act of 1954 —Exchange of Military Information and Material With Allies*, 85th Cong., 2nd sess. (1958), p. 41.

[115] See JCAE, *Hearings*, 86–1, p. 12.

the antiproliferation principle was described as hypocritical both by the Soviet Union and by some of the allies.[116]

Unlike the other six agreements, the 1959 agreement with France was a "purely commercial" arrangement for sale of enriched uranium for construction of a prototype reactor for a nuclear-powered submarine. The discriminatory treatment given this recalcitrant ally continued to rankle; it even prevented implementation of the agreement.[117] Already the French had snubbed earlier United States efforts to place American nuclear weapons in Europe and had begun to retrench French forces assigned to NATO. The outcome of negotiations over a cooperative nuclear agreement was one more step in a long series which separated the two allies further and further. Americans had earlier viewed the French "security system" as unreliable; but in the late 1950's under General de Gaulle, its reputation greatly improved. Meanwhile, to some Europeans Americans, in their readiness to publish material usually kept out of the public press in Europe, seemed to be straining at security gnats while swallowing publicity camels. On their side, the Americans found in the several cases of prominent European defectors who allegedly carried atomic secrets across the Iron Curtain justification for denying much-wanted information to their allies. The 1964 agreements, which further eased restrictions on nuclear information to NATO and allied officials to facilitate joint strategic discussion and nuclear planning, contained the possibility of discrimination between members. This was true despite the potential increase in cases where NATO itself would be a party.[118]

American defense and atomic energy officials did not regularly recognize that there was a positive side to information-sharing in the field of nuclear weapons, that "exchange" could be a two-way affair. Usually they seem to have considered only the "benefits" to be conferred on

---

[116] *Ibid.*, p. 26.

[117] See *New York Times,* October 16, 1962 and April 2, 1963. However, it did not prevent the sale of Boeing jet tankers (twelve C-135 F's) to France, without which the independent French nuclear strike force could not have become effective.

The agreements to sell enriched uranium proved sufficiently ambiguous that the United States found an excuse to discontinue shipments in 1964 because of an alleged divergence in the two parties' views of the purpose to which the fuel was to be put. The United States claimed the fuel was for a "hunter-killer" type of submarine; the French were using it to develop a Polaris type, which the United States regarded as outside the scope of the 1959 agreement [*New York Times,* April 17 and 20, 1966].

[118] Joint Committee on Atomic Energy, Subcommittee on Agreements for Cooperation, *Hearings, Agreement for Cooperation with NATO for Mutual Defense Purposes,* 88th Cong., 2nd sess. (1964) (hereafter referred to as JCAE, *Hearings,* 88–2), esp. pp. 11, 34, 35 and 42.

others,[119] although occasionally they would admit that they had learned something in return.[120] Often Americans were too impatient to wait for the reverse benefits. Professor Eugene P. Wigner, in testimony before the Senate Committee on National Policy Machinery in 1960, declared that "if a line of work abroad appears to be promising we jump at it, even though, as a result of agreements, its accomplishments would be available to us anyway." He deplored the waste and declared that the "temptation to have a finger or even fist in every pie should be resisted." [121]

Since the scientific community should exist without national *or international* barriers between countries, or at least between democracies, the fifteen nations of NATO do not necessarily constitute a more logical group for general scientific cooperation than any smaller or larger group.[122] Yet scientific questions of immediate and specific concern to NATO, notably those relating to nuclear and electronic developments basic to alliance strategy, could be tackled on an alliance level, as have some other scientific and technological problems of a military nature. Secrecy rules which restrict the sharing of knowledge among the members may be justified if their observance in fact prevents the adversary from catching up with Western military developments. This potential advantage, however, needs to be weighed against the possibility that the

[119] When a JCAE member asked about the Department of Defense's opinion of the proposed nuclear cooperative agreements, the general being questioned simply replied that they would be implemented "without risk to our national defense" [JCAE, *Hearings,* 86–1, pp. 54–55]. An exception to the one-sided view of "exchange" was praise of the Anti-Submarine Warfare Research Center at La Spezia by Admiral George W. Anderson before the House Committee on Armed Services [*Hearings on Military Posture,* 87th Cong., 2nd sess. (1962), p. 3662].

[120] For an example, see the testimony of the Chairman of the Atomic Energy Commission regarding cooperation with the British, JCAE, *Hearings,* 86–1, p. 60. The situation was quite different with respect to the peaceful uses of atomic energy. Here there was a much more equal exchange.

[121] Senate Committee on Government Operations, Subcommittee on National Policy Machinery, *Hearings, Organizing for National Security,* Part II, 86th Cong., 2nd sess. (1960) p. 370. The Director of Research and Development of the Department of Defense told a subcommittee of the House of Representatives Committee on Armed Services that in the field of avionics there was a good exchange of *information* between Britain and the United States, but this did not prevent separate development [*Hearings on Military Posture,* 88th Cong., 2nd sess. (1964), pp. 7608 and 7611–12].

[122] Much less should NATO serve to restrict scientific interchange as it apparently did when owing to an understanding by Germany's allies to refuse travel permits to East Germans, scientists from that region were to be excluded from meetings of an international scientific union in the United States [*New York Times* (International ed.), June 24, 1963].

gap might be broadened if contributions could be made by all fifteen members. It not only is wasteful but could also be dangerous for one member to attempt to keep all the sophisticated technology to itself. A number of the other allies are cooperating in nuclear and space research for peaceful uses in organizations such as the European Center for Nuclear Research (CERN), the European Atomic Community (Euratom), the European Launcher Development Organization (ELDO) and the European Space Research Organization (ESRO); but the large sums for research on military projects, by enabling one member to enjoy most of the impressive spin-off for non-military uses, create ill will among others in the alliance.[123]

One advantage of freer interchange of technological knowledge in the alliance is suggested by democratic theory. A loyal opposition can keep the government on a course to which the latter could not be reliably held by yes-men. Similarly, the better informed the other members are, the better they can judge and make constructive suggestions about strategy, and the healthier are the relations between them and the giant members. Today the European members still seem constantly out of phase with American strategic thinking. Visits to centers of American study of strategy are useful in themselves, especially if they stimulate a dialogue rather than a lecture.

ARMS CONTROL. The United States has failed to coordinate its NATO policy with its arms control policy in a variety of ways. NATO itself has not been a suitable instrument for Soviet-Western arms control negotiations, partly because the Soviet Union would have countered by insisting that NATO negotiate with the Warsaw Pact organization, but perhaps even more because NATO is a device by which its members negotiate with each other; it wholly lacks organs and ambassadors to negotiate with outsiders. Thus United States negotiations with its major European allies over a variety of issues, only one of which was a common Western policy on arms control, and United States negotiations with Russia on another range of issues, only one of which dealt with arms control, pursued separate and sometimes conflicting courses.

At the same time that one part of the United States government was facilitating the wider deployment of tactical nuclear weapons and

---

[123] Unlike scientific knowledge, military intelligence cannot be easily exchanged on an alliance-wide basis. In this field, the United States exchanges information with those who have information to offer. NATO could merely provide a framework.

intermediate-range ballistic missiles in Europe (controls, to be sure, remained in American hands), another was conducting disarmament negotiations with the Soviet Union.[124] Undoubtedly the overseas deployment of these weapons strengthens the Americans' negotiating position on arms control if the United States is willing to use them as counters for bargaining purposes, but the United States government as a whole has evidently not eliminated apparent contradictions among its varied efforts to achieve peace and security via regional defense arrangements on the one hand and via arms control on the other.

The American response to Soviet protests about deployment of nuclear weapons was that these were not really being passed on to third parties for use at their own discretion but were distributed in accordance with NATO plans, an absolute veto over their use remaining with the United States government.[125] Yet the arms and missiles were not provided to NATO as NATO, but to individual members willing to receive them. Similarly, when opponents of the MLF declared that it would promote proliferation, the proponents claimed that the force would be assigned to the alliance and would not be subject to the sole will of any European participant.[126] The vague hints of some American negotiators pressing for the MLF that the United States might consider eventually abandoning its veto further weakened the credibility of the American response to Soviet protests and demonstrated a lack of coordination between NATO and arms control policy-making.[127]

---

[124] See Bernhard G. Bechhoefer, *Postwar Negotiations for Arms Control* (Washington: Brookings Institution, 1961), p. 362, regarding the 1957 United Nations Disarmament Committee discussions, in which the Western states insisted on the right to transfer weapons.

[125] So long as the weapons were on European soil, it is true that only safety-catches were being shared.

[126] Robert Stephenson, a writer for the London *Observer*, described some of the earlier American probings of British and French willingness for a "nuclear partnership" as an "almost metaphysical endeavour to define a nuclear trinity which is both indivisible and separate" [*The Observer* (London) June 24, 1962]. The same might be said for the argument that the MLF would reduce rather than increase diffusion. For a contrary argument, see Osgood, *The Case for the MLF,* pp. 49–52.

[127] See *Washington Post,* February 19, 1963, and letter of Alastair Buchan in *The Times* (London), June 26, 1963. The confusion was exemplified when the Director of the Arms Control and Disarmament Administration, testifying before the House of Representatives Committee on Foreign Affairs regarding a proposed treaty to prevent proliferation, told of an American suggestion to the reluctant Russians that an escape clause could be included to permit the Soviet Union to withdraw if the MLF were to be established and the Russians continued to regard it as "proliferation" [*Washington Post,* January 27, 1965]. A minor uproar resulted. See also *New York Times,* July 27, August 2, and September 1, 1965.

In arms control negotiations the countries with which the United States consulted or collaborated from the summer of 1957 onward were the more powerful NATO allies whose interest in arms control the United States acknowledged. The negotiations with the Communist-bloc countries were always conducted by individual members, with the United States as a leader. The proposals were "cleared" by the NATO Council, but NATO as an entity did not otherwise participate. In any case, NATO itself had no nuclear weapons.

Leading members of NATO had quite different opinions, resting on the interpretation of their respective national interests, as to concessions safe to make in the many arms control negotiations.[128] In 1957 neither the French nor the British were interested in a test ban, at least if it were unaccompanied by the assurance that the United States would share nuclear information with them; and the Germans were more concerned about disengagement proposals. The United States has felt enough constrained by the membership of those three in the North Atlantic alliance to make its proposals conform to their desires. This kind of collaboration tends towards a package offer, which, as in 1957, may repel the adversary or permit him to make a response which would strain or split the coalition.[129] But NATO itself did not elaborate an arms control plan, although the subject was constantly discussed within the organization. No doubt there were rigidities enough without the formal involvement of the whole organization; the members' differing interpretations of what was needed for stability in the military confrontation might have immobilized the alliance.[130] One NATO official, General Norstad, stood out because of his serious concern with the problem, elaborating ideas and not merely reacting negatively to others' proposals.[131] For whatever reason, almost everyone else connected with NATO and with making United States policy regarding NATO hesitated to develop a de-

[128] Consider the interesting case of Canada, so sure of the United States nuclear guarantee that it declined to become a nuclear power, as it easily could have done [see Leonard Beaton, "To Slow Down the Nuclear Race," *New York Times Magazine,* March 8, 1964, p. 35].

[129] See Bechhoefer, *op. cit.,* p. 410. A package may permit trade-offs between two otherwise unnegotiable issues, but if the package is for the convenience of a coalition negotiating with a monolithic adversary, to provide a common front, then the costs of a package have to be weighed against the benefits of combined influence. The opponent, by picking and choosing, may split the coalition.

[130] See Buchan and Windsor, *op. cit.,* p. 194.

[131] He did not participate in the 1957 discussions when the allies were first consulted [House of Representatives Committee on Foreign Affairs, *Hearings, Mutual Security Act of 1957,* 85th Cong., 1st sess. (1957), p. 547].

sign for security which joined building up of arms with acceptance of arms controls.[132]

In the 1960s the United States took certain military measures which clearly could be related to arms control, although it did not take them in the context of arms control negotiations. The renewed emphasis on conventional warfare capability, coupled with the preparation for a "flexible response," the removal of the Jupiters and Thors, the hardening or dispersing of strategic nuclear weapons, and even the "hot line"—all contributed to stability. Certain NATO allies disapproved of some of these moves—moves which involved them, but in which they could not participate.[133] Nevertheless, these measures did contribute to the prevention of surprise attack, accidental nuclear war, and escalation, subjects which all the NATO allies were prepared to discuss.

Some of the leading allies were, moreover, opposed to one important arms control objective, prevention of proliferation. On this, the United States was probably more in agreement with the Soviet Union than with at least one of its close allies. When Secretary Dulles negotiated on arms control in 1957, he placed solidarity among the NATO allies first, however this might affect the prospect for some kind of an agreement with the Soviet Union.[134] In the 1963 conference which produced the test ban treaty, on the other hand, the United States chose to collaborate only with Britain in seriously negotiating with the Soviet Union.

The United States view in the late 1950s was somewhat ambivalent about the "two keys" form of proliferation that resulted from the transfer to some of its allies of atomic weapons, although with a veto on their use remaining in American hands. Such was not the case with the sharing of the knowledge underlying nuclear technology for military use, even though much of the anxiously protected American monopoly of such information has been a wasting asset wastefully reproduced by allies of the United States. Had the United States government heeded earlier pleas of Europeans and Americans to be more liberal towards NATO

[132] The 1965 British proposals for discussion of a test ban treaty at the resumed Geneva disarmament conference are a notable exception [*New York Times,* July 27, 1965].

[133] How might they react to a stabilizing suggestion of General Sidney F. Griffin that the two superpowers make a public statement that neither would come to the aid of any nation making first use of nuclear weapons? ["Untangling an Alliance," *Orbis,* Fall, 1963, p. 472].

[134] See Stebbins, *The United States in World Affairs, 1957,* p. 136; and Bechhoefer, *op. cit.,* pp. 427 and 431.

allies in sharing nuclear technology, responses at that time would have been less destabilizing than action taken only after a number of years of following a rather futile policy. Meanwhile the alliance might have grown stronger in mutual confidence, at no real cost to the goal of discouraging proliferation.[135]

Part of the difficulty in reconciling United States arms control policy with its NATO policy has derived from one of the Soviet objectives in embarking on what were ostensibly arms control negotiations, namely, the elimination of NATO itself. Because Americans have thought of NATO primarily as a military instrument for deterring war through arms, they have been loath to use it as a bargaining device in deterring war through damping down the arms race. NATO as a relationship among some of the major Western powers could be used by the United States in negotiating about arms control with the Soviet Union, but not NATO itself as a military organization. One of the reasons why the United States had difficulty reconciling its policies regarding NATO with its arms control policies was that the government in practice continually distinguished between some NATO allies and the North Atlantic alliance at the same time at which it was verbally obscuring the difference.

Tacit understandings and implicit agreements between the United States and the Soviet Union to remove causes of miscalculation are forms of arms control, but they have aroused the other allies' suspicions of a "deal behind their backs." It is not clear how such arrangements could be made NATO-wide and at the same time remain tacit or informal, especially as the United States is under pressure to loosen its hold on the alliance. If the tacit and implicit arrangements do not seem to include all of the NATO members, however, the aggravated disunities in NATO may raise the Communist adversary's fears that NATO military policy may get out of control, with a single irresponsible member acting as catalyst in a war neither superpower wanted.[136]

MAINTAINING THE COMMUNITY

POLITICAL CONSULTATION. Acceptance of the principle of collective defense implies agreement to support the broad purpose for which

---

[135] The secrecy policy looked hypocritical—or at least inconsistent with providing other countries with materials for "peaceful uses of atomic energy." No matter what the safeguards, it was conceivable that the possessors could, if they willed and understood the principles of conversion, engage in unpeaceful uses.

[136] Cf. Buchan and Windsor, *op. cit.*, pp. 134–36.

the principle of collective defense was adopted and to accept the necessity for some kind of foreign policy coordination among the members. Despite occasional fears among two of the major members of NATO that the United States would negotiate away their interests in its separate dealings with the Soviet Union, the United States has played the game faithfully in NATO with respect to issues involving Communist threats to the NATO area. It has not pushed beyond limits set by France and Germany in negotiating a detente with Russia. On the crucial question of Berlin it has stood firm and acted more decisively than the others; at the same time it has urged its allies to follow suit, to provide the military strength necessary to support their declared foreign policy.[137]

A *collective* NATO policy for the areas beyond the treaty commitment would be improbable, even if it were desirable. To what extent, however, have American moves in such areas stimulated disunity in the alliance? More than any other member the United States has interests in other parts of the world. This raises two kinds of problems within the alliance. One concerns members who have interests different from those of the United States, such as France and her interests in North Africa; and the other concerns members who do not wish to be involved outside the NATO area, which is generally the case with the smaller states and sometimes, for particular issues, the case with one or another of the larger states. Here the United States has been faced with what has been called "one of the most difficult tasks of diplomacy: how to soft-pedal awkward commitments without extinguishing the vital ones, and how to endorse non-alignment of others without being repudiated by one's allies." [138] A minimum step in fulfilling this task is to put the United States' position before the North Atlantic Council or an appropriate committee of the council. For some years this country's representatives have done so as faithfully as any member and more than some.[139]

Since not even the most powerful state can conduct a completely independent foreign policy, the United States has often been motivated in its consultations within NATO by the desire to obtain support, or at least to minimize opposition, by explaining its actions. American readiness to inform allies regarding a contemplated move outside the NATO

---

[137] At least since 1960.

[138] George Liska, *Nations in Alliance: The Limits of Interdependence* (Baltimore: The Johns Hopkins Press, 1962), pp. 284–85.

[139] Even though such a presentation may on occasion stir up more controversy than if not made, an alliance depends on confidence, which requires frankness.

area and to delay action long enough to hear and weigh their responses has depended somewhat on anticipated reactions. Occasional failure to give the allies an opportunity to respond has been conducive neither to harmony within the alliance nor to its strength.[140] The Eisenhower Doctrine, guarantees regarding Quemoy and Matsu, the Lebanon landing, the providing of small arms to Tunisia—all these actions in the 1950s were taken with only the most perfunctory communication with the NATO Council.

"Consultation" in NATO has been likened to a bank account, upon which the members feel free to draw for diplomatic aid when in trouble. Because of the privacy of consultation in NATO we do not know how close the United States has sometimes come to overdrawing its account. However, complaints by some of the other members about lack of support by the United States suggest that the latter has made deposits less frequently than withdrawals.[141] Its blanket guarantee against Soviet aggression in the NATO area is, however, a "deposit" so enormous that the allies may hesitate long before declining to honor an American claim.

The United States drew heavily on its credit at the time of the Cuban missile crisis; but credit was granted willingly despite a feeling of impotence on the part of allies faced with the possibility of global nuclear war in an affair about which they were not well informed. The unity which buoyed up the United States at the time was seriously endangered later when the Americans pressed for economic measures against Cuba which were contrary to the perceived interest of most of its NATO allies and which in any case did not seem to them (or to many unofficial American observers) likely to be effective in destroying the Castro regime.[142] The NATO allies were even less willing than were some of the United States'

[140] American representatives sometimes have trouble staying ahead of the news agencies, especially in view of the time differential between Paris and Washington; see statement of former Permanent Representative W. Randolph Burgess, in "Practical Considerations about Cooperation," in Cerny and Briefs (eds.), *op. cit.*, p. 194.

[141] For example, the Dutch in the case of Dutch New Guinea, the Portuguese regarding Goa—to say nothing of Angola—and the Belgians regarding the Congo. The other members were also indifferent, to be sure; but in the spring of 1961 the United States even went so far as to vote against Portugal on a United Nations resolution regarding Angola, rather than merely abstaining.

[142] See *New York Times,* December 17, 1963; January 28, 1964; February 10, 1964; February 19, 1964; and Philip Geyelin, "The Cuban Embargo Myth," *Reporter,* April 23, 1964, pp. 18–19.

allies in the OAS, who have not directly felt the danger of the Cuban government, to weaken themselves for a cause which they regarded as remote from that in which they were aligned with the United States. Moreover, here as in other situations the allies differed with the United States about proposed measures without having much opportunity to discuss their difference in NATO before the United States acted.

American officials, in admitting that the economic deprivation was less important than the psychological effects, revealed a tendency to use NATO (and the OAS) as though the issue were before the United Nations. Unlike the United Nations, the two regional organizations cannot be effectively employed as places for making fellow members stand up and be counted against their preferences. Constant harping by Americans on the theme of isolating Castro has made some allies wish for a more variegated orchestra and a different tune; others have become deaf.

Another threat to the unity of NATO—and to that of any other international organization—is ill-considered shifting back and forth from bilateral to multilateral action.[143] The former type of diplomacy is usually necessary in preparation for multilateral consultation and can be an effective spur to overcome the inevitable inertia in the organization. However, when it fails to use the organs of the alliance for multilateral action, the United States weakens the alliance. Others are then likely also to act outside it, as the French began to do in 1963 in connection with the war in Vietnam. Although the North Atlantic Council was "briefed" on a United States conception of the MLF in February, 1963 and was kept informed of bilateral and multilateral discussions with reference to it, up to 1965 there had been no formal Council consideration. General Lemnitzer commented in July, 1963 that SHAPE had not been asked for its opinion.[144] In November, 1964 at a critical point in the diplomatic history of the proposal, Secretary General Brosio told the

[143] This tendency, so noticeable in inter-American policy, is an important source of Latin-American officials' distrust of the United States. One of numerous examples was the United States action in unilaterally withdrawing the Alliance for Progress team from the Dominican Republic in September, 1963, when the United States broke off diplomatic relations with that country.

[144] See General Lemnitzer's remarks at the WEU Assembly, reported in *NATO Letter,* July–August 1963, p. 20. Of course, the general question of nuclear controls and nuclear sharing had been discussed in the North Atlantic Council and SHAPE for several years.

NATO Parliamentarians' Conference that the MLF had not been discussed "within NATO itself"; some of his hearers sensed a certain feeling of rivalry with the group of officials of various member countries who were discussing it.[145] Had the United States pressed the British to take their proposed NATO police action for Cyprus to the North Atlantic Council in early 1964, the British would undoubtedly have been turned down; but in the process NATO would have deprived the Soviet Union of any effective basis for accusing the alliance of seeking a new bridgehead in the Eastern Mediterranean.[146] Systematic American dependence on bilateral actions is likely to have a cumulatively corrosive effect on the alliance.

Sometimes not trying at all is wiser than trying to get potentially divisive support through NATO. By not pressing hard for Spain's entry into NATO and not seeking to use NATO to enlarge a potential schism between the Soviet Union and its satellites, the United States avoided a possible disruption within NATO. Like the other NATO allies, the United States has avoided the temptation to exploit internal political differences of fellow members in cases in which opponents of the government held views about NATO issues more congenial to its own, as happened in Britain in 1963–64. American inhibitions have been less when it was a question of helping a relatively friendly government maintain itself.[147]

Once disagreements between members of the alliance become acute, the United States cannot stand aside.[148] To allow other members to take the peace-making lead, as in the Cyprus case both in 1958 and 1964, was one way to strengthen the other members' attachment to the organization, as the United States has also found to be the case in the

[145] *Washington Post*, November 17, 1964. Nor had the extra-NATO working groups discussing the MLF reported to him by the time of the NATO ministerial meeting in December [*Baltimore Sun*, December 14, 1964]. Undersecretary of State Ball told the JCAE in July, 1964 that "discussions of the MLF are going forward using the facility of NATO, but it is not a NATO proposal as such" [*Hearings*, 88–2, p. 19].

[146] *New York Times*, February 8, 1964. Apparently the British were hoping to use the allies but not the alliance, in which Cyprus was not in any case a member.

[147] Thus the United States in 1964 pressed for adoption of the MLF before the German elections which were to take place the following year.

[148] With a commonly conceived external threat, the NATO members were less inclined to yield to intra-alliance hostility than were members of the OAS.

OAS. Leaving some of the initiative to others is becoming easier (and in fact harder to avoid) in NATO; for the United States is no longer trying to serve at the same time as "both partner and paymaster." [149] Free nations must choose freely. This is another reason why American attempts to get its NATO allies to toe the line in Cuba have been self-defeating: freedom to trade at will is to the European allies almost as sacred a principle as non-intervention is to the Latin-American countries.

The use of NATO for protection against Communist expansion and the concomitant effort, especially when reciprocated on the other side of the Iron Curtain, to relax tensions between the two camps are in potential conflict and have posed an increasingly awkward problem for the United States. A non-aggression treaty between NATO and the Warsaw Pact does not seem to solve the problem, for reasons cogently expressed by General de Gaulle on July 29, 1963:

. . . France does not like this assimilation between the Atlantic Alliance and Communist servitude, seeing also that there is no need of a pact in order for France to declare she will never be the first to attack, it being understood that she would defend herself with the means she may have against anyone attacking her or her allies.

The Germans would hardly disagree with this view.

Coordinating NATO and détente policies is difficult both for the United States and its NATO allies; the United States has not made full use of the organization to achieve this coordination. A start was made at the December, 1963 ministerial meeting of the North Atlantic Council. In line with Secretary Rusk's remarks at the time, the joint communiqué issued after the meeting referred to "limited measures to reduce tension" and hope for "a genuine and fundamental improvement in East-West relations." [150]

FOREIGN ECONOMIC POLICIES. What passes for United States foreign economic policy is a mixed bag of measures which variously are in-

---

[149] The phrase is Douglass Cater's, referring to the United States in inter-American affairs ["The Lesson of Punta del Este," *The Reporter*, March 1, 1962, p. 22].

[150] See reports of Secretary Rusk's speech, *New York Times*, December 17 and 18, 1963, and the communiqué (*ibid.*, December 18, 1963). Such expressions were unprecedented in earlier communiqués. In a speech to the Foreign Service Institute on March 23, 1966, President Johnson referred to the value of a strong NATO in promoting the reconciliation of Western and Eastern Europe.

consistent with each other in their economic effects; are sometimes in conflict with declared American military and political objectives; are transparently designed to promote narrow private or sectional interests, though ostensibly to promote national security; are damaging to the economic interests of the allies of the United States without any commensurate gain to the United States itself; are so narrowly focused that they alleviate one problem while they exacerbate others; or are ineffective as cold war measures. Our concern, however, is not to pass judgment on the general rationality or propriety of these policies but to ask how they impinge on the values which the United States hopes to realize through participation in NATO and other international organizations.

If contradictory policies only negated each other, their significance for the United States' foreign relations would be small. But some of them, such as the agricultural subsidy system with its resultant surpluses disorganizing the markets in which indispensable allies must sell their own products, make a mockery of the professed goal of trade expansion and encourage the protectionist aspects of Europe's economic policies, including Common Market policies. A quota on Icelandic fish in the mid-1950s turned that small ally towards the Soviet Union for trade and jeopardized the military-base rights enjoyed by the United States for NATO purposes.

The "security" rationale of some United States restrictions on the importation of specific commodities has rubbed rather thin in recent years. The mandatory quotas on imports of lead, zinc, and petroleum that were imposed in the later 1950s were especially hard on friendly countries in the Western Hemisphere.[151] The "Buy American" Act for government purchases, which dates back to an era of economic stringency, has provided hidden subsidies to domestic industries in a weak competitive position; it has also continued to produce animosity among allies, and especially in Great Britain.[152] One wonders whose security is being protected, when the high-cost shipping industry in the United States is shielded from competition with shipping which is the mainstay or one of the chief income-earners of some of the other NATO countries

---

[151] See Richard P. Stebbins, *The United States in World Affairs, 1959* (New York: Random House, 1960), p. 82.

[152] See Percy Bidwell, "Raw Materials and National Policy," *Foreign Affairs,* October 1958, p. 145. Some of its provisions were relaxed in 1960 for Canada [Eayrs, *op. cit.,* p. 69].

or when restrictions are periodically imposed on imports of petroleum from Canada.[153] In the Canadian case, the industry was expanded at United States urging during the Korean War.[154]

The balance of payments problem, a genuinely serious problem for the United States but one which the United States has not been willing to deal with by measures which might check its economic boom, has provided the occasion for a series of measures which undermined objectives being promoted in NATO, the OECD and GATT. Thus in 1960 President Eisenhower directed that United States forces in Europe purchase their coal from American suppliers, despite the higher cost, with half of the largest contract to be carried in United States-flag vessels.[155] Among the examples of Department of Defense pressure to obtain NATO contracts for an American concern was the case of the Greek government's choice of a target missile for the NATO missile-firing installation on Crete. To prevent the award being given to a French target-missile enterprise the United States caused the Greeks to cancel their initial selection of the French product and tried hard to reverse the German support for it. The result was an indefinite delay in the use of the NATO facility.[156]

A country which is spending huge sums on forces abroad to meet its alliance commitments must make every effort by sales abroad to earn the foreign exchange to support those forces. Nevertheless, in its zeal to sell military items it ought not to undermine its alliance relationships. There have been numerous reports that the International Logistic Negotiations program has increased United States arms sales to $1,500,-000,000 per year at some cost in the form of ruffled allied feelings and good will.[157] More than that, in the specific case of competition with Britain over arms sales to Germany, the United States has further weak-

---

[153] See Stebbins, *The United States in World Affairs, 1959*, p. 82; *ibid., 1961*, p. 149; Slessor, "Cuba, Skybolt, and the Congo," *loc. cit.*, p. 273. A Department of Commerce official stated in 1964: ". . . the purpose of the construction-differential subsidy is to subsidize American shipyards, not American shipowners. . . . this subsidy should put the shipowner in the position he would have been in but for the build-American requirement" (*New York Times*, April 8, 1964).

[154] Eayrs, *op. cit.*, pp. 69–72.

[155] *New York Times*, August 23, 1961; House of Representatives Committee on Armed Services, *Hearings on Military Posture*, 87th Cong., 2nd sess. (1962), p. 3417.

[156] L. L. Doty in *Aviation Week and Space Technology*, March 1, 1965.

[157] See Jack Raymond, "Traffic in Arms Again Rising," *New York Times*, May 30, 1965; "The Hard-Sell Arms Race, U.S. Style," *Newsweek*, June 14, 1965, p. 59.

ened Britain's ability to maintain the armed forces in Germany which NATO defense arrangements envision. It is not yet clear whether Secretary McNamara's call for a NATO "common market" in arms reflects a willingness by the United States to treat foreign arms manufacturers on a par with American arms suppliers, as well as a call for American manufacturers to be fully freed to compete abroad with European suppliers.[158]

As the "giant among nations," at least in the Atlantic alliance, the United States has often taken actions of small consequence to itself but with by-product effects on its allies which are disproportionately large.[159] Members who are both smaller and less given to preachment follow similar practices, but these are less likely to attract the unfavorable notice of the alliance as a whole.

Because the other allies are smaller and have so much less possibility of being self-sufficient, they must either contribute to the productive strength of the alliance what they produce best or make very little contribution at all. United States economic policy often fails to take account of this necessity despite a general policy of trade liberalization.[160]

It may be granted that most of the foreign economic problems faced by the United States are better solved through channels other than NATO.[161] Nevertheless, the United States when dealing with NATO problems has often ignored the economic implications for the well-being of the rest of the community. For example, Admiral Burke replied negatively to a question in the Senate Armed Services Committee on March

[158] *New York Times,* May 31, 1965, and *Economist,* June 5, 1965, pp. 1126–27. The whole question of arms sales is too complex for simple judgments about correct policy.

[159] Peter Kenen's *Giant Among Nations* (New York: Harcourt, Brace and Co., 1960) contains numerous other examples of contradictory foreign economic policy.

[160] Cf. Lincoln Gordon, "Economic Aspects of Coalition Diplomacy—The NATO Experience," *International Organization,* November, 1956, p. 542, where he states: "Economic resources . . . are fungible. This implies that physical efforts should be concentrated where they can be secured at the lowest real cost, and the form of resource transferred to make up the differences is a matter of secondary importance. Unfortunately, the logic of this principle was never fully explained to publics or parliaments, especially in the United States."

In a sense this division of labor has happened unintentionally; with the United States providing such a large part of NATO's defense expense other members felt freer to devote their own resources to non-military activities except when being induced by the American grant-in-aid programs.

[161] See William Diebold, Jr., "The Changed Economic Position of Western Europe: Some Implications for United States Policy and International Organization, *International Organization,* Winter, 1960, pp. 17–18.

13, 1959 regarding the eligibility of other NATO members to participate in shipping ground troops to Europe if the Berlin situation became
more critical.[162]

The contradictions between economic and alliance policies do suggest
that the members are essentially competitive in economic matters despite their military dependence upon each other. Interallied economic
conflicts become more prominent in times of military relaxation. Since
1962 the United States has made a number of relatively fruitless efforts
to get NATO support for trade restrictions against countries in the
Communist bloc.[163] These efforts were bound to conflict with economic
interests the members felt to be stronger than any alleged security concern, especially because foreign trade was much more vital to them than
to the United States. Even though the United States was able to get
the North Atlantic Council to approve a resolution discouraging sales of
large-gauge oil pipe to the Soviet Union in 1963, this condemnation was
not strong enough by itself to prevent the British from defying the
United States preference in view of the many domestic arguments in
favor of it.[164] (The British, after all, had a balance of payments problem
as serious as the Americans'.) If not all potential suppliers agree, one is
likely to be the beneficiary; thus the effort at common action aggravates
the split.

The British government's policy on economic trade with the Communist bloc has diverged most from the American; the British see such
trade not as harmful but as positively helpful. They think that it de-
creases the satellites' dependence upon Russia and increases peaceful
contacts with the Russians themselves and may lead to reduced tensions.[165] Other allies lean more and more in this same direction, and
there are increasing doubts within the United States as to the effective-

---

[162] Senate Committee on Armed Services, Preparedness Investigating Subcommittee, *Hearings, Major Defense Matters,* Part I, 86th Cong., 1st sess. (1959),
p. 141.

[163] See *supra.*

[164] On this conflict, see articles in *Christian Science Monitor,* January 1 and 7,
1963, and March 27, 1963; *Washington Post,* March 22 and 30, 1963, April 2
and 9, 1963; C. L. Sulzberger, *New York Times* (International ed.), June 15,
1963; *New York Times,* editorial, April 13, 1963. During the oil-pipe controversy
the United States was importing cheap chromium from Russia at the expense of
the traditional suppliers, Turkey and Rhodesia.

[165] After the wheat sale to Russia the previous year, signs began to appear in
1964 that the Johnson administration was reexamining its policies regarding trade
with Communist countries. One reason for a National Security Council review
of this question in April was said to be allied reactions [*New York Times,* April 19,
1964].

ness of economic boycotts. To the others, American policy too often has looked like a "beggar thy foe at the expense of thy neighbor" policy. The gigantic sale of American wheat to the Soviet Union in 1963 was a harbinger of change in American policy, as proponents of the older, more restrictive view (the less trade the better) lost ground to those favoring selective relaxations on trade with particular Communist countries in order to multiply fissions in the Eastern bloc. NATO provides a good forum for the exchange of views on this subject but a poor agency for implementing the increasingly resented American economic boycott proposals. United States pressure for such action provides the other allies with a convenient way to prove they are independent of the giant.

The United States will no doubt continue to pay some price for its pluralistic political organization in the form of a continued pursuit of often incompatible trade and defense policies; given the domestic political influences of various special interests, this is inevitable, as it would be for any other state. It is a question, however, whether the price of pluralism cannot be brought down—particularly as international organizations such as NATO help to make clear the broader interest the pursuit of which is jeopardized by government action that promotes the narrower interest.

TIMING AND STYLE. The way in which the United States has taken decisions affecting NATO sometimes has been as important in its consequences for the unity of the organization as has been the substance of the decisions. Although American utterances of the type exemplified by Secretary Dulles' famous threat in the mid-1950s about an "agonizing reappraisal" have been less noticeable in later years, a similar patronizing and irritating attitude sometimes lurks close to the surface. American officials on occasion say, for example, that United States military decisions will "so far as possible" take the alliance into account.[166] With such an example before them, the French under President de Gaulle could find some justification for their far more disunifying moves prior to actual withdrawal.

One action affecting the alliance directly was very awkwardly handled, namely, the nomination of the officer to succeed General Norstad as SACEUR. Only General Lemnitzer's own exceptional qualities and his previous position as the highest-ranking United States military officer overcame the obvious displeasure of some of the allies at the heavy-

---

[166] As, for example, Under Secretary of Defense Gilpatric said of the proposed thinning out of United States forces in Europe in October, 1963.

handed procedure followed. Clearly the decision had been made in Washington without the appropriate inquiry as to the other allies' views, views which were unlikely to be adverse anyway.[167] On other occasions the United States has seemed more concerned with appearing to share power and to defer to its allies' wishes than has in fact been the case. The MLF proposal and the preceding offers of IRBMs to individual allies are illustrations. (See the first section of this chapter.) Thus Europeans were told in very compelling terms that the initiative was theirs regarding a multilateral deterrent; they could and did take this and other such declarations with a grain of salt.

More disintegrating to the morale of the alliance is the attitude of omniscience which some Europeans think they observe among Americans, particularly in the field of strategy.[168] This may be all the more galling because of the information advantage which American negotiators, with access to the tremendous fact-gathering apparatus of the United States, often enjoy. Tact in intra-alliance negotiations may be especially necessary if the allies are not to resent the restraints which lack of information imposes on them. The certainty among important American officials that they were right, often reinforced by their preoccupation with political struggles within their own government, has led to clumsy behavior towards allies whose support is important for the alliance.

As an example of insensitivity and ill-timing, one need only mention the sequence of Skybolt cancellation, Nassau Conference, and De Gaulle's absolute refusal to accept the role assigned to him at Nassau by the untrustworthy "Anglo-Saxons." Other examples are the abrupt way in which the United States announced the closing of certain logistical and communications bases in France in September, 1963 and the handling of the Big Lift operation during the same fall.[169] The unprece-

---

[167] In order to move General Maxwell Taylor from the position of President's Military Adviser to that of Chairman of the Joint Chiefs of Staff the current holder of that post was suddenly proposed for the Supreme Commander's position —before the occupant of that office was slated to retire. The other members of NATO could not conceal the fact that they had not been consulted. On this action, see *New York Times,* July 26, 1962.

[168] Cf. Bernard Brodie, "What Price Conventional Capabilities in Europe?", *Reporter,* May 23, 1963, p. 33, regarding the Americans' unwillingness to take challenges seriously; and Henry Kissinger's complaint that except for England the Americans have dealt too long with others "psychotherapeutically" ["The Unsolved Problems of European Defense," *Foreign Affairs,* July, 1962, p. 541].

[169] On closing the French bases, see *New York Times,* September 29, 1963, and *Economist,* October 5, 1963. The French regarded the United States negotiations with Germany, to which the bases were moved, as double-dealing and

dented detail deliberately published about the German-American armaments collaboration in November, 1964 was obviously and inappropri-
ately directed at President de Gaulle's demand that the Germans review
their willingness to join the MLF. This heavy-handed tactic failed.[170] It
was probably an expensive use of the alliance when President Johnson
sought to deter Turkish military action in Cyprus in June, 1964 by writing to President Inönü that, inter alia, Turkey could not expect automatic NATO support if the Russians attacked Turkey as a result of the
latter's action against Cyprus.[171]

Whatever the American shortcomings in implementing more fully the
possibilities inherent in balanced, collective forces, combined action,
coordination, and community maintenance, the United States has had a
difficult choice. Vigorous and self-confident leadership sometimes
drowns out other members' proposals or objections and reduces the
chance for constructive tension within NATO. The other members are
inured to the American penchant for action, any action so long as it involves movement.[172] To have both a thick skin and a delicate touch
may be hard for the leading power in an alliance, but it is essential for
effective leadership.

United States policy towards NATO affairs paradoxically has shown
both steady persistence in pursuing unpopular causes and rapid and confusing twists of policy, as exemplified in the various forms of the MLF
proposal. Secretary Rusk told the Jackson Committee on December 11,
1963 that some actions appear "verbally inconsistent" because the
situations themselves are contradictory." [173] This may help to account
for inconsistencies in almost simultaneous official statements on matters
relating to NATO. Another reason, to be examined in the following
chapters, may be found in the organizations that make these decisions.

---

objected to the Americans' talking to Germans about "subleasing" bases on French
soil.

[170] *New York Times,* November 12 and 15, 1964; *Newsweek,* November 23,
1964; *Washington Post,* November 18, 1964; *Wall Street Journal,* November 16,
1964.

[171] *New York Times,* January 14 and 16, 1966.

[172] For example, the United States proposal for a test ship to try out the feasibility
of the MLF, which President Kennedy was reported to favor "as a means of
demonstrating some action" [*New York Times,* October 5, 1963].

[173] Jackson Committee II, *Hearings,* Part VI, p. 390. A conspicuous example
in the 1960s was the effort to redress the balance of payments problem and
satisfy the desire for allied participation in the development of military equipment to strengthen NATO.

CHAPTER SEVEN

NATO AND AMERICAN DECISION PROCESSES: THE EXECUTIVE BRANCH

IN CHAPTERS V AND VI NATO qua NATO seldom appears as either subject or object of a decision made by United States officials. If it did, NATO might figure more prominently in the competition among Washington's "quasi-sovereignties" to determine in any given case who speaks for the American government. The end products of the processes of competition and consensus-building are decisions and actions of the government as a whole, but in practice this is not as clear as it seems. Executive agencies form the executive branch. They do not form a unity; in a sense there is no such thing as *the* executive branch, but only a federation of agencies which seldom all agree upon any subject. Thus when Dean Acheson advises, as a "first step" towards NATO grand strategy, that the United States develop a plan to be proposed to NATO, "upon which the entire executive branch, civilian and military, is united," the counsel is utopian.[1]

It has often been easier to get agreement in NATO than in Washington. Coordination is a less utopian objective than unity; but Max Beloff's analysis of the problem of coordination in England—an analysis in which the question, whether specific departments carry on their exter-

---

[1] "The Practice of Partnership," *Foreign Affairs*, January, 1963, p. 252. Properly to acknowledge his sophistication we should note Mr. Acheson's remarks before the Jackson Committee in April, 1966. He said, "Government itself is an alliance," and added that determining its position "depends on what part of the dinosaur you tap" [*New York Times*, April 28, 1966].

nal relations "in line with general policies of the Government," was posed—leads to no prescription directly applicable to American problems.[2] Closer to the schizophrenic realities was a journalist who wrote that "the United States was prevented by law" from taking a particular action.[3] That the United States government is a composite of quasi-sovereignties is particularly clear in the case of decisions relevant to, but often not explicitly related to, NATO.

THE PRESIDENCY

Above and apart from the other executive branch participants in the American decision process is the group which constitutes "the Presidency." This includes the man in the White House and, to some extent, those in the Executive Office of the President, who number about two thousand employees, plus the secret thousands of the Central Intelligence Agency. In its impact on the responsibilities and functioning of the Presidency NATO exemplifies an historical trend dating back to the end of the nineteenth century. As a result of the country's greater involvement in foreign affairs, a trend accelerated since World War II by the exigencies of the nuclear age, executive power has expanded both absolutely and relative to legislative power. This centripetal pull of decision-making towards the White House in the sphere occupied by NATO is not merely due to the fact that NATO affairs are foreign affairs but also to the fact that they usually concern more than one department of the United States government. Even when President Eisenhower was shielded from immediate contact with other kinds of policy-making, Secretary Dulles dealt directly with him on matters relating to NATO. The office of the President's Assistant on National Security Affairs, formally established only in 1953, has also served to keep the Presidency close to decisions affecting and affected by NATO.

Not only do American officials look to the President and the Presidency for ultimate guidance regarding matters which affect NATO; so do many officials of the other NATO countries and in the Secretariat. Thus few except Frenchmen regarded President Kennedy's promotion of a "Grand Design" as an act of supererogation.

Because of NATO the President has special responsibilities. It is for

[2] *New Dimensions in Foreign Policy* (London: George Allen and Unwin, Ltd., 1961), p. 162.
[3] *New York Times,* November 6, 1963.

him to nominate SACEUR; but even more important, his is the dreadful responsibility for "pressing the button" of nuclear war in defense of the NATO area. He has had other duties relating to NATO, such as making a "determination" for projects to be undertaken in the Mutual Weapons Development Program and approving cooperative nuclear agreements with particular members.

Other Presidential functions of immediate concern to NATO derive from his constitutional roles. The alliance depends upon him as Commander-in-Chief of the United States defense forces to fulfill the constantly reiterated promise that American troops remain in Europe. As spokesman for the United States in foreign affairs, each President in turn has pledged general support to NATO at the beginning of his term of office, assurance which is vital to the existence of NATO. The President is also, by virtue of his constitutional position, able to make other pledges, such as that arms control negotiations with the Soviet Union shall be carried on in close consultation with NATO. When United States military aid was important to most NATO members (and even when it was reduced to providing "modern" weapons and more comprehensive aid only to Greece and Turkey), the President's primary responsibility for the budget came into play. At least as significant for NATO has been the President's general responsibility for laying down the main lines of United States defense policy and of defense expenditures. The adoption of the New Look policy, the later reemphasis on strong conventional warfare capability, and the stress on the Polaris-armed nuclear submarine are three examples of the exercise of this general responsibility. The President's duty to guide the economy affected NATO when President Eisenhower sponsored the "long haul" concept for defense expenditures and when he and his successors took steps to meet the balance of payments problem.

NATO is heavily dependent on the President of the United States. Does it then matter to its members who is elected to this office? The policies of American Presidents, and especially their defense policies, have differed markedly in ways that affect NATO; but at no time have changes of administration posed a major danger for the alliance. So far as support for NATO is concerned, there has been a clear continuity from one administration to the next; and the party platforms of both national parties have in recent elections contained favorable references to NATO. On the other hand, European "fears of the worst" regarding the outcome of presidential elections may somewhat limit the President's power to lead the whole alliance.[4] In any case, in the heat of a presidential campaign as one administration draws to a close, the president may have neither the wish nor the power to conclude agreements which would bind his successor on a variety of matters of interest to other NATO members.

While Europeans' fears regarding Presidential elections have so far proved groundless, their estimate that a new President means new policies of great significance for NATO has been repeatedly confirmed. The changing fortunes of General Maxwell Taylor in his successive roles as Army Chief of Staff by appointment of President Eisenhower, as informed critic of the Eisenhower military policies with which he disagreed, as personal military adviser to President Kennedy and later, as Chairman of the Joint Chiefs of Staff under him, and then in 1964–65 as President Johnson's Ambassador to South Vietnam symbolized doctrinal changes that have greatly affected defense policy and therefore NATO too. With changes in the Chief Executive, the administration of security policy has also altered noticeably as a result of differences in the type of high-echelon officials involved. Furthermore, Presidential election campaigns have tended to create a hiatus in negotiations of indirect importance to NATO, as in the case of negotiations about the EDC early in the 1950s and about arms control later in that decade.[5]

Such are the political functions and constitutional responsibilities of the President in matters relating to NATO. He has not, however, always possessed the power to meet those responsibilities. Here lies part of the explanation for the gap between declaratory policy and action policy noted in preceding chapters. To protect his own preeminent political position the President has been obliged to gain the support of many other

[4] Governor Rockefeller as Presidential aspirant and Senator Goldwater as Republican nominee both advanced proposals to "strengthen NATO" in the 1964 campaign. Their introduction of NATO issues into the campaign apparently did not reassure Europeans that the United States was indeed a unity on foreign policy questions. For example, the Republican platform contained such items as "this Administration has created discord and distrust by failing to develop a nuclear policy for NATO." The Democratic Platform stated, inter alia, "Control and use of nuclear weapons must remain solely with the highest elected official in the country," a view disputed by Senator Goldwater so far as tactical nuclear weapons were concerned.

[5] For early examples see Dean Acheson, *Sketches from Life* (New York: Harper and Brothers, 1959), pp. 53–56, and Harry S Truman, *Memoirs* (Garden City: Doubleday and Company, 1956), vol. II, p. 260.

decision-making groups, official as well as unofficial, and such bargains as he may find it necessary to make to win that support seldom are made with NATO's interest as his primary concern. Thus pressures by him on NATO allies to boycott Cuba were intimately related to Congress' reluctance to provide funds he had requested for the Alliance for Progress. Some of the President's public speeches have not been intended simply to teach the American public and to communicate assurance to NATO allies and warnings to NATO foes; they have also been directed towards administrative subordinates, who have sometimes been insensitive to pleas for implementing established policy. Where the subordinates have not been in accord, they have on occasion followed a different path when they doubted the President's will or capacity to force the issue.

The President's most urgent efforts to promote a multitude of foreign and domestic interests have rarely been directly related to NATO's requirements.[6] Postponable actions have tended to lose out, especially since the President's prestige abroad has at any given moment been less immediately useful to him than an unimpaired domestic political position. Despite a growing need, the administration put off a reappraisal of the United States role in NATO until it was forced to action by De Gaulle's rude blasts at the beginning of 1963, by which time much damage had already been done. In some critical choices in earlier years the Presidency had taken insufficient account of their relevance to NATO, despite general acceptance of the idea that before the President urged a particular action in one sphere he should be made aware of its impact on other spheres of action. The New Look policy of the first Eisenhower years is an example of a policy with undesired by-products for NATO. Despite journalists' perennial claims that NATO was in crisis no single incident concerning NATO so acute as to preempt the President's attention occurred for many years. Even De Gaulle's January, 1963 action against the British ostensibly concerned only the EEC. Such action-forcing processes as the annual cycle of budget-making seldom involved NATO directly; and when they did so indirectly, as in the case of the cancellation of Skybolt, the impact on the alliance had lower priority than other considerations.

[6] A rare case in which a President's advisory committee gave major attention to NATO was the Draper Committee dealing with military aid [President's Committee to Study the U.S. Military Assistance Program, *Composite Report*, 2 vols. (Washington, 1959)]. But President Eisenhower did not directly follow its recommendations in his next budgetary appeal to Congress [House of Representatives Committee on Appropriations, *Hearings, Mutual Security Appropriations for 1961*, 86th Cong., 2nd sess. (1960), p. 2326].

The President needs, says Richard Neustadt, to reach down into the administration for details of approaching situations important to his powers of choice. And there is a tug-of-war between his own free-wheeling requirements and the orderly procedures of the middle-level administrators.[7] In this process NATO concerns, such as the MLF proposals, have tended to get one-sided treatment rather than a fully balanced consideration. The case of the MLF also illustrates the possibilities open to the President for bringing in foreign pressures to modify resistance within his own government. Here we see an interdependence between NATO and the President which suggests that this organization is an additional tool for consolidating his position on an issue. But where NATO has not been at the focus of concern, as it was not during the Cuba crisis of 1962, its members have found themselves on a par with Congress. In that case, they were informed promptly but only after the critical decisions had been made.

What about the other side of "consultation"—when foreign governments are consulting the United States? This aspect of NATO can be important to the President in making decisions where time is of less significance. Access to knowledge of their proposed actions could come through the North Atlantic Council, where fourteen nations face the United States and each other.[8] NATO's value as an informational resource depends partly upon the Presidency's not being hard of hearing, but also upon there being no risk that the United States might appear indecisive when asking allies' opinions. Usually the President seeks more direct communication, either through the American ambassadors in the capitals of the NATO countries or through his own itinerant representatives. Reliance on the ad hoc envoy is regarded as a blight by the regular ambassadors to allied capitals, as well as by the United States ambassadors to NATO itself. Among other disadvantages, the special negotiators, it is claimed, are in no position to develop the frank relationships which characterize the work of the Permanent Representatives to the

[7] Senate Committee on Government Operations, Subcommittee on National Security Staffing and Operations, 88th Cong., 1st sess. (1963) (hereafter referred to as Jackson Committee II), *Staff Report, Administration of National Security—Basic Issues,* pp. 8–9.

[8] An example of the administrative usefulness of NATO during the period of extensive military aid to Europe was the habit of the American defense planners to depend upon the Standing Group's determination of need rather than, as in the case of other countries, the Joint Chiefs' own estimates [Senate Special Committee to Study the Foreign Aid Program, *The Military Assistance Program of the United States: Two Studies and a Report,* Committee Print, 85th Cong., 1st sess. (1957), p. 101].

North Atlantic Council. This frankness is also missing in direct encounters between heads of state. Furthermore, itinerant negotiators appearing at irregular and unpredictable intervals confuse those allies singled out for special attention.

Timely communication of relevant details, securing consensus, and expediting decisions of the President are related to that official's administrative methods. Eisenhower's administration relied heavily on the National Security Council and other formally constituted committees with responsibility for the general security policy of the United States rather than for NATO specifically. During this period when the use of committees was common, individuals in other NATO countries complained about the lack of leadership in the alliance. In the interest of consensus, clearly defined responsibility fell by the way.

President Kennedy abruptly altered the methods within the Presidency. The European allies then got a taste of forceful leadership and action, which in many cases proved too strong for them.[9] If vigorous American leadership meant less systematic consulting within the United States government, it also meant that sometimes American policy congealed before NATO allies had had time to speak. Thus United States policy often appeared unilateral, however lofty and multilateral the "Grand Design" on which it was said to be based. The President's Assistant for National Security Affairs became even more important in the decision-making process than his Eisenhower predecessor. Expedition was often at the expense of the sensitivities of key allies.

The Bureau of the Budget leaves few records that show its real influence from one administration to another. Certainly during the Eisenhower administration it seems to have had the initiative in setting overall limitations for defense spending, and always it has some influence over all spending, of which defense spending is most significant for NATO.[10]

[9] Richard Neustadt's observation that the traditional autonomy of field commanders disappears with the President's new need to control details has special relevance to his relationship to NATO [see Jackson Committee II, *Hearings*, Part I, p. 77].

[10] See Richard P. Stebbins, *The United States in World Affairs, 1959* (New York: Random House, 1960), p. 68, and Charles H. Donnelly, *United States Defense Policies in 1959*, House Doc. No. 432, 86th Cong., 2nd sess. (1960), pp. 26 and 56–57. During the Eisenhower administration it was customary for an overall limitation on defense expenditures to be set for a long period. See testimony of Paul Nitze in Senate Committee on Government Operations, Subcommittee on National Policy Machinery, 86th Cong., 2nd sess. (1960) (hereafter referred to as Jackson Committee I), *Hearings*, Part VI, p. 872 and Part VII, p. 9, in which he reported that in the previous administration other officials were consulted by the Bureau of the Budget at the beginning of the process.

The activities of the Bureau of the Budget have, however, been hard to disentangle from those of budget-cutters in the regular departments with whom Budget Bureau officials work closely at various levels.[11]

When President Kennedy downgraded the National Security Council by convening it less regularly and less frequently, he had to develop other devices for achieving the ends it had served. The need remained for focus, coordination, and orderly presentation of alternatives in deciding issues in which more than one department had a legitimate concern; these included issues affecting NATO. One device was the ad hoc committee that specialized in a particular problem and dissolved at completion of its work; a good example was the Berlin Task Force, the nature of whose duties required that it concern itself with NATO.[12]

Whatever the device, the difficulties in getting consensus of any kind among those with a legitimate concern—who can be numerous in NATO-related issues—militates against reconsideration if a policy proves outdated or otherwise ineffective. Thus proposals for the MLF existed side by side with appeals for greater stress on conventional warfare capability for NATO; in the Eisenhower administration, the nuclear strategy for NATO remained out of step with changes in technology and power partly because those who could initiate a new policy were unwilling to disturb the existing consensus. The "tortured collective effort" decried by George Kennan (describing United States foreign-policy making in general) was too painful for repetition.[13] The same obstacles stand in the way of those who see possibilities for fruitful alliance cooperation not yet tried. Such efforts usually require action by more than

---

For the practice during the McNamara regime, see his statement, House of Representatives Committee on Armed Services, *Hearings on Military Posture,* 87th Cong., 2nd sess. (1962), pp. 3163 and 3193.

[11] A 1952 reorganization of the Bureau of the Budget added, among others, two new program divisions, "Military" and "International." On some aspects of the role of the Bureau as they applied especially to security policy and foreign policy, see Arthur Smithies, *The Budgetary Process in the United States* (New York: McGraw-Hill Book Co., 1955), pp. 44, 80, 240 and 243; House of Representatives Committee on Appropriations, Subcommittee, *Hearings, Department of Defense Appropriations for 1957,* 84th Cong., 2nd sess. (1956), pp. 546–47; Senate Committee on Appropriations, *Hearings, Department of State . . . Appropriations for 1957,* 84th Cong., 2nd sess. (1956), pp. 428 and 434 ff., and reply to Senator Jackson by McGeorge Bundy in September, 1961, reprinted in *Foreign Service Journal,* May, 1962, pp. 42–45.

[12] For some other coordinating devices, most of them informal, see testimony of Secretary Rusk, Jackson Committee II, *Hearings,* Part VI, pp. 395–96.

[13] For a representative sample of Kennan's views on this subject, see "America's Administrative Response to its World Problems," *Daedalus,* vol. 87, No. 2, 1958, reprinted in Jackson Committee I, *Selected Materials,* pp. 225–39.

one agency, and one or more may hold back. The reluctant agency then requires a push from the President, but what power does he have? The experience of the Mutual Weapons Development Program suggests that in the field of interallied cooperation the public to whom the President might appeal for support either does not exist or is relatively uninfluential. If the President acts without consulting some legitimately concerned officials, as apparently occurred in the Nassau case, there are likely to be subsequent rapid shifts of the government's position. Defects in the policy consensus show up promptly, and late precinct returns may alter the outcome.

DEPARTMENT OF STATE

Assessing the impact of NATO on the functioning of the Department of State and the impact of the Department's processes on NATO, we find again that NATO is only one of the elements which have together changed the foreign policy environment in which the Department must operate. (Other foreign offices have had to cope with some of the same changes in environment.) The distinction between "domestic" and "foreign" policy has grown more obscure. "Foreign" policy concerns of the United States have expanded with the increasing interest of other governmental agencies whose concern with a foreign policy question most often flows from more immediate domestic concerns. Huge programs, calling for foreign operations involving foreign aid, propaganda, and secret intelligence have an uneasy relationship with a department traditionally without "operations." Multilateral diplomacy and regional groupings, of which NATO is only the most prominent example, have become common. The relationship between science and policy has been recognized, somewhat belatedly, in the Department of State. Military and political affairs are intermingled, particularly in the NATO field.

In responding to these changes the Department has greatly expanded. Its larger size and greater complexity of organization complicate the tasks of those who seek to advance particular foreign policy interests. Similarly, the response to new needs through the frequent reorganization of the Department and of its relationship with other agencies has only intermittently helped make NATO more effective.[14]

[14] For a history of "Organizational Reform in the Department of State and the Foreign Service," see William Gerber in Stephen D. Kertesz (ed.), *American Diplomacy in a New Era* (Notre Dame: University of Notre Dame Press, 1961), pp. 386–418.

Some characteristics of the Department of State which affect NATO, often adversely, long antedate the North Atlantic Treaty. The Department has practically no domestic constituency smaller than the whole nation, a factor of special importance in Congressional relations. Furthermore, instead of seeming to represent any particular element of American life, to its critics it often seems that "the State Department represents foreigners." In the case of NATO this claim is not entirely without substance. The Department of State, unlike Defense and Agriculture, spends no money to speak of in the United States. This accounts in part for its domestic political weakness. Its product is intangible and unweighable, and the criteria for its success are almost purely subjective. It does its work most effectively out of the glare of publicity, a chance rarely afforded it. Like the Department of Defense, it depends heavily upon a professional corps with strong traditions, the Foreign Service. Most of its personnel are generalists, not specialists in anything except international politics and negotiation, fields others seldom recognize as requiring expertise.

The primacy of the State Department in foreign affairs is frequently and explicitly acknowledged by other executive leaders. The extent to which the Department in fact asserts its primacy is significant to NATO, for it is this Department which is politically responsible for NATO affairs. Unlike the Department of Defense, the Department of State lacks a visible "operation" connected with NATO. State is, in fact, overshadowed by Defense, with which it must collaborate closely. To balance this weight the Department of State has the power implicit in being "at the end of the cables."

Secretary of State Acheson, however initially reluctant to respond to Pentagon pressure for German rearmament, was eventually persuaded of the need to support the Pentagon on this issue. He did, however, couple his support with the assertion of a political requirement for negotiating with NATO allies over German rearmament. He sought the creation of an integrated NATO military command for Europe, a command which came into being several years before there was any significant German rearmament.[15] Secretary Acheson also exercised his authority, along with his two colleagues from Defense and Treasury, in working out the

[15] See Laurence W. Martin, "The American Decision to Rearm Germany" in Harold Stein (ed.), *American Civil-Military Decisions* (Birmingham: University of Alabama Press, 1963), pp. 646–54; Dean Acheson, *Sketches From Life* (New York: Harper and Brothers, 1959), pp. 41–43.

Lisbon arrangements; thus he illustrated what Dean Rusk later observed, that "power gravitates to those who are willing to make decisions and live with the results. . . ." [16] Such individuals are at least as likely to turn up in the White House staff as in the Department of State. But the latter has the steadiness and the staff capable of considering all aspects of a foreign policy problem; as a result, its actions are less likely to confuse allies.

The Secretary of State occupies an anomalous position as the right-hand man of the President; he is supposed to keep all the United States agencies in line so far as foreign relations are concerned, but he has no substantial domestic political leverage.[17] Thus, as spokesman for NATO interests he cannot always prevail, however great his formal authority; the most he can do is to assure that these interests get expressed when all factors of a decision are examined. During the Eisenhower period of committee operations, the Department might have lost a good deal of its primacy, including the coordinating responsibility for NATO affairs, had it not been for the strong personal leadership of Secretary of State Dulles. Even he, however, failed to exercise his full authority in important respects. Mr. Dulles' lack of knowledge of or interest in defense decisions taken in the 1950s (apart from his very general agreement with New Look military policies and his strong affirmation of "massive retaliation") left decisions with important foreign policy consequences to be made in the Defense and Treasury Departments.[18]

President Kennedy dismantled some of the elaborate committee structure of the previous administration. He made sparing use of the National Security Council and let it be known that he wanted no large

[16] "A Fresh Look at the Formulation of Foreign Policy," *Department of State Bulletin,* March 20, 1961, reprinted in Jackson Committee II, *Selected Papers,* p. 28.

[17] "The responsibilities of the Secretary are wider than those of his Department" [Jackson Committee II, *Basic Issues,* p. 7]. See Paul Nitze's testimony in Jackson Committee I, *Hearings,* Part VI, p. 857, for a good summary of the responsibilities of the Secretary of State, and also American Assembly (Don K. Price, ed.), *The Secretary of State* (Englewood Cliffs: Prentice-Hall, 1960).

[18] See Henry M. Jackson, "Organizing for Survival," *Foreign Affairs,* April, 1960, p. 451. According to General Maxwell Taylor, when Secretary Dulles finally changed his mind about a single strategy, he was only half successful in weaning Department of Defense officials away from it [*The Uncertain Trumpet* (New York: Harper and Brothers, 1960), pp. 55, 57 and 65]. However, he did play a major role in preventing Defense officials from redeploying American troops out of Europe [Glenn H. Snyder, "The 'New Look' of 1953," in Warner R. Schilling, Paul Y. Hammond, and Glenn H. Snyder, *Strategy, Politics, and Defense Budgets* (New York: Columbia University Press, 1962), p. 436].

organization between himself and the Secretary of State. This did not mean that the Secretary immediately assumed the full coordinating responsibility which had formally been his all the time. Secretary Rusk had no more domestic political leverage than his predecessors. The President himself did a good deal of the coordinating through ad hoc arrangements and through his Special Assistant for National Security Affairs. At one critical juncture for NATO affairs, in the Nassau meeting, at which important decisions were taken, the Secretary did not even participate; he was returning (with a stop-over in Ireland) from a ministerial-level North Atlantic Council meeting. (Like foreign ministries in many other governments, the Department of State was left to clear up the disarray created by the precipitate actions of those impatient with careful staff work.)

Reflecting on his experience as SACEUR, General Norstad complained that too often "too many people become involved in this process of policy formulation and they bring in too many preconceived ideas. . . . Confusion results. . . . Policy . . . must be established at the top. . . . In the foreign field . . . the particular responsibility belongs to the Secretary of State . . . and to his associates. . . . Perhaps we should ask ourselves whether our practice really faithfully reflects this conclusion." [19] The principle is easier to establish than the practice. Thus, although Secretaries Rusk and McNamara regularly affirmed their very close cooperation and although Secretary McNamara usually deferred to the Secretary of State on "large questions" such as reforms in the structure of NATO, he regularly took the lead in "small questions" in the field of operations, such as missile withdrawals.

Below the cabinet level, the record of State-Defense cooperation is mixed, but is improving. An area important to NATO in which the Department of State is authorized to exercise general supervision is military aid. Indeed this Department took the initiative in establishing the mutual security program; its special responsibility has been to examine aid programs from the point of view of United States foreign policy. The military officers assigned to work out the programs and implement them frequently had a narrower view of the goals of military aid than did the State Department officials who were to approve programs for particular countries. In the 1960s, however, teamwork seems to be the rule, at least so far as one can judge from testimony before Congressional com-

[19] Jackson Committee II, *Hearings,* Part I, p. 12.

mittees.[20] NATO (in reality SHAPE) has played a role in the process. The SHAPE staff worked out requirements upon which the military aid program for Allied Command Europe was based, and SACEUR has regularly appeared before Congressional committees to explain and support that program.

In the 1950s the concentration in Paris of both NATO and international organizations to promote European economic cooperation, as well as the then-existing need to bring together interallied negotiations regarding American military aid and programming of that aid, brought about the organization of the United States Mission to Regional Organizations (USRO). This unusual type of representation abroad, in which State and Defense (and the Treasury also) are involved, includes missions serving at NATO and the OECD, successor to the OEEC. Reports from USRO, as from all other United States missions abroad, are addressed to the Secretary of State; and it is through the Department of State that United States positions are transmitted to USRO, however much or little the instructions may be drafted jointly with the Treasury and Defense Departments.[21]

The Department of State has another important NATO-related responsibility: to prepare for the regular ministerial meetings of the North Atlantic Council (which are attended by the Secretaries of State, Defense, and the Treasury). As with other international conferences whose subject matter cuts across several departments, the Department of State regularly takes the lead in preparing coordinated position papers for these semiannual meetings.[22]

An incidental effect of the increase in interdepartmental collaboration in fields such as NATO occupies is to enhance the role of the Under

[20] Secretary Rusk told the Senate Committee on Appropriations in August, 1961, that the "critical center" for total United States policy regarding a country was the Assistant Secretary of the regional bureau, but that there were almost daily contacts between appropriate officials in the Department of State and the Department of Defense in this field of activity [*Hearings, Foreign Assistance Appropriations for 1962*, 87th Cong., 1st sess. (1961), p. 104].

[21] Michael H. Cardozo, *Diplomats in International Cooperation: Stepchildren of the Foreign Service* (Ithaca: Cornell University Press, 1962), p. 76. The Defense Representative in USRO (DEFREPNAMA) reports both to the Secretary of State and to the Secretary of Defense.

[22] According to a member of the Policy Planning Council describing procedure in the 1950s, staff experts prepared positions on issues, often aided by members of the Department of Defense, which were then circulated within interested agencies. Prior to his departure for the meeting, the Secretary of State met with staff members to discuss these papers and resolve problems in doubt. On the basis of these meetings he revised or approved the papers and took major decisions to the President [Jackson Committee I, *Selected Materials*, p. 103].

Secretaries of State, who lighten the burden upon the Secretary of State.[23] Under Secretary Ball has been a frequent visitor to NATO headquarters in Paris and to other European capitals, pressing United States positions on its allies and co-members of international economic organizations. United States-NATO relations also exemplify the general trend toward greater decision-making in Washington and less in the missions abroad, a trend deplored by those who think more decisions could be taken promptly and effectively in the country missions. Indeed the Permanent Representative to NATO, although styled an ambassador, has even less scope for independent action than the many ambassadors about whom it has been said that ". . . 'Washington clearance' often means that a junior officer in Washington is second-guessing a senior officer in the field—and second-guessing him on matters the latter is better qualified to decide than an equally experienced officer in Washington." [24]

Innovations in the structure of the Department of State to permit effective American participation in international organizations have been difficult to fit into its traditional administrative arrangement; for the line (operating) bureaus, as opposed to the staff bureaus, are based mainly on geography.[25] The United Nations as a multifunctional universal organization presented such complexities that from the beginning there has been a special unit in the Department of State concerned with its affairs; for many years this has been headed by an Assistant Secretary of State. The name and organization of this unit have changed over the years (its present name is the Bureau of International Organization Affairs); it has had certain difficulties in becoming accepted.[26] NATO is confined to one region and to only the politico-military function; and the unit created in 1962 to deal with its affairs, the Office of Atlantic

[23] See Jackson Committee II, *Basic Issues,* p. 4.

[24] *Ibid.,* p. 14. This problem is common throughout the administration of foreign affairs.

[25] The problems of adapting have been further complicated when foreign aid questions were combined with those relating to NATO and OEEC operations [Lincoln Gordon, "The Development of United States Representation Overseas," in American Assembly, *The Representation of the United States Abroad* (first ed., New York: The American Assembly, 1956), pp. 29–36].

[26] Thus Lincoln Bloomfield referred to its position as "servant of policy directives not its own," described the "internal brokerage function," where multilateral diplomacy had to be practiced two ways, and observed the tendency to "cross-sterilization of ideas" ["United States Participation in the United Nations," in Stephen D. Kertesz (ed.), *op. cit.,* pp. 489–90]. Illustrative of the struggles this Bureau has to wage against the geographical organizations is the long period in which its preference for IAEA safeguards on United States-arranged nuclear

Political-Military Affairs, is far more modest in size and design than the bureau dealing with United Nations activities. The political-military office and the Office of Atlantic Political-Economic Affairs function under a Deputy Assistant Secretary for Atlantic Community Affairs in the Bureau of European Affairs. (NATO questions were formerly dealt with by the Office of Regional Affairs in the same bureau.) This new political-military office faces difficulties similar to those raised by the United Nations; like the Bureau of International Organization Affairs, this small office is neither quite "staff" nor quite "operating." Unlike the Bureau, the Office of Atlantic Political-Military Affairs cannot look to its own special advisers situated within the other bureaus, advisers who would provide a NATO "presence."[27] The Office of Atlantic Political-Military Affairs

provides the primary organizational support in the Department of State for U.S. participation in the North Atlantic Treaty Organization. The complex organizational structure of NATO and the intimate interrelations of political and military-strategic problems that characterize its functioning make RPM [Office of Atlantic Political-Military Affairs] an extremely busy and important office. The staff of RPM has a close working relationship with G/PM [Office of Deputy Assistant Secretary of State for Politico-Military Affairs].[28]

This official description did not mention the handicaps of the Office flowing from its newness, lack of continuity in personnel, and unconventional function.

---

supplies to other countries could not prevail over the geographical bureaus' concern for the individual recipients within their domain [John W. Finney in the *New York Times,* March 23, 1964].

[27] At various times the Bureau of International Organization Affairs has had some minor responsibilities or service functions related to NATO, as when it presented the NATO science program to Congressional committees, along with a number of other somewhat disparate science programs [Senate Committee on Foreign Relations, *Hearings, Foreign Assistance Act of 1962,* 87th Cong., 2nd sess. (1962), p. 293]. A member of the forerunner of this bureau informed a Congressional committee in January, 1952 that one of its new duties was to ensure that the United States position in NATO was consistent with the United Nations Charter [House of Representatives Committee on Appropriations, *Hearings, State . . . Appropriations for 1953,* 82nd Cong., 2nd sess. (1952), p. 103].

Treatment of OAS matters is somewhat similar to that used for NATO matters; such questions are handled within the Bureau of Inter-American Affairs [Robert E. Elder, *The Policy Machine: The Department of State and American Foreign Policy* (Syracuse: Syracuse University Press, 1960), pp. 79–80].

[28] "Memorandum on the Department of State's Politico-Military Organization and Staffing," Jackson Committee II, *Staff Reports and Hearings,* p. 414. Thus some NATO problems are also considered by the staff of the Deputy Assistant Secretary of State for Politico-Military Affairs.

Both the offices dealing with Atlantic affairs and the Bureau of International Organization Affairs probably were considered part of the elaborate apparatus in the Department of State to which Secretary Rusk referred when he called "layering" a prime organizational problem.[29] If the responsible country desk officers were to be brought higher up in the organization and closer to the major decision levels as he proposed, might this not be done at the expense of this other type of agency, which in a sense does intervene? Actually, in their establishment, the two Atlantic affairs offices were buried fairly deep in the formal hierarchy, although the Deputy Assistant Secretary for Atlantic Community Affairs has been able to exert influence disproportionate to his position in that hierarchy. (Department of State organization for OECD affairs poses similar problems.)

The very complexity of the problems presented by NATO has facilitated an individual specialist's having access to the Secretary of State. Meanwhile, if there are differences of opinion in the Bureau of European Affairs between the Atlantic affairs offices and the country desks, they are likely to go to the Assistant Secretary for settlement, or even further up. Such controversies may be infrequent, but they can occur. For example, if one of the Atlantic affairs officers detected, in a cable ostensibly dealing with another problem, a matter concerning NATO, he might use the occasion to have the Department's position clarified so as to resolve potential differences. As the successive bursts of United States pressure for the MLF illustrated, a few dedicated partisans of a proposal may become very influential on a single policy front, regardless of their places in the formal hierarchy.

After some preliminary shifts and the discomfort expected in fitting new organizations in with old ones, USRO, the "theater-command" type of mission, has settled down into a multiagency embassy headed by the United States Permanent Representatives to NATO.[30] USRO has been at the Porte Dauphine, the headquarters of other members' delegations to NATO and to the economic organizations and the civilian headquarters of NATO. This permitted personnel from one member country to have easy contact with those of another. USRO has a political, a military, and

[29] Jackson Committee II, *Hearings*, Part VI, p. 398.
[30] See Lincoln Gordon, "The Coordination of Overseas Representation," in American Assembly, *The Representation of the United States Abroad*, rev. ed., Vincent M. Barnett, Jr., editor (New York: Frederick A. Praeger, 1965), at pp. 226 and 239–43, and Ben T. Moore, "American Representation to International

an economic section, the last being headed by an official who is also ambassador to OECD.[31] Thus coordination of policies and procedures at the European end is facilitated. Nevertheless, this type of regional mission continues to have organizational problems; coordinating arrangements in Washington may not parallel those in Paris, and this hinders unified guidance and instruction for negotiators.[32]

Another organizational problem inherent in the regional mission is that of the relationships between it and the American embassies stationed in the individual member countries. This is not so much a question of authority as of the appropriate planning unit for particular purposes. The regular ambassadors are supposed to head their "country teams" regardless of what agencies are included. USRO is not part of such a country team, and from the country ambassador's point of view is somewhat of an administrative anomaly.[33] One solution, not a very satisfactory one, is the avoidance of contact. With respect to some functions, however, a modus operandi has been developed.[34] For dealings with many of the countries in NATO the mutual exchange of information between USRO officials and the American embassies now works well.

Policy is made in the national capitals of the member countries, and it is almost inevitable that the regular American ambassadors will carry more weight in those capitals than will the Permanent Representative to NATO, who must deal with those countries through *their* permanent representatives. Thus the ambassador to the regional security organization is really dependent on his colleagues in the North Atlantic Council and upon bilateral discussions between Washington and the national

---

and Multilateral Organizations," *ibid.,* pp. 187 and 205–14; and Ben T. Moore, "United States Overseas Representation to International and Multilateral Organizations," in American Assembly, *The Representation of the United States Abroad,* first ed., pp. 165–68.

[31] The combination of representation to two different kinds of international organization with non-congruent membership may help to explain the American tendency to mix up "alliance" with an economic enterprise. As successive steps to disengage France from NATO take effect and NATO's functions are moved elsewhere, the Permanent Representative may no longer head a multi-agency embassy.

[32] Jackson Committee II, *Basic Issues,* pp. 12 and 16.

[33] There have been four United States ambassadors in Paris at the same time: one to France, one to NATO, one to the OECD, and one to the Development Assistance Committee [*ibid.,* p. 15]. On the general question of coordination in the field, see Jackson Committee II, *The Ambassador and the Problem of Coordination,* Committee Print.

[34] See Cardozo, *op. cit.,* p. 82.

capitals of the member countries, regardless of his formal responsibility or the personal prestige he brings to his post. He needs unified guidance in carrying on negotiations in his multilateral setting, instruction which must come in many cases from the Assistant Secretary of State for European Affairs. The importance of that officer thus tends to grow.[35]

Another American organizational problem affecting the activities of NATO arises from the establishment of a separate Arms Control and Disarmament Agency. Arms control and disarmament have been hived off from the Department of State, where they formerly, it is true, were not given the continuous expert attention they deserved.[36] This separation has complicated even further any attempts to stimulate meaningful action on arms control in or by NATO.[37] However, whenever an ACDA proposal is to be negotiated, it must first be approved by the President, the National Security Council, and a "Committee of Principals," which is led by the Secretary of State and includes the heads of several interested agencies.[38]

[35] Jackson Committee II, *Basic Issues,* pp. 12 and 16. From the point of view of NATO the Department of State organization contains an anomaly: Greece and Turkey are not included in the responsibilities of the Bureau of European Affairs but are under the Bureau of Near Eastern and South Asian Affairs. Thus the formal organization reflects a real difference between these two NATO members and the others.

[36] See Bernard G. Bechhoefer, *Postwar Negotiations for Arms Control* (Washington: Brookings Institution, 1961), p. 591; Charles H. Donnelly, *United States Defense Policies in 1961,* House Doc. No. 502, 87th Cong., 2nd sess. (1962), p. 71; House of Representatives Committee on Foreign Affairs, *Hearings, To Establish a United States Arms Control Agency,* 87th Cong., 1st sess. (1961), esp. pp. 3 and 21.

[37] In the 18-nation negotiations on a proliferation agreement at Geneva in August, 1965, the uneasy compromise between ACDA's concern for a treaty and the Department of State's concern for some kind of NATO nuclear sharing resulted in a highly ambiguous United States proposal which the Soviet Union quickly rejected. The United States had already disregarded warnings from Britain and Canada, who did not join in the proposal [*New York Times,* August 17 and September 1, 1965].

See Laurence W. Martin, "Disarmament: An Agency in Search of a Policy," *Reporter,* July 4, 1963, pp. 22 ff. For the administrative organization of ACDA, which includes a Bureau of International Relations, see Senate Committee on Foreign Relations, *Hearings, Review of Operations of the Arms Control and Disarmament Agency,* 87th Cong., 2nd sess. (1962), pp. 13–14.

[38] The others are the Secretary of Defense, Chairman of the JCS, Chairman of AEC, Director of CIA, Director of ACDA, Special Assistants to the President for National Security Affairs and for Science and Technology, Administrator of NASA and Director of the USIA. See *ibid.,* pp. 22, 26, and 27; Arms Control and Disarmament Agency, *Fourth Annual Report to Congress of the ACDA,* 1965, p. 28. From the highest to the lowest staff levels the Joint Chiefs of Staff and Defense Department officials also participate in arms control discussions. The Director

The very existence of NATO and of agencies to coordinate United States policy in NATO with other areas of foreign policy raises additional coordinating problems. An early example was the increase in work of the Bureau of Economic Affairs, which was concerned with questions of economic defense mobilization in Europe as well as at home. That some office should work to counteract the natural parochialism of the geographical and functional subdivisions of the State Department is perhaps less recognized than that this department should do so for outside agencies with interests in the NATO area. In the National Security Council and various interdepartmental coordinating groups such as the Berlin Task Force, the Department of State has played a leading role.[39]

Coordination sometimes takes place in the field through regional conferences of heads of missions. However, most coordination must take place in Washington, where there is a multitude of agencies, each watchful of its prerogatives. State-Defense coordination is more developed than that between State and other departments such as Agriculture and Commerce, if only because tasks of coordination between State and Defense are greater.[40] Appreciation of the need for political-military collaboration in national security policy did come earlier, a need exemplified by, inter alia, membership in NATO.[41]

---

of ACDA advises the Secretary of State and President in this field, while under the Secretary of State's direction he has primary responsibility for arms control matters [Charles H. Donnelly, *A Compilation of Material Relating to United States Defense Policies in 1962*, House Doc. No. 155, 88th Cong., 1st sess. (1963), pp. 81–82].

[39] On these coordinating problems and the role of the Department of State, see Paul Nitze's testimony, Jackson Committee I, *Hearings*, Part VI, p. 865; Secretary Rusk's testimony, Jackson Committee II, *Hearings*, Part VI, pp. 410–11; Lincoln Gordon, "Coordination of Overseas Representation," *loc. cit.*, pp. 237–38 and 244–48; Jackson Committee II, *Basic Issues*, pp. 8–9; Senate Committee on Foreign Relations, *Hearings, International Development and Security*, 87th Cong., 1st sess. (1961), p. 27; Joseph Kraft, *The Grand Design* (New York: Harper and Brothers, 1962), pp. 25–26; and Jackson Committee II, *Staff Reports and Hearings*, pp. 104–12.

[40] Jackson Committee II, *Staff Reports and Hearings*, pp. 374–75. The State Department and National Science Foundation cooperate in the NATO science program [House of Representatives Committee on Appropriations, *Hearings, Mutual Security Appropriations for 1961*, 86th Cong., 2nd sess. (1960), p. 541, and House of Representatives Committee on Foreign Affairs, *Hearings, Foreign Assistance Act of 1962*, 87th Cong., 2nd sess. (1962), p. 749].

[41] Similarly, with respect to some international economic organizations, an interdepartmental interest in international finance is recognized through the National Advisory Council on International Monetary and Financial Problems, chaired by the Secretary of the Treasury, but in which the Department of State is represented.

Formal coordinating mechanisms, however, are far less important than the various kinds of informal contact between responsible officials in different but related agencies. These have grown markedly between the Departments of State and Defense, although Louis Johnson, during his brief tenure as Secretary of Defense, practically forbade such contacts without his permission, even when he himself was seeking via the National Security Council clarification from the Department of State of foreign policy matters with military implications.[42] Informal, lower-level contact between State and Defense has the great advantage that the proposals of the two departments can be better integrated into a common policy if the interested parties have not previously made up their own minds before coming together and thus have not already developed institutional loyalties impeding cooperation.[43] Formal requirements which give every agency which conceivably might have an interest a right to be consulted are what Robert Lovett has called the "foul-up factor." [44]

Formal coordinating mechanisms such as the National Security Council are no substitute for vision among the responsible officials, as can be seen in that body's failure in 1953 and 1954 to examine the long-term implications of the reliance on nuclear weapons implicit in the New Look military policy and on the doctrine of massive retaliation.[45] Readiness to consult together, such as has marked the relations between Secretaries Rusk and McNamara, is no substitute either. It did not prevent the occurrence of a Skybolt crisis when, after consultation, the resulting action still reflected an underestimate of diplomatic costs.

It is true, however, that where the principal officers of agencies concerned maintain close contact with each other (admittedly not an easy task) integrated policy becomes more likely. NATO's requirements occasionally bring the Secretaries of State, Defense, and the Treasury together. Dean Acheson, describing the intricate and multifaceted negotiations during the North Atlantic council meeting at which the Lisbon

[42] Walter Millis, Harvey C. Mansfield, and Harold Stein, *Arms and The State* (New York: The Twentieth Century Fund, 1958), pp. 235–36.

[43] They should not be *representatives* but collaborators. See Paul Nitze's testimony, Jackson Committee II, *Hearings*, Part VI, pp. 865–66 and 876.

[44] Testimony, Jackson Committee I, *Hearings*, Part I, pp. 14–15. A minor example of this tendency was the requirement for the Mutual Weapons Development Program that each particular project be cleared by, among others, the Department of State [President's Committee to Study the United States Military Assistance Program, *Composite Report*, vol. I, p. 36 and, *idem*, Vol. II, p. 171].

[45] See Paul Nitze's testimony, Jackson Committee I, *Hearings*, Part VI, p. 883.

goals were fixed, singled out this fortunate juxtaposition of the American principals (including the Mutual Aid Administrator) to help explain their success.[46] Combined delegations to NATO meetings are much less complicated than, for example, those sent to GATT meetings, where there may be as many as ten different agencies represented.

An indispensable factor in coordination as well as integration is easy flow of the information required by the decision-makers. Within a department there may be impediments to the flow upward to the principal offices and also (but less noted) from the top down. Where some agencies, such as the CIA, are formally independent, even greater obstacles impede the flow.[47] Where they are not formally independent, there still may be procedural hindrances. Sometimes information can flow too freely. From its own offices in the field the State Department offices in Washington tend to be swamped with unassimilated or unassimilable information.[48] Officials in USRO have felt the effects of this plethora, because they found themselves not being heard when they did communicate with the deluged Washington authorities. This was the more unfortunate because, with fifteen nations represented at NATO headquarters, information can be very rapidly interchanged on specific questions.

Turning to budgeting procedures, we see that the deadlines for making up the federal budget set quite inflexible time limits to decisions relevant to NATO.[49] The Skybolt controversy sprang in part from this difficulty.[50]

Perhaps out of executive loyalty, perhaps from a feeling of impotence, individual officials in the Department of State do not appear to have

[46] *Sketches from Life,* p. 48. He continued: "For difficult action was required by all their Departments; and man's inhumanity to man is never revealed more starkly than by one colleague to another far away at the end of a cable line pleading for help with a fervor which in Washington always seems hysterical. As it was, even joining as the others did in the recommendations which we sent to the President, we had to ask his intervention to tell their Departments to stop arguing and do what he had approved. Authority fades with distance and with the speed of light."

[47] See Jackson Committee II, *Hearings,* Part VI, p. 407.

[48] Jackson Committee II, *Basic Issues,* p. 12: ". . . the rule seems to be: Report Everything."

[49] Considering that the budget process may take as long as 16 to 18 months and involve as many as 45 levels of authority [Elder, *op. cit.,* p. 219], this is a large-sized intractability.

[50] See "Secretary Rusk's News Conference of December 10," *Department of State Bulletin,* December 31, 1962, p. 1001. After referring to the budget process, he also said at that time, "If decisions or prospective decisions on these [research and development plans] affect our allies, we consult with our allies."

made as strenuous efforts before Congressional committees to alter the budget itself as have some of those in other departments. Secretary Dulles would not follow the example of some military representatives by revealing changes made by the Bureau of the Budget when he was prompted to do so by a Congressional committee member.[51] He was also apparently not much interested in the size of, or allocations within, the defense budget.[52] Only in the 1960s did the Department of State begin to participate in the annual planning and budget exercise of the Department of Defense.[53] An important exception was military aid; in this field the Department of State strongly supported budgetary requests of the Department of Defense before Congressional committees.[54]

The Department of State and the related USIA have somewhat larger public relations duties due to NATO, whose own information service is severely limited. Among these activities have been exchange programs enhancing the understanding of the United States among individuals and groups from the other NATO members.[55] In the 1950s the USIA focused on the NATO theme in its propaganda directed to European countries.[56] The Department of State has expended relatively little effort to enhance appreciation of the role of NATO among American citizens. This probably reflects strict Congressional limitations on the Department's Bureau of Public Affairs which gives political information to the public in the United States. Influential Congressmen oppose the

[51] Senate Committee on Appropriations, *Hearings, State . . . Appropriations for 1957,* 84th Cong., 2nd sess. (1956), p. 428. He said, "We have got to live with them [the Bureau of the Budget]" [p. 434].

[52] "Since 1945 not one Secretary of State has appeared before a military appropriations committee to discuss the relationship between the budget and the nation's foreign policy" [Warner R. Schilling, "The Politics of National Defense: Fiscal 1950," in Schilling, Hammond, and Snyder, *op. cit.,* pp. 256–57]. See also testimony of Paul Nitze, Jackson Committee I, *Hearings,* Part VI, p. 883, and Maxwell Taylor, *op. cit.,* pp. 55 and 65.

[53] See "Memorandum on the Department of State's Politico-Military Organization and Staffing," *loc. cit.,* p. 415.

[54] Now that certain items formerly carried in the budget under "mutual security aid" have been shifted to the category of "contributions to international organizations" in the budget of the Department of State, the role of this department may increase, but not significantly.

[55] For example, a "NATO program" jointly sponsored by the Departments of State and Defense arranged American visits for information-media specialists from other NATO countries, who "then contributed articles favorable to the United States and the unity of purpose in the common defense against Communism" [*Department of State Bulletin,* March 14, 1955, p. 141].

[56] Senate Committee on Appropriations, *Hearings, State . . . Appropriations for 1957,* 84th Cong., 2nd sess. (1956), p. 223; *ibid.,* 85th Cong., 1st sess. (1957), p. 503.

use of government funds for what they regard as "selling the State Department line." The main public relations job regarding NATO has appropriately been assumed by able and willing private groups operating among the "attentive public."

NATO almost always operates outside the limelight of American domestic politics. This apolitical aspect of NATO can be discerned when we compare the politically prominent Americans who man the United Nations delegation with the semi-professional or professional diplomatists in American delegations to NATO meetings. NATO presents a very different public relations problem, not unique to this organization, in that the various audiences to whom information about it are addressed have somewhat conflicting publicity requirements. At times this produces the kind of censorship about which General Maxwell Taylor complained when someone in the Department of State claimed that his description of the nakedness of NATO might frighten the allies and therefore blue-pencilled an article intended for *Foreign Affairs*.[57]

What about NATO's effect on the State Department's role in planning for national security? A study prepared for a subcommittee of the Senate Committee on Government Operations dealing with the "Administration of National Security" (the Jackson Committee) called attention to the inadequacy of planning, either in the field or in Washington, to coordinate country policy with regional policy; it found that "this is one of the major problems of staffing and organizing for national security." [58] Witnesses before the subcommittee often referred to the undesirability of separating planning from operations. "Planning is critically dependent on the unplannable flashes of insight which are usually sparked by worrying and wrestling with actual problems." [59] Except in the military field, NATO is not the kind of organization which continuously poses "actual problems" for United States officials. (France's withdrawal in 1966 was, however, an "actual problem.") Planning thus has most often taken the form of drawing blueprints for organizational innovation or for correcting policy. On this kind of planning activity, a type which tends to intrigue many Americans in and out of government, NATO has had an impact. When the Kennedy administration was preparing itself for office, a task force led by former Secretary of State Acheson dealt with the role of NATO; it was this task force that stimu-

[57] *Op. cit.*, pp. 190 and 192.   [58] Jackson Committee II, *Basic Issues*, p. 12.
[59] *Ibid.*, p. 5.

lated the meetings of individuals who helped to draw up the "Grand Design" for the "Atlantic Community." [60]

United States membership in NATO, as in other international organizations, has an impact on the work habits, attitudes, and skills of the diplomatists assigned to tasks involving the organization, and on the kind of personnel needed for future participation in it. The "new diplomacy" requires in its practitioners new characteristics as well as those traditionally associated with diplomatic activities. For some it means new specialties, which in the case of NATO includes a combination of military with political knowledge, and in the OECD and GATT, political-economic expertise. For others it requires special knowledge of regions (such as Western Europe) as well as of particular countries. For those in USRO, it has meant knowing how to assess the impact of a policy on not one but fourteen countries. Also required of some is a capacity for expediting, coordinating, stimulating, catalyzing, and generally directing specific foreign policy programs.[61] These new requirements modify and complicate the task of recruiting and training qualified personnel and of defining promotion criteria. Even protocol problems arise when the outward symbols of prestige are not accorded the new type of diplomats in their exercise of non-traditional capabilities.[62] Recognition of the need for change comes slowly in a bureaucracy with entrenched habits and a disposition on the part of the professional corps, associated with the older ways of conducting foreign policy, to feel hostile to change.[63]

Gradually, adjustments may be discerned, however, and many are associated with NATO. The younger Foreign Service Officer is less likely than in the early postwar period to shun assignment to a mission dealing with an international organization as detrimental to his career.

[60] Joseph Kraft, *The Grand Design: From Common Market to Atlantic Partnership* (New York: Harper and Brothers, 1962), p. 27.

[61] See Cardozo, *op. cit.,* esp. pp. 76–77, 84–85, 89, 114–16, 119–21, and 133–34; Moore, "American Representation to International and Multilateral Organizations," *loc. cit.,* pp. 213–14; Paul Nitze's testimony, Jackson Committee I, *Hearings,* Part VI, pp. 859–60; The Committee on Foreign Affairs Personnel, *Report, Personnel for the New Diplomacy* (Washington: Carnegie Endowment for International Peace, 1962), esp. pp. 6–7 and pp. 47–59.

[62] See Cardozo, *op. cit.,* pp. 122–25; Moore, "American Representation to International and Multilateral Organizations," *loc. cit.,* pp. 221–22.

[63] Senate Committee on Foreign Relations, *Administration of the Department of State,* Committee Print, 86th Cong., 2nd sess. (1960), p. 18; and "A Letter of Resignation," *Foreign Service Journal,* September, 1962, pp. 8–10.

His career prospects may even be improved, although the chance remains that those empowered to pronounce on his qualifications for advancement may not yet be habituated to the new outlook.[64] There is still a reluctance to accept secondment to the secretariat of an international organization (especially on the part of those Foreign Service Officers who have a distaste for foreign administrative methods). However, a large difference between organizations is recognized. Those which offer a real opportunity to "shape" the environment are regarded as more desirable, while those which are bogged down in bureaucratic red tape and wrangling over national prestige (especially certain United Nations organizations) are considered unattractive. NATO falls somewhere in between the two kinds of organization, but its Secretariat has very few Americans. The pull continues to be towards service in a national capital, where the main policy is made. Regardless of whether or not they favor service with an international organization or with a mission to one, a growing number of officers have had such experience at some point in their careers. Gradually, new attitudes develop and, for some, a deeper interest in collaboration for a common objective which ignores nationality.

One assignment with growing appeal is service as political adviser to the highest-level military commands. SACEUR has such advisers; and various major United States military commands have "Political Advisers" (POLADs) assigned to them, one of such posts being to the European Command. As one POLAD has written, "In the European Command virtually every problem also raises the relationship with NATO." The POLAD, as a special staff officer responsible solely to him, is supposed to be the commander's consultant on political, political-military, and economic questions.[65] Another recent trend, the exchange of personnel between the Department of State and Department of Defense, should develop the type of officer useful for NATO assignments. Similarly, State Department personnel have been "detailed" to other departments, including Commerce and Treasury, and to the White House,

---

[64] Secretary Rusk has hinted that promotion boards may not always give the same weight to precepts concerning untraditional experience which have been urged by high executive officials [Jackson Committee II, *Hearings,* Part VI, pp. 408–09].

[65] Richard B. Finn, "POLAD—A Permanent Institution," *Foreign Service Journal,* February, 1962, pp. 51–53. See also "Memorandum on the Department of State's Politico-Military Organization and Staffing," *loc. cit.,* pp. 417–19. General Ridgway [*Soldier* (New York: Harper and Bros., 1956), p. 246] wrote of this indispensable aid to SACEUR.

where they work as an integral part of that agency for an extended period.[66] Some Foreign Service Officers study at the various war colleges, including the National War College and NATO's own Defence College.[67]

In view of the giant role of the United States government in NATO, such intermingling of American personnel is probably as important as intermingling at NATO headquarters or with counterparts in other allied countries, a development much more difficult to discern except perhaps for a few examples of it in Canada and Great Britain.[68] The Department of State's Foreign Service Institute has received some students from allied governments. Training and service together are supposed to be highly effective ways to develop common perspectives among officials and to produce coordination through psychological conditioning.[69] The possibilities of interchange in training have hardly been explored by the United States Foreign Service, much less realized.[70] The military seem to have gone much further, perhaps because the relative generosity of Congress towards them has allowed them to do more. Perhaps because diplomats are trained to *represent* their government and are conscious of the dangers of "local-itis," they are also more immune from psychological attachments to such an international organization as NATO than are their military co-workers.

At the highest grades of the Foreign Service and among top-level officials, careers of an increasing number of individuals also have touched NATO at some point, directly or indirectly.[71] Many of these persons

[66] "Department of State Details to Other Agencies," Jackson Committee II, *Hearings,* Part VI, Exhibit II, pp. 439–40, and *idem, Staff Reports and Hearings,* pp. 573–74.

[67] But not nearly enough do, according to those who are encouraging this kind of training. See Raymond L. Thurston, "Education at the Top of Government," *Political Science Quarterly,* June, 1966, p. 255.

[68] For example, some United States Foreign Service Officers have attended the Imperial Defence College in Britain and the Canadian National Defence College [Jackson Committee II, *Hearings,* Pt. VI, p. 417].

[69] For a British example, see Lord Strang, "Inside the Foreign Office," *International Relations,* April, 1960, p. 19.

[70] In 1964 the Department of State inaugurated a program to give to its own officers training as "Atlantic Affairs Specialists," who would be "experts in the multilateral and regional aspects of Western European and Atlantic developments" [*Atlantic Community News,* March 3, 1964, p. 1].

[71] A partial listing would include Edward Martin, Walter Stoessel, Burke Elbrick, Hugh Cumming, Martin Hillenbrand, Livingston Merchant, Theodore Achilles, William Rheinstein, Raymond L. Thurston, Douglas MacArthur II, George Perkins, Robert Bowie, Thomas R. Finletter and W. Randolph Burgess.

tend to be unusually strong supporters of the organization. This tendency, plus the personnel trends noted above, give the Department of State much needed weight when the department carries out its rather slippery task of coordinating the United States with a coordinating international institution.

DEPARTMENT OF DEFENSE

The Department of Defense, like the National Security Council and the Joint Chiefs of Staff, is an organizational innovation of the past quarter-century. It was created in response to the same changes in the United States role in world politics that led to United States membership in NATO, SEATO, and the OAS. Membership in NATO brings the Department of Defense together with the Department of State at many points, as we have already noted.[72] It is Defense which must provide the forces and equipment which the United States government has allocated to NATO. Defense officials have had to implement the military aid program, and they must find the staff for NATO commands.

In view of the gigantic size of the Department of Defense, its worldwide operations, and the fact that it spends about half the national budget (several billion dollars of it abroad), membership in an organization like NATO makes only a small imprint on this establishment.[73] Furthermore, the kinds of issues which have shaken the Department since World War II have for the most part touched NATO only very obliquely. Despite continual affirmations about NATO's crucial importance to United States security, membership in that organization is but one response to changing conditions which would have greatly affected the Department of Defense in any case.[74] Among them are the revolution in weapons development; the changed use of many weapons, i.e., not only for defense but also for deterrence (less for actual firing and more

[72] That coordination seemed important to Department of Defense officials as well as to those in the Department of State may be seen from Secretary McNamara's statement that "one of my first objectives was to establish a close relationship, both personally with Secretary Rusk, and also formally and officially at all levels of the Defense Department with corresponding levels in the State Department. . . . The relationships are close, frequent and cordial" [House of Representatives Committee on Armed Services, *Hearings on Military Posture,* 87th Cong., 2nd sess. (1962), pp. 3205–6].

[73] See William W. Kaufmann, *The McNamara Strategy* (New York: Harper and Row, 1964), p. 168, for dramatic figures on the size of the Department of Defense establishment.

[74] For example, Secretary McNamara stressed its importance in each of his annual statements to Congress on "The Military Posture."

for demonstrating and communicating); the global military operations of the United States; the rapid changes in the nature of security threats; the elaboration of different kinds of international peace-keeping machinery in which the United States participates; and the growing demand for arms control.

Adapting the Department of Defense to such changes has been a continuous and difficult process. One cannot legislate consensus among the armed services, and the Joint Chiefs were in the early postwar years more successful in compromising the issues of budget and role which divided them than in producing an integrated defense policy responsive to America's needs and commitments. The Secretary of Defense did not then have in the Department the staff to generate policy. The vast knowledge of the first Comptroller, Wilfred McNeill, and the impotence of other high Defense officials combined to make his office of great importance in budget allocations which were, in any case, developed in accordance with guide-lines not always derived from calculations of external threat or alliance commitment.[75]

Successive reorganizations were designed to strengthen the offices of the Chairman of the Joint Chiefs of Staff or of the Secretary of Defense in the interest of taking more account of world-wide political, as well as scientific and technological, changes and less account of parochial service interests in developing defense policy. Establishing the unified and specified commands in 1959 made it easier to relate foreign political objectives, including the fulfilling of NATO commitments, to military capabilities. President Eisenhower's last Secretary of Defense, Thomas Gates, put new life into the office of Secretary by attending Joint Chiefs of Staff meetings and making, when necessary, on-the-spot-decisions.[76]

Strong and controversial personalities as well as organizational shifts have put their mark on the administration of the Department of Defense. Defense Secretaries Wilson and McNamara and certain senior military officers such as Generals Taylor, LeMay, Ridgway and Gavin, as well as Admirals Radford and Rickover, were among the individuals who shaped the way in which the Department of Defense reacted to issues related to NATO as well as the substance of defense policy.

Secretary McNamara's somewhat abrupt transformation of the Office of the Secretary of Defense into an efficient engine for decision threw

[75] See Schilling, Hammond, and Snyder, *op. cit., passim.*
[76] See Paul Y. Hammond, *Organizing for Defense* (Princeton: Princeton University Press, 1961), Chapters ix–xiii.

into relief the whole backlog of unresolved alliance problems examined in Chapters V and VI. Whatever feeble hold the other allies had on American defense policy was, if anything, weakened just as they were beginning to ask for more control. Furthermore, the increased effectiveness of American armed forces was matched by a tightened control over them, and especially over the "American key" of the "two keys" nuclear armed forces. The new vigor of the Department of Defense, spilling over into an alliance whose European members exhibited greater economic than defense strength, ran counter to a general demand by these members to participate more fully in the "collective" security. The McNamara techniques in planning-programming-budgeting (which later spread to England and Germany) raised some doubts that certain imponderable political elements could be practicably combined with measurable units of comparison. Thus political considerations often brought the Department of Defense into conflict with the Department of State.

The reforms associated with Secretary McNamara and his collaborators decidedly improved the *effective* security of the alliance members.[77] These reforms could not overcome some of the long-term ill effects to the alliance of the budgetary and strategic conflicts associated with Secretary Wilson and Chairman of the Joint Chiefs of Staff Radford, in which the Army leaders in the first years of the Eisenhower administration lost out to those favoring the New Look and increased reliance on nuclear weapons. Army leaders frequently pleaded their case in terms of the commitments of the United States to its allies, although there were other grounds upon which they opposed New Look military policies. Secretary Wilson specifically denied more than a vague commitment to the NATO allies, and Admiral Radford denied seeing any connection between NATO commitments and the new policies.[78] The important role played in politics by the Chairman of the Joint Chiefs of Staff in the Eisenhower administration boded ill for a regional security organization in which he was not much interested.

Budgetary ceilings imposed early in the budget cycle and in the absence of any fresh calculation of changing threats to national security aggravated interservice rivalries. In the first Eisenhower administration

[77] Cf. Kaufmann, *op. cit.*, esp. chap. v, and James L. McCamy, *Conduct of the New Diplomacy* (Harper and Row, 1964), pp. 96–101. See Charles J. Hitch, *Decision-Making for Defense* (Berkeley: University of California Press, 1965) for a discussion of the process by which new defense policies were formulated.

[78] Maxwell Taylor, *op. cit.*, pp. 83, 98 and 128; James M. Gavin, *War and Peace in the Space Age* (Harper and Brothers, 1958), pp. 139, 158, 159, 161, 431, and 455–56; Ridgway, *op. cit.*, pp. 283, 287–89, 308, 311, and 314–16.

budgets such rivalries were usually resolved in favor of the Air Force, whose interest in NATO has largely been a function of its interest in access to overseas air and missile bases; it had little interest in building up military airlift capability to complement Army efforts in meeting the latter's NATO commitments.[79] After the mid-1950s the fortuitous development of ballistic sea power and second thoughts about the role of tactical nuclear weapons in the era of Soviet atomic plenty changed greatly the terms of interservice competition. By 1960 the United States Air Force in central Europe was operating under the general direction of SHAPE, with the evident purpose of making possible some kind of air-ground defense of Europe at least long enough to enforce a "pause" on any Soviet attacker. Nevertheless, Air Force officers in Europe were worried about the new stress on conventional warfare in 1961.[80] By 1965, however, the United States' missile power in Europe had been built up as dramatically as its ground forces had been strengthened.

The naval forces of the United States are only loosely associated with NATO; although the Atlantic and Mediterranean Commands of NATO are held by United States naval officers, the United States, like the other members, assigns no ships to them in peacetime. Thus, given the Navy's as well as the Air Force's role, it is not surprising that it is the Army that is most deeply involved in NATO.

When in 1958 the service departments were removed from the chain of command and the defense forces were reorganized into unified commands, controversies over missions and over responsibility for new weapons diminished, with indirect benefit to NATO. Symptomatic of the reduced tendency of a given service to fight for its own special interests was the Navy's failure to protest against the MLF, a proposal not popular among naval officers. Nevertheless, strong opposition to a multilateral fleet composed of nuclear-powered, Polaris-armed submarines very quickly converted the proposal into one involving surface ships.[81]

[79] Ideologists of strategic air power have sometimes been rather emotionally "pro-NATO" and "anti-UN" because they saw in the "reform" of NATO the opportunity to mount a great anti-Communist crusade. On the other hand, their interest in the overseas bases of NATO allies declined as strategic air and missile power developed an intercontinental capability.

[80] See Hanson Baldwin in *New York Times,* October 2, 1961.

[81] Admiral Anderson, then Chief of Naval Operations, told the House of Representatives Committee on Armed Services on February 16, 1963, that "we had some concern that we might have to give away information on nuclear propulsion and we are satisfied that it is recognized that we must safeguard this information, and there is no suggestion at this time that this would be given away to the detriment of the United States. My position has been that we have to maintain approximately (deleted) leadtime . . ." [*Hearings on Military Posture,* 88th Cong., 1st sess.

This shift was reminiscent of the shift implied in the vague offer Secretary Herter made to the North Atlantic Council in December, 1960 regarding Polaris submarines, following opposition in the Pentagon to the development of the Norstad idea of land-based strategic missiles.[82]

Essential support functions remain with the service departments; this has implications for the fragmented logistics of NATO forces.[83] Concentration on mission rather than agency has not been pressed to its logical conclusion. Decisions relating directly to NATO, however, are made at a level higher than that of the service secretaries.[84]

With respect to more specific ways in which NATO has some impact on the Department of Defense, the principal organizational change arising from this alliance and from other international obligations, including military aid and arms control commitments, was the creation in 1953 of the office of Assistant Secretary for International Security Affairs. This office, which evolved from that of Special Assistant for International Security Affairs (created in 1950), looks after the NATO and United Nations interests of the Department of Defense. It is responsible for negotiations regarding military-base rights and for the programming of military assistance; it develops Department of Defense positions for questions to be considered in the National Security Council. On alliance matters it communicates directly with appropriate offices in the Department of State and with the unified commands.[85] The quality of the man appointed to this Assistant Secretaryship and his working relations with the Secretary are clearly of great importance in integrating political and military considerations as they affect alliance security policies.[86]

(1963), p. 963]. He said, when pressed by Representative Arends, that he would argue against mixed-manned Polaris submarines. Most of his further reply was deleted.

[82] See Robert E. Osgood, *NATO; The Entangling Alliance* (Chicago: University of Chicago Press, 1962), p. 233.

[83] See Roswell L. Gilpatric, "An Expert Looks at the Joint Chiefs," *New York Times Magazine*, March 29, 1964, pp. 11, 71–72.

[84] Secretary of the Army Stahr, Senate Committee on Appropriations, *Hearings, Department of Defense Appropriations for 1962*, 87th Cong., 1st sess. (1961), p. 74.

[85] For its specific responsibilities see Jackson Committee I, *Interim Report*, 86th Cong., 2nd sess. (1960), p. 9; also Timothy Stanley, *American Defense and National Security* (Washington: Public Affairs Press, 1956), Chap. v. Stanley cites the report of a participant in the decision to rearm Germany that this proposal was discussed in ISA-JCS-State conferences but never formally with the NSC, "although it was cleared with each member individually."

[86] Frank Nash, Struve Hensel, Gordon Gray, John Irwin, Paul Nitze and John McNaughton have all occupied this office with distinction. See *ibid.*, p. 48, for

Another response to the need to coordinate aid and representation to NATO was the creation of the military section of USRO. The Defense Adviser and Defense Representative North Atlantic and Mediterranean Areas heads a group of about one hundred. His deputy is a general, and nearly half of the group are military personnel. Most of the divisions of this section (for example, Production and Logistics, and Multilateral Finance) have as part of their duties representation on appropriate NATO committees.

Among the other ways in which the United States defense establishment is geared into NATO the following should be mentioned. The Secretary of Defense and high officials in his department are as much a part of the delegation to the ministerial meetings of the North Atlantic Council as are the Secretary of State and his assistants. The Chairman of the Joint Chiefs of Staff, or his deputy, sits on the Military Committee of NATO and was a member of the former Standing Group. SACEUR, after General Eisenhower's day, has had a double role, the second responsibility being to head the European command of the United States forces. However, most of the second task has been delegated to his deputy in that command.[87]

Defense officials often reiterate that their military planning must "take account" of allied forces which might operate in conjunction with United States forces, or be related to them, but the connecting organizational links between NATO planners and the long-range defense planners in the Pentagon appear to be quite loose. Otherwise, the McNamara promise at Athens and the subsequent briefings by American defense planners in various European capitals could hardly have had the element of novelty attributed to them. The major responsibility for United States strategic plans lies with the Joint Chiefs of Staff, who do have, through their chairman and the Military Committee of NATO, at least a point of communication with their opposite numbers.[88] The

---

observations on some of the earlier Assistant Secretaries. They came from other Defense posts, the Executive Office, the Department of State, and RAND.

[87] Owing to the Cuban crisis, General Lemnitzer did not become SACEUR until January, 1963, although he was appointed CINCEUR the preceding November, since NATO members desired General Norstad to remain after his scheduled retirement until the situation became more settled. The United States and Canadian Chiefs of Staff, to whom the Commander-in-Chief of NORAD reports, are also the Canadian-United States Regional Planning Group, which in turn "reported" through the Standing Group (until its dissolution in June, 1966) to the NATO Military Committee.

[88] For the place of the JCS in the planning structure, see Admiral Radford, House

Joint Chiefs played an important early role in pressing for German rearmament, on the strong initiative of and through the persistence of the Army staff planners. The Joint Chiefs' interest flowed from their fears of a long, dangerous commitment to a "collective" defense which was not under the effective control of the United States.[89]

The plan for German rearmament within some NATO context was carefully worked out in conjunction with State Department officials; but planning such as that for nuclear weapons in the 1950s was carried on in considerable isolation from those outside the Department of Defense, with the ill effects for NATO strategy already noted.[90] Strategic target planning has been under the direction of the Commander of SAC, although this duty is separate from his other responsibilities. He reports to the Joint Chiefs of Staff on plans made by a group composed of officers from each service, representatives from the unified commands which are concerned with strategic warfare, and a liaison from the staff of the Joint Chiefs. Since 1963 a NATO liaison group has also been included, providing a further point for communication and coordination of United States and NATO war plans.[91]

With both the Joint Chiefs of Staff and the Office of International Security Affairs organized to deal with NATO-related questions, the Department of Defense has within it agencies with overlapping but different perspectives working on policies of relevance to NATO. This increases the possibility that NATO policy will be considered against the full range of American security interests.

A great deal of planning takes place at lower levels in the military services.[92] Probably here may be found the corrosive effects of the

---

of Representatives Committee on Appropriations, *Hearings, Department of Defense Appropriations for 1957,* 87th Cong., 2nd sess. (1956), pp. 274–76; Maxwell Taylor, *ibid.,* pp. 443–44; Charles H. Donnelly, *United States Defense Policies in 1958,* House Doc. No. 227, 86th Cong., 1st sess. (1959), p. 117; Gilpatric, *op. cit.,* Secretary McNamara has made extensive use of studies by the joint staff of the JCS [Kaufmann, *op. cit.,* p. 238].

[89] Cf. Martin, "The American Decision to Rearm Germany," *loc. cit., passim.*

[90] See Chapters V and VI *supra.*

[91] Charles H. Donnelly, *United States Defense Policies in 1960,* House Doc. No. 207, 87th Cong., 1st sess. (1961), p. 27; General Thomas S. Power, "The Nature of the Deterrent System," *Air Force Magazine,* March, 1965, p. 67. Of the NATO group General Power wrote that they "are kept current of our planning as it affects their own operations and thus can assist, on a day-to-day basis, in coordinating NATO's war plans with ours."

[92] Also at lower levels are the numerous committees to coordinate with NATO on research undertakings [House of Representatives Committee on Armed Services, *Hearings on Military Posture,* 88th Cong., 2nd sess. (1964), p. 7846].

"military-industrial complex" deplored by President Eisenhower.[93] In recent years many persons have criticized the piecemeal nature of United States military planning. Such criticisms have not been met despite major budgetary reforms of great importance for rational planning and the tightening up of administrative processes under the McNamara regime. Where goals are plural, "fragmentation" is not a defect in administrative processes but an expression of multiple purposes. Unfunctional fragmentation may be remedied by efficient administration; functional fragmentation only by consensus-building.

The planning-programming-budgeting reforms of the McNamara regime provided a centripetal counter-pull to the centrifugal tendencies caused by each Defense agency's normal concern that its role in planning not be diminished. Since calculations regarding NATO have always entered more readily into strategic planning than into budget-making, the bringing together of these two streams of decisions increases the prospects that the resources and requirements of NATO will have an impact on budget decisions.

The American military aid program for the NATO allies has depended upon both interdepartmental and interallied collaboration. Thus it provides an illustrative case for noting participant roles in defense planning. From the beginning, military aid permitted allied forces to be trained and equipped to perform some essential military functions at a cost smaller than that which would have been incurred if these particular tasks had been carried out by American forces. Here was one standard by which the United States military decided how much, to whom, and for what they would recommend military assistance. Besides SHAPE and the MAAG missions, important agencies in the process were the Commander-in-Chief of United States Forces in Europe, the Joint Chiefs of Staff (which reviewed requests to ensure that they dovetailed with American military needs), the Director of Military Assistance (usually a military officer) in the Office of the Assistant Secretary for International Affairs, and the service departments, which calculated the supply requirements and carried out the programs.[94] At various stages the comptroller of the Department of Defense participated.

---

[93] Also probably here allied countries would find serious obstacles to the acceptance of their own military production for United States forces or NATO installations.

[94] The first Director of Military Assistance was General Lemnitzer, who some years later became SACEUR.

Bureau of the Budget, State Department, and foreign aid officials worked with those in Defense from the beginning of the programs, both in the field and in Washington.[95] Some questions were also considered by the National Security Council. The Secretaries of Defense and of State and the President himself eventually reviewed the programs.

The relation between NATO force goals and readiness indices for member countries, on the one hand, and United States defense planning, on the other, is difficult to define. The plans of SACEUR and other NATO military commands are submitted, formerly via the Standing Group, to the Military Committee, who in turn recommend action to be taken by the North Atlantic Council. The United States Joint Chiefs of Staff are, however, represented on NATO military groups; and SACEUR, being also an important American general, submits his plans with some knowledge of trends in Pentagon thinking. One may speculate that force goals and readiness indices established for the United States in NATO bear a close relation to estimates established by the Joint Chiefs.

The other NATO governments have always been free, in theory at least, to accept, reject, or alter the estimates for their respective countries. So long as they remained dependent on the United States for military aid (in 1966 only Greece and Turkey were recipients), the United States' role in making the estimates and in getting them accepted and implemented was large. As aid ceased, American influence in decisions on the equipping and training of the other members' forces lessened. Also lessened was the unprecedented American access to information regarding members' defense establishments and a not wholly spontaneous allied willingness to collaborate with the Americans in defense planning which was made possible by that access. While European defense planners may have accustomed themselves during the period of enforced collaboration to recognizing that a viable alliance with the United States is the foundation of their national security policies, there still remains the European allies' recollection of how they had felt compelled to accept United States decisions about important aspects of their defense.[96] (The grant-in-aid principle followed for a few NATO members in

[95] The role of the Department of State in this process has already been indicated earlier in this chapter.

[96] For information on the administration of military aid as it relates to NATO, see President's Committee to Study the United States Military Assistance Program, *op. cit.*; Gordon, "The Development of United States Representation Overseas," *loc. cit.*, pp. 25–35; Senate Special Committee to Study the Foreign Aid Program, *op. cit.*, esp. pp. 102, 111, and 147; Paul C. Davis and William T. R. Fox, "Ameri-

the mid-1960s had made the recipient a much more voluntary participant in the process, but American defense officials still had a major voice in deciding what should be aided.)

American leadership in NATO continues to affect ways in which the Department of Defense functions. For example, the Secretary of Defense's diplomatic activities have steadily expanded. Secretary McNamara has made numerous trips to Europe, not just for North Atlantic Council meetings, but to press United States views on officials at NATO and more particularly on defense ministers and prime ministers in the members' capitals. He has also received his counterparts for negotiations in Washington. Most of his concern has been to increase the European contributions to NATO. On occasion he has also assumed the more dubious role of salesman, pressing American military equipment on the allies, presumably for balance of payments reasons. Meanwhile, he and his assistants also have shared to some extent the State Department's function of defending and explaining NATO members' behavior before Congressional committees. In the case of the Skybolt controversy Secretary Rusk left the task of dealing with the disappointed British government to the Secretary of Defense (whose decision had caused the disappointment).[97] Secretary McNamara also assumed the responsibility for urging the British to maintain substantial armed strength in the Far East. He, as well as

can Military Representation Abroad," in American Assembly, *The Representation of the United States Abroad*, rev. ed., *op. cit.*, pp. 150–56. Also Senate Committee on Foreign Relations and Committee on Armed Services, *Hearings, Mutual Security Act of 1951*, 82nd Cong., 1st sess. (1951), pp. 135, 174, and 691; Senate Committee on Foreign Relations, Subcommittee, *Hearings, Military Assistance*, 82nd Cong., 1st sess. (1951), p. 39; Senate Committee on Foreign Relations, *Hearings, Mutual Security Act of 1954*, 83rd Cong., 2nd sess. (1954), p. 142; Senate Committee on Foreign Relations, *Hearings, Mutual Security Act of 1960*, 86th Cong., 2nd sess. (1960), pp. 95–97 and 103; Senate Committee on Foreign Relations, *Hearings, International Development and Security*, 87th Cong., 1st sess. (1961), pp. 25, 27, 594, 597, 601–03, 641–46, 672–73; Senate Committee on Foreign Relations, *Hearings, Foreign Assistance Act of 1962*, 87th Cong., 2nd sess. (1962), p. 270; Senate Committee on Appropriations, *Hearings, Foreign Assistance and Related Agencies Appropriations for 1962*, 87th Cong., 1st sess. (1961), pp. 149–50 and 274; House of Representatives Committee on Appropriations, *Hearings, Department of Defense Appropriations for 1957*, 84th Cong., 2nd sess. (1956), p. 65; House of Representatives Committee on Appropriations, *Hearings, Mutual Security Appropriations for 1961*, 86th Cong., 2nd sess. (1960), pp. 2318, 2320, 2326–28, 2373–74, and 2376–77; and House of Representatives Committee on Foreign Affairs, *Hearings, Mutual Security Act of 1959*, 86th Cong., 1st sess. (1959), pp. 154 and 391.

[97] See "Secretary Rusk's News Conference of December 10," *loc. cit.*, p. 1001.

General Taylor, then Chairman of the Joint Chiefs, and Assistant Secretary for International Affairs Nitze, took a part in the negotiations with individual NATO governments about the MLF.

Similarly, a new role for military personnel has opened up, a role which is traceable in good part to military aid programs and to NATO and other security organizations. For want of a better term, we call it the "politico-military" role: representing, advising, and collaborating on the international level. This is the task which corresponds to the new function of Foreign Service Officers.[98] In fact, the military somewhat antedated the Department of State in recognizing the need for special education and training in this field. A military man aspiring to become a general officer today is expected to have had some politico-military experience in the Pentagon or at SHAPE or a similar post. "Alumni" who have served together in the various joint defense organizations, including the NATO Defence College and such American institutions as the National War College, feel special bonds with each other, at home and abroad.[99] Like the diplomats who have served at international organizations, however, the military still fear they may incur certain career promotion problems as a result of having served in so untraditional a post.[100] When officers have returned to the Pentagon, they may find themselves overruled or ignored when they espouse "North Atlantic"-oriented views, as opposed to narrowly American views; but the gradually accumulating experience in joint defense assignments of American military personnel has raised the general confidence level between United States and other NATO military officials. Such experience in a regional security organization or in the mission to it go hand in hand with a close collaboration with foreign-service personnel rarely experienced before World War II. Adjustments are called for between two quite different traditions with very different working procedures. For one example, it is hard for many military officers to practice the patience required of diplomats or to be satisfied with untidy, loose "understandings." For another, the military men "must contemplate some eventualities that the statesman cannot afford to acknowledge" because of political inhibitions.[101]

---

[98] See Davis and Fox, *op. cit.,* pp. 173–80.

[99] William A. Knowlton, "Early Stages in the Organization of SHAPE," *International Organization,* Winter, 1959, pp. 17–18.

[100] This difficulty appears to be diminishing.

[101] Such as the "forward strategy" laid down for NATO in the early 1950s. See E. Vandevanter, *Some Fundamentals of NATO Organization* (Santa Mon-

Another phenomenon in the Department of Defense associated with the NATO period is the use of consultants and of studies made by civilian experts in the field of strategy.[102] This development hardly owes anything to the emergence of international organizations, but other NATO members have been affected directly and indirectly through the stimulus given by such outsiders to the more traditional thinking of the military. A noteworthy change in the legal position of American military forces abroad due to NATO (and other alliances later) was the United States' acceptance of local jurisdiction over military personnel for some kinds of crimes, an acceptance embodied in the "Status of Force Agreements."

In spite of formal and informal arrangements for coordinating military policy with foreign policy, lapses from time to time have needlessly unsettled the alliance or some of its members.[103] Thus defense officials sometimes make public statements without regard to their NATO implications, and on occasion one part of the gigantic Department of Defense takes an action independently of related parts.[104] Secretary McNamara's statement on January 30, 1963 (shortly after De Gaulle's explosive veto of Britain's entry into the EEC) that the United States would stay in the driver's seat of NATO so long as it carried so much of the load seemed a tactless way to underline an unpalatable truth. Such incidents have not grown more numerous over the years, but the other allies' sensitivity has increased. In any case, to some NATO members the Defense Department's occasional impolitic candor did not seem to harmonize with State Department assertions of "interdependence." [105]

---

ica: RAND Corporation, 1963) for this and other differences (pp. 29–31). In the case cited, the diplomats from the foreign ministries did not dare to examine some possibilities which the military men were forced to look into.

[102] Some of these experts eventually became high officials in the department.

[103] This is part of a general problem which needs more attention to ensure consistency of instructions—and binding authority behind these instructions—which go out to missions and military commanders; see Jackson Committee II, *Basic Issues*, p. 8.

[104] One of numerous examples of the former was Under Secretary of Defense Gilpatric's speech in October, 1963 about the possibility of withdrawing some American contingents from Europe as a result of improved mobility. In the latter category was the report that the United States was planning to lease some of its logistics bases in France to the German government—apparently without consultation with the already very touchy French or with American officials in Bonn [*New York Times*, Sept. 28, 1963].

[105] See Buchan, "NATO Divided: Nuclear Weapons, Europe and the United States," *New Republic*, December 29, 1962, pp. 13–16. If the guarded hints from State Department sources about the eventual end of the exclusive United States

Whether or not McNamara reflected the official United States position, if indeed any one position was "official," the allies had difficulty finding for themselves in Secretary McNamara's nuclear strategy the role they desired.

The Department of Defense also must deal with the Atomic Energy Commission on matters involving NATO. Since 1955 the law has required the Commission to cooperate with the Department of Defense in working out nuclear exchange cooperative agreements with allied governments.[106] Unlike State and Defense officials, those in the AEC for the most part lack numerous personal contacts with governments overseas. The Commission does have a Division of International Affairs, which is concerned occasionally with NATO matters and even with NATO staff, but the AEC's responsibilities make it more concerned with secrecy and "security" for American nuclear arrangements than with alliance responsibilities.[107]

We have seen that decisions relating to NATO reveal characteristics found in other areas of foreign and security policy-making: watered-down compromise; contradictory policy; "paper policy," (cases characterized by a wide gap between declaratory policy and action policy); stalemate; slowness of process; "radar" policy (policy reflecting no clear purpose, but which results from the tendency of participants in the decision process to act on the basis of calculations as to what other participants may do or want); leaderless policy; indecision; crisis-oriented policy; outmoded policy; hand-to-mouth policy-making; and "gyroscopic effect" (policy once set tends to persist). All these attributes flow from the diversity within the United States government of groups of participants in the decision process, participants with separate sources of

---

control over nuclear weapons committed to NATO were a reliable index, the two departments were diverging in their views. In any case, State Department officials did not ostentatiously support Secretary McNamara's insistence on unified control.

[106] Joint Committee on Atomic Energy, Subcommittee on Agreements for Cooperation, *Hearings, Agreements for Cooperation for Mutual Defense Purposes,* 86th Cong., 1st sess. (1959), p. 64.

[107] See Harold P. Green and Alan Rosenthal, *Government of the Atom: The Integration of Powers* (New York: Atherton Press, 1963), pp. 75–78, for the general isolation of the Commission from other parts of the government and its subordination to the Joint Committee on Atomic Energy. The committee, in turn, seems to regard the AEC as far more "reliable" on security questions than the Department of Defense [Joint Committee on Atomic Energy, Subcommittee on Agreements for Cooperation, *Hearings, Agreement for Cooperation with NATO for Mutual Defense Purposes,* 88th Cong., 2nd sess. (1964), p. 25].

political support.[108] When an element outside that government, such as NATO, is added, building the consensus requisite for action is, if anything, further complicated. We ought not, therefore, to expect continuities and orderliness in policy-making regarding NATO which would be uncharacteristic of policy-making in general.[109] Regarding innovation in defense programs, Samuel P. Huntington has commented that "the emergence of an autonomous organization strengthens the program in competition with other programs and usually leads to a marked increase in the resources allocated to the program." [110] There appears to be no good reason why this should not be equally true of an autonomous international organization, and in fact such a development could be observed in the early history of NATO. Later, however, as other international organizations emerged, it was they who had the special attention-getting advantage of newly-won autonomy. Nevertheless, the large number of agencies in the United States government with roles in the decision process affecting NATO assured the alliance multiple access to the United States. As the temporary attention-getting effects of autonomous organization have declined, the more permanent effects of protracted, intimate, and routinized contact have grown.

United States membership in NATO has altered the position of various parts of the executive branch in relation to each other and to Congress. It has provided new ways for them to influence and be influenced by the NATO allies, and it has made the NATO institutions themselves participants in the "legislative politics" of the executive branch.

A giant among allies, the United States, by joining in an organized Atlantic alliance, has strengthened the voices within the country of those with a larger vision of an Atlantic security community as well as the voices of those outside who see America's security and their own country's as tied together. Thus, in the political dialogue of gargantuan

---

[108] Warner R. Schilling, *op. cit.,* pp. 19–26 and 222; he also drew on Gabriel Almond, Roger Hilsman, and others. See also Samuel P. Huntington, *The Common Defense* (New York: Columbia University Press, 1961), pp. 26 and 166 ff.; Roger Smith (pseud.), "Restraints on American Foreign Policy," *Daedalus,* Fall, 1962, pp. 705–16, esp. pp. 713–14; and James L. McCamy, *op. cit.,* esp. chaps. iv–vi.

[109] On this general problem, see Roger Hilsman, "Congressional-Executive Relations and the Foreign Policy Consensus," *American Political Science Review,* September, 1958, pp. 739–40.

[110] *Op. cit.,* p. 198. See also Karl W. Deutsch, *The Nerves of Government* (New York: The Free Press of Glencoe, 1963), for the consequences when there is a "degeneration of steering capacity or coordination" which occurs when a decision-making organization grows large [pp. 225 ff.].

America preoccupied with making its own policy, offstage actors gain the nation's ear. And within the nation, the effect of membership has been to give the same groups a better chance to gain the all-important ear of the President himself.

The President in turn finds that, while NATO membership and its attendant commitments constrain him to listen to new voices, they also strengthen his position vis-à-vis Congress. Furthermore, making himself accessible to the alliance partners has given him new access to them.

Participation in NATO has generated an additional need for coordinating foreign and military policies. Especially during the tenure of McGeorge Bundy, this brought prominence to the role of the President's Special Assistant for National Security Affairs. On occasion this official seemed to be performing what has traditionally been a State Department role, to coordinate the whole of United States policy as it impinges upon the outside world. Furthermore, the Department of State shares with other United States government agencies the making of decisions regarding NATO which it then has the responsibility for formulating and promoting in NATO. It is both the instrument for translating United States preferences into NATO actions and the channel and filter through which the alliance communicates with the American government. State Department responsibility may often exceed its power, for decisions about the defense budget and coalition military planning arrangements taken by others may decisively shape United States relations with NATO.

On its side, the Department of Defense has progressively become a more effective instrument for generating defense policy. The consequent strengthening of the Secretary of Defense has enhanced his role in counsels regarding NATO policy, perhaps in the process weakening the Department of State's efforts to "represent" the NATO allies just as these have come to seek a greater role in NATO strategy and policy. On the other hand, this same strengthening of the office of the Secretary of Defense and the organization of unified commands have made it easier and more likely for American defense policy to be related to his estimate of NATO's needs. So has the development of specialized career patterns for military officers involved in politico-military questions.

Since NATO questions regularly involve two different departments, State and Defense, whose professional experts are trained to approach problems quite differently, the harmony already achieved is at least as noteworthy as the remaining discord. Self-consciousness about political-military coordination has at last begun to bear fruit. However, since the Department of State's prime concern is to promote and protect American interests by strengthening the consensus between the United States and its allies, while that of Defense is concentrated on physical actions for protecting the country, the latter is likely to envelop the former wherever consensus-seeking leads to inaction. Those responsible for military defense will step in to settle unresolved questions unless they are held back.

We should not unduly stress the distinction between the political experts presumably lodged in the Department of State and the military experts in Defense, for some genuinely politically oriented officials serve also in the Department of Defense. The issues in which NATO has been concerned do not divide either along political or military lines, but partake of both. None of these issues involves the fundamental character of the alliance itself. Thus the main difference between Department of State perspectives and those of Defense are likely to be in breadth of perspective.

An observation made by Sir Solly Zuckerman regarding "judgment and control in modern warfare" applies with even greater force to the multipurpose policy-making of the United States government: ". . . the more vast, the more heterogeneous, the more scattered any organization becomes, and the more complicated its component parts . . . . the more difficult it is to control and to concert its multitudinous activities to a single common purpose." [111] Questions relating to NATO have to compete for attention with a thousand and one other concerns of the appropriate policy-makers in the executive branch, and also, as we shall see in the next chapter, in Congress.

[111] "Judgment and Control in Modern Warfare," *Foreign Affairs,* January, 1962, p. 293.

CHAPTER EIGHT

NATO AND CONGRESS

ONLY the very large questions of policy relating to NATO have affected or been affected by decision-making in the legislative branch of the
United States government. Responsibility for day-to-day diplomacy and
for military strategy belongs to the executive branch. Congressional attention is directed mainly to domestic questions, and few members of
Congress expect to get reelected on the basis of their efforts to improve
international relations. Nevertheless, many of them have had to concern
themselves with NATO as they dealt with particular aspects of national
security and foreign policy. As is also true of the executive branch, it is
hard to separate out NATO's impact on Congress and Congressional-
executive relations from the impact of wider developments of which
NATO is a part.[1]

After the United States led in forming the alliance, four important
policy questions raised by American membership in NATO involved
Congress: providing military aid, stationing United States troops
abroad, sharing the expenses of the free world's upkeep, and providing
for the nuclear defense of the alliance. In dealing with these questions
specific Congressional powers were differentially important.

CONGRESSIONAL POWERS

Exercise of the Senate's treaty-confirming power, once the North Atlantic alliance had been accepted, has rarely been a way of expressing

[1] For an early postwar discussion of Congressional behavior in this field see
Robert A. Dahl, *Congress and Foreign Policy* (New York: Harcourt, Brace, 1950);
the recent American Assembly volume on *The Congress and America's Future*,
edited by David B. Truman (Englewood Cliffs: Prentice-Hall, 1965) contains
several pertinent articles, including Samuel P. Huntington, "Congressional Responses to the Twentieth Century," pp. 5–31; Richard E. Neustadt, "Politicians
and Bureaucrats," pp. 102–120; and Holbert N. Carroll, "The Congress and National Security Policy," pp. 150–75.

Congressional concern with NATO. Treaty action was also taken on the accession of Greece, Turkey, and Germany and on the Status of Forces arrangements. But this action simply legitimated "policies initiated by the executive to deal with problems . . . identified by the executive." [2]

Similarly, protection of Congress' constitutional power to declare war necessitated a careful wording of the guarantee contained in Article 5 of the North Atlantic Treaty and the inclusion in Article 11 of the provision, "This treaty shall be ratified and its provisions carried out by the Parties in accordance with their respective constitutional processes." [3] Once NATO was established, these special treaty and war-declaring powers were of much less importance than more general Congressional powers.

Most of the functions of Congress which might be affected by United States membership in NATO, including those arising from its power to raise armies, are performed in conjunction with the executive. Congress has had the ability, however, to play a relatively independent role in two aspects of NATO: activities requiring money and those involving American atomic energy facilities.

When military aid to the NATO allies was vital to the success of the alliance, the need for Congressional approval provided some opportunities for the legislative branch to participate in NATO policy. However, the only important case in which Congress did not in general merely follow, if grudgingly at times, the executive lead was the first authorization of "mutual aid." The House of Representatives, responding to the objections of its Foreign Affairs Committee, balked at the size of the first mutual defense assistance proposals. Authorization was withheld until a compromise, brought about by Senator Vandenberg, was reached between the Senate and the House, which provided that United States military aid must be conditioned upon the recipients' drawing up a plan for integrated defense to be approved by the President.[4] As the importance of military aid to NATO allies diminished, the leverage which Congress might have employed began to disappear.

[2] James A. Robinson, *Congress and Foreign Policy-Making* (Homewood, Ill.: The Dorsey Press, 1962), p. v.
[3] Harry S. Truman, *Memoirs* (Doubleday and Company, 1956), vol. II, p. 249. The need was political rather than legal.
[4] Holbert N. Carroll, *The House of Representatives in Foreign Affairs* (Pittsburgh: University of Pittsburgh Press, 1959), pp. 128–29 and 300–03. See also Arthur H. Vandenberg, Jr. (ed.), *The Private Papers of Senator Vandenberg* (Boston: Houghton Mifflin Co., 1952), pp. 503–08.

The increasing unpopularity of foreign aid in Congress has provided an additional stimulus to efforts, especially by the Senate Foreign Relations Committee, to put at least the NATO infrastructure expenses of the United States into the regular defense budget rather than to continue them under "foreign aid." This change would be consistent with the regularly reiterated argument that "aid" to the allies and especially contributions to the regular expenses of the alliance itself are part and parcel of America's own defense. Even appropriations committees have come to regard as relatively mandatory the financial burdens which the United States has accepted as its share in the upkeep of NATO's defenses.[5]

In their supervisory role over United States participation in NATO members of Congress have been mainly interested in how well the other members of NATO are playing their part and how fully they are paying their share. Eliciting information of this kind is a task familiar to the legislators, who often make public what they learn in order to put pressure on the executive branch. In the case of NATO, however, much of the information so elicited must be kept secret since it involves delicate political matters in other governments. Appropriate Congressional committees have from the beginning been given privileged, very secret information derived from NATO's Annual Review and other NATO sources; they have demanded it as necessary to put a favorable case before the whole House or Senate. Committee members have claimed that their colleagues depended upon committee understanding of the detailed issues; they have used the privilege and the information responsibly.

Occasionally a Congressional committee has prepared a report concerning NATO or, more frequently, concerning questions related to NATO. These reports have usually been friendly to the committee's concept of the alliance and frequently critical of other members' performance in the alliance. It would be difficult to say what influence, direct or indirect, such reports have had on the United States government's policy—to say nothing of alliance policy; members frequently complained that their reports were ignored. Members of Congress are generally well aware of their weakness as initiators of policy, although some of them do not cease trying. A perennial question (asked less frequently in recent years) is why Spain cannot be included in the alliance.

---

[5] See House of Representatives Committee on Appropriations, *Hearings, Mutual Security Appropriations for 1961 and Related Agencies,* 86th Cong., 2nd sess. (1960), pp. 2348 and 2441.

That Congress, in spite of its limitations, nevertheless continues to be important in NATO affairs is demonstrated by the regular appearances of each succeeding SHAPE commander before Congressional committees to report on the state of the alliance. SACEUR's account, as well as the appearance of State and Defense officials who are responsible for aspects of United States policy in NATO, give individual committee members the opportunity to ask provocative questions.

To speak of Congress in general rather than of specific committees or leaders is to miss the main foci of influence. Each committee—indeed, within the House Appropriations Committee, each subcommittee—is likely to have a different perspective, and jealousy between the House and Senate is well known. There is somewhat greater coordination between related committees in the Senate than in the House of Representatives.

The prestige of the Senate Committee on Foreign Relations and of its renowned chairman, J. William Fulbright (and Senator Theodore F. Green before him), has aided the committee in providing strong, if benevolently critical, support for NATO and its members. (An earlier chairman, Tom Connally, was of a different breed.) Less support could be expected from the House Foreign Affairs Committee, especially early in NATO's existence. At first the administration had been less careful to cultivate its good will; furthermore, instead of being one of the most powerful committees in its chamber this committee has had to fight hard for recognition.[6] The armed services committees of the two houses have both occupied a high position. Although not inclined to question the usefulness of NATO, these committees have been disposed towards taking a parochial view, making whatever contribution they might to the strength of NATO by pressing for improvements in the United States defense forces. On procurement matters members have been particularly concerned that the sources be American. (Considering the furor over the TFX contract in 1963, one wonders what would happen if one competitor were foreign?) Since the members have been more interested anyway in the "nuts and bolts" and "real estate" questions than in overall defense matters, this attitude is hardly surprising.[7]

[6] Carroll, *The House of Representatives in Foreign Affairs*, pp. 134–35, 137, 273, and 275.
[7] See Warner R. Schilling, "The Politics of National Defense: Fiscal 1950," in Warner R. Schilling, Paul Y. Hammond, and Glenn H. Snyder, *Strategy, Politics, and Defense Budgets* (New York: Columbia University Press, 1962), pp. 65–66;

Coming to the powerful House Committee on Appropriations, we find a very different picture, one of scarcely concealed ignorance and indifference regarding international organizations. This committee, the despair of the Department of State, conducts much of its business in great secrecy, secrecy which is preserved even between one subcommittee and another.[8] The subcommittee responsible for foreign operations has been for some years chaired by the notorious foe of foreign aid, Representative Otto Passman, who had strong support from the powerful late chairman of the parent committee, Clarence Cannon. It tends to serve as a "conduit" for grievances and exposures.[9] Passman's suspicion that under cover of a military alliance the administration has been expanding all kinds of welfare activities for non-Americans has been shared by other colleagues.[10] Even General Norstad as SACEUR did not escape his challenge: "General, you are competing with a lot of other different programs. . . ." "There is not a member of this committee who would ever meat ax this program. . . . When Congress has worked its will I hope you will have sufficient money to carry out your commitments. I cannot imagine Congress approving a figure anywhere near what has been requested, but you can rest assured that this committee will lean over backward to take no more than just the fat out of the program. . . . You must keep in mind that the economy can stand just so much." [11]

Administration leaders generally look to the Senate to restore appro-

---

Samuel P. Huntington, *The Common Defense* (New York: Columbia University Press, 1961), pp. 134 and 138; and Lewis A. Dexter, "Congressmen and the Making of Military Policy," in Robert L. Peabody and Nelson W. Polsby (eds.), *New Perspectives on the House of Representatives* (Chicago: Rand, McNally, 1963), pp. 305–24.

[8] See Carroll, *The House of Representatives in Foreign Affairs*, pp. 140–62.

[9] Ernest Griffith, "Congress and United States Foreign Policy," in Stephen D. Kertesz (ed.), *American Diplomacy in a New Era* (Notre Dame: University of Notre Dame Press, 1961), p. 375.

[10] House of Representatives Committee on Appropriations, *Hearings, Mutual Security Appropriations for 1961 and Related Agencies*, 86th Cong., 2nd sess. (1960), pp. 543, 551–52, 557, and 560.

[11] *Ibid.*, pp. 515 and 532–33. Often in the past, however, committee members' bark has been worse than their bite. Another subcommittee cut the funds requested for mobile medium range ballistic missiles in 1963 despite support from the Joint Chiefs of Staff, the NATO Command, the Pacific, United States, and Alaskan Commands [Charles H. Donnelly, *United States Defense Policies in 1963*, House Doc. No. 335, 88th Cong., 2nd sess. (1964), p. 23]. And Secretary McNamara complained in 1965 that Congress had twice refused funds to make the theater air bases invulnerable [House of Representatives Committee on Armed Services, *Hearings on Military Posture*, 89th Cong., 1st sess. (1965), p. 343].

priations cuts made in the House.[12] But the Senate Appropriations Committee has had in its membership such old-fashioned isolationists as Senators Ellender, Bridges, McCarran, and Ferguson, who were disposed to question appropriations that could be construed as "international." There were also on the committee Senators with doubts or objections specific to NATO. For example, Senator Dworshak told General White, Chief of Staff of the Air Force, in April, 1961 that in saying SAC was America's main protection he did not mean to "disparage NATO, [but] there is a Maginot Line mentality among too many Americans regarding NATO." Senator Chavez then said, "May I add, General, I think all of us are rather sympathetic to the idea of NATO and the so-called free world but our greatest confidence is in our own military. You will find the American people also feel that way." [13] The constituent whom members of the appropriations committees have constantly in mind is "the taxpayer," who often fails to see the connection between higher taxes and greater national security.

From the point of view of NATO operations probably the most important Congressional body is the somewhat autonomous and extremely powerful Joint Committee on Atomic Energy. Its importance derives not from NATO's impact on it, but from its power to decide questions vital to NATO. At least three Presidents have tiptoed around this committee. It has a dominant position in Congress and has also taken over unprecedented powers of an executive type, rather quickly gaining the upper hand over the Atomic Energy Commission.[14] JCAE members are highly conscientious, non-partisan, and strongly loyal to their committee, but they are short on international experience. They have a narrow conception of national security, and during much of its life the committee has been more interested in building up and protecting American nuclear development than in gearing such development into foreign affairs. In international matters their primary concern has been to prevent pro-

[12] Thus Secretary Dulles personally appeared to ask restoration, inter alia, of funds cut by the House Committee on Appropriations which were intended to strengthen NATO's performance in political and economic areas [Senate Committee on Appropriations, *Hearings, Appropriations for State, Justice, Commerce, and the Judiciary for 1957*, 84th Cong., 2nd sess. (1957), pp. 406–07].

[13] Senate Committee on Appropriations, *Hearings, Defense Appropriations for 1962*, 87th Cong., 1st sess. (1961), pp. 306–07.

[14] For the powers, functions and behavior of this committee see Harold P. Green and Alan Rosenthal, *Government of the Atom: The Integration of Powers* (New York: Atherton Press, 1963).

liferation of nuclear weapons. Unlike the appropriations committees and many others in the House, this joint committee is strongly staffed. It has effectively opposed sharing its jurisdiction over some international nuclear questions with the Senate Foreign Relations Committee. In 1963 it secured the right to review all of the Atomic Energy Commission's budget requests, including military items not formerly part of its jurisdiction.[15]

The committee has carefully controlled all nuclear cooperative arrangements with other countries while simultaneously protecting its own prerogatives, and its members have regularly leaned towards trying to keep nuclear secrets rather than sharing them. (In this respect their actions have accorded with opinions expressed in the armed services committees, whose members have also been apprehensive regarding the loss of American control over nuclear questions.) On a number of occasions the committee has effectively (if not always formally) prevented a more liberal nuclear policy toward NATO allies, and particularly toward France.[16]

As soon as the MLF proposals of the administration became public, the committee sprang to action. Within a few days the Polaris-type submarine proposal was changed to one involving surface ships; there is strong evidence pointing to a JCAE role in this change.[17] A secret report of the committee based on an inspection of American nuclear installations in Europe in 1960 was one of the important factors in bringing about the removal of the Thors and Jupiters in 1963.[18] A reading of the committee's hearings confirms that its members have known how to bring out important considerations that were either being ignored or being deliberately hidden from view by Administration witnesses. In so doing, the committee has clarified neglected points. Its views have been

[15] *New York Times,* July 21, 1963.
[16] See Robert E. Osgood, *NATO: The Entangling Alliance* (Chicago: University of Chicago Press, 1962), pp. 226 and 230–31; *New York Times,* October 18, 1962; Richard P. Stebbins, *The United States in World Affairs, 1959* (New York: Random House, 1960), pp. 65–66, and *ibid.,* 1960 (New York: Random House, 1961), p. 126.
[17] *Washington Post,* February 20, 1963. Vice-Chairman Holifield warned again in April, 1963 that it was necessary to be "extremely cautious" about the MLF proposal and described as "extremely constructive" a plan for an interallied force of national units, with the United States retaining a veto on the use of nuclear weapons [*ibid.,* April 17, 1963].
[18] House of Representatives Committee on Armed Services, *Hearings on Military Posture,* 88th Cong., 1st sess. (1963), pp. 273–81.

as worthy of attention as administration views in a field in which so little can be objectively determined. The big question in the 1960s has been whether or not the committee would bow to pressure for relaxing United States controls over American nuclear weapons as it eventually gave way, in part, to such earlier, far less radical changes as were involved in the nuclear agreements of the 1950s.

It is not only in the Joint Committee on Atomic Energy that members of Congress have shown an increasing interest in NATO affairs. For example, after some delays Congress authorized and financed a United States commission of private individuals to attend a conference of Atlantic states in Paris in January, 1962. Reporting in June, 1962, the commission made strong recommendations for greater unity and integration.[19] Probably more important than this report in influencing attitudes of individual members of Congress towards NATO and the other allies are the annual NATO Parliamentarians' Conferences. (The United States began to send delegations after the conferences had already been started.) United States delegations try to arouse interest among the allied delegations in questions of American concern, such as a unified trade policy vis-à-vis the Communist states and cooperation in aiding development in Latin America, two of the issues raised in 1963. Whether or not they develop transnational interests with their counterparts in other NATO countries the American delegates do at least become better acquainted with each other. The reports coming out of these conferences tend to be wide-ranging, somewhat arbitrary in the items selected for emphasis, and more concerned with economic questions than NATO is officially. The Senate publishes the report in its own series. Since there can be no Congressional delegates to the North Atlantic Council as there have long been on the team which represents the United States each year at the United Nations General Assembly, this unofficial conference has played a part, if only a minor one, in the acculturation of Congress to NATO. Like the meetings of the North Atlantic Council, the Parliamentarians Conference has provided the opportunity for the American participants to have discussions with leaders of particular foreign governments.

[19] United States Citizens' Commission on NATO, *Report,* June 18, 1962, House Doc. 433, 87th Cong., 2nd sess.

CONGRESSIONAL PROCEDURES

Do Congressional procedures hobble potential efforts to use member-ship in NATO more effectively? Two notorious hindrances to legislative action, the filibuster in the Senate and the Rules Committee in the House, have not entered into the picture here. The use of riders, or even regular legislation, to restrict the freedom of action of the administration has occasionally prevented a more cooperative behavior with particular allies in the trade field. The Buy American Act and requirements that government-financed exports in particular programs be transported in ships at least 50 percent American are examples. Apart from the con-trol which Congress exercises over the State Department's personnel practices via the appropriations process, there has been no evidence of the kind of interference in appointments which has occasionally oc-curred in areas other than those relating to NATO. Non-partisanship characterizes Congress' treatment of questions related to NATO even more than that of other foreign policy questions.[20] So far, there have been no formidable interest groups aligned for or against the alliance, at least at the prevailing modest level of international cooperation. Thus, Congressional committees have been able to exercise independent judg-ment on NATO-related questions.[21]

A principal obstacle to more effective participation in a more inte-grated NATO is the almost chaotic fashion in which Congress—especially the House—carries on business, resulting in such fragmented or contradictory policies that the best-organized administration cannot counterbalance the effect. The incoherence flowing from two equally powerful chambers dealing separately with issues is only partially re-duced by resort to joint conference committees to reconcile differences; the eventual outcome is often closer to administration policy. Yet even the incoherence of Congress has its compensations. Thus the fact that every program must be authorized by Congress (often yearly) and

---

[20] The first evidence of any specific party interest in NATO—and it was benev-olent—was the formation of a House Republican "Task Force" for NATO, in-itiated by Representative Quie of Minnesota, which made recommendations on November 20, 1963, and again in May, 1964 [*Atlantic Community News,* Novem-ber 1963, p. 1, and December, 1963, p. 4; *New York Times,* May 15, 1964]. Senator Goldwater's use of the nuclear control issue in the Presidential campaign of 1964 was not a Congressional question.

[21] An unproved suspicion exists that some very large providers of defense items are so influential as effectively to prevent more alliance-wide cooperation in arms supply, but in any case such lobbying is not against the alliance itself.

therefore defended before an authorizing committee in two separate chambers and then at the appropriations stage be justified before two other very differently oriented committees has two effects. (1) The appropriations committees cannot completely carry the field. (2) Although annual authorization keeps the departments on a short string, it gives the Departments of State and Defense more voice, because they have an opportunity to present their views before the other (authorizing) committees, where they are more respectfully heard.

Each committee and each house is highly jealous of its prerogatives and therefore markedly competitive with its rivals. Programs or projects which are not particularly popular with Representatives or Senators are unlikely to have strong advocates among the weaker of the competing committees, such as the House Foreign Affairs Committee. Within the very strong House Appropriations Committee questions related to NATO are divided up among secretive subcommittees, and the answers are not subsequently coordinated. Coordination is a word unpopular in Congress and especially in this committee.[22] Added to this confusion, many questions of interest to the NATO allies, such as questions pertaining to monetary policy, the merchant marine, tax laws, and disposition of farm surpluses, are the "property" of diverse committees having "constituents" different from those of the Department of State or Department of Defense. Even the staffs of the committees—where they are qualified to deal with NATO aspects of the matter under review— have stayed aloof from each other and in any case have been far too few in numbers for gathering and sifting the information members of Congress need to make rational judgments.

In May, 1950 Secretary of State Acheson tried an experiment not repeated. On his return from the meetings of the North Atlantic Council in London, he met informally with the members of both houses of Congress, reported on the meetings, and made himself available for questioning. Instead of concentrating on the matters touched on in his report, the members asked questions that were quite irrelevant, ones that ranged over the whole field of foreign policy.[23] In their committees, on the other hand, members of Congress usually see only the trees, not the

---

[22] Carroll, *The House of Representatives in Foreign Affairs,* pp. 195 and 207–08. Ernest Griffith has argued that there are certain advantages at times in "strategic or tactical obfuscations" [*op. cit.,* p. 385].

[23] Dean Acheson, *A Citizen Looks at Congress* (New York: Harper and Brothers, 1956), p. 80.

forest. For example, the concept of a *regional* organization does not seem easy for members to grasp; most of the questions deal with specific countries. This corresponds to the common American tendency to confuse *allies* with the *alliance* or the organization.

CONGRESSIONAL-EXECUTIVE RELATIONS

The zeal with which different segments of the United States government protect their own decision-making powers is particularly noticeable when the competing segments are two coequal branches, Congress and the executive. To foreign observers, and potential victims, the separation of powers appears to be an inherent defect of the United States Constitution—as, for example, during six of President Eisenhower's eight years in office when Congress was organized by the opposition Democratic Party. So far as NATO is concerned, however, competition between the two branches of the government has not markedly hindered the executive in making effective use of NATO during its first sixteen years. Validating and modifying executive initiatives has been accepted by most members of Congress as their function in this field.[24] Some criticism could be heard but there has been no outright veto of administration action on a NATO matter, for no clear alternative was apparent.

The Foreign Relations Committee report favoring the North Atlantic Treaty stated that the treaty would "in no way affect the basic division of authority between the President and Congress as defined in the Constitution." Less than two years later the executive's interpretation of this division became a matter of extensive Congressional inquiry after President Truman had assigned ground troops to Europe as part of the United States contribution to an integrated NATO command. The clash of opinion over this action exposed several different but overlapping conflicts: old-time isolationist vs. new generation internationalist arguments, strategic air power vs. ground forces, Pacific vs. European priorities. Some Senators who did not clearly take sides on any of these issues were nevertheless concerned as to whether or not the President

[24] See Roger Hilsman, "Congressional-Executive Relations and the Foreign Policy Consensus," *American Political Science Review,* September, 1958, pp. 725–44; Robinson, *op. cit.,* pp. 13–14; Hubert H. Humphrey, "The Senate in Foreign Policy," *Foreign Affairs,* July, 1959, pp. 525–36. Even in other fields Congress tends, at its best, to make its contribution through what David B. Truman calls "the stabilizing and legitimating processes of autonomous criticism and consent" [*op. cit.,* p. 2].

had overstepped his powers. Elaborate hearings were held by a joint session of the Senate Foreign Relations and Armed Services committees on the Wherry Resolution. This resolution, introduced by a member of neither committee, was so worded as to give Senators the opportunity to express their concern that the President's actions in NATO be accounted for to Congress. The demand for formal consultation before the President sent troops to the NATO command in Europe was dropped, but the executive branch did not forget Congress' desire to have reports on major actions relating to NATO.[25] (Administration leaders claimed they had been making such reports all along.)

After the Senators had expressed the frustrations which flowed from the declining ability of the legislative branch to control events in the new era of cold war, Congress settled back to a general acceptance of the United States commitment. Not even the rearmament of Germany and its entrance into NATO aroused Congressional hostility. Quite to the contrary, this move ran in the direction of Congress' preference that the Europeans do more in their own defense.

Congress could have hindered the implementation of the treaty by withholding funds, but for many years it cooperated in providing military assistance to complement the commitment, although members seldom demonstrated a clear understanding of the extent of that commitment. (Few understood that the commitment to "the defense of Europe" was a commitment to support a strategy jointly concerted with the North Atlantic allies. Even when they did, they assumed that the strategy would be more or less dictated by the Americans, with European concurrence induced at least in part by a desire for American aid.) Even the House Appropriations Committee was resigned, if resentful; but it resisted, usually unsuccessfully, the idea of providing funds to persuade other states to put up funds of their own for projects of interest to NATO. In any case, the administration had a number of means for getting around such recalcitrance. It could use contingency funds, deficiency appropriations, and transfers, none of which devices found

[25] Senate Committee on Foreign Relations and Committee on Armed Services, *Hearings, Assignment of Ground Forces of the United States to Duty in the European Area,* 82nd Cong., 1st sess. (1951), esp. pp. 38–41, 53–56, 70–72 and 584. See also Walter Millis, Harvey C. Mansfield, and Harold Stein, *Arms and the State* (New York: Twentieth Century Fund, 1958), pp. 344–49; Huntington, *The Common Defense,* pp. 320–25; and Vandenberg (ed.), *op. cit.,* pp. 570–71.

favor with the Appropriations Committees. Only in its third year of operation did the NATO Science Program come up specifically before these committees.[26]

State Department officials (and those in other departments) perennially complain that especially in matters involving requests for money or regulation of trade Congressional committees tend to fasten them into an administrative strait jacket. For fear of losing control, Congress has regularly refused to authorize aid over periods longer than a year, even though longer-term arrangements could improve the efficiency of the programs and make the negotiation of them with other countries much easier for the administration. Similarly, flexibility in international bargaining tends to be hindered by import quotas, shipping requirements, and agricultural-disposal measures enacted by Congress. Although these restrictions do not affect NATO directly, they have an indirect effect in their reduction of the diplomatic maneuverability of the executive. In one area Congressional restrictions have directly affected NATO: the series of acts relating to atomic energy control have tended to set boundaries to American diplomacy with NATO countries.

Congressional leverage, except for money questions, arises mainly where the executive needs legal authority to embark on new programs. Thus, even if the administration had persisted in the MLF proposal and had reached agreement on it with some NATO allies, the American contribution to the fleet would still have had to be approved by Congress; and the MLF was unpopular among members of Congress of many different hues. The fact that the Joint Chiefs of Staff have two masters, Congress as well as the President, could conceivably enable the former to put pressure on the executive in NATO matters, but this has not happened so far.

Numerous devices blur the jurisdictional lines between Congress and the executive in areas of concern to NATO; the most important is the contingent veto. This procedure requires the executive to lay certain kinds of orders before some appropriate Congressional committee for a specified period during which the committee may vote to recommend Congressional disapproval. The Joint Committee on Atomic Energy has such powers. Action to nullify an executive order on recommendation of

---

[26] House of Representatives Committee on Appropriations, *Hearings, Mutual Security Appropriations for 1961 and Related Agencies,* 86th Cong., 2nd sess. (1960), pp. 534–38.

the JCAE is by concurrent resolution, which is not subject to the veto of the Chief Executive.[27] So far no conflict relating to NATO has erupted from use of the contingent veto. Another device is the requirement that the President specifically declare it to be in the national interest to make an exception to a general restriction laid down by Congress. This the President has had to do in order to continue military assistance to a number of NATO allies who had, in defiance of Congress, traded with Communist countries in the earlier 1950s.[28]

When Congress is showing a general tendency to support the State Department's diplomacy, an administration may not strongly oppose Congressional constraints. Thus the "self-commitment" resulting from a legislative ban on nuclear sharing has on occasion suited the diplomacy of a government bent on preventing proliferation, even among allies.[29] A Department of Defense lukewarm to the idea of a mobile medium-range missile could claim that Congress' failure to appropriate adequate funds prevented the development of this weapon of such great importance to the establishment of a NATO nuclear force.[30] A change of administration may bring a different attitude. Secretary of State Rusk begged Congress to comprehend the fact that once a card had been played, as for example, by Congressional restrictions on aid, it was gone, and United States diplomacy was thereby deprived of a potential trick.[31] When contradictory or confusing instructions are given by Congress (which is quite possible in view of the way it legislates), the administration is not likely to be overly troubled. Such ambiguities permit it a choice of direction.

Although Congress labors under severe handicaps, especially in its lack of either relevant detailed information or acquaintance with the

---

[27] Green and Rosenthal, *op. cit.*, p. 145.

[28] *Department of State Bulletin,* December 24 and 31, 1956, p. 988.

[29] Senate Committee on Government Operations, Subcommittee on National Security Staffing and Operations, *Hearings,* Pt. VI, p. 387.

[30] Osgood has pointed out that the 1954 law giving the Joint Committee on Atomic Energy unusual powers regarding nuclear cooperation agreements "enabled Congress to administer the legal criteria for sharing with a discrimination among allies that the executive branch would have found embarrassing [*NATO: The Entangling Alliance,* p. 402]. See also Thomas C. Schelling, *The Strategy of Conflict* (Cambridge: Harvard University Press, 1960), esp. pp. 26–27, for the general advantages of "self-commitment." Congressional restrictions on military aid gave the administration in 1964 a way to restrain Greek and Turkish action over Cyprus; see James Reston, *New York Times,* August 19, 1964.

[31] Charles H. Donnelly, *United States Defense Policies in 1964,* House Doc. 285, 89th Cong., 1st sess. (1965), p. 70.

broad strategy of the administration, it continues to try to spur the executive into adopting policies not part of the accepted government program though favored by some officials in the executive branch. During the late 1950s many members of Congress tried to get the Eisenhower administration to raise the effectiveness of the armed forces by expansion and modernization. The Senate Preparedness Investigating Subcommittee, under Senator Symington's chairmanship, conducted a formal inquiry on "Major Defense Matters." In similar and related efforts some members of Congress pointed up ambiguities in nuclear defense policy for NATO and the neglect of conventional warfare capability.[32] At least when Secretary Wilson headed the Department of Defense such activities were of no avail, for he ignored both Congressional chiding and Congressional acts while maintaining parts of the defense forces at a low level. The hitherto odd sight of Congress appropriating defense funds unasked for by the administration—and also unspent—became relatively common, especially for congressionally favored items such as particular types of aircraft. Some of the appropriations could have been meaningful to NATO, such as those intended in 1959 and 1960 to modernize the army and improve airlift capabilities, as well as to hasten missile development. These pressures on defense officials by members of Congress helped lay the foundation for ready acceptance of the McNamara reforms; Eisenhower's last Secretary of Defense, Thomas Gates, was already moving in that direction. These reforms in turn altered the United States position in NATO, but relatively seldom had a member of Congress during the slack years asked of a Defense Department witness what effect defense cuts or inadequate preparations might have on the allies.

Depending upon the department, committee, and issue, the executive and legislative branches have many times worked together in fields relating to NATO. Close collaboration between the executive and the Senate Foreign Relations Committee began at the birth of the treaty, with initiatives taken by both President Truman (aware of his predecessors' difficulties) and the author of bipartisan foreign policy, Senator Vandenberg. The "Vandenberg Resolution" paved the way for the treaty; the

[32] Examples appear in House of Representatives Committee on Foreign Affairs, *Hearings, Mutual Security Act of 1959*, 86th Cong., 1st sess. (1959), pp. 21 and 80, and House of Representatives Committee on Appropriations, *Hearings, Department of Defense Appropriations for 1957*, 84th Cong., 2nd sess. (1956), pp. 116–18 and 495–96.

report of the Senate Foreign Relations Committee favoring its ratification specifically mentioned executive-legislative cooperation in emphasizing its own important advisory role.[33]

The Chairman of the Senate Foreign Relations Committee, Senator Green, offered in 1959 to propose a resolution using the wording of the North Atlantic Council on the Berlin crisis—but Secretary Dulles declined the offer as injecting an element of inflexibility into United States diplomacy.[34] Early in the life of the alliance, the executive took little care in dealing with the House Foreign Affairs Committee, an omission for which it paid a price.[35] The consent of these committees was necessary for longer-range matters, but when crises occurred, the executive took quick action without consultation, whether it was in Korea or Berlin.[36] In the October, 1962 Cuba crisis Congress was on a par with the allies in being informed—elaborately, but after the decisions had been taken. (An exception was Senator Fulbright, who was in the inner circle of advisors.) Both allied and Congressional circles understood the necessity for this procedure. The Senate Foreign Relations and House Foreign Affairs committees have conducted some hearings in recent years the purpose of which was at least as much to afford the administration (principally the Department of State) a chance to present its case as to let the legislative branch criticize executive positions or ventilate its opposition. As Senator George was retiring from elective office, he accepted an assignment from President Eisenhower to conduct an inquiry, in his newly retired capacity, into non-military aspects of NATO, which he did with enthusiasm. (This study coincided with the "Three Wise Men" investigation into peaceful uses of NATO.) [37] As NATO faced its major crisis in 1966, both Senator Jackson and Senator Fulbright arranged a series of hearings in their respective committees in order to deal specifically with NATO problems.

Intractable problems can arise out of the clash between Congressional desire for publicity and administration desire for executive privilege;

[33] Harry S Truman, *op. cit.,* vol. II, pp. 242–44 and 250–51; Senate Executive Report No. 8, 81st Cong., 1st sess. (1949); and Vandenberg (ed.), *op. cit.,* pp. 403–08.

[34] Senate Committee on Foreign Relations, *Hearings, United Foreign Policy,* 86th Cong., 1st sess. (1959), pp. 11–12.

[35] Carroll, *The House of Representatives in Foreign Affairs,* p. 328.

[36] See Robinson, *op. cit.,* pp. 4, 50, 54, and 63.

[37] *Department of State Bulletin,* May 28, 1956, pp. 879–90 and *ibid.,* June 25, 1956, pp. 1066–67.

such conflicts may sometimes affect United States relations in NATO. Several different audiences are involved, and the information often includes foreign governments' budgets and plans, publicity about which would erode confidence within the alliance. The executive's attitude towards publicity may explain the absence of a regular State Department report to the Senate Foreign Relations Committee after the semiannual ministerial meetings of the North Atlantic Council.

At the request of the Senate Foreign Relations Committee, Secretary Dulles used to give committee members a panoramic report of foreign relations at the beginning of each session, very little of which appeared in published form. Information on a general level was not always the answer to Congressional desires. The enthusiastic response the House Armed Services Committee gave to Secretary McNamara's innovation in giving each year an extremely detailed picture of the country's "military posture" (compared to earlier cut-and-dried reports) suggests that a genuine need was being fulfilled. Secretary McNamara has also been ready to give explicit answers to Committee members' questions. His annual reviews have paid especial attention to NATO, and members' questions about the alliance suggest much greater enlightenment than heretofore. Late in the day President Kennedy began a similar type of briefing with the Joint Committee on Atomic Energy.[38]

In contrast to the Foreign Relations and Foreign Affairs committees and Armed Services committees is the House Appropriations Committee, which under the long chairmanship of the late Representative Cannon seemed not to desire any potentially weakening contact with the executive branch.[39]

There remain many ways of improving procedures: better formal liaison between members of the executive branch (e.g., State Department officials) and willing members of Congress; more continuous informal contact by administration officials with interested and appropriate committee members; resistance by members of Congress to the temptation to pit one part of the administration against another, especially within

[38] A.P. dispatch in *Greenwich* (Conn.) *Time,* January 18, 1963. The Congressmen's pleasure with Secretary McNamara's frankness gradually declined and did not carry over to other matters, such as the TFX affair, on which the views of some committee members strongly diverged from the Secretary's.

[39] See Carroll: "aloof, discouraging advance consultation . . ." [*The House of Representatives in Foreign Affairs,* p. 329]. A change may eventually take place under his successor, Representative Mahon, who had made defense his speciality [*New York Times,* May 13, 1964].

the Defense Department; better preparation of the State Department position for Congressional committees; a more coordinated presentation of national security questions, especially one which will eliminate contradictions between testimony given by one part of the administration to one committee with that by another to a different committee; and—the most utopian reform of all—better coordination in Congressional procedures, particularly those involving budget decisions. Nevertheless, the unavoidable fact remains that policy for NATO is part of the whole military policy of the United States, and this is a subject which no Congressional committee has yet been able to debate very intelligibly; in fact, none has even made much of an attempt. Most members of Congress tend to see defense matters as a subject for "experts" except when the matters involve expenditures in the member's constituency. Apparently they do not so view diplomatic questions, feeling no inhibitions in opposing the Department of State on specific questions.[40]

Hindering better Congressional-executive understanding about matters pertaining to NATO are perspectives in the executive branch regarding "what Congress will take." To the outsider, State Department and White House officials have seemed unnecessarily timid over the years in educating Congress to the obligations of, as well as benefits from, more wholehearted cooperation in such an international organization as NATO. The short-term gains from avoiding direct confrontation may have had to be secured at a long-run cost. Quite different has been the steady indoctrination given by the executive in the need for foreign aid. Nor has Secretary McNamara been afraid of trouble in presenting very frankly the defense facts of life. His boldness has scored some astonishing successes, despite the apprehensions for their favorite services that he has aroused among some members of the armed services committees. In the face of certain Congressional opposition, he was far less bold in pursuing the idea of a common arms market, tentatively proposed to the allies in May, 1965.

Neither Secretary McNamara nor the military officials who have appeared before Congressional committees have clearly spelled out the meaning of international cooperation and the difference between this

---

[40] See Schilling, *op. cit.*, chaps. iii–iv; Senator J. William Fulbright's speech at the University of North Carolina [*New York Times*, April 6, 1964]; Dexter, *op. cit.*, pp. 312 and 314; and Carroll, *The House of Representatives in Foreign Affairs*, pp. 163, 184, and 190. Perhaps the difference can be accounted for partly because the Department of State deals with goals as well as instrumentalities.

and persuading the other allies to accept American decisions, probably because they did not think it their job to do so. Such elucidation is a job for the political expert, whose expertise is supposed to be preeminently the specialty of the Department of State. The successful political bargainer cannot reveal his techniques, and foreign-policy makers have to persuade two different constituencies, Congress and foreign governments, while avoiding contradictory arguments. Thus allies who disapproved of the embargo on trade with Cuba in 1963–64 could hope that American pressures on NATO members to follow the United States lead were being exerted to gain Congress' consent on some other issues. But were the same committees involved or the same segments of Congress? If not, such a maneuver would be fruitless.

Critics of executive timidity towards Congress regarding NATO affairs may note a possible parallel with executive behavior in matters pertaining to international cooperation in the field of trade. After some abortive attempts to obtain Senatorial approval of the proposed International Trade Organization President Eisenhower resigned himself to the more modest GATT, which has performed fairly effectively in a sphere somewhat more restricted than that projected for the ITO. Again anticipating (and thus almost inviting) Congressional disapproval of a more liberal trade policy, the Eisenhower administration so fashioned its proposals for replacing the OEEC with the OECD as to mute the latter's potential significance in trade negotiations. Once created, however, the OECD began to look at trade questions as well as other aspects of foreign economic policy, even though it was not a vehicle for formal tariff negotiation. Even so, the parallel is not complete, for the economic groupings are organized and operate quite differently from NATO. Furthermore, their activities touch more directly specific influential interests within the constituencies of many members of Congress.

The caution with which the executive proceeds in the light of possible Congressional opposition may be viewed as one way the "government" demonstrates its accountability to a representative organ. The United States alone among the alliance members has a legislative body powerful enough to enforce such accountability when the administration deals with matters relating to NATO. To a minor extent Congress performs this function for all members of the alliance, as when it hears and comments on the reports of SACEUR. That accountability has not been a more prominent feature of Congressional-executive relations in NATO affairs is due partly to uncoordinated Congressional procedures and to lack of executive initiative in educating the legislators. As an independent branch of government Congress could help to develop a broader consensus on NATO's functions while also forcing the executive to refine its NATO-related actions which require defending before Congressional committees.

We constantly hear of the "nuclear crisis" in NATO, but little about a potential "nuclear crisis" in the United States government. A key committee for the success of the executive's proposals for some kind of nuclear sharing in NATO is the Joint Committee on Atomic Energy. This committee's jointness was a rational adjustment to a new problem difficult for Congress to handle in a customary way. Ironically, this jointness gives it the legal and political power completely to frustrate the executive on NATO-related questions, a power greater than that of any other Congressional committee in recent years.[41] On the other hand, the committee has the rare opportunity to play a creative role in fashioning a sensible, down-to-earth response to legitimate allied demands for more participation in NATO's nuclear defense. In 1963 and 1964 we observed a novel political process. The administration had been seeking the consent of its NATO allies to the MLF *before* bearding the JCAE in its den, apparently with the hope of having allied support to strengthen its hand.

In the fall of 1965 Chairman Chet Holifield, perhaps to bury the MLF forever, began to speak of the need to share with the allies genuine participation in NATO's nuclear strategy. Members of this committee also put pressure on the administration through the press to reveal the not greatly publicized extent to which the NATO allies already took part in their own nuclear defense through the arming of their aircraft. The members continued to stress the committee's role in ensuring United States control over the weapons.[42]

The dispersal of functions and heterogeneity of perspective in the legislative branch, combined with the diffusion of power in the executive branch, together make for great caution and conservatism in dealing with new conditions in foreign affairs. If the domestic-affairs oriented Congress were called on to support efforts to distribute the burdens

---

[41] See Roger Smith (pseud.), "Restraints on American Foreign Policy," *Daedalus,* Fall, 1962, p. 706.

[42] *New York Times,* October 21, 1965; November 16, 21, and 23, 1965.

within NATO more in accord with the principle, "from each according to that member's overall capacity," the new division of labor would encounter strong opposition from vested interests well represented in one committee or another. It is small wonder, then, that the United States has often responded belatedly or inadequately to the need for greater mutuality among the allies in providing for the common defense. A further explanation for unexploited opportunities made possible by membership in NATO may be found in the political process of the alliance itself, which we consider in the next chapter.

CHAPTER NINE

DECISION-MAKING IN NATO AND THE UNITED STATES GOVERNMENT

A DISCUSSION of the impact of NATO membership on United States policy-making would be incomplete without considering how policy is made in NATO itself, a process in which the American government is intricately involved. The usefulness of the organization to the United States, its reactions to demands for organizational changes that would permit greater participation by the other members, and the giant member's success in relating itself through NATO to fourteen other allies each different from the other—all these depend in part on how NATO is organized to carry on the alliance's affairs. That NATO functions as a cooperative enterprise for both military and political purposes complicates the organizational problems which the alliance faces in the 1960s. Contrary to President de Gaulle's intimation, NATO is not another part of the United States government; neither is that government free to ignore what the other members do in the organization.

Reliance on nuclear weapons has sharpened interest in how NATO operates and what changes are desirable for changing conditions. The suggested reforms can only be touched upon briefly here in order to assess their potential consequence for American policy-making. Whether one evaluates the adequacy of the organization from the United States viewpoint, from that of the alliance itself, or from that of other members considered jointly or severally, certain characteristics are commonly assumed to be desirable in a cohesive organization. Among them are that all members enjoy a certain equality of respect and status no matter how differentiated their functions, that the organization be reasonably efficient, that it be responsible to the members, that its activities be coordinated, and that the members feel engaged. These five desiderata sometimes conflict with each other, complicating the task of those who would evaluate NATO's procedures. We shall nevertheless keep them in mind while examining the various facets of the organization.

THE NORTH ATLANTIC COUNCIL

The North Atlantic Council is primarily a "decision-ratifier." Apart from that, it is at the most a "planning and consultative body" somewhat remote from the centers of power.[1] The inability of the North Atlantic Council to "take decisions" (except in the form of recommendations to governments) has suited the United States government. The latter has, in any case, no fear of being bound by anything the Council might do, for the unanimity rule prevails. The United States can, when it chooses, use the Council as a convenient instrument for reaching fourteen allied governments simultaneously. It has indefatigably sought North Atlantic Council support for diplomatic interests around the world, and its representatives have heard in the Council different evaluations of events of common interest. The United States has urged the members to consult with each other in the North Atlantic Council before taking a major step in areas of joint concern.[2] Through the Council it has also tried to promote the habit of coordination among members for their policies in various fields and has supported conciliation efforts when other members came into conflict with each other.

By participating as an equal in a fifteen-member organization the

[1] See Senate Committee on Government Operations, Subcommittee on National Security Staffing and Operations, 88th Cong., 1st sess. (1963) (hereafter referred to as Jackson Committee II), *Basic Issues*, p. 16; Institute for Strategic Studies, *The Evolution of NATO,* Adelphi Papers, No. 5 (London, 1963), esp. remarks of Harold Watkinson, p. 36; and Secretary Herter at the Atlantic Convention in Paris, *New York Times,* January 9, 1962. Less complimentary descriptions include "platform for unilateral national assertions about what alliance doctrine ought to be" [Alastair Buchan and Philip Windsor, *Arms and Stability in Europe* (New York: Frederick A. Praeger, 1963), p. 157] and "clearinghouse for individual national aspirations and anxieties" [Alastair Buchan, *NATO in the 1960's* (rev. ed., New York: Frederick A. Praeger, 1963), p. 115].

[2] For American officials the North Atlantic Council is less valuable as a source of information than it is for officials of some of the other countries whose governments are less talkative, and in any case the Council seldom *creates* information, but merely circulates it.

United States can on occasion more easily turn to the smaller members for support against the other large states. For their part, the smaller members often count on the United States to uphold them against the pressures of a bigger European ally. In any case, they gain greater access to the giant member because of the Council. The Americans need not be concerned because the formal status of the United States is no different from that of less powerful members. Not only does its huge military establishment magnify its voice, but the enormous diplomatic establishment supporting its delegation can blanket those of all the others.

Through the Council the United States may share with many others the onus for turning down excessive or otherwise unwelcome demands from individual members as well as for putting pressure on a backsliding member to make its full contribution or to act in accordance with its NATO commitments. On the other hand, in Council discussions a particular member under pressure from the United States can deflect the pressure by reference to the performance level of other allies.

Knowledge of the working of the North Atlantic Council is limited; for sharp discussion, informal exchanges, and often successful appeals for concerted action on minor issues go on in the relatively private regular meetings of the 15 Permanent Representatives. Nevertheless, the blandness and apparent ineffectiveness of the Council's public actions have provoked proposals for reform from many directions. Some critics overlook the fact that negotiating for some kind of agreement is only one of the North Atlantic Council's many functions. The danger remains, however, that if in order to maintain cohesion abrasive initiatives are avoided and issues only indirectly related to the military alliance are evaded, the substance may be lost in the process. Tacit understandings are useful only at top levels: below these levels there must be concrete, detailed agreement on any common course of action. And however great the influence of the North Atlantic Council operating under its present subtle methods, there is no gainsaying that it does not have a very tangible job to perform. It is not called upon to reach decisions based on hard bargaining; and through it nothing of great value can be granted or withheld.

A more vigorous North Atlantic Council would be one in which the other members played a more active role. This, however, poses a dilemma for the giant in a legally equal alliance; for paradoxically, the

United States would have to take the lead in bringing such a change about. On what kinds of issues is the United States prepared in the North Atlantic Council to see the unanimity principle abandoned? Are there some in which it would favor having the Council decide by simple majority? In any competition with the larger European NATO members for the support of the nine or ten others, how would the United States fare? Would the Council be the agency for concerting alliance-wide foreign policy, at least for the NATO area? Would its staff and committees develop proposals on which the Council would act? Given an affirmative answer to these questions, how would the United States draw the line between policies to be determined multilaterally in NATO and those which it would determine unilaterally for parts of the world where NATO does not operate? Could the members' willingness to accept responsibility for the advice proffered become the measure of their participation in United States decisions for non-NATO areas? Past experience suggests that American officials prefer a "strong" Council only when it furthers their own policies.

The United States has not been notably successful in gaining support through NATO for its policies to protect other parts of "the free world." How successful it would be in gaining North Atlantic Council agreement to a comprehensive and unified military strategy for the whole alliance, covering nuclear and non-nuclear forces alike, is problematical. What is the prospect that the Council might instead generate its own strategy? If the prospect is indeed slight, would other indispensable NATO members consider NATO as any more satisfactory than before?

Perhaps the United States could accept the principle of decisions made by NATO itself, expecting that a council of fifteen would only come to some innocuous, watered-down policy acceptable to every member. Note that the problem of using NATO for shared control over nuclear weapons has faced the Council since at least 1960, but it did not formally debate the issue until forced by events to do so in December, 1964.[3] Committees, especially large committees, are noted for "steriliz-

---

[3] The communiqué issued after the December, 1964 ministerial meeting of the Council stated, "Ministers examined the problems confronting the Alliance in the field of conventional and nuclear weapons. A thorough exchange of views on these problems took place and will be continued." But the communiqués for the ministerial meetings of December, 1963 and May, 1964 failed to mention these problems directly, and that of May 24, 1963 simply noted that "Ministers [In deference to the French this form had replaced 'the Council'] . . . approved the steps taken to organize the nuclear forces assigned or to be assigned to SACEUR."

ing" ideas; they cover up differences with obfuscating generalization; and if an agreement is once registered, they may be unwilling or unable to go through the "searing" process of changing the policy when conditions change.[4] If the United States were to decide to seck a fifteen-nation agreement through the Council, this government—like other governments—would find it difficult to give detailed instructions for flexible multilateral negotiations. Wider latitude to its envoy would be necessary. If the Council were to acquire greater influence over the military, and especially the nuclear, defense of the alliance, some kind of executive committee device more effective than the Standing Group would probably be necessary.[5] Perhaps Secretary McNamara's suggestion of May 31, 1965 for a "select committee on nuclear strategy" would help to meet the need. No matter how the smaller members would be represented, whether on a rotating basis or by the Secretary General, their assent to this way of solving a very perplexing problem would be difficult for the United States to secure, even if it wished.

An alternative to breaking the unanimity principle, which is solidly embedded in the North Atlantic Council's procedures, would be provision for abstention from voting by partners not willing to join an undertaking under NATO auspices. Such projects would require only the assent of those desiring to participate in them, rather than the general approval of all members.[6] Already there are numerous NATO undertakings in which only the interested join, but these were originally accepted by the whole Council. They include the establishment of the La Spezia antisubmarine warfare center, the Small Arms Ammunition Panel, AGARD, and consortia for the production of NATO-approved weapons or airplanes.[7] None of these examples approaches in impor-

---

[4] Henry Kissinger used these adjectives to describe the National Security Council in the 1950's.

[5] Klaus Knorr, *A NATO Nuclear Force: The Problem of Management* (Princeton: Center of International Studies Policy Memorandum 26, 1963), pp. 7 and 14; General Norstad's suggestion, "The Longer Second Look," *Atlantic Community Quarterly*, March, 1963, pp. 48–49. See also E. Vandevanter, *Some Fundamentals of NATO Organization* (Santa Monica: Rand Corporation, 1963), pp. 52–73 for some of the difficulties arising from various proposals to increase the effectiveness of the North Atlantic Council.

[6] SEATO's rules of procedure were changed to permit a majority to take some collective stand if no member voted *negatively* [*New York Times*, April 19, 1964]. Thus France abstained from one item in the SEATO communiqué following the ministerial meeting of its Council in the spring of 1964.

[7] The OECD convention specifically allows for abstention by a dissatisfied member which would not invalidate an agreement but simply make it inapplicable to

tance the proposals for some kind of alliance nuclear force, which raise two questions for the United States. How separate can a defense force be without disintegrating the alliance? Who are the indispensable members in a force which does not encompass the whole alliance? (Portugal does not fall under SHAPE's area of command, and its small participation in NATO affairs accords with its peripheral position; but if France is to remain permanently outside the SHAPE command, the effect would be incomparably more serious.) [8]

Part of the dissatisfaction with the way the North Atlantic Council has operated relates to its system of semiannual ministerial sessions. They seem gradually to have become cut and dried; in fact, the United States has tried to keep them toned down.[9] Meetings are scheduled at fixed intervals and may take place at times inconvenient to participating governments for domestic political reasons or at times unrelated to those moments when critical decisions need making. However, regularly scheduled meetings do force the governments to prepare "positions," an especially salutary pressure on the cumbersome American government. They also provide welcome opportunities for the foreign ministers of the larger countries to meet informally prior to the regular sessions without arousing undue speculation about "crises of confidence." In addition, they provide a kind of clearing house for reciprocal requests from officials of the various ministries during the valuable corridor political talk. Unlike the regular weekly meetings of the Permanent Representatives, ministerial sessions attract the attention of the press. This is bound to magnify and usually to distort alleged points of conflict among the members, because reporters have to produce interesting news. At least twice the Department of State has publicly objected to the manner in which news was handled at such a session. Such problems are inevitable when the world is watching discussions which are supposed to be "secret."

The most widespread criticism of the North Atlantic Council relates

---

that member. Secretary General Stikker suggested a similar arrangement for NATO. See also Timothy Stanley, *NATO in Transition* (New York: Frederick A. Praeger, 1965), p. 379.

[8] There is the precedent of Switzerland, not a member of the United Nations but host country to several organizations in the United Nations system. France, in March, 1966, refused even to be host to SHAPE after it withdrew from NATO.

[9] The December, 1963 meeting did not even last the allotted three days. The May, 1964 meeting was, however, made lively by, inter alia, the opposition to the French position. But the December, 1965 meeting was regarded as so little newsworthy by the *New York Times* that probably for the first time, this paper did not publish the communiqué issued at its conclusion.

to its composition for regular meetings. A reform commonly suggested is that the Council at all times consist of cabinet-rank officials, fully responsible members of their respective governments—not, as is now true except for the semi-annual ministerial sessions, merely diplomatic representatives of their governments. Americans who would change the Council variously suggest, in view of their particular constitutional arrangements, "high-level" statesmen, or persons close to the main seat of government, "senior respected citizens," or widely acknowledged public leaders.[10] Occasionally a comparison is made with the United States representative to the United Nations; he is a far more regular attendant at Cabinet meetings and presumably thereby participates more directly in some decisions than do most diplomats. But New York is closer to Washington than is Paris. President Eisenhower promised that the Permanent Representative to NATO, by attending both Cabinet and National Security Council meetings, would be made privy to the government's deliberations, and the Representative has attended from time to time. Since both the National Security Council and the Cabinet in the United States are only as influential as the President wishes, such a status is not by itself very important. The majority of the other Cabinet members have huge domains to administer; but the United States Ambassador to NATO has neither department nor country responsibility, and thus has no ground to stand on.

An alternative would be for NATO to follow an OECD practice. In that organization council meetings are supplemented by periodic gatherings of officials of the member governments with comparable operating responsibilities. Meeting unobtrusively and regularly, they can avoid having to explain either to the press or to a Congressional committee about their "instructions" or about the promises they have made. The conferences can be informal, and the exchange of information and intentions can be useful to each. As their knowledge of and confidence in each other grows, a group *esprit* is said to develop. Governments are not thereby committed, but avoidable frictions are reduced and the way is opened to the discovery of common courses of action. The Assistant Secretary of State for European Affairs, the Assistant Secretary of De-

---

[10] For some examples see Stanley, *op. cit.,* p. 380; James W. Fulbright, "Partners with a Future," *NATO Letter,* February, 1963, p. 13; Henry A. Kissinger, *The Necessity for Choice* (New York: Harper and Brothers, 1961), pp. 166–68; and Robert Strausz-Hupé, James E. Dougherty, and William R. Kintner, *Building the Atlantic World* (New York: Harper and Row, 1963), pp. 292 ff.

fense for International Security Affairs, the President's Special Assistant for National Security, and the Assistant Secretary of State for Policy Planning, for example, might develop the habit of conferring with their NATO opposite numbers. Along these lines an Atlantic Policy Advisory Committee has recently been holding periodic meetings attended by senior foreign ministry officials whose specialty is policy planning or regional affairs.[11] However, procedures which work fairly well in an economic organization are not necessarily applicable to a politico-military organization. Thus many United States offices have no genuine counterparts in other members' governments. Furthermore, there may be confusion between discussion of the individual members' intentions and negotiations to alter them, and regular diplomatic representatives would then fear that their own function would be eroded away.

No one can reasonably expect a foreign minister with the heavy global tasks of the American Secretary of State to take a serious, working part in the weekly meetings of the North Atlantic Council. The same holds true for the Secretary of Defense, although a special meeting of defense ministers, such as that held in May, 1965, may on occasion be convened. Proposals that NATO ministers follow the practice of the Council of Ministers of the Six overlook numerous difficulties; a busy individual can still only be in one place at one time. Rather early in NATO's existence the principals of both the Council and other groupings came to have deputies; these later became "permanent representatives." At least as instructive a model is the Executive Board of the International Monetary Fund. Neither delegates nor international civil servants, the Executive Directors are often present or former officials of their respective countries' treasuries, ministries of economics, or central banks. Although those from the major members are often "instructed" by their governments, they are also likely to have drafted their own instructions.[12]

If responsible officials below ministerial rank and without such titles were to come together under the North Atlantic Council's aegis to discuss problems common to their specific jobs, how would official representatives of the governments involved take account of the discussions?

[11] Stanley, *op. cit.*, pp. 379–80. This practice is along lines suggested also by Robert Bowie.
[12] Ervin P. Hexner, "The Executive Board of the International Monetary Fund: A Decision-Making Instrument," *International Organization*, Winter, 1964, pp. 77–78 and 84–86.

Perhaps some lesson could be derived from the experience of the Deputy Director of the State Department's Office of Inter-American Affairs, who for some time also served as alternate United States delegate to the OAS. Since in NATO the responsible officials would not be "representatives," they could not work for some agreement; but the experience of "learning" together about common problems, in the manner of the working parties of the OECD, might be much more important. An additional advantage for the United States government would be the closer acquaintance among *American* officials who took part in such NATO activities, resulting in coordination by personal relationship. A WEU Assembly's plea for "responsible ministers" who could defend their policies in their respective parliaments would appear to be inapplicable in the United States system. Cabinet and sub-cabinet officials who could testify effectively before appropriate Congressional committees might be a rough equivalent; but on occasion relatively little information might be forthcoming, due to the exercise of "executive privilege." Not one but several changes in procedure made simultaneously probably may be required to revitalize the North Atlantic Council. A United States lead in their acceptance would demonstrate the importance of NATO to this government in its policy-making. The obstacles to inaugurating these are great, however. Like other organizations, NATO has developed "traditional" ways of operating which set the heavy weight of custom against innovation, and officials in the Department of State are specialists in the caution which results from carefully considering every proposal from all points of view.

THE NATO SECRETARIAT

Critics of NATO have called its Secretariat, as well as the Council, "weak," with the implication that only an act of collective will is needed to make them "strong." Some administrative problems are inherent. They arise from variations among the members in fiscal years, in bureaucratic customs and attitudes, and in pay scales; this last tends to isolate the Americans from others and helps to keep most of them out of the Secretariat altogether.[13] Dissatisfaction does not relate to the performance of NATO's housekeeping or service functions, e.g., fiscal ad-

[13] For a description of the personnel system, see M. Margaret Ball, *NATO and the European Movement* (London: Stevens and Sons, Ltd, 1959), p. 59, which also draws on Lord Ismay's Report to the North Atlantic Council, May, 1957 [*NATO Letter*, Special Supplement, June, 1957].

ministration, economic and statistical studies required by the Annual Review, and the administration of the infrastructure projects. Such difficulties as arose here flowed mainly from the extremely complicated rules which have to be followed when up to fifteen countries are conducting a joint program.[14] Indeed, American officials have told Congressional committees that they are satisfied with the way in which representatives of the United States participate in all stages of the budgeting for NATO's overhead and infrastructure. Furthermore, there are suitable procedures for relating programs such as the NATO Science program to the appropriate United States agencies.[15] Although the Annual Review has disappointed American officials because of the lack of immediate response to their spurs for greater activity, it remains important as the "pledging session" among representatives of sovereign states; and the visits of Annual Review teams to the member governments, which are part of the process, serve an American purpose in spreading United States views in appropriate places.

A more substantial complaint of reformers is that the Secretariat makes no dynamic contribution to proposed joint policy in a way comparable, for example, to that made by certain efficient agencies in the United Nations Secretariat. Part of the difficulty is due to the way the North Atlantic Council uses the Secretariat's services. The Council works through committees, subcommittees, study groups, and the like, which far exceed a hundred in number. Many of them are coordinate in authority and manned by representatives from each member. The Secretariat's energies are largely consumed in staffing these committees and providing their chairmen. Whether or not the committee system is a drag on the potential efficiency of the Secretariat, it does mean that a third-party, international, professional point of view coming from the Secretariat is less likely to be presented to the Council than some mixture of national views.[16] The advantage of an international organization for mediating within the alliance by raising an objective standard is thus not

[14] For an example of how infrastructure costs are estimated, see House of Representatives Committee on Appropriations, *Hearings, Mutual Security Appropriations for 1961,* 86th Cong., 2nd sess. (1960), p. 2375.

[15] See House of Representatives Committee on Appropriations, *Hearings, Mutual Security Appropriations for 1961,* 86th Cong., 2nd sess. (1960), pp. 545, 548–49, 552–53, 2347 and 2566; *idem, Hearings, Department of Defense Appropriations for 1962,* 87th Cong., 1st sess. (1961), pp. 462–63.

[16] For observations on how the committees worked in the 1950s, see Ruth Lawson, "Concerting Policies in the North Atlantic Community," *International Organization,* Spring, 1958, esp. pp. 167 and 178. A more recent description appears in Stanley, *op. cit.,* pp. 385–87. For a devastating picture of how the administrative

fully exploited.[17] If it were otherwise, the United States might find difficulty in accepting such views in areas close to the vital center of American security policy.

The Committee of Political Advisers does make use of groups of experts (drawn largely from the outside and from many specialties). They meet prior to the ministerial sessions to prepare working papers on the field of their knowledge. The documents are forwarded to the Council by the Committee of Political Advisers, which is assisted by the Division of Political Affairs in the Secretariat. This committee, chaired by the Assistant Secretary General for Political Affairs, meets about once a week to discuss informally events which might concern NATO; it prepares reports for Council debate and strives to anticipate problems before they have become crises.[18] It provides background material, not the clarion call for action desired by some critics; and its reports are only indirectly related to military doctrine. And even this committee, unless firmly directed, tends to scatter its efforts.

For the United States, with its immense information-gathering and evaluation facilities, the services of NATO's Committee of Political Advisers may appear only indirectly or marginally useful. The deliberate pace of the Secretariat also troubles Americans accustomed to the appearance of speed. Yet the United States gains, and so do the other members, if Secretariat officials manage quietly to serve the objectives of particular delegations in such ways as redefining issues and thus reducing unfunctional national differences at no cost to the collective interest. To some extent this has been done through informal relationships between Permanent Representatives and important mission members on the one hand and some key members of the Secretariat on the other.

An important function of the Secretariat is the preparation of the Secretary General's annual report to the Council. This official has, through the personalities of the successive incumbents, become politically significant. The bigger powers have not always welcomed manifestations of

---

system worked in the field of cooperative weapons production see E. Vandevanter, *Coordinated Weapons Production in NATO* (Santa Monica: Rand Corporation, 1964), pp. 8–13 and 17–34.

[17] See Lord Franks, "Cooperation Is Not Enough," *Foreign Affairs,* October, 1962, p. 33.

[18] NATO Information Service, *Facts About the North Atlantic Treaty Organization* (Paris: NATO, 1962), pp. 72–73. For example, it asks particular governments about actions they may have taken as reported in the press and discusses the reply the following week [Max Beloff, *New Dimensions in Foreign Policy* (London: George Allen and Unwin, Ltd., 1961), p. 72].

this development.[19] Without the Secretary General's drive the Secretariat would seem even weaker. No matter what the personal style of each incumbent, for the smaller members this official has become the "conscience of the alliance," in much the same way as has the Secretary General of the United Nations. His availability as mediator among the members makes him a desirable collaborator for even the most powerful member, especially in interallied controversies such as the disputes over Cyprus.

There are relatively few Americans in the Secretariat, but several have occupied high-level positions, and two have been chief political advisers of the Secretary General. The non-American complexion of the Secretariat is sometimes called a "balance" to the American-dominated SHAPE, which is a kind of military secretariat. Some critics think too large a number of the Secretariat are civil servants seconded from member governments who tend not to remain long enough to provide continuity. Others regard the movement back and forth between the Secretariat and national governments as an asset in building solidarity, a result which would not seem to affect Americans directly, since so few are involved.

Compared to American or other exclusively national agencies, many of the NATO agencies appear inefficient; in any event, they exhibit characteristics frequently found in multilaterally organized activities: great inertia, top-heavy and complicated administration to accommodate the sensibilities of the lesser powers, wide variation in the qualifications of the personnel. Getting a common undertaking under way takes a long time. Member governments drag their feet; and the pace of common action is set by those who hold back the most, who seldom include the United States. (A proposal to set up a technological institute under NATO auspices was misclassified as "secret" and took twelve months to get declassified.[20]) For Americans the inducement to seek an objective through NATO's machinery is therefore reduced.

Loss of efficiency can, however, be more than offset by gains in other directions. A prime example is the NATO Defence College, an institu-

---

[19] Note reactions to Secretary General Stikker's expression of his views on a non-aggression pact at the May, 1962 ministerial meeting of the North Atlantic Council in Athens [*New York Herald Tribune*, May 6, 1962].

[20] *New York Times*, November 17, 1962; *Report of Ninth NATO Parliamentarians' Conference*, House Report No. 1478, 88th Cong., 2nd sess. (1964), p. 39. For comments on the "political infighting" in some NATO science programs, see William A. Nierenberg, "The NATO Science Program," *Bulletin of the Atomic Scientists*, May, 1965, pp. 45–48.

tion which is not dominated by Americans.[21] Although the quality of its course of instruction may not equal that of the best defense colleges in the large NATO countries, the alliance has gained, as graduates of the NATO Defence College have moved into responsible positions in their own countries' armed forces. In many cases the College not only increased the professional capabilities of its graduates, but also imbued them with loyalty to NATO and made them more appreciative of allied countries. As with those returning from service in other NATO institutions, participants return to their own countries and also tend to maintain their personal NATO contacts. Americans who participate in the NATO Defence College have a special opportunity to see the United States as others see it.[22] The personal "engagement" with NATO of the alumni, foreign and American, is an asset to the United States.

The "natural" inefficiency of international "mixed-manned" administrative arrangements may be mitigated or even eliminated in agencies where Americans have the leverage (and the tact) to enforce their own standards. Much American dissatisfaction with the NATO Spare Parts and Maintenance Administration has disappeared as a result of insistence on procedures which prevent staff members from securing special advantages for their own countries.[23] Furthermore, critics should not lose sight of the efficiency often gained by integrated effort. The infrastructure system under SACEUR's direction, even with the cumbersome administrative arrangements, is much more efficient than the chaotic national systems of logistical support for NATO forces in central Europe.[24]

A CONSULTATIVE ASSEMBLY?

If the NATO Secretariat seems often to operate in a vacuum, how much greater might be the vacuum in which a consultative assembly

---

[21] C. T. Honeybourne, "The NATO Defence College," *Journal of Royal United Service Institutions,* 1962, vol. 107, pp. 57–60; and "From One Course to Another," *NATO Letter,* October, 1962, p. 11.

[22] Especially in the seminars dealing with NATO's political problems. See Richard Stillman, "NATO Defense College," *Military Review,* January, 1964, pp. 32–41, esp. p. 36; *idem,* "Collective Education Fosters Collective Military Security," *NATO's Fifteen Nations,* August-September, 1965, pp. 66–70.

[23] See House of Representatives Committee on Foreign Affairs, *Hearings, Mutual Security Act of 1962,* 87th Cong., 2nd sess. (1962), p. 174 [regarding reform of NATO Spare Parts and Maintenance Administration]; *idem, Hearings, Foreign Assistance Act of 1964,* 88th Cong., 2nd sess. (1964), pp. 637–39.

[24] See F. W. Mulley, *The Politics of Western Defense* (New York: Frederick A. Praeger, 1962), pp. 188–90.

would operate! Those proposing such an institution, on the other hand, desire and expect it to make NATO more accountable, to stimulate it to greater activity, and to increase the sense of cohesion in the alliance. For such results to follow, they believe NATO should imitate some of the European multilateral organizations which already have consultative assemblies. Some of its proponents specifically stress the need for a representative body the resolutions of which would have binding effect on the North Atlantic Council and which would have the right to obtain information and receive replies to questions it might put to the North Atlantic Council.[25]

In some instances these proposals reflect greater familiarity with the parliamentary than the presidential system of government. They also reflect the desire of those lacking influence over their own government's policy regarding NATO to have some impact, and certainly more impact than is possible while the United States continues to dominate the alliance. The proponents tend to overlook the relatively ineffective role played up to now by other consultative assemblies, including that of WEU, which has a slender connection with NATO. Even when WEU Assembly resolutions have been accepted by the members' parliaments, they have frequently not been implemented.[26] A link is missing between the actions of these consultative assemblies and the systems of making decisions in the member countries, even where, as in WEU, the members are drawn from the parliaments of member states. The gap would be even greater if the United States were one of the members.

Members of the WEU Assembly and its committees have tried, generally without much success, to elicit information from the Secretary General of NATO and from SHAPE. The facts they seek are often "classi-

---

[25] For some discussions on the need for a consultative assembly see *ibid.,* pp. 241–42; *Report of Eighth NATO Parliamentarians' Conference,* Senate Committee on Foreign Relations Print, 88th Cong., 1st sess. (1963), pp, 8–9; *Report of Tenth NATO Parliamentarians' Conference,* Senate Committee on Foreign Relations Print, 89th Cong., 1st sess. (1965), pp. 10–11 and 28; Stanley, *op. cit.,* pp. 396–99; Senate Committee on Foreign Relations, *Problems and Trends in Atlantic Partnership II,* Senate Doc. No. 21, 88th Cong., 1st sess. (1963), pp. 47–49; Frank Munk, *Atlantic Dilemma* (Dobbs Ferry, N. Y.: Oceana Publications, 1964), pp. 137–39; and J. Allen Hovey, "Interparliamentary Consultation and Atlantic Cooperation," unpublished Ph.D. thesis, Columbia University, 1965. The eleventh NATO Parliamentarians' Conference continued to urge such an assembly [*NATO Letter,* December, 1965, p. 13].

[26] See Forschungsinstitut der Deutschen Gesellschaft für Auswärtige Politik, *Der Stand der europäischen Sicherheit* (Frankfort am Main: Alfred Metzer Verlag, 1962), p. 154.

fied." Furthermore, the Assembly includes numerous representatives of opposition parties whose inquiries create embarrassment for those in NATO who must work, in their relations with any particular member state, with the government of the day. The Permanent Representatives on the North Atlantic Council tend to reply that they are not "responsible" but simply "representative," and thus lack authority to reply.

The reformers are dissatisfied with the NATO Parliamentarians' Conference because of its unofficial character and lack of legal powers. Yet it does hear reports from the top officials of both Secretariat and SHAPE, including reports on the current status of problems discussed by the previous year's conference.[27] These officials find good relations with the Conference desirable because of the support it can supply. After a formal study the 1963 Conference decided not to recommend the creation of a new consultative assembly, but the 1964 and 1965 Conferences were more enthusiastic.[28] Americans in both Congressional and executive branches have been relatively cool to such a change.[29] Compared to members of parliaments of other member states, members of Congress already have much more power to learn what is going on in NATO if they wish to exercise it. They would gain little from a change and might see their present influence diluted. State Department officials have worried about how the actions of American members of a consultative assembly could be coordinated with government policy if they were also officials. If the members were not members of Congress, their authority would not likely be recognized by the legislative branch. If they were members of Congress, there would be relatively little difference from the existing situation.

Those who are agitating for a consultative assembly miss the fact that parliaments do not provide the points at which many kinds of policy relevant to NATO are made, nor are political parties agents in working out and confirming such policy. Nevertheless, concern about accountability would become more widespread and acute if the North Atlantic Council

[27] On the other hand, the Military Committee of the Tenth Parliamentarians' Conference complained that progress on the previous year's recommendations could not be reported due to the failure to receive the requisite information [*Report,* p. 13].

[28] See footnote 25.

[29] See Carol E. Baumann, *Political Co-operation in NATO* (Madison: University of Wisconsin, 1960), pp. 81–92, and Ball, *NATO and The European Movement,* pp. 68–70. Among the exceptions were Senators Kefauver and Fulbright and Representative John Lindsay.

should become more than a representative body and take on a life of its own more like that of the commissions of the European Communities. If the United States grew readier to accept such an increase in the Council's power, the question of an assembly would have to be faced seriously. Meanwhile, the NATO Parliamentarians' Conference has continued to be a useful sounding board and vehicle for stimulating action on small-sized problems.[30]

Critics have also deplored the scattered location of the various civilian and military headquarters of NATO. With the North Atlantic Council and the NATO secretariat in Paris (and SHAPE in the nearby Paris suburb, Rocquencourt) and the Military Committee and the old Standing Group in Washington, an ocean has separated the Council and what were intended to be its military advisers. SHAPE's proximity to the political center of the alliance may have contributed to its growth in influence and functions at the expense of the Military Committee, even though SHAPE was formally only headquarters of one of four regional commands subordinate to the Military Committee. The move of the Military Committee from Washington to Europe, which the Council decided upon in June, 1966, in order to bring the Military Committee close to NATO's political headquarters, may show whether it was proximity or the inherent importance of Allied Command Europe which have led SACEUR to play an outstanding role.

Suggestions, now overtaken by events, that the North Atlantic Council meet on American soil also reflected a desire to bring the Council and the military organs of NATO closer together; but there was the further wish to bring the whole NATO decision-making process closer to points at which American policy is being made. It seems unlikely to have aroused the kind of uneasiness Latin Americans have expressed at having the OAS secretariat housed in Washington, where it is supposedly under the thumb of the giant member. SEATO's headquarters, so remote from the main focus of important policy-making as to make it easily forgotten, illustrate a disadvantage to the small-power members in an organization's not having its seat in Washington, one which the Latin-American critics of the OAS may have overlooked. Western Europe is not Southeast Asia, however, and the analogies between NATO and the other regional security

---

[30] Secretary General Stikker advised the Conference that his staff was instructed to follow the debates carefully and prepare analyses to serve as additional guidance to NATO, but that the obligation of the members of the Conference was to seek to influence their *own* governments [Hovey, *op. cit.,* p. 76].

organizations should not be overdrawn. Having the North Atlantic Council, as well as the Military Committee, in Europe gives the Secretaries of State and Defense the occasion for trips to several European political centers and not merely to the capital at which the current semiannual ministerial session is being held.

That the members' delegations have been housed at the Porte Dauphine in Paris along with the civilian headquarters has encouraged closer informal working contacts between the Americans and others. Such informal proximity is frequently more important than official communications, as the United Nations has often demonstrated.[31] Presumably, the host country should become especially sensitive to the potentialities of the organization, but in what way? President de Gaulle is said never to have visited SHAPE.[32]

Other reformers would have had *both* Military Committee and Standing Group eliminated altogether and their advisory function carried on by a different office (such as a Minister of Defense in the Secretariat) or else have had them reinvigorated and given more staff.[33] Unhappiness with location is related to a more deep-seated criticism: the North Atlantic Council lacks an effective "general staff"; and the Military Committee and Standing Group, especially the latter, which were to advise it, have permitted national rivalries to be expressed at the expense of collective action in the common interest. The vacuum has been filled by an American-dominated SHAPE and an American strategy. If strategic planning is to be more generally shared by the other members and if the various parts of the NATO military operations (including the Atlantic Command) are to be more closely articulated, some staff changes giving a larger role to officials of the other NATO members would be necessary.

[31] Informal working contacts are all the more important because the living arrangements and salary scales of Americans abroad, where they are numerous and gregarious, as in Paris, do not facilitate social contacts with NATO personnel from other member countries.

[32] See C. L. Sulzberger, *New York Times*, January 8, 1962.

[33] In 1964 the staff of the Standing Group was "internationalized," a German general was made director, and places were opened to non-Standing Group countries [*NATO Letter*, July–August, 1964, p. 26]. An example of proposals to improve the "civilian-military planning staff" may be found in Stanley, *op. cit.*, pp. 387–88. General Sir Richard N. Gale, after he had served at SHAPE, suggested that the tenuous connections between the three supreme commands might be remedied by having the Supreme Commanders form a council to make concrete proposals, with the Standing Group serving as the executive staff ["A Critical Appraisal of N.A.T.O.," *Journal of the Royal United Service Institutions*, Vol. 106, 1961, pp. 154–63].

As both former Secretary General Stikker and Secretary McNamara have emphasized, decisions on strategy, force goals, and budget need to be brought together. In dealing with these interrelated questions the North Atlantic Council is more or less dependent upon SHAPE for military advice; but this "Supreme Headquarters" was originally intended only as an operating agency in Europe, one which reflected American policy chiefly because it was through this command that United States forces essential to the defense of Europe were related to forces locally available.[34]

The United States is called on to recognize NATO's need to adapt to the growth of Europe's own military capabilities and potential and to the expansion of the alliance's political as opposed to strictly military concerns. How can the tie which binds SHAPE so closely to the United States be loosened without destroying the efficiency of the military machine in Europe? If planning is too far removed from operations it becomes unrealistic and ineffective; inserting more political offices into the military planning system could impede action. SHAPE is, after all, the most successful manifestation of the alliance.[35]

THE SUPREME ALLIED COMMANDER EUROPE

Neither the radical alterations proposed in the decision-making machinery of the alliance, and especially that relating to SHAPE, nor the agitation in behalf of the proposals appealed to General Norstad or to his successor. General Norstad warned of the demoralizing consequences of continual reappraisals of the modus operandi, especially when they lead to proposals not thought through.[36]

No assessment of the position of SACEUR or his command can be separated from the personality of the individual who longest held this post. General Norstad was in SHAPE for twelve years and was

[34] For the process by which NATO requirements are worked out in Washington and then presented to the other members see Senate Committee on Foreign Relations, *Problems and Trends in Atlantic Partnership II,* p. 30.

[35] Cf. Vandevanter, *Some Fundamentals of NATO Organization,* for weighty arguments against these proposals, esp. pp. 29–33, 46–47, and 67–73.

[36] See Jackson Committee II, *Hearings,* Part I, p. 14; also *NATO Letter,* July–August, 1963, pp. 20–21. Others who have participated in SHAPE fear that too much tinkering with the admittedly defective organization might vitiate the military effectiveness of NATO and endanger a reasonably well-functioning supreme command; see, e.g., General James E. Moore "The Military Effectiveness of NATO," in Karl H. Cerny and Henry W. Briefs (eds.), *NATO in Quest of Cohesion* (New York: Frederick A. Praeger, 1965), pp. 162–66 and 175.

SACEUR for six. He made the most of his right to communicate directly with the governments of the member states and was on easy terms with prime ministers and defense and foreign ministers of other NATO countries as well as with the President of the United States and several Congressional committees.[37] However, SACEUR and the Secretary General could only communicate with each other informally; the formal connection was through the Military Committee or Standing Group in Washington. Informal contacts between SHAPE and civilian NATO officials were, nevertheless, continual and productive of much "lateral coordination." [38] In contrast, formal relationships between SACEUR and his "masters," the Military Committee, have been via a liaison staff which was less influential and lacked his knowledge of essential technical detail.[39] General Lemnitzer has followed his predecessor's example in giving top priority to establishing good relations in various NATO capitals and becoming better acquainted with the appropriate ministers. He has also followed General Eisenhower's precedent in reporting frequently to the President and to high American officials.

General Eisenhower refused to jeopardize his international status by taking on major duties regarding the American military aid program.[40] However, in a kind of dual role, each SACEUR made important recommendations during the whole of the period of assistance from the United States. Another dual role began with General Eisenhower's successor. General Ridgway asked for and was granted the additional title of Commander-in-Chief of the United States Forces in Europe; this arrangement avoided the need for coordination, which Ridgway said was often synonymous with red tape and delay.[41] His successors have continued to have the two appointments, although the duties as a commander of

[37] In commenting on the importance of communication in building up confidence levels General Norstad said, "It helps when you can pick up a telephone and can talk to the President of the United States from time to time" [Jackson Committee II, *Hearings*, Part I, p. 26]. See also House of Representatives Committee on Foreign Affairs, *Hearings, Mutual Security Act of 1959*, 86th Cong., 1st sess. (1959), pp. 466 and 474.

However, because of SACEUR's ambivalent position his relations with parts of the Pentagon have not been so easy; see William W. Kaufmann, *The McNamara Strategy* (New York: Harper and Row, 1964), pp. 36–37.

[38] James Moore, *op. cit.*, 175 and Vandevanter, *Some Fundamentals of NATO Organization*, pp. 25–28.

[39] Gale, *op cit.*, pp. 156.

[40] Senate Committee on Foreign Relations, *Hearings, Mutual Security Act of 1951*, 82nd Cong., 1st sess. (1951), p. 45.

[41] Matthew B. Ridgway, *Soldier* (New York: Harper and Bros., 1956), p. 238.

American forces have been very largely delegated to a Deputy Commander. General Eisenhower also set the precedent that SACEUR and SHAPE stay out of "diplomatic" questions, such as the admission of Spain.[42] Furthermore, from the beginning, each SACEUR has insisted that the officers at SHAPE be truly international and take no instructions from their own governments regarding their NATO duties; respect for the spirit in which integration has been implemented at SHAPE has steadily grown.[43] Many American officers at SHAPE had attended the National War College and thereby or in other ways had acquired a political sophistication desirable for their sensitive duties.

SACEUR has served two kinds of master and has performed such diverse functions as planner, adviser, and commander that reformers have doubted their compatibility. The consensus-building endeavors of SACEUR, which depend upon his staying out of the glare of publicity and preventing any conceivable breaches of confidence, probably would have been more successful without the complications of nuclear weapons. Even so, they were highly effective with all but the largest allies. Furthermore, the difficult task of "command" by persuasion, requisite in an international military organization, has been successfully met. As the most important military officer of the fifteen-member organization while at the same time the nuclear agent of the President of the United States, SACEUR had an ambivalent position, a position with the vices of its virtues.[44] Because of this relationship it was feasible for the United States to provide such weapons to NATO, but the special position of

[42] Senate Committee on Foreign Relations, *Mutual Security Act of 1951*, 82nd Cong., 1st sess. (1951), p. 21.

[43] Note the citation accompanying the award of an honorary degree by Oxford University to General Norstad, *The Times* (London), June 27, 1963. Other commentaries on the international spirit at SHAPE may be found in Field Marshal the Viscount Montgomery of Alamein, *Memoirs* (Cleveland: World Publishing Company, 1958), p. 461; Vandevanter, *Some Fundamentals of NATO Organization*, pp. 61–62 and 64–65; Lt. Col. Rolf Ehle, "Spirit of NATO Staff," *Military Review*, November, 1963, pp. 35–39; and Lt. Col. Jack E. Carter, "The International Staff Officer," *NATO's Fifteen Nations*, December 1964–January, 1965, pp. 49–52.

The question was raised in 1964 as to how long French officers with such "international" attitudes would be allowed by President de Gaulle to remain at their NATO posts (*New York Times*, May 24, 1964). By 1965 they were under French Government orders not to participate in certain activities of SHAPE. In a sense this confirmed the international character of SHAPE, because their activity there could not be reconciled with De Gaulle's views on integration. In March, 1966 De Gaulle announced complete withdrawal.

[44] For the virtues, see Vandevanter, *Some Fundamentals of NATO Organization*, pp. 46–50.

SACEUR emphasized that the United States had not really relaxed control over these nuclear weapons. Yet neither General Norstad nor General Lemnitzer (despite the fact that the latter had previously been the highest American military officer) could—if they wished—dominate American strategic policy as it involved NATO. Their influence in the Pentagon diminished regarding nuclear strategy, the more *European* and independent they appeared.

Meanwhile, those in the alliance who wished a larger role for their own nationals tended to think of SACEUR as an *American* officer, a situation which their governments willingly accepted in an earlier era.[45] That SHAPE military doctrine as expressed by SACEUR did not always correspond with the particular developments in thinking among Pentagon strategists did not register with some European critics. So long as the United States continued to provide most of NATO's nuclear defense, SHAPE was unlikely to develop into anything resembling a functional equivalent of the "High Authority" in the European Coal and Steel Community. Yet, if SACEUR were to be a European, the valuable links that previous American SHAPE commanders had with different portions of the United States government would disappear; and the alliance would lose much of its strength. Meanwhile, the trust that most of the allies put in those who did head this command was a great asset to the United States.

Part of the dilemma may be obviated as American officers come to occupy fewer subordinate command posts in SHAPE and the other commands; the number has been declining somewhat in the 1960s.[46]

[45] See Harry S Truman, *op. cit.*, vol. II, pp. 257–58. Two former United States officers at SHAPE have complained that some Washington authorities also mistakenly thought SACEUR would be subject to their orders [Vandevanter, *Coordinated Weapons Production in NATO*, p. 67, and James Moore, *op. cit.*, pp. 164–65].

[46] For a long time Americans officers appeared in practically every alternate layer, partly at the wish of the smaller powers; see House of Representatives Committee on Foreign Affairs, *Hearings, Mutual Security Act of 1957*, 85th Cong., 1st sess. (1957), pp. 540–41; Laurence I. Radway, "Military Behavior in International Organizations: NATO's Defense College," in Samuel P. Huntington (ed.), *Changing Patterns of Military Politics* (New York: Free Press of Glenco, 1962), p. 118. Illustrative of recent changes was the appointment of a British Commander of the ACE Mobile Force, earlier under an American general stationed in Germany [*NATO Letter*, March, 1964, p. 26]. On the other hand, former Secretary General Stikker reported in 1965 that a study of 200 generals and flag officers assigned to NATO showed that about 100 were American or British, while the Germans occupied only 25 such posts [Dirk Stikker, "NATO—the Shifting Western Alliance," *Atlantic Community Quarterly*, Spring, 1965, p. 14].

French demands for more recognition in the distribution of commands, however, have worked in the opposite direction; for earlier rebuffs and subsequent French withdrawals made later NATO concessions to the French even less likely. Even before De Gaulle's pronouncement of March, 1966 there appeared no way out of this dilemma, at least if it were considered outside the context of the whole question of French disaffection. Prompt recognition of German claims to more command posts could go a long way in satisfying the legitimate prestige requirements of one of the strongest supporters of NATO and could deflect other more risky kinds of claim. This has been one of many very good arguments made for reorganizing or abolishing the Standing Group. By the mid-sixties there should be suffcient numbers of well-trained *anciens* from the NATO Defence College to permit substitutions from other countries for American officers, if the natural opposition to losing footholds for control can be overcome.

Americans are by no means the only or most conspicuous claimants preventing more flexibility in the command structure. Some suggestions for dividing the command over conventional forces from that over nuclear forces—so far as they exist in Europe—stem from European desires for greater opportunities for control over the latter. If such a division were to be made only for "strategic weapons," such as some versions of the MLF would require, the motivation could be traced to *American* desires to retain control. To both types of suggestion General Lemnitzer insisted that "defense is indivisible." [47] Disintegration of the SHAPE command would be inconsistent with American interests in the long run.

CIVILIAN CONTROL

Command issues are clearly political in the sense that different governments are vying for influence or protecting what they have. These controversies emphasize a frequent criticism of NATO as it now stands: that there is insufficient civilian control by the North Atlantic Council over the military arm of NATO. Since only the latter, primarily in

[47] Speech to WEU Assembly published in *NATO Letter,* July–August, 1963, pp. 20–21. He made a similar criticism of certain aspects of the British proposal for an Allied Nuclear Force, which would have removed some elements from his command. In a comparable concern about command questions, the Germans were resisting in 1964–65 British proposals which would have the effect of weakening SACEUR's position, since the Germans were strongest in SHAPE.

SHAPE, has something specific and tangible to do, how is one to prevent NATO's military tail from wagging the civilian dog? In some ways the Council's plight resembles that of Congressional committees which try to keep control over the United States military establishment without the sources of information and perspectives vital to exercising such control.

One solution to the Congressional committees' problem is to acquire more knowledgeable staff for their own use. This is not unlike what numerous reformers propose for the NATO Secretariat, including those who think in terms of a Minister of Defense to aid the Secretary General. Nevertheless, the elaboration of administrative machinery beyond critical needs should be avoided if NATO wishes to escape the fate of the OAS, which is almost drowned in seas of committees, commissions, secretariats, semi-independent agencies, and the like.[48] NATO's organization should also profit from the lesson presented by those United Nations agencies which spend much time arguing and deciding on procedural matters while the substance escapes them.

The many informal facilities for communication between officials of SHAPE and members of the Secretariat help to promote the merging of civilian and military perspectives, even though, in the formal structure, this contact only appears to take place at the apex. Some such interchange also comes from the contacts between member governments and their military representatives at SHAPE as well as their military officers who are part of the international staff.[49] On the other hand, former Secretary General Stikker complained that cooperation between the *higher* civil and military authorities (i.e., the Military Committee and Standing Group) was highly unequal. He reported that the civil side provided all sorts of opportunities for the military to participate in its deliberations, but that the military "refuse the presence of civil authorities at their meetings, refuse to provide agenda and records of meetings, and refuse to make working papers available." [50]

[48] See John C. Dreier, *The Organization of American States and the Hemisphere Crisis* (New York: Harper and Row, 1962), pp. 119 ff.

[49] One means for military-civilian communication has been the "SHAPEX" Conference held annually by SHAPE, attended by the North Atlantic Council, Chiefs of Staff of the members, the Standing Group and senior officers in the NATO commands, to discuss major problems faced by the alliance. Specialists from member countries, both in and out of government, have also attended [*NATO Letter,* September, 1963, p. 26]. Still another means is the office of Political Adviser to SACEUR.

[50] Stikker, *op. cit.,* p. 14.

Criticism that the North Atlantic Council lacks control over the military side of NATO often boils down to dissatisfaction with the amount of *alliance* control over United States policy-making relevant to NATO. This lack of power is inevitable as long as most of the members make contributions so small compared to the American shares that they neither feel the incentive to demand nor appear to have a legitimate claim to a large voice in the joint planning. The United States has always done whatever it considered additionally essential to make good on any deficiencies in the military arrangements of NATO or of the other members.

The disappearance of the patron-client relationship in military aid provides an opportunity for different attitudes to prevail—for the Europeans to assume the larger burden in the common defense which the Americans desire and for the Americans to recognize the larger share in making common policy which the Europeans desire. The United States could be more sure of its allies' judgment if there were quiet ways of introducing appropriate NATO officials more directly into the planning which goes on in the Pentagon. Even symbolic gestures can promote greater understanding; such a gesture was the arrangement for NATO Defence College students to visit defense facilities in the United States in addition to those in European member countries which the students had previously visited.

Would the United States officials be psychologically prepared to accept informed criticism of American-generated defense ideas? Perhaps some of them might find encouragement from experience in a neighboring field. Apart from the Annual Review in NATO itself, there are relevant cases in other organizations. OECD studies and resolutions have been taken seriously by, and sometimes regarded as valuable support for, those American officials who wish to alter United States foreign economic policy (or even such domestic economic policies as those pertaining to taxation). When the United States finally agreed to an international committee organized under the OAS to help sift Alliance for Progress projects and suggest priorities, it found part of the onus for making embarrassing judgments on their partners' performances could be borne by that interallied group and shifted from the United States. A similar development is conceivable whenever the United States is readier to share strategic planning with the alliance, not merely with selected allies.

Many problems will remain unsolved, despite organizational or procedural improvements to accord with changing conditions. The political tugging and hauling is continuous, merely taking different and more constructive forms depending upon the channels provided. Some of the changes necessary to keep NATO as vital as American officials declare the United States objective to be will require changed attitudes and ways of doing things inside the United States government. Americans will need to find new compromises between the demands for equal respect from the other members and efficiency within the organization, between responsibility of NATO to all its members and coordination of national activities, between United States leadership and the engagement of all the other members. Not all the reforms touched upon above would effectively serve these purposes, and current practices would sometimes better be left alone.

CHAPTER TEN

THE APPEALS OF PLURALISM
AND THE COSTS

ON THE fifteenth anniversary of the signing of the North Atlantic Treaty President Johnson declared that it was "a tested and recognized foundation stone of America's foreign policy" that Americans would never turn back to "separated insecurity" and that "we are eager to share with the new Europe at every level of power and at every level of responsibility." [1] If these statements were more than ritual—and even ritual has its significance—they imply that NATO is a useful instrument to the United States in pursuing its foreign policy objectives. That it also must be useful to the other members goes without saying, else it would have quickly disappeared. Its value to them enhances its value to the United States. But some uses the United States has sought to make of NATO have at times competed with each other.

A political process special to the postwar world, although not unique to NATO, has thus developed. Through the years there have been feedbacks in this process which altered NATO's functioning. (Some changes in the environment have been of course quite independent of NATO, though relevant to it.) They have produced a need for adjustments, to which the United States has not always responded as readily as the President's proclaimed eagerness for sharing power and responsibility might suggest.

NATO has not been an end in itself. This is clear from the ways in which the United States government has behaved. What is not clear is the meaning that has been attached to "NATO" in officials' statements

[1] *New York Times,* April 4, 1964. Similar sentiments were expressed two weeks later in a major foreign policy speech [*ibid.,* April 16, 1964].

at particular times. Were they thinking (or at least speaking) of NATO as an organization, as distinguished from an alliance or from an American guarantee to allied members? Or were they using it as shorthand for certain allies (particularly France, Britain, and West Germany)? The public's confusion regarding the difference between the organized alliance and the allies has been even greater. (Thus Americans have found difficult to comprehend General de Gaulle's reiterated support for the alliance as a commitment and his opposition to the idea of the organization.) These distinctions are important in judging the range of American choice. In this study we have stressed NATO as an *organized* relationship between several states. Given the cold war, some form of multilateral policy-making and cooperation was almost inevitable. The choice of instruments for the United States was to this degree limited, providing the goals were those actually pursued. The need for joint action meant that there would be some kind of reciprocal impact between the collectivity and the United States; but, as we have seen, the American focus was seldom on the need for adjustments by the United States to the evolving organizational needs of the alliance.

THE UNITED STATES USE OF NATO

In a variety of ways NATO has been an instrument of American policy (as it has also been an instrument of that of other members), though not all of the roles envisaged for it by American policy-makers are wholly compatible. It has provided the organizational framework for the highly successful Western effort to deter Soviet aggression. The "German problem," though unsolved, has remained within manageable limits largely because of the way the Federal Republic has been involved in NATO activities. Using NATO as a vehicle for exercising American influence has, however, become more difficult the more successfully NATO has been used to revive European defense capabilities and the Europeans' will to defend themselves. Americans have less and less been able through NATO to persuade their European partners to help themselves according to a "made in America" defense strategy—even though some of the American projects for cooperation would have achieved substantial defense economies within the NATO framework. The allies have begun strongly to resist American pressures, even those for increased coordination and cooperative activity. For most of the allies such resistance grew more out of renewed self-confidence than out of bitter resentment of United States power. (Canada, the other non-European member, though in many ways the most dependent of all upon the United States, also has increasingly felt free to withstand such pressures.)

The North Atlantic Council has been useful for simultaneous political communication with fourteen allies (and for seeking their diplomatic support), but the hope of many Americans that NATO might form a nucleus for some vaguely defined but more institutionalized "Atlantic Community" has not been realized. The United States has not regarded NATO as a suitable instrument for general economic cooperation and has found it somewhat refractory for putting economic pressure on Communist countries. Proposals to expand NATO's functions have been a focus of controversy within the alliance in the 1960s.[2]

Some of the reasons why the United States has not been able to accomplish through NATO all that various American officials have hoped for flow from perspectives of United States government officials on the role of the giant member.[3] The American nuclear guarantee and, in the early years of NATO, military aid were vital to the success of the alliance. It was practically inevitable that the United States government should in consequence expect to formulate the strategic plans and guide the general policies of NATO, as well as to demonstrate by its own example what NATO military forces could achieve. But leadership also meant putting Americans into the majority of leading positions, and the need to stimulate others to action sometimes made the Americans insensitive to the need for demonstrating that NATO was a reciprocal relationship. An exception is to be found in the legal domain; the unprecedented Status of Forces Treaties originated in a need created by NATO. Unlike the partners of the United States in SEATO and the OAS, the NATO allies were sufficiently self-confident in their dealings with the giant not to be immobilized by suspicion of "intervention" in strictly domestic affairs; their concern was rather that they also should be able to participate in decisions on affairs of mutual concern.

How did United States defense policy differ from what might have

---

[2] Cf. the neatly defined "concepts" cutting through much of the fog, which are offered in Stanley Hoffmann's "Discord in Community," *International Organization*, Summer, 1963, pp. 521–49, esp. pp. 524–31.

[3] But if adaptation to change in accordance with "reality" requires some clearly defined failure of means to reach a goal, as Hadley Cantril suggested [in Lloyd Free, *Six Allies and a Neutral* (Glencoe: The Free Press, 1959), p. xiii], such a failure has not occurred.

been expected in the absence of NATO? American forces organized under NATO auspices or made available to NATO constituted a relatively small portion of the total United States striking power, especially in view of SAC. They were nevertheless the forces most vitally important to United States defense planning, aside from SAC. American participation in NATO shaped defense decisions as to the size and form of military aid given the allies, the stationing of American ground forces in Europe, certain cooperative research and development projects, and the acceptance of a few standardized items approved by NATO's military authorities. However, in the New Look–massive retaliation era, American defense planning seemed to take little cognizance of NATO forces. American pressure resulted in NATO acceptance of heavy reliance upon tactical as well as strategic nuclear weapons; many analysts have since felt this to have been a mistake. Budgetary decisions in the mid-1950s reducing American conventional or ground forces were apparently taken without much regard to their impact on NATO planning, on the decisions of NATO allies regarding their own force levels, or in general, on the credibility of American commitments abroad.

Changes in the stationing of American intermediate-range ballistic missiles were made "in the framework" of NATO planning, but were not an integral part of NATO plans, which could only react to the changes. When the Thors and Jupiters were replaced by Polaris missiles, the connections with NATO became even more tenuous, although some Polaris-armed submarines were "committed" to NATO. In the case of the intermediate-range missiles some allies had something to say about their deployment, but neither the alliance nor any ally had any responsibility for defining the military requirements which governed their design.[4]

When military doctrine changed in the United States and "flexible response" became the theme, the European allies proved hard to win over to a new policy which required more of them, but continued to deny them an important voice in the nuclear arm of their "collective" security. The United States government began devising schemes to satisfy this legitimate concern and yet allow itself to retain nuclear control. The MLF proposals would hardly have been conceivable if NATO did not exist. All these conclusions apply only to American defense responses in

[4] See forthcoming study by Michael Armacost on "The Thor-Jupiter Controversy in the United States Government," based on unpublished Ph.D. thesis, Columbia University, 1965.

the Atlantic area; in other parts of the globe the United States has pursued its defense planning without much reference to NATO, although it counted on NATO to hold the fort in the region outside North America most important to United States security. In comparison to the OAS and SEATO, however, American defense authorities have paid close attention to NATO; this indicates that there is real substance to their frequent reiterations of the importance of the North Atlantic alliance.

Although United States officials have formally recognized a connection between arms and arms control policies, American arms control efforts have not been exerted through NATO. From 1957 onward the United States consulted *allies* in and out of NATO in negotiating for reductions in arms. NATO was not a major instrument in forwarding this aspect of foreign policy; both the United Nations and the International Atomic Energy Agency played larger roles. Since NATO's very existence was part of the controversy with the Soviet Union over steps towards disarmament, the United States might not in any case have been able to promote certain objectives in this area through the alliance. However, the Soviet Union's desire to weaken if not to destroy NATO gave it an incentive to bargain with the United States over arms control. American views and those of other major members were sufficiently divergent to make almost impossible a joint policy of much significance. The question of a still broader fifteen-nation consensus thus hardly arose. Nevertheless, the habit of diplomatic collaboration built up in NATO caused the United States to be more solicitous of its allies' views than might otherwise have been the case, even to the extent of following apparently inconsistent policies regarding arms control and nuclear weapons for the alliance.

In formulating and implementing United States foreign aid policy (outside the military field) NATO was used in only a very minor way. It was a channel for urging larger European contributions to economic assistance for developing areas; but the United States helped create the OECD in part to meet this need more effectively. Since the members themselves (except Greece and Turkey) were hardly in need of economic aid after the midfifties, NATO's function was even less important in this field than that of the OAS and SEATO; all three alliances played minor roles in influencing the allocation of American economic assistance.

Other organizations were available for cooperation in lowering barriers to foreign trade—or raising them, in the case of exports to the Communist countries. Allies in neither NATO nor the OAS received special consideration when United States tariff policy was determined, and quotas or similar restrictions were occasionally imposed on products or services of high economic importance to some of these countries. The United States was more amenable to suggestions or pressures emanating from the OECD and GATT than from NATO. It responded vigorously to another organization in which it was not a member, the EEC; and it participated not only as one manager and contributor to the International Monetary Fund but also in 1963 as a prospective consumer of its services.

United States policy respecting decolonization differed from that of certain members of NATO. Their views tended to be identified in the minds of the ex-colonial countries with a nonexistent NATO stand on these issues. Although the United States followed no clear pattern, it was blamed by both sides. United States behavior in various colonial crises was very little affected by its NATO membership; in crises of decolonization American action was shaped far more by membership in the United Nations.

Among the diplomatic issues vital to American security, only with respect to Berlin and German reunification was United States policy coordinated with NATO or through NATO with its major allies. In Laos and South Vietnam the United States played its part as if SEATO scarcely existed. In questions relating to Castro's Cuba, the OAS followed fairly reluctantly the leadership of the giant member.

As the foregoing brief summary of the impact of NATO on United States foreign and security policies suggests, the United States has not fully exploited potentialities of membership in this organization. With respect to defense matters, the United States seemed almost to be moving away from rather than towards the ideal of balanced, collective forces in the 1960s; in any case it has been slow to recognize the new basis on which collective defense must be balanced. No attempt was made to expand the small area in which forces were integrated, NATO's Central Europe Command, to other command areas, notably the Atlantic and Mediterranean. (An important decision was taken, however, in the late 1950s to integrate air defense.) Heavy emphasis on nuclear deterrents during the massive retaliation days sapped later European interest in the doctrine of flexible response and the particular balance of collective forces which all-round acceptance of that doctrine would have implied. The United States continually came up against the question of who was to decide on the division of labor, but it did not adequately recognize the importance of this question.

Earlier American practice sometimes got in the way of later efforts to promote cohesion in NATO. For example, military aid was provided to individual members on the basis of bilateral agreements, although it was set in terms of NATO requirements. Much more could probably have been accomplished through standardization and cooperative arrangements such as the Mutual Weapons Development Program. Among the numerous obstacles were lack of interest among lower echelons in the United States defense agencies, American efforts to redress the balance of payments through sales of United States military products, and European suspicions that United States producers would continue to flood the market for armaments.

On the highly controversial question of command and control of nuclear weapons for defense of the NATO area, we conclude that the final order to fire them, if the time should ever come, ought to remain in the hands of the President of the United States, as the executive for the alliance, but that far more can be done in sharing the decisions leading up to such an order. The MLF proposal evaded this critical question. Confidence-promoting measures necessary to satisfy the other allies on the matter of unified command and control have been late in coming and have had to overcome serious obstacles raised by earlier American failures to share more fully nuclear knowledge. Genuine allied participation in strategic planning would also require the United States to act more consistently as a partner rather than as an independent agent in affairs related to the others' interests outside the immediate NATO region. Several times in the late fifties and early sixties this government deployed its forces in non-European areas without adequate warning to its allies and apparently without much reference to NATO plans, although at no time with such devastating consequences as followed the Suez venture of two of its main allies. Unless the United States uses NATO as a confidence-building device with its major allies, it will lose its chance to forestall such ventures. Even when the United States has taken unilateral measures having the effect of a degree of informal arms control, these actions have raised suspicions among some of the larger members of the alliance that the United States was making a deal with the Soviet Union behind their backs.

In 1956 the United States began to take seriously the opportunity NATO offered for political consultation. To identify any instance in which American diplomatic behavior changed as a result of NATO consultations or followed advice given by others in the secret meetings of the North Atlantic Council would be difficult. Aside from rather liberally giving information about United States views on political matters around the world and expressing willingness to listen, this government has mainly "consulted" in NATO in order to summon up diplomatic support for its own already elaborated policy. Such support is likely to be forthcoming only on a quid pro quo basis, something not always recognized by Americans. And support will not be given if its effect clearly runs counter to what another member views as its interest; the Cuban embargo case was one in which the United States failed to get via "consultation" allied agreement to trade restrictions which it sought.[5]

In international economic matters, the United States has attempted to follow contradictory policies. (So have many of the other allies.) Greater harmony might be achieved by concentrating on strengthening allies rather than on weakening the foe, whose economic well-being does not necessarily run counter to American security interests. Economic concessions to allies, though not made *through* NATO, could take the edge off dissatisfaction with American dominance in the security organization. A similar effect would clearly follow if the United States government paid more attention to the timing and style of its actions relevant to NATO, so as to lessen the impression of an attitude of superiority and to eliminate some of the twists and turns of official policy.

For the United States NATO has been a means to organize consensus, but not on all foreign policy matters. With sensible restraint the Americans have avoided using NATO as a caucus on issues before the United Nations. They have not attempted to force Spain's acceptance

[5] The case was somewhat similar when the United States sought economic aid in its Vietnam struggle. A typically restrained view was expressed by Foreign Minister Lange of Norway on May 28, 1964: "It is questionable whether our limited resources for international development assistance should be used in such a manner. This does not imply lack of appreciation for the ungrateful task of protecting security interests in many parts of the world which circumstances have thrust on the U.S.A." [*News of Norway,* June 4, 1964, p. 1].

into the alliance, or to extend further the minor excursions of NATO into the fields of foreign trade and foreign aid. Since NATO is not an all-purpose instrument—though it may be a multipurpose agency—one should avoid imputing failure to the organization if it carries out only the functions which it was expected to perform. Among these, insufficient attention has been paid to its role in managing the "German question," which might otherwise be even more unmanageable. It has clearly been in United States interest—as also in its allies'—that Germany should find its way back to respectability and usefulness in a comprehensive alliance in which its position would not be dominant. Also, the readiness of the United States to pay the costs for arrangements more or less ordered by Americans—has prevented a fuller testing of a possibly more substantial role which the other allies could play.

In the sixteen years of NATO's life there have nevertheless been striking proofs that through it the United States has strengthened its own security position by strengthening its allies. On political issues it has found in NATO an expedient channel for a fifteen-nation exchange of views clarifying positions and sharpening perceptions of the real world of demands and techniques used to further them. The special contributions of the smaller members probably could not have been secured outside NATO. These achievements had to be paid for; "a collective policy requires those who take part in it to do some things they might not do if they were acting alone, and not to do some things they would privately like to do." [6] Among the costs were some restraints on action in the United Nations and greater rigidity of policy, especially in dealings with the Soviet Union. Perhaps the number of cumbersome inconveniences increases more rapidly than the number of states with which the United States must find accord, even if some states are less difficult than others. But these inconveniences need to be balanced against the conveniences, and some have been overcome by devices American officials describe as "within the framework of NATO." The problems of coordination are nevertheless large, even if in one sense the organization itself is a coordinating device.

A large part of the coordinating process must take place within the United States government, where the preliminary "battle of Washington" tends to overshadow the struggles within the alliance. The responsibility for coordination falls primarily upon the Department of State.

[6] *Economist,* May 16, 1964, p. 690.

Experience with the United Nations and its specialized agencies, particularly in the administration of foreign aid, suggests ways in which a more adequate mechanism than currently exists could be devised also for NATO. Thus, the office of the Assistant Secretary of State for International Organization Affairs is a focal point for consideration of a number of United Nations agencies, and he plays an important role in the budgeting procedures for these agencies.[7]

There is no Assistant Secretary for NATO Affairs; but the Assistant Secretary for European Affairs, to the extent that he concentrates on Atlantic Community questions, elevates the importance of NATO affairs in the State Department hierarchy. Also, there are increasingly effective means of coordination between the Department of State and Department of Defense; not least of these are the informal relations between officials in the two departments responsible for NATO-related matters. In any case, NATO issues of consequence go to the top of the executive branch.

Basic obstacles to coordination nevertheless remain. They stem from the generally disintegrative tendencies of the executive branch of the United States government, from the combination in NATO of functional and regional characteristics in a way that does not correspond to the prevailing organization of the Department of State, and from the absence of strong political levers for the Department of State to employ in coordinating activities with the much larger Department of Defense. In that department, furthermore, a special Assistant Secretary deals with NATO matters and related types of international affairs; and it is through that department that the American government communicates with SACEUR and other American military officers in NATO commands. An important development, partly traceable to NATO, is the increase in numbers of personnel in both State and Defense who might be called politico-military experts, who in themselves provide a coordinating capability.

A comparable type of expert for Congressional-executive matters often helps to overcome the disadvantages of the insufficient liaison between Congress and the administrative agencies, but he appears to be in insufficient supply among agencies interested in NATO affairs. Some

[7] See Harlan Cleveland's testimony regarding his "two hats," House of Representatives Committee on Foreign Affairs, *Hearings, Foreign Assistance Act of 1962*, 87th Cong., 2nd sess. (1962), p. 712.

Congressional committees help to supply this deficiency, but the way in which Congress divides its work among existing committees limits their effectiveness in Congressional-executive rapprochement. The one Congressional committee, the Joint Committee on Atomic Energy, that does in effect share administrative powers is not well tuned to NATO's requirements; yet it possesses extremely important powers over NATO-related matters. The NATO Parliamentarians' Conference, although unofficial, has helped to brdge the gap between administrative officers responsible for NATO affairs and Congressmen interested in NATO questions, but here again on each side jurisdictional concerns have stood in the way of greater coordination.

Coordination through individuals by means of "indoctrination in the common purpose" can also occur when American officials serve at some stage in their careers in NATO offices or in the USRO delegation. More military personnel than State Department personnel appear to be so affected, partly because the NATO secretariat itself has few seconded Americans in it.

The special relationship which the President as Commander-in-Chief of the United States forces has had with NATO's most important military commander, SACEUR, has made NATO a more flexible resource for American policy-makers. Certain features of the American governmental process further increase NATO's utility. Although NATO questions only intermittently occupy the President's attention, this organization can at times be helpful to him when he negotiates with the domestic quasi-sovereignties ostensibly part of his executive branch responsibility, as well as with Congress. The powers of Congressional committees to ask questions at length about almost any subject administered by the executive branch provide an opportunity, though Congressmen have seldom fruitfully employed this instrument to increase NATO's usefulness to the country. Nevertheless, Congressional criticisms concerning the military posture of the United States did help to prepare the ground for sharp improvements in that posture in the 1960s, with indirect consequences for the strength of NATO as well. Despite persistent questioning about the adequacy of other members' contributions, Congress has remained fairly generous in providing funds for American participation in and the pursuit of defense policy in NATO. The regular appearances of SACEUR before several Congressional committees have helped to give the members a sense of participation in an organization otherwise apparently beyond their ability to influence.

This study did not find that serious impediments to an effective use of NATO have arisen from the "arbitrary" timing of Presidential elections, the treaty-ratifying powers of the Senate, or the separation of powers between executive and legislature. Grudgingly, perhaps, but inevitably, Congress has followed the lead of the executive in matters directly related to NATO. When the executive's freedom of action is limited by statute, as it is by the atomic energy control legislation, it does not inevitably find this "self-commitment" a disadvantage in negotiating with other members of the alliance. In other cases the boundaries between executive authority and Congressional authority can be brushed over for easier accommodation of the United States government with an international organization.

There remain in the American system of policy-making some serious obstacles to more effective use of NATO. The President, acknowledged to be the leading official of the alliance (not the organization), has so many high-priority responsibilities that his attention is focussed on NATO only at intervals. The "tortured collective efforts" necessary to define an official policy in the United States mean that it may jell too early or too late or linger after the circumstances calling it forth have disappeared. Among the administrative obstacles to an effective link between NATO policy and related questions is the splitting off of the arms control agency from the Department of State. The unreadiness of Defense Department officials to incorporate strategic planners from NATO into their own planning process can seriously impede the sharing which the organization needs so greatly. Likewise, the preoccupation with secrecy of many members of Congress has prevented sharing information which long ago could have built up greater confidence in the alliance if it had been provided at an early stage. Furthermore, Congressional restrictions in the economic field lessen the willingness of the allies to accept United States leadership in meeting security problems. Congressmen also tend, more than those in the executive branch, to look at *allies,* singly or in numbers, rather than at their relationship in the *alliance organization,* and to act accordingly. If the executive branch had been less timid in educating Congress to the need for reciprocity in an alliance or other collective international effort, NATO's usefulness could also have been enhanced.

Such an effort would have required that administrative leaders themselves become more conscious of the commitments and therefore of the inescapable costs as well as of the usefulness of NATO. In the American system of government such consciousness is often aroused by pressure groups. A number of opinion leaders have sought to promote a better appreciation of NATO. Organizations interested in the Atlantic Community have grown up in the 1960s the membership of which contains political leaders in and out of Congress.[8]

Most of these groups also concern themselves with the OECD, the economic organization for the Atlantic (as opposed to purely European) partners, and they take an interest in the European Community organizations. But these are only the beginning of the many different joint approaches which the United States can make to problems facing the states of the Atlantic world.

THE USES OF OTHER INTERNATIONAL ORGANIZATIONS AND BILATERAL DIPLOMACY

In the range of foreign and security policy choice which United States participation in an international organization affords, NATO stands alone. It is the only one that affects significantly the range of choice on military matters. But NATO functions other than security tend to overlap those more appropriately performed by larger or smaller organizations—or differently composed groups of states—such as SEATO, ANZUS, the OAS, and CENTO. The United States is not even a member of some of these organizations, although it may have representation to them or provide assistance through some informal type of associate participation. In others, European states which do not belong to NATO are useful contributors to the building of the new European institutions.

Does the United States government wish to get help in regulating trade in strategic materials with Communist countries? There is COCOM, but the European Coal and Steel Community is also empowered to impose quotas on Communist oil imports into the Europe of the Six if there is danger of undue dependence on those imports.

Is the United States concerned about the hunger, poverty, and acute dissatisfactions of the more than seventy underdeveloped countries? Numerous agencies connected with the United Nations are available to

---

[8] For example, the Atlantic Council of the United States, the American Council of the Atlantic Association of Young Political Leaders, and the House Republican Task Force on NATO Unity. Whether or not such groups produce a more sentimentalized conception of NATO, their activities properly directed could make officials more regularly aware of this organization when policies related to it are being considered.

tackle their problems of trade and aid; GATT, the International Bank, the International Monetary Fund, and OECD's Development Advisory Committee may be especially useful; and both the OAS and SEATO provide a framework for special assistance to their needy members. In addition, various consortium arrangements have been made between individual countries or private enterprises in them working together with some of the above-mentioned agencies. Through these even the EEC has participated in development aid projects for countries in Latin America.

Does the United States wish to see some scientific advances, especially in atomic energy or space, that would be more difficult or less rewarding if done either by Americans or by Europeans, working alone? The multilateral groupings available for this purpose include (but are not confined to) ESRO, ELDO (in which Australia is also a partner), Euratom, and the IAEA. On issues of immediate concern to NATO there are other, smaller groups also working. Military standardization progresses through a rather informal cooperation program involving Australia, Canada, Great Britain, and the United States; this program can also serve as a catalyst for more extensive multilateral cooperation.[9] An Ambassadorial Group, consisting of representatives from Great Britain, France, Germany, and the United States, meets in Washington to plan political strategy for Berlin; the group often refers its views to the North Atlantic Council, although it has no connection with NATO.

In the rich variety of multilateral agencies we should not lose sight of the older, bilateral avenues for pursuing American foreign policy objectives. In American relations with unaffiliated Sweden and Spain the United States perforce depends upon bilateral diplomacy. Of particular importance are the quiet ways this country works with its northern neighbor inside and outside the alliance; there are, for example, committees at the cabinet level composed of responsible officials from the Canadian and American governments and joint committees of members of the two countries' legislative bodies. Similar close arrangements exist with the British government; one of several results beneficial to the alliance as well as to the two immediate parties was the agreement for the BMEWS station at Fylingdale in Yorkshire which grew out of such a two-nation group. Among the various advanced countries the infinitely complicated network of information-sharing on military, economic, and

---

[9] See J. H. Barnes, "International Cooperation in Army Research and Development," *Military Review,* January, 1963, pp. 48–56.

political matters defies description and requires little formal organization.

For government-to-government action, however, bilateral negotiations have limitations which on occasion a multilateral approach can overcome. The United States maintains official relations with more than one hundred governments; but its most extensive opportunities for cooperation lie with the advanced states which are members of the North Atlantic alliance or the OECD, or SEATO. High American officials continue mainly to deal directly with the capitals of these countries rather than indirectly through an organization such as NATO, in which the matters of common concern can also be dealt with. Apart from the normal day-to-day operations of bilateral diplomacy, such bilateral (or trilateral or quadrilateral) negotiations (especially when they take the form of meetings between heads of states) sometimes arouse suspicions that a bargain to the disadvantage of the other interested members is about to be made. They can even embarrass the particular partner so favored.[10] Despite the frequent assertion that other countries, especially if they are small, prefer to make, state by state, individual arrangements with the United States, their officials observe that the state which dispenses can also withhold and, in so doing, create intense dissatisfactions. The smaller states may on many issues exert more influence as a group than if they negotiated separately. This fact has not escaped the notice of American officials, who sometimes find a combination of smaller states in NATO, for example, useful collaborators when differences arise between the United States and one of the other larger members. Furthermore, organizations such as NATO and OECD help to shift some burdens from the United States whether of financing or of obloquy.

With such a variety of approaches open, the United States can more easily conduct a flexible policy, choosing one or more instruments according to the stage in the negotiations and the objectives pursued.[11] Rational choice of "the organizational venue" and reduction of incongruities among United States policies in the various international organizations, however, are difficult without better coordinating mechanisms in

[10] For example, the United States-German arrangements on the purchase of arms, November 13, 1964.

[11] See the forthcoming study by Henry G. Aubrey, "Economic Cooperation —the Case of the OECD," prepared under the auspices of the Council on Foreign Relations, New York, chaps v and vi.

the United States government, as we have observed earlier. The ultimate success of each choice will further depend upon the planners' vision of how future events may impinge on the chosen policy and how the immediate choice will affect the world ten years or so hence.[12] Other partners' preferences also affect the outcome of a choice, a simple fact occasionally unnoticed by American officials who in addition may fail to observe *changes* in these preferences.[13]

Many NATO members have become disenchanted with the behavior of the United Nations General Assembly and Security Council, as the character of the world body has changed in composition and general orientation.[14] Their attitude, and the changes from which it sprang, have made the position of the United States difficult. For most purposes, however, the American government may find NATO and the United Nations quite compatible and complementary; they are instrumentalities having for the most part rather different functions.[15] Such conflicts as have arisen were mainly over the issues of decolonization and disarmament. On the second issue the United States is likely to be on the same side as its European allies and on the first issue is only partly differentiated from them.[16] However, as William M. Jordan has pointed out, the house of the United Nations has many mansions, and in most of them the claims of the North Atlantic alliance create no difficulties for American choices. One function the United Nations performs which no less-than-global organization could do: it provides a giant communications and negotiating center for all parts of the world.

As was formerly true of conflicts among members of the OAS, conflicts between NATO members have not been brought to the United Nations; the Cyprus conflict is the exception. The second flare-up of this

[12] Cf. Robert Bowie's remarks, Senate Committee on Government Operations, Subcommittee on National Policy Machinery, *Hearings,* 86th Cong., 2nd sess. (1960), Part VI, p. 889.

[13] Note American efforts in 1962 to keep European neutrals out of an organization to which the United States did not belong, the EEC. Such backseat driving is bound to be frustrated. See Gordon Brook-Shepherd, "Does Europe Need Its Neutrals?" *Reporter,* May 24, 1962, pp. 29–32.

[14] As one writer put it [Edmond Taylor, "NATO After Spaak: A Loss and a Warning," *Reporter,* April 13, 1961, p. 17], they tend to think of NATO as "a kind of large family, while the U.N. is a capricious tribunal." It seems irresponsible, unwieldy, even, in ex-Secretary General Spaak's words, "hypocritical."

[15] Cf. Francis O. Wilcox, "The Atlantic Community and the United Nations," *International Organization,* Summer, 1963, pp. 683–708.

[16] As Secretary Rusk has explained divergencies in NATO members' votes in the United Nations, the allies behave as members of a free society.

conflict almost inevitably came before the United Nations, since Cyprus was not a member of NATO.[17] This dispute, involving in addition to Britain the two members of NATO that are least "Atlantic" and most different from the other members, shows what can happen when an organization expands; for the new members had rather different value systems and were united with the original members chiefly by a common threat. Greece and Turkey were welcomed because they border the Iron Curtain and are willing to maintain large armies. Moreover, these two countries might have gone to war at once had they not been in NATO.

The suspicions of the "third world" regarding NATO ("militaristic countries" with a "vested interest in the status quo") and the OECD (a "wealthy white man's club," despite Japan's accession in 1964) hinder the United States from using these organizations extensively in dealings with the underdeveloped countries. This applies particularly to NATO, which unlike the OECD, has little to offer such countries. No matter how useful these agencies may be in keeping the peace of the world or in promoting its prosperity, they are suspect by their very membership. Even GATT's "action program" for developing countries did not deter these countries (or the Soviet Union) from running a parallel conference in Geneva in 1964, under United Nations auspices, at the same time that GATT was meeting. On the other hand, advanced countries not members of NATO may welcome joint activities promoted by the organization, such as the proposed International Institute of Science and Technology, should the United States and others wish to "improve NATO's image" by making it appear more than a military grouping dedicated to upholding the status quo.

There is a double problem of coordinating United States policies with respect to the various multilateral regional security organizations to which it belongs. There is the need to secure coordinated (or at least not incompatible) actions from NATO, OAS, and SEATO in support of the totality of American security policies. As the main link between these three organizations, the United States alone is in a position to define and prescribe for this problem. (For CENTO it is Britain which is the formal link, but even in CENTO the Americans are influential and active "observers.")

The second need for coordination arises within the United States gov-

---

[17] The first occasion grew out of Greece's hope to profit from anticolonial sentiment in the United Nations.

ernment. There is hardly any place in the administrative structure below the highest levels, however, where policies toward each of these organizations may be harmonized, except informally. Spontaneous new relations are being formed between the numerous economic organizations, such as those between the OECD and OAS in its economic manifestation and between the EEC and the economic agencies of the OAS. There are, however, many more economic organizations to be linked together. Regardless of their articulation, American foreign economic policy remains highly uncoordinated, in part because of Congressional restrictions on the ability of the administration to choose more rationally.

INHERENT OBSTACLES TO MORE RATIONAL USE

No matter how well organized the United States government may be for effective use of NATO and other multilateral organizations and no matter how large the supply of feasible instruments, some conditions in the world of international politics remain intractable. The first is that the United States is the giant even among the large and powerful states in NATO, and there are inherent difficulties in acting as an equal among unequals. Mutually acceptable ways to share alliance burdens when the giant also has global responsibilities have yet to be discovered. Since NATO is even more important to the security of some of the European members than to that of the United States, it might seem politically feasible for them to carry a larger share of the burden than they are now carrying, but this would also mean more sharing of the command. Fortunately, there are ways of blurring the differences in power and in interest, as the Annual Review indicates. Americans, even though the main strategic initiatives are theirs, must accept the need in a partnership for a flow of frank criticisms; the main current of criticism necessarily moves from the smaller members to the initiators of policy. The others have more scope for "heresy" than the necessarily conservative world leader. After all, the difference between the United States and the others is not that it is independent; it is only less dependent.[18]

Another factor limiting the utility of multilateral action through international organization is the differing perceptions among members of the process of change within the two blocs. Shifts in Soviet political tactics

[18] See John W. Holmes, "The Advantages of Diversity in NATO," in Karl H. Cerny and Henry W. Briefs (eds.), *NATO in Quest of Cohesion* (New York: Frederick A. Praeger, 1965), p. 289, and Geoffrey Crowther, "Reconstruction of an Alliance," *Foreign Affairs,* January, 1957, p. 175.

are often mistaken by some of the NATO members as changes in Soviet strategy. Until President de Gaulle's rude shocks occurred the United States showed equally poor perception in not recognizing that the growing polycentrism in the Western bloc requires changes in its perspectives of its own role.

A third limitation arises from the blending into one organization of states with different, even if mostly democratic, constitutions. Members accustomed to the parliamentary system have difficulty appreciating how the American system operates, and vice versa. The obstacles are more serious in an organization the more members there are with less responsible political systems; NATO is in this respect better off than, for example, the OAS.

Even events in the internal politics of different member countries, particularly the fact that some state is always getting ready for a "crucial" election, make rapid adjustments or effective proposals almost always seem untimely in these alliance organizations.[19] Even when they do not look as if they are intruding into "domestic" affairs, the Americans are nevertheless going to affect such politics no matter what they do or fail to do. The Atlantic alliance has nonetheless been notable for the absence of one member's attempt to intervene in another's internal affairs. Furthermore, stability of government policy has distinguished the alliance; even the shifts in France and Turkey, though internally radical, did not immediately alter their NATO orientation.[20]

Another extremely intractable obstacle is the division of Germany. Despite the successes in stabilizing the German situation over a long period, no solution is even yet visible which will satisfy the West Germans and their allies. Meanwhile, if the allies of the Federal Republic, especially France, Britain, and even the United States, begin to thin out their NATO-assigned forces in Western Europe, the Germans will outnumber them even more strikingly; and West Germany has no overseas military involvement to drain away its forces. This situation will require very careful adjustments in the use of NATO to prevent an unsettling change in power due to weakening the organization.

[19] A change in government in a particular country may not affect that state's *membership* in NATO, but it can alter the ways that state *participates.*

[20] In judging De Gaulle's impact on the functioning of NATO in the early years of his regime, his sabotage of the military command system and his contribution to France's internal stability must be set off against each other. In the United States, the differences between the two parties regarding NATO affairs are minimal.

A basic dilemma related to several of the foregoing obstacles faces the United States. How can the Americans revitalize NATO without dominating it to the point of destroying it as an effective international institution? [21] Military implementation of alliance policies requires clear, specific commitments well in advance of their possible use. Well-defined and acceptable delineations of function are difficult among fifteen very different powers of disparate size, especially when there are many built-in arrangements to ensure that the national viewpoints are not forgotten in the zeal for common action. During NATO's first sixteen years the United States stepped into every breach: the others did what they would, the United States what Americans believed it must. This solution is becoming less and less agreeable to all concerned. The United States tended to harden its position on NATO matters early, thus avoiding the possibility of subjecting that position to allied pressures, pressures which might disrupt the alliance. But by evading controversy at an earlier stage the United States reaped eventual ill will. Again we come back to the need for opening up some hitherto exclusively American strategic planning to the aspiring Europeans. [22]

Another way to make the alliance more vital while avoiding American domination would be for each member to accept more specialized roles in the various fields of joint activity—not the now disliked sword and shield division—but a broader differentiation of activity in which some members would offer economic concessions in lieu of diplomatic or military contributions, and vice versa. Such an effort would recognize the unpalatable observation of a former official in SHAPE: "Politically and economically, an ally in the grand scheme is at the same time a rival in the interior maneuvering—and he is an opponent today, not at some unknown point in the future." [23] It also would require recognition that the resources of the member countries could be pooled to redistribute more equitably, as well as more rationally, the burden now so heavily carried by the leader. In any case the Americans should not forget the impor-

[21] The United States has to sail between the Scylla of SEATO, which it dominates to the point where that alliance is almost a paper international organization, and the Charybdis of the OAS, which it cannot dominate and which lacks the vitality of NATO.

[22] As a leading Social Democrat in Germany, Fritz Erler, has remarked, the American decision process is already so clumsy that a few more interjections from outside would not make the situation very different! [Institute of Strategic Studies, *The Evolution of NATO,* Adelphi Papers, No. 5 (London, 1963), p. 28.]

[23] E. Vandevanter, *Some Fundamentals of NATO Organization* (Santa Monica: Rand Corporation, 1963), p. 29.

tance of the leader's style, and the frequency with which American leadership has been resented because the voice of the United States was too loud, too peremptory, too confused, too disunified, and heard too often and too soon.[24] Listening may prove more effective than shouting on some occasions.

THE EFFECT OF NATO ON UNITED STATES RELATIONS WITH PARTICULAR STATES

Although in this study "NATO" has meant the whole alliance, we must not overlook the character of American relations with particular countries and how these relations are affected by the organization. As Laurence Martin has remarked, the "special relationship" between the United States and Great Britain could hardly be extended to other allies without dilution, but "something of the same sense of being less than foreign to each other" could be developed elastically.[25] Close as Anglo-American relations have been, Americans believe that Britain can do still more to alleviate the giant's problem in the Atlantic alliance. The United Kingdom, like the United States, assumes many responsibilities for keeping the peace in the non-European world; and its spokesmen occasionally refer to these non-European concerns in explaining why Britain does less in Europe than its American critics call for. So long as NATO is needed to fold West Germany into the Atlantic Community, Britain's NATO partners must discourage any interpretation of her role outside Europe which weakens her force in Europe.[26] The maintenance of British military power in Germany, which the French desired so much in the mid-1950s as a counterweight to the prospective German rearmament, continues to be of interest to the Americans, who want to see both British and German forces strengthened.

---

[24] See Aubrey, *op. cit.*, chap. vi. On the other hand, Mayor Willy Brandt reported in June, 1964, "I know from my recent visits in Washington that the leading Western power wants to hear much more than 'Yes, Sir.' It wants its friends to think and act alongside, and to share common responsibility with it. That will not make things simpler or easier, but it will be more interesting politically. It will expand the variety of methods and possibilities" [*Atlantic Community Quarterly*, Fall, 1964, p. 407].

[25] Laurence W. Martin, "The Future of the Alliance: A Pragmatic Approach," in Arnold Wolfers (ed.), *Changing East-West Relations and the Unity of the West* (Baltimore: The Johns Hopkins Press, 1964), p. 238.

[26] See criticism of the British White Paper on Defence of February, 1965, in the *Economist*, February 27, 1965, pp. 862–63.

Examples of the British temptation are the article, "Is NATO Irrelevant?", by the defense correspondent, *The Times* (London), April 6, 1964, and Quintin Hogg, "Britain Looks Forward," *Foreign Affairs*, April, 1965, pp. 413–14 and 419.

Meanwhile, however, the French under President de Gaulle have come to believe that they can handle the German problem more effectively by themselves, in a "Europe of the Two" or in a purely Continental framework of the "Europe of the Six." (France, nevertheless, was in March, 1966 still maintaining in Germany a ground force of 65,000 men, a considerably larger NATO contingent than that of the British.[27]) German loyalty to NATO has often been interpreted as a way of assuring to Germany the support of its single most useful collaborator —the United States. France's concern for her relationship with Germany and Germany's for her relationship with the United States set the stage for Franco-American competition. The two have been competing not only for influence on other members of the alliance but also for status in the international world as a whole. A large part of this protracted Franco-American rivalry and conflict over the organization of the alliance would have no meaning outside the NATO context.

Competition between France and the United States arose in part from France's high estimate of the power which a nuclear weapons capability automatically confers on the possessor, an overemphasis first encouraged by American action in the 1950s. American pressure on the Germans to purchase their armaments in the United States seemed to deny France an alternate route to enhanced power and prestige, via the building of its conventional arms capability; the pressure was successful in spite of French efforts at more Franco-German exchanges in this field.[28] There was in addition an aversion to what Foreign Minister Couve de Murville called "ready-made solutions"; his term suggests that even if the solutions were good, the French would not like them. However, the competition with the United States also reflects latent French jealousy aroused by the way French leaders perceived the "special relationship" of the United States and Britain. By way of contrast, Americans do not resent special relationships between Britain and Commonwealth countries or special British influence in other parts of the world. (They did tend to ignore the Commonwealth relationship in trying to push the British into Europe, purportedly for the sake of strengthening NATO.) American and British interests, if not always parallel, have for the most part not conflicted; those of France and the United States have,

[27] *New York Times,* April 2 and April 19, 1966. There were, in addition, 4,000 in the French Air Force in Germany. The future status of these ground and air forces formally withdrawn from NATO command was being negotiated in the summer of 1966.

[28] Here it was not the formal relationships of the alliance which were involved.

a condition difficult for an alliance to contain.[29] Responsibilities can be divided and interests traded off, but dovetailing or splitting the difference is nearly impossible when matters of status are involved. All these problems arise in part because the four countries involved are the most powerful states outside the Communist bloc. An alliance with such a nucleus cannot help being somewhat unstable, and its organization will inevitably be marked by competition among them.

The effect of NATO on United States relations with Germany is of prime significance. Undoubtedly the United States would be attentive to German demands if there were no organized alliance, but the responsiveness of American officials is greatly increased because of NATO. The whole scheme of the MLF, for example, would hardly have been conceivable without NATO and Germany's membership in it. German desires for unification could be so interpreted as to deny American assertions that NATO is a purely defense organization; they cause the United States to be especially careful in dealing with the country which makes NATO meaningful to the Germans—the Soviet Union.[30]

What of NATO's consequences for the close defense relationship between the United States and Spain? In many ways and without allied objection Spain also is informally and unobtrusively articulated with NATO's military plans through American actions, which are extensive in Spain. United States military arrangements in that country in large part complement antecedent arrangements made in the NATO countries. NATO did not stand in the way of base arrangements which the United States was able to secure in Spain. In fact, the two parties to the 1963 agreement regarding the Rota base and its use for Polaris submarines stated that it formed a "necessary and appropriate" part of "security agreements for the Atlantic and Mediterranean areas." [31]

NATO might have been expected especially to influence United States relations with one non-European country, i.e., Canada. In fact, the ways

[29] Raymond Aron, *Paix et Guerre* (3rd ed., Paris: Calmann-Levy, 1962), pp. 461–63. He cites Suez as the exception in Anglo-American relations (*ibid.*, p. 476). See also Jean-Baptiste Duroselle, "De Gaulle's Designs for Europe and the West," in Wolfers (ed.), *op. cit.*, pp. 171–201.

[30] Assertions that *NATO* impedes a détente between the two superpowers do not bear up under scrutiny, but one or two members of NATO might conceivably inhibit the United States. Except for Germany and France, other members have been more sympathetic to such a development than is the United States.

[31] *Economist*, October 5, 1963, p. 33. Germany and France also have certain bilateral cooperative military arrangements in Spain [*New York Times*, November 28, 1965].

in which the two North American neighbors integrate North American defenses are not closely related to their alliance with the European members. Canada's preference for non-nuclear forces, even in Europe, has not been much altered by association with one or two allies having very different views, and this is ironic in the country Americans trust perhaps more than any other. If the Canadians were to take a more active role in NATO, some observers believe they would find in it an important outlet for the frustrations inherent in their unequal but symbiotic relationship to the Americans. The very closeness of the United States and Canada impels Canadians in NATO to appear constructively different, not just a front for the United States; and Canadian leaders have sought to play a stabilizing role in the alliance.

THE UNITED STATES AND THE NATO POLITICAL PROCESS

One reason for the uniquely intimate connections between the United States and Canada is that prolonged experience in collaboration is self-sustaining. Trust grows among the individuals who are responsible for facing common problems together; and it can survive periods of bad governmental relations, as during the Diefenbaker interlude. The more this kind of personal interchange among other members of NATO takes place, the more likely the participants are to understand each other's perspectives, even those they do not share. This is one of the unmeasurable and often unnoticed advantages of the political exchanges in the North Atlantic Council. If such exchanges culminate in joint decisions, they come to public attention only at a very late stage in such collaboration. Much of the time the participants are neither negotiating nor seeking agreement on quasi-legislation; they are simply feeling each other out.[32]

Compared to this task of political communication, the alliance's military tasks, however difficult to execute, are easy to define, in part because they focus on more specific problems. The military questions, which Senator Fulbright has mockingly claimed are often considered the "heart and soul" of foreign policy, are relatively predictable and controllable. Even in military collaboration, however, the gains accruing to the collaborators are somewhat hypothetical, while the liabilities for such collaboration are immediate. The examination in NATO of strategy, resources, and goals, begun in 1963 and which focuses otherwise

[32] See Aubrey, *op. cit.,* chaps. v and vi.

diffuse "consultation," is a particularly valuable exercise in bringing the political and military aspects of the alliance more closely together.[33] This "exercise" shows how NATO may act as a catalytic agent to influence to some extent the making of United States policy and the policy itself.

Americans may hope that other members will realize more clearly as a result of this particular exercise that they enjoy greater benefits from NATO than they have so far paid for. They are more likely to act on the realization and assume a larger share of the NATO burden, however, if the United States itself follows through on its promises to share more of the inner discussion over the strategy which is said to make the payments seem worthwhile. Since this exercise takes over some of the functions no longer effectively carried out by the Annual Review, it may presage some shift in influence away from American predominance. If the members recognize that the resources of their complex but interrelated economies may be effectively pooled and perceive that contributions to the common defense may take a great variety of forms, then the burden-sharing, though intricately organized, can be harmoniously agreed upon. The way would then be open to more allied sharing in the key decisions. One difficulty perennially facing the United States is that others believe, so far correctly, that the Americans will always make up the balance, if the objective is something the Americans strongly desire. But the principle of "from each according to that member's total capacity" would require changes in United States economic policy which the domestic-affairs oriented Congress might not support.

More contacts between "responsible" officials in the different allied governments might enlighten their governments as to a more rational distribution of burdens. The United States began to promote such contacts in 1964; and ultimately they should probably include those responsible for the purse strings—the legislators, or at least members of the appropriate legislative committees.

Problems of responsibility and accountability are not so acute in NATO as in the European Communities. Perhaps this question has remained relatively dormant because the effective head of the most visible operation in NATO—SACEUR—has taken his accounting responsibili-

---

[33] There remains a tendency for some American military officials to think there is a "right" decision and to be reluctant to entrust what they regard as matters for the expert in their profession to political personnel with a more tentative approach.

ties very conscientiously, both to the other allied governments and to the executive and legislative branches of the government which contributes the largest portion to NATO's defense. His close relations with the other allied governments, in fact, give some of their ministers and legislators information to which they might not have had access within their own governments. But SACEUR's special relationship to the United States does raise another question broached by an English critic of the EEC: how to draw the line between being informed and being instructed by a government.[34] Through their military representatives to SHAPE the members already have an informal means of guidance which provides an additional way of making the integrated command responsible to the individual allies. Since NATO's operations are those in which *governments* are participating, not a "supranational" agency working through groups inside governments, it is not perfectly clear how the *representative* character of members of the permanent Council could be entirely eliminated. Each must be responsible to his own government, which has its own ways of ensuring responsibility to the governed within its jurisdiction.

Does such responsibility require that the unanimity rule always prevail in Council activities? For some matters anything less than unanimous agreement would render a decision almost meaningless and would be unacceptable to many members.[35] For other matters it is almost inconceivable that the United States itself would be willing to be bound to do something against its will, and there would be no way to force American action.[36] On matters not of vital moment but rather of convenience, e.g., cooperative undertakings for military research and development, NATO already has arrangements in which only those participate who are interested and willing to contribute; the others merely

[34] William Pickles, "Political Power in the EEC," *Journal of Common Market Studies,* vol. II, No. 1 (1963), p. 75. The "instruction," however, could be stimulated by that government's representatives in the international organization.

[35] Similarly, when only three-fourths of the OAS voted for (rather than abstaining from) a proposal to permit internal security fact-gatherers under the OAS to operate in Latin America, the action was not even a symbolic victory for the United States, a strong proponent.

[36] See Fritz Erler's observation that if "a majority is supposed to force the hand of the United States, such a body would destroy the credibility of the deterrent" [Institute for Strategic Studies, *The Evolution of NATO,* p. 28]. Where the United States has agreed to a double-veto arrangement, however, as in the case of the "two-keys" device for tactical nuclear weapons, the United States might be *prevented* from taking an action.

acquiesce in the general proposal. The MLF, as proposed by the United States, however, seems to have been a kind of specialized cooperative enterprise of a life-and-death type requiring the agreement of all, even if it did not require all members' participation. Even though force at the disposal of the MLF were to include only a small fraction of the nuclear arsenal available to protect the alliance, there would have to be a higher confidence level than yet exists in NATO to dispense with unanimity in using that force. If that level were sufficiently high to make some kind of weighted majority vote acceptable, it should be sufficiently high for the President of the United States to remain the nuclear agent for NATO.

Could such a scheme as the MLF have created sufficient confidence to permit decisions on a less than unanimous basis for the alliance as a whole? If it could, it would have been because the MLF required the United States to perform a long-postponed task (which might have rendered the MLF unnecessary), namely, greater sharing of knowledge and participation in strategic planning. The unanimity requirement can halt some positive action; yet it also makes difficult a retrogressive step disruptive to the alliance.

One should not overlook how large already is the sphere in which member governments of NATO—with the notable exception of De Gaulle's—are indoctrinated with a common purpose. Through constant reciprocal surveillance of defense forces that each has assigned to NATO the allies have maintained a remarkable degree of unity in defense arrangements not involving the strategic nuclear force. Drawn together for security reasons, they have found that security cuts across many different kinds of policy; and they have thus been able to perceive its ramifications more clearly.[37] The shock of Suez revealed this to all concerned, especially the United States. In the 1960s President de Gaulle was administering new shocks to NATO. However otherwise damaging to the alliance, some such shocks have apparently been necessary to arouse the giant to realize that an effective alliance permits a wider range of choice not only to the United States but also to its allies.

How far can an Atlantic ally go in non-participation before the organization is fatally affected? This depends in part on how important that member is to the alliance and in part on what alternate arrangements the non-participating signatory to the North Atlantic Treaty then makes. To

---

[37] Just as "growth" issues cut across different economic policies dealt with in the OECD, as pointed out by Aubrey [*op. cit.*].

many observers France's collaboration had seemed indispensable; and President de Gaulle's announcement of March, 1966 that France would withdraw from the organization might therefore have been interpreted as sounding its death knell.[38] The other fourteen members have not so interpreted the decision. They propose to go on. While not denying that the organization's efficiency has been reduced, they evidently do not believe it to have been irreparably damaged.

The United States has less to lose than France in a world without NATO, but France as a non-participant in a world with NATO is in a far different position from France in a NATO-less world. Thus, France's withdrawal must be assessed in terms of the degree to which it cripples the functioning of NATO. A government enamored of the idea of *grandeur* apparently does not wish merely to supply real estate to its allies for the carrying on of *their* organized alliance. We have yet to see what price France is willing to pay in opportunities forgone to affect its allies' policies. By ceasing to be the site of NATO military and political activity it may lose one kind of influence; by choosing to be a special case with which the others will have to make special arrangements it may gain another. There are practical limits to acting on the temptation to be a spoiler so long as a member wishes to retain the advantage of association, and this advantage includes the certain and effective United States military support only possible through the organization.

We cannot predict in 1966 how unwise De Gaulle's decision will one day be judged. The costs to France appear to us great both in security and in prestige, and the free ride France will take on the others' contributions to European defense does not comport with "greatness." The cost to NATO and to the United States is certain. From 1966 onward, the Americans must pay a higher price for the security derived from NATO. It may be that the United States is paying a higher price because it avoided paying a lower price in past years—a price of permitting more sharing in strategic planning on behalf of the alliance and more attention to French sensitivities when German cooperation was being ardently sought.

More reasonable and practical than withdrawal would be (or might have been) the forming of intra-alliance blocs. In either case, President de Gaulle is faced with the fact that every country with which he would

---

[38] Seldom noted is the fact that the French have not been urging other members of NATO to disengage, but have merely acted by themselves.

like to work in special intimacy also has important links with the United States.[39] If the United States were to welcome the development of informal allied groupings within NATO, groupings which already have geographical, historical, and cultural counterparts, it might find the organization tougher and more resilient as a result. Since such groupings are likely to overlap, depending upon the reasons for their formation, they would form a "mutually compensatory pattern" or a political "infrastructure." [40] This is the way the political process works in the United States, and Americans should expect and welcome the counterpart in the Atlantic alliance.

Linked to alliance cohesion is the question of new tasks for NATO, to accord with changing needs. Once a political organization is established, its leaders often seek new functions to extend its power and theirs. But some added functions may instead impair the performance of the original function. Just as many voices earlier were calling for the extension of NATO into economic fields (under Article 2), so in more recent years some supporters have bid NATO look to the periphery to meet a Communist peril that is no longer primarily in Europe. There is danger in diverting attention from what is still the central front, where the most critical issues between the Soviet Union and NATO members —divided Germany and exposed Berlin—remain festering. To do so is to offer temptations to a Communist regime which has never publicly abandoned its extreme demands in Europe nor the military posture to pursue them. As General Lemnitzer has pointed out, NATO keeps this vital area stable and thus enables the United States to deal more securely with threats in other regions.[41]

Many of the tasks long ago said by United States leaders to require integration or cooperation in NATO have been only superficially accomplished. For one thing, NATO actions have not overcome the general scarcity of scientific and technical personnel of which the Ameri-

---

[39] See *Economist*, May 12, 1962, p. 536. The United States has not always resisted the temptation, disintegrating to NATO, to encourge the bilateral development of these lines.

[40] See George Liska, *Nations in Alliance: The Limits of Interdependence* (Baltimore: Johns Hopkins Press, 1962), p. 114, and Carol E. Baumann, *Political Cooperation in NATO* (Madison: University of Wisconsin, 1960), p. 73. Alliances within alliances may be divisive as well as cohesive, as Prime Minister Wilson warned in December of 1964, but this depends on whether the organization divides the same way on every issue.

[41] Lyman L. Lemnitzer, "NATO's Military Posture," *NATO Letter,* October, 1965, pp. 26–27.

cans suddenly became aware in 1957; there have been only modest efforts at stimulation and joint activity since then. Meanwhile, this scarcity has engendered new tensions within the alliance; for many allied countries see their own specialists lured to better-paying American employers. A growing threat to the alliance and its leading members is cutthroat competition in the armaments market, in the sale of both new and old military equipment. Enthusiasts for functional international organization cite advantages which also could apply to Atlantic regional collaboration: a cutback on projects important as national prestige indicators but otherwise unprofitable, consolidation of scattered efforts, and coordination to avoid duplication and waste.[42] To this list might be added objectives wholly beyond the technical possibilities of any one member. Thus the NADGE (NATO Air Defense and Ground Environment) program is meeting a common need which no single European country can undertake on its own.[43]

Some functions now performed by NATO or by groups under its auspices were formerly perceived as purely domestic concerns; it was hardly imaginable before the 1950s that member states would subject themselves to the kind of cross-examination that takes place in NATO and the OECD. There are limits, however, to how far even the leader of any state can go in broaching "internal" questions regarding the others' affairs; to question, for example, the length of service of military forces an ally assigns to NATO may appear to be "intervention." Americans have expressed concern in NATO as to the quality of the other allies' military contribution; but since to question quality is to question the prior actions of governments, it is in effect a criticism of those governments.

One kind of leverage which operates in the European Communities is not available: pressure by private economic groups affected by the joint enterprise. As Arnold Wolfers has pointed out, "inward-directed cooperation" is harder for sovereign governments to achieve than "outward-directed cooperation."[44] One factor favoring the adaptation of NATO to new needs is the ever increasing and highly complex trans-

[42] Cf. Inis L. Claude, Jr., *Swords Into Plowshares,* 2nd ed. (New York: Random House, 1959), chap. xvi.

[43] See *New York Times,* February 28, 1965. Another important task requiring much more support is that performed by the ACE Mobile Force.

[44] *Discord and Collaboration* (Baltimore: Johns Hopkins Press, 1962), pp. 27–29. The former does not depend upon an outside threat to motivate the would-be cooperators.

national web of unofficial experts on and promoters of Atlantic affairs. They constitute a transnational political elite with influence on the member governments.[45]

The United States government has found that a large purse enables it to stimulate joint activities and concrete programs within NATO. It is much harder to get the members of NATO to agree on rules which bind them all. Even where such agreement is not possible, diplomatic consultation in NATO may still serve a more modest goal: to prevent mutual harm by timely exchange of views and information.

Misled by the dramatic progress of the European Communities, some would-be reformers of NATO's organization overlook the differences in function which make the Communities' structure an inappropriate model for NATO. Such a structure would be too cumbersome to be usable for collective defense of fourteen or fifteen countries. Another danger is that solutions appropriate for a particular but transient military technology become so rigidly bureaucratized as to make them inapplicable as new weapons systems become operational. Thus those who worry that the most visibly lively part of NATO, i.e., SHAPE, is dominating the main body, the North Atlantic Council, quite properly call attention to other aspects of the alliance which have been relatively neglected. They do not always observe that SHAPE, too, operates through persuasion rather than authority. Since SHAPE is heavily influenced by American perceptions, this observation is especially pertinent for the United States.

UNITY VERSUS DIVERSITY

The Canadian publicist, John Holmes, has questioned indiscriminate demands for unity in the Atlantic community; since a high value is placed on diversity in the polities and societies of most of the members, it ought to be at least as valuable in the wider community.[46] Fascination with unity for its own sake, both unity of view and unity of organization, is partly the product of a press the reporters for which have to

---

[45] This development resembles what Chadwick Alger ["The External Bureaucracy in United States Foreign Affairs," *Administrative Science Quarterly*, June, 1962, pp. 50–78] has called the "external bureaucrats" in the American administrative system. One might also note that the members of the Constitutional Convention of 1787 had also been seeing each other at intervals for several years.

[46] "Canada and the United States in World Politics," *Foreign Affairs*, October, 1961, p. 117. See also Henry A. Kissinger, *The Troubled Partnership* (New York: McGraw-Hill Book Company, 1965), pp. 225–36.

make their news dramatic and simple. It also reflects the aspirations of articulate leaders, including officials in the United States government in the 1960s. To some extent they fear differences in view and policy among the allies within NATO, which is already clearly divided on several questions. But to some extent also, the proponents of unity are inspired by a vision, now clearly outdated, of a monolithic adversary. Perhaps they are also misled because membership in NATO does affect the status of an ally in international politics. They vainly search for some neat, simple design to cover as many aspects as possible of the multiple American interests which require international cooperation. Meanwhile, they do not see that the various member states perceive their needs quite differently—and that much of what unity there is lies in the American conception of what the others should want or do. They are continually rediscovering that military allies may be economic competitors. (Just one example is the politically explosive question of agricultural prices and protection which has deeply divided the six members of NATO who belong to the Common Market.) Indeed, a major source of tension in NATO itself has been that the economic and strategic trends have been moving in the opposite directions, the first tending toward greater influence in European hands, the second requiring more concentrated control in American hands. Why do the economic and military activities need to be brought together in one overarching organization?

Each country in NATO has relations with others outside the alliance which it does not share with its fellow members in NATO. Just as there may be overlapping functions, there are overlapping regions and overlapping organizations for the politico-military and economic functions. Thus it is important for those in NATO not to be cut off too sharply from other parts of the world and for them to prove by deeds that they are ready to share some of their advantages. The global concerns of the United States do not permit Americans to be so cut off, even though Americans regard NATO (or OECD) as the nucleus of their outward-looking relationships. Some problems cannot be dealt with on a regional basis, as supporters of the United Nations remind us; NATO and the United Nations have complementary, not competing functions.

There are a number of ways in which the United States can accommodate to the diversity of organizations and ensure for itself the wide range of choice implicit in the foregoing arguments. Collaboration already takes place between international agencies, not only among those affiliated with the United Nations but between them and regional groups and between regional groups with different memberships. Some states do not have to be members of an organization to enter into collaboration with it.[47] Officials of different agencies of the United States government confer with their counterparts in affiliated governments through the OECD, GATT, NATO, the Bank, or the Fund, depending upon the objective sought. When the semiannual ministerial sessions of the North Atlantic Council take place, treasury officials of non-members, such as Japan or Switzerland, may convene with their opposite numbers either just before or just after the strictly NATO sessions. The NATO Parliamentarians' Conference feels no inhibitions about addressing numerous proposals to the OECD.

Much of the discussion about an overarching Atlantic organization originally stemmed from the fear that the European Communities might in the flush of success wall themselves off from other countries, and particularly from the United States. This fear helps to account for the numerous arguments about an "ellipse"- versus a "dumbbell"-shaped Atlantic "community." The nomenclature later shifted to "partnership" between two "equally strong" entities—"Europe" and the United States. (Where was Canada, and where was the United Kingdom, in this vision?) And there was talk of NATO providing the "political" structure while the OECD formed the "economic" structure. Various American proposals for a unified Atlantic Community provided ways for the United States to influence developments in Europe. Not surprisingly, the proposals originating in Europe often exhibited features which might have reduced American and increased European influence. This divergence, and the almost exclusive preoccupation of some of the American proponents with a Communist threat which seemed less urgent to many in Europe, have blocked progress toward practical realization of aspirations for transatlantic integration. In any case, the American proposals were not directly relevant to the Soviet threat—unless Washington was to be the seat of a new Empire of the West and Moscow was seen as the new Byzantium.

Occasionally, proponents of a formal Atlantic Community have been concerned with the proliferation of organizations, which were occasion-

---

[47] Thus Germany, which does not belong to the United Nations, contributed substantial sums to the United Nations Cyprus peace-keeping expedition. The United States plays a leading role at CENTO without belonging to it.

ally duplicating each other's functions. Their very numbers also caused government officials to grow walleyed in trying to keep track of them. However, a veteran in the campaign to reduce the number and rearrange the functions of the crazy quilt of public authorities in an American metropolis would be dubious about the chances of doing this on an international scale once the organizations have become established. In any case, there is always this advantage to diversity: if an objective cannot be reached through one organization, another can be tried. After Britain failed to enter the EEC in 1963, the United States and Britain were ready to seek some other way of closer association with the Continent through WEU, thus avoiding the danger of transferring the conflict to NATO. Those who would consolidate organizations must face the question of who is to be included and who excluded. In a period when government leaders hope they are seeing a lessening of tensions with the Soviet Union, to attempt to draw the lines more sharply may be counterproductive.

The very existence of NATO and comparable organizations attests to the belief that there can be multiple loyalties, as do the existence of federal systems and confederations. According to one student of these allegiances, loyalties are expandable, they may be complementary, and what begins as a means relationship can eventuate in a loyalty based on implicit acceptance of an end.[48] Groups like GATT and the Fund occasionally serve to act as a bridge between the loyalties that exist among the privileged members of the Atlantic organizations and those existing among less advantaged countries elsewhere.[49]

Numerous advocates of some stronger European organization within or outside the Atlantic "partnership" stress the indivisibility between a country's political power and its defense capabilities, and they especially regard nuclear weapons as a sign of such power. This belief runs counter to long experience in international relations where militarily weak countries have under particular circumstances been able to achieve remarka-

---

[48] See Harold Guetzkow, *Multiple Loyalties: Theoretical Approach to a Problem in International Organization* (Princeton: Center for Research on World Political Institutions, 1955), esp. pp. 58–62. He also noted that where two loyalties conflict, one can be repressed. Something similar may occasionally occur when conflicts within NATO are grounded by the lightning rod of the United Nations (in Ernest Gross's words), as happened at the time that the Suez cease-fire resolution required the United States to make a choice.

[49] There can also be a conflict between loyalty to an ally and to the alliance, as has occasionally occurred in Anglo-American relations.

ble diplomatic successes. Failure to recognize that political power cannot be defined solely in terms of military power leads many observers into chicken-and-egg arguments about whether economic union should precede political union and whether either or both require military union. True, NATO in the early 1950s provided a security underpinning which made possible the remarkable economic rebirth of Europe. But here we seem to have a paradox. Economic liberalization, especially the lowering of trade barriers, seems easier in an expanding market, while the relaxing of national barriers to military cooperation appears easier in periods of contracting security.[50]   Arguments about which must come first overlook another consideration: a pluralistic approach is to be favored whenever it is feasible. Governments such as that of the United States have concerns not extensively served by any existing types of integration, concerns such as the expansion of human rights and the spread of democratic governmental practices. Atlantica may grow function by function, but it need not be through a unified organization.

There remain certain advantages to talking about an Atlantic "community" even if it does not exist; Coral Bell has referred to the "political uses of illusion." [51] Such an illusion blurs the lines between different classes of states, so that the gradations are not so painfully visible. It liberates the imagination from earlier preconceptions and sterile arguments about universal versus functional integration and reveals new ways to pursue old goals. (As Paul Nitze said of NATO in 1959, much more was feasible through this organization than was immediately apparent.[52]) It tempts American leaders to make promises which they can then be called upon to keep, as President Johnson did in the quotation beginning this chapter. It answers a requisite of American politics, a myth to give leaders the courage to choose and their followers courage to accept the choice.

We have been dealing with ways in which NATO has affected the range of American choice without explicit attention to the meaning of this relationship to the international system in general.[53] NATO has de-

[50] For the economic tendency, see Pierre Uri, *Partnership for Progress* (New York: Harper and Row, 1963), p. 28.

[51] *Negotiation from Strength* (New York: Alfred A. Knopf, 1963), p. 211.

[52] "Alternatives to NATO," in Klaus Knorr (ed.), *NATO and American Security* (Princeton: Princeton University Press, 1959), p. 278.

[53] A colleague, Wayne Wilcox, calls this "a study of the effect of a partially structured segment of international politics in the foreign policy of the hegemonic power."

veloped in a changing environment; the changes have been both technological and political. The adversary against which NATO was organized
is behaving differently from the way it was behaving when the alliance
was established, perhaps because NATO has worked; and the collaborators are increasingly engaged in the normal political give-and-take of a
common enterprise. Some of this interallied bargaining has related to the
scope of the enterprise—how much military and diplomatic integration
to attempt—and some to its extent—whether or not to confine cooperation to Europe. But much of the discontent of the other allies stemmed
from dissatisfaction with the weight of the giant partner. The process by
which the United States makes its own policy has been so cumbersome
that positions tended to harden at the wrong time; the policies themselves have often been more tuned to the needs of American agencies
than to alliance needs; and the United States has seemed to the other
allies to resist change too long.

In its participation in NATO and the other international organizations the United States has endeavored to cope with truly "outsized
problems," military and economic problems which could not be handled
alone even by a country as large, wealthy, and powerful as the United
States. At the same time, transnational, supranational, and cosmo-
politan groupings, both governmental and private, were being established at a very rapid rate, weaving a pattern reminiscent of the pluralistic states that compose this "community." [54] Even the opposing parties
within one member state tended to have (somewhat attenuated) constituencies in associated states. In NATO what we now see is an organization at the international level which is roughly analogous to the special-
purpose authority familiar to the student of American metropolitan government.[55] In both the metropolitan area and the Atlantic Community
cases a need became manifest which could not be met by any existing
government acting alone. In theory, the need might have been met by
"centralization," transfer of function to government at a higher level. A
more practical alternative turned out to be creation of a functionally

[54] For example, three consortia, each composed of European and American
companies, reputedly spent millions of dollars in the competition to win con-
tracts for the $300,000,000 NATO Air Defense Ground Environment project
[*Wall Street Journal,* July 2, 1965]. The winning consortium, with American,
British, Dutch, and French members, made a low bid of $280,000,000 [*New York
Times,* June 30, 1966].

[55] See Matthew Holden, Jr., "The Governance of the Metropolis as a Problem in
Diplomacy," *The Journal of Politics,* vol. XXVI (1964), pp. 627–47.

specific organization with membership limited to interested political units.[56] It is too soon to say whether an essentially single-function organization such as NATO can grow into a multifunction organization which would more and more exhibit the characteristics of "government." We are, however, aware of the aptness of President Kennedy's simile, that the Atlantic community grows, not like a volcanic mountain, but through gradual accretion as does a coral reef.

In this process have American actions in NATO merely helped to prevent an unwanted event, Soviet expansion in Europe, or have they also helped to reshape the structure of international politics? American officials agree that NATO, acting alone, can not have a marked impact on world order. It needs to be accompanied by various kinds of economic organization; but in these economic organizations only some of the decision-making processes are similar to those appropriate to an alliance, which is an association of *governments*. Americans are beginning to recognize that if a broader community is to be built, its common institutions will have to carry on a variety of functions and there will have to be a multiplicity of interallied devices for communication. For these various organizational devices to have vitality the members must see that the benefits of participation are allocated among themselves with reasonable equity and be able to respond to each others' needs.[57]

There have been many American failures to exploit the full range of choice made possible by participation in NATO, but the organization has helped to focus attention and resources on a crucial security problem. It has strengthened the United States for bargaining with the Soviet adversary. It has helped build consensus between the United States and the other allies. It has been used to implement United States military policy. The burden of proof lies with NATO's critics to demonstrate that a different kind of organized alliance would do as well what NATO is now doing. Only then may NATO's critics legitimately focus public

[56] Fred Riggs distinguishes between the functionally specific and the functionally diffuse governmental structures and develops the model of a "prismatic system," a transitional state between fused and refracted, where for every function there is a corresponding structure ["International Relations as a Prismatic System," *World Politics,* October, 1961, pp. 144–81].

[57] This is a proposition discussed in Karl W. Deutsch, Sidney A. Burrell, Robert A. Kann, Maurice Lee, Jr., Martin Lichterman, Raymond E. Lindgren, Francis L. Loewenheim, and Richard W. Van Wagenen, *Political Community and the North Atlantic Area* (Princeton: Princeton University Press, 1957), chap. ii.

debate on goals which would be better served if the prescriptions of the critics were followed.

It may be clever to say the king has no clothes on when he is in fact naked. But when he is arrayed, even if somewhat unspectacularly, it is dangerous to deny it.

ONE MODEL OF AN
ORGANIZED ALLIANCE

THE REAL NATO is infinitely more complex than the simplified version of it carried in the heads of those participating in its work. They are likely to see it, as will the participants in any organized alliance, in terms of what their respective countries can get out of it. They may or may not perceive whether the organized alliance efficiently serves some larger collectivity than their own nation-state; and if it does, they may or may not care. In Chapter IV we discuss the way NATO and other organized alliances have been perceived by the Americans who shape American policy toward them.

What kind of model of an organized alliance may be constructed by disinterested observers? Their models, too, will be greatly simplified versions of reality, but the simplification as far as possible ought to be self-conscious and deliberately related to the central question being asked. *Our* central question is "How does American participation in an organized alliance affect the range of choice of American policy-makers?" Other observers may have very different concerns; those, for example, who want to know whether organized alliances help or hinder, or are irrelevant to, man's progress toward the creation of a world government might develop a very different kind of model.

We think, then, of NATO (and other organized alliances) as instruments of governments. We ask about each of them: (1) Which are the member states? (2) What are the geographical limits of the alliance commitment? (3) What is the scope of the commitment within the defined geographical limits? With respect to any given organized alliance these are questions of fact. When we turn from commitment to performance we may ask further: (4) What actions by member governments were (or were not) or could have been (or could not have been) taken through the alliance organization to achieve what objectives? And (5) with what effect? These latter questions, relating to actual and potential performance, are central in the present study; and we are interested both in recording actual past performance or actual missed opportunities and in estimating future utilities. Our model, however, is one which permits us to relate our historical experience with organized alliances to potential experience with them on the assumption of rational choice by the specified member state.

So far as the geographical limits of an alliance commitment are concerned, the commitment may apply only to the area occupied by the members, to a general region including this area, or to the entire world. There may be variations in the extent of combined operations up to but not including complete integration of *all* defense forces, with one command, one general staff, and one governing body—conditions only to be found in a sovereign government. Among the ways combination may occur are (1) provision by a single state, compensated or not by the others; (2) equal contributions in administration and financing by all; (3) unequal participation in the operations; (4) financial contributions by one, the rest or part of them carrying out the service; and (5) performance by each member of its own agreed-upon portion of the common enterprise in accordance with commonly accepted rules. (All these methods have in fact been employed in NATO.) Some states lying within the region in which the alliance operates may not participate. They may seem to the members to have nothing to offer the alliance or may be ideologically repulsive to them or may have strong reasons to be unaligned. On the other hand, the participation of some states may seem to be so important that without such "key members" the organization would appear to be pointless. The one common factor in any alliance is that all members face the same foe or foes, explicitly or implicitly.

What modifications of national practice may occur as a consequence of or as part of the raison d'être of an organized alliance? NATO experience and proposals made regarding NATO suggest the following. The allies may agree to a unified strategy for their forces. They may establish a joint command or commands. There may be balanced forces on a collective basis, with each participant contributing to a common pool what it can best provide. The weapons and vehicles may be standardized, even if provided separately by the participants. They may be produced jointly, or the production may be balanced through specialization by different members. Research and development for more advanced or improved types of armament may be jointly undertaken. There may be a joint maintenance and supply system. A single communications system or at least a coordinated series of such systems may also serve an alliance. Transport may be pooled. The alliance may provide a common infrastructure for the use of the forces. The personnel may be trained together. The allies may share intelligence through the organization.

All these potentially joint operations assume that the members are agreed on what they mean to do with the defenses in which they are cooperating, since security questions are inseparable from political objectives. Thus some kind of diplomatic coordination seems to be required, whether the members conduct their diplomacy on alliance-related matters severally or collectively.

In the absence of joint diplomatic representation on behalf of the alliance there may be different degrees of political consultation among the allies to harmonize their own diplomacy. The first step toward diplomatic coordination would be sharing information. Then might come discussing what steps should be taken by different members. A further step towards a collective diplomacy would be members asking advice on what their national diplomacy should be. An even greater adaptation would be participants taking the advice determined upon jointly. There would also be variations according to whether the subject of consultation is a joint operation, one related to it, or one with only tenuous relevance to the purpose of the organization.

What about the decision-making apparatus for such an alliance? One would expect a permanent body to make or advise on policy, composed either of representatives of the participating states or of active members of their governments, perhaps with deputies. They will require a secretariat to perform housekeeping functions and to prepare subjects for deliberation. There will also be some kind of defense organization, with commanders selected by the allies jointly. A high court does not appear to be necessary; the performance of functions of the organization will not be likely to pose justiciable issues, unless the members care to subject themselves to judicial decision regarding the performance of their commitments. There may also be a parliamentary assembly, perhaps composed of members of the individual members' legislatures, but an unlikely development if the main activities of the alliance are conducted by the individual members.

A somewhat similar model may be constructed for an international organization dealing with economic matters, such as trade regulations, fiscal policy, social security, labor policy, subsidies and concessions, and rules of fair competition, or some of these. There will be three major differences, however. The economic organization will more likely engage in the making of rules applicable to individual members, will concern itself with private enterprise rather than with the strictly governmental activities which are involved in defense, and will not envisage a common foe. Thus its methods for making decisions may be quite different from those employed by an organized alliance.

Whether pertaining to a defense or an economic organization, some problems are inherent in developing an organization along the lines of the models suggested above. The larger the number of participants, the more difficult it is to reach concrete decisions jointly. The organization must accommodate to differences among the individual members in size, wealth, location, and place in the international political system. Deeply rooted opposing interests within the domestic political systems of the participants will be hindrances to the achievement of the shared objectives. Where will the line be drawn between security and economic functions? Or between either of these and other kinds of foreign and specific diplomatic issues? How will the organization be related to other existing organizations, global, regional, and functional?

Just as the organization will have to adapt to specific key members, so another crucial problem will be the adaptation of the participating state's decision-making processes to the additional medium for policy determination. Within the member state there must be new forms of coordination, new institutions for gearing military power to political objectives, and new roles for the various branches of government. In democratic countries, new questions of responsibility to the governed arise. All of these adjustments involve not only questions of effective government but also other political issues of the first order: of who would influence whom and how.

APPENDIX B

FUNCTIONS OF COMPARABLE INTERNATIONAL ORGANIZATIONS

FOR THOSE with an interest in comparative analysis of the role of the United States in both NATO and other international organizations, the following outline of objectives and methods of some organizations may be of interest.

SEATO

A pale reflection of NATO, after which it was to some extent modeled, is the Southeast Asia Treaty Organization. Created in 1954 after the French defeat in Indo-China and the division of that country, SEATO was meant by its founders, who were led by the United States, to put the Communists on notice that they could expand no farther without encountering grave risks. SEATO's members are the three large Western powers with an interest in Southeast Asia—the United States, Britain, and France; two smaller "Western" members of the Commonwealth—Australia and New Zealand; and three Southeast Asian countries willing to be allied with these five—the Philippines, Thailand, and Pakistan. The dichotomy in the membership has been as influential in SEATO's development as have its relations with the Communist world.

George Modelski has called SEATO "a device by which three great powers . . . have undertaken to support and protect a number of small states of South-East Asia . . . against the extension of the influence of other great powers, principally Communist China and the Soviet Union." According to the same author, SEATO has symbolized the concern of the United States in Southeast Asia affairs and has made clear that in the appropriate circumstances American power might be exercised in the defense of these small states.[1] Soon after its founding, Britain and France became absorbed by their concerns in other regions and increasingly lost effective interest in SEATO. A reviving interest was observable in 1963–64 as events in Laos and Vietnam grew more critical, but for the most part these European members have acted as a brake when energy was desired by some of the others. Various United Nations agencies might have been suitable instruments for attacking the economic and social conditions in the SEATO area, but the founders believed in 1954 that a regional security organization was necessary to combat Communist armed aggression or subversion.

Other Asian countries have almost always kept their distance from SEATO, since two of the members have been almost inevitably linked with colonialism.[2] The imperialist tinge allegedly imparted by French and British membership is all the more ironical, since France, after at first making a small military contribution, strongly opposed later suggestions for military action and Britain tried to keep SEATO's range of commitments as narrow as possible. As for the Asian members themselves, they tended to look upon SEATO as a special channel to economic aid, regarding themselves as more reliable recipients than the non-aligned.

Unlike NATO, SEATO has no integrated command nor any forces assigned to it. Its two principal military functions are coordinating the defense plans of the members for that area and improving the capabilities of the members to implement these plans if necessary. Military (especially naval) exercises have been regularly held. Military facilities have been replanned and built in order to aid the movement of allied armed forces.

To deal with problems of subversion a committee of experts on "security" (composed of members of national intelligence services and police forces) meets twice a year to exchange information and make recommendations regarding both the internal and external threats. For both the East Asian members and the more politically advanced states these are sensitive questions; the members, for different reasons, have not pushed this type of cooperation vigorously.[3]

Economic assistance is one way to alleviate problems in disturbed areas which might otherwise become ripe for Communist subversion. Those who can render such assistance have, however, tended to prefer other instruments to SEATO. In any case, most of SEATO's operations, in this as in the military field, involve "one-way traffic," with the help all going in the same direction.

The most critical problems which SEATO members have faced in Southeast Asia, those of Laos and Vietnam, have not proved amenable to effective

[1] George Modelski (ed.), *SEATO: Six Studies* (Melbourne: F. W. Cheshire, 1962), pp. 3–4. We have drawn much of the material about SEATO from this work.

[2] A few, such as Nationalist China, have on one occasion or another participated in a particular SEATO activity, or at least sent an observer.

[3] See Modelski, *op. cit.*, pp. 32–33 and M. Margaret Ball, "SEATO and Subversion," *Political Science* (Victoria University of Wellington), pp. 25–39.

action by the alliance, although they have provided lively topics of discussion within its Council. When Pakistan came to an agreement with Communist China concerning part of the area disputed by Pakistan and India and by India and China, the alliance faced a new kind of attrition. It was no longer merely inability of the members to agree on a common policy for combating Communist expansion that inhibited SEATO action.

SEATO has a small permanent staff in Bangkok and a common budget (both staff and budget are smaller than those of the United States Information Office in Thailand). The budget has been a little more than $1 million annually, most of it composed of contributions calculated according to a formula in which the United States puts up 25 percent, Britain 16 percent, Australia and France 13.5 percent each. The staff has been recruited by the member states, not chosen by the Secretary General. All SEATO activities must be finally ratified by the SEATO Council, but for the most part its discussion has simply set the general tone for the organization. A half-yearly conference of Military Advisers, including the United States Commander-in-Chief, Pacific, the Australian Chief of the General Staff, the British Commander in Singapore, and others of appropriate position, has exercised most of the military influence. Detailed plans have been worked out by the Military Planning Office, made up of delegations of the national military planning officers, who have been constantly in session. This office is the organization's military core.

The member states have maintained some continuous contact on political issues in Bangkok through the Permanent Working Group, meeting several times a week, and the Council of Representatives, convening at least once a month. The Permanent Working Group's main task has been administrative supervision. The annual ministerial meetings of the Council serve mainly to review the reports of the organs and to express in broad terms national positions on political problems in the region.[4]

OAS

Even for the specialist in Latin-American affairs, it is very difficult to describe the Organization of American States, much less the inter-American system, of which it is a part and for which it is often used as a synonym. Ambassador Dreier has called the entire system a juridical and procedural jungle; the OAS is thoroughly entangled in it. The whole complex represents an accretion of functions over half a century and reflects a tradition much older than that. However, the "Treaty of Rio de Janeiro" dates only from 1947 and the organically related Charter of the OAS (the "Act of Bogota") only from 1948. Further difficulty arises because the OAS has represented different things to different participants and has varied through time. The differences are especially marked when we compare the perspectives of the United States government with those of the other members. The OAS has

---

[4] For organizational details see Modelski, *op. cit.,* pp. 17–29.

been called the "institutional manifestation" of the inter-American system.[5] We shall discuss only a few aspects of the organization, those dealing with security and economic cooperation.

To most Latin-Americans security—especially security from extra-hemispheric aggression—has not been an important function of the system. For them the OAS and the whole inter-American system have been primarily useful in regularizing relations with the colossus of the north. When the Treaty of Rio de Janeiro and the Charter of the OAS were framed, however, the cold war was becoming very evident to the United States. As a regional guarantee, the Treaty of Rio was a forerunner of the North Atlantic Treaty. Such regional arrangements for "collective self-defense" were specifically provided for in Article 51 of the United Nations Charter, put there largely on the initiative of the Latin-American states, who together with the United States had already negotiated the Act of Chapultepec prior to the UN Charter conference at San Francisco. There was a long tradition of giving inter-American procedures priority in dealing with hemisphere controversies, a tradition which the members did not wish to have weakened by the actions of a universal organization in which they were likely to have less weight.[6] Memories of the threat of Fascist expansion and subversion in the Western Hemisphere in World War II were still fresh and colored the perception of those who drafted the treaty; they desired a regional guarantee against new threats from outside the hemisphere. However strong the Latin-Americans' fear of external aggression in general, they did not take the Communist threat very seriously for a long time.

Long before the Communist intrusions into the Western Hemisphere Latin America had problems susceptible to treatment by an organization like the OAS. Continuing danger of conflicts between member states, particularly in the Caribbean area, intense poverty and economic underdevelopment, and the need to find some satisfactory accommodation between the immensely powerful United States and the weak but very proud and independent Latin-American states all have been faced—even if not decisively dealt with— by parts of the organization. Serious obstacles to the success of their operations have been the almost neurotic attachment of the Latin-American states to the idea of non-intervention and the cultural gulf between them and their giant Northern neighbor. For thirty years before 1965 the United States

[5] John C. Dreier, *The Organization of American States and the Hemisphere Crisis* (New York: Harper & Row, 1962), p. 11. Much of the following description of the OAS depends on this work; on the same author's "The Organization of American States and United States Policy," *International Organization*, Winter, 1963, pp. 36–53; and on Northwestern University, "The Organization of American States," a study for the Senate Committee on Foreign Relations, Subcommittee on American Republic Affairs, *United States-Latin American Relations*, Senate Doc. No. 125, 86th Cong., 2nd sess. (1960) [hereafter referred to as NU, OAS], p. 220.

[6] See Charles G. Fenwick, *The Organization of American States* (Washington, 1963), pp. 512–32 and Dreier, *The Organization of American States and the Hemisphere Crisis*, p. 26.

had followed a non-interventionist policy; the OAS made it easier for the United States to continue to do so. Thus very gradually the older bonds which had held all the American republics together—aversion to an alien system thrusting itself into their hemisphere—could reassert themselves. When the United States finally turned an attentive ear to the economic demands of its poorer neighbors to the south, interest in hemispheric cooperation was revived.[7] (In 1966 it is too soon to assess the impact of the 1965 United States and OAS actions in the Dominican Republic.)

Until very recently international development assistance came mainly through the United Nations and its specialized agencies, which have carried on programs in Latin America much more impressive in many cases than those of similar inter-American agencies. Carrying on both United Nations and inter-American programs at the same time has presented numerous problems in coordination.[8]

According to Ambassador John Dreier, the OAS Charter not only codified and restructured agreements which already had existed; it also affirmed a strong emotional attachment to certain ideals of inter-state conduct, containing, as it did, a body of doctrine and "some pure rhetoric." [9] There are 112 articles in the OAS Charter, including chapters on "Social Standards" and "Cultural Standards."

The procedures employed by the OAS resemble those used in the United Nations. Indeed, many of them were deliberately copied from UN provisions. The key provisions of the Rio Treaty are the members' obligation to regard an armed attack on one as an armed attack on all and to come to the assistance of the attacked; to consult about collective measures in case of the threat of armed attack or other danger to the territorial integrity and independence of the American states; and by a two-thirds vote to put into effect specified sanctions. While no state may be required to use its own armed force in a collective action contrary to its will, the United States has surrendered any absolute veto power over non-military sanctions, something which it has not done in NATO, SEATO, or the United Nations.

Until the Cuban crisis of 1963 the sections dealing with collective action against an outside threat had not been invoked. Instead, articles were employed which were more closely related to procedures for pacific settlement of disputes than to collective security measures. Until the Cuban revolution

[7] Membership in the inter-American system has never included one of the hemisphere's countries, Canada, earlier because of United States objections, and later because of Canadian indifference. However, the hemisphere defense area of the "American States" which was to be covered in the Rio Treaty's guarantee did include Canada but not by name (Article 4 of the Inter-American Treaty of Reciprocal Assistance).

[8] One highly regarded OAS agency is the long-established Pan American Health Organization, which is now affiliated with the World Health Organization for actions in the Western Hemisphere.

[9] Dreier, *The Organization of American States and the Hemisphere Crisis,* p. 32.

these procedures worked quite successfully in preventing the spread of violent conflict, although they did not provide a basis for a more permanent solution of some of the controversies involved. They have been effectively used despite the fact that what many once regarded as an indispensable pillar of the inter-American system, the Treaty of Pacific Settlement, is unratified by most of the members, including the United States.

Unlike the United Nations, the OAS has no body with the powers of the Security Council or the General Assembly to hear political controversies, unless aggression is already about to begin or has taken place; this is one of the many features of the system which reveal the Latin-American states' reluctance to delegate power to others whom they do not trust. Nor has any machinery for the collective use of armed force actually been used, although there are treaty provisions for sanctions. (A near case was that involving Costa Rica and Nicaragua in 1955, when members were called upon to expedite delivery of military planes ordered by Costa Rica. The United States planes arrived the next day, radically changing the military situation.[10] Another case involved the peace-keeping forces that some members added to the overwhelmingly large United States forces after the Dominican uprising in 1965.)

The Cuban and Dominican crises in 1959 presented a truly revolutionary situation, one which the Latin-American members were afraid to face directly. At most they were willing to have the OAS study the problems and issue reports. This earlier Dominican crisis passed, and a different regime came to rule in 1961–1962 without the OAS having played any significant role in the process. (In the 1965 Dominican crisis the OAS played an important and very controversial role.) Unlike the earlier conflicts, the Cuban affair was one in which the giant Northern member was immediately involved. Fidel Castro's initial assumption of power was accepted without any member calling for OAS action. As his regime turned spectacularly toward the Communist bloc, the United States sought support from the OAS in dealing with this development. However, the Latin Americans were—in general— even more hesitant about using the OAS than in the earlier Dominican case. It was not until President Kennedy revealed the presence of Soviet missile bases in Cuba that the OAS rallied and gave its hearty support to the American moves. A few members even supplied ships to help in the temporary blockade. Two or three of the Latin-American states have since experienced Cuban infiltration and have led in attempts to secure some OAS action to protect themselves.

The kind of collective security through military measures which NATO provides would be inappropriate in the inter-American situation. In any case, neither the United States government nor the others have been prepared to undertake joint OAS military operations. Naval exercises, held periodically, are conducted by the United States with only certain of the Latin-American

[10] *Ibid.*, pp. 63–64.

naval forces. The United States has also granted small amounts of military aid bilaterally. The OAS chiefly acts, in the military defense of the continent, as a vehicle for coordinating military policy under the leadership of the United States. For continuing consultation when it is not a question of emergency or general policy, the Inter-American Defense Board (which is not a part of the OAS) serves a minor function. This is a hold-over from World War II collaboration, but another wartime agency, the Committee for Political Defense, was not reconstituted, owing to Latin-American fears that the United States could use it for intervention purposes.[11] In 1962 the OAS established an Inter-American Defense College to give courses in military, political, social, and economic factors in the inter-American system.[12]

Although the Alliance for Progress may ultimately make a great change, the record of the OAS in economic fields and in social development has been unimpressive, despite provisions in the OAS Charter for these activities and for economic consultation. Part of the difficulty lay in the difference of views between the Latin-American countries and the United States regarding United States responsibility for rendering very extensive governmental aid to the poorer countries to the south and the desirability of working through mililateral rather than bilateral channels. (The United States has contributed to OAS projects, but not on the scale of its bilateral programs.) Another source of dissatisfaction and inaction lay in the field of trade, with several Latin-American countries resenting United States import restrictions on some of their key products—lead and oil, for example—and American opposition to international commodity stabilization agreements. In the trade field many of the problems were not in any case hemispheric or at least could not be readily solved without regard to the rest of the world.

With the formation of the Alliance for Progress a new role more satisfying to the Latin Americans has developed for the OAS, which had already participated in its formation. Increasing responsibility for OAS organs to review the social and economic development plans of potential aid recipients has been agreed to by the United States government. The OAS has also arranged for planning sessions to discuss taxation, agricultural reforms, and housing and has sent joint technical missions to help members formulate development plans in order to qualify for American aid.[13]

The prospect of specific aid for specific performance may help to remove one of the reasons for OAS failures in the economic field, the tendency to regard as "action" the adoption of resolutions calling for broad programs the implementation of which has been far beyond the scope and ability of the available agencies. The public pillory function of OAS meetings should now also diminish. Included in the Alliance for Progress procedures is a provision for an annual review of its programs, to be made by the Inter-

[11] *Ibid.*, pp. 44–46 and 49–50.   [12] *New York Times,* October 10, 1962.
[13] See the summary of OAS activities in *International Organization,* Summer, 1962, p. 658.

American Economic and Social Council, which submits pertinent recommendations to the Council of the OAS.[14]

The OAS continues to suffer from fragmentation, complexity, large representational demands on countries not well endowed for such tasks, an elaborate network of checks and restraints, and as a way of not affronting the juridically equal members, the practice of accepting for its agenda all suggestions offered, without clear priorities.[15]

From the maze of the inter-American system we have selected only a few instrumentalities for comparison with NATO. What was supposed to be the supreme organ of the OAS was the continuing series of Inter-American Conferences, to be held every five years. None has been held, however, since 1954; and the value of the Conference is much in question. Instead of the Eleventh Conference, which has not met, there have been two "Special Inter-American Conferences." The second, held at Rio de Janeiro in 1965, directed that major organizational reforms be prepared for action in 1966 and recommended an annual meeting for some new kind of supervisory body.[16] Between Conferences, a Council of the Ministers of Foreign Affairs can deal with serious political problems; but in practice the permanent Council, acting as a Provisional Organ of Consultation, has through a "judicial stratagem" assumed important political functions. It sits in Washington, as the governing board of the Pan-American Union (for more than fifty years the "bureau" or secretariat of the inter-American system's international organization), and can meet for instantaneous action.[17] Nevertheless, the Secretary General is not empowered (formally) to call attention to threatening situations as can his counterparts in the UN and NATO. The Inter-American Peace Committee, which dates from 1940 rather than from the Act of Bogota creating the OAS, has played an important role in a number of the pacific settlement cases since the war.

ECONOMIC AGENCIES

NATO and SEATO, like the OAS, were regional approaches to regional problems. Many economic problems are global and thus require instrumentalities like those which have been organized under United Nations auspices. In this very superficial comparison we confine our discussion to the International Bank of Reconstruction and Development, the International Monetary Fund, and the General Agreement on Tariffs and Trade. (GATT's only connections with the UN are the fact that the latter's Economic and Social Council sponsored the conference giving it birth and the fact that it is a substitute for an aborted UN specialized agency, the International

[14] Secretary of the Treasury Dillon described this procedure in his testimony August 23, 1961, before the Senate Committee on Appropriations [*Hearings, Foreign Assistance Act of 1962,* 87th Congress, 1st sess., p. 206].

[15] Cf. NU, OAS, pp. 1–2 and 48.   [16] *New York Times,* November 25, 1965.

[17] See Dreier, "The Organization of American States and United States Policy," p. 53.

Trade Organization. There are of course other specialized agencies, as well as divisions within the UN secretariat itself, that concern themselves with economic questions.)

The Bank and the Fund were established at Bretton Woods in 1944 just prior to the great-power discussions leading to the formation of the United Nations. They were especially designed to prevent or discourage restrictive national practices which had proved injurious to all commercial states prior to World War II. Availability of capital and the liquidity of monetary systems were questions of concern to developed countries; these countries had recognized a mutual interest in financial cooperation for objectives unobtainable by unilateral action. The Bank lends, for reconstruction or development, funds it has raised through selling its own bonds in the world's capital markets; it also guarantees private loans. The Fund maintains orderly exchange arrangements among its members, promotes convertibility of currencies, and supports weakened currencies through its pool of currencies. Although the member governments supply reserves in both organizations, operations of the Bank and Fund must pay for themselves.[18]

The immediate postwar years saw commercial conditions in most of the interested countries so deranged by the war's destruction that neither agency could play the role envisaged for it. Taking their place, for the most part, was massive American economic assistance for reconstruction (coupled with new European agencies). Eventually the advanced countries returned to more normal conditions. By that time new roles began to be discerned which looked towards mobilizing aid to underdeveloped countries—on a purely business basis. The Bank acquired two affiliates, the International Finance Corporation and the International Development Association, designed specifically to meet the "soft loan" needs and other particular economic requirements of the underdeveloped countries. The Fund was slower than the Bank in coming to play a part in the problem of developing areas. Expanding world trade and strengthened European currencies have brought about an expansion in its activities, the purpose of which is to maintain a stable, well-oiled international payments system.

These agencies were established and began functioning during the wave of internationalist feeling which made popular anything attached to the United Nations.[19] This wave was soon spent, and different attitudes reappeared with

[18] Peter Kenen, *Giant Among Nations* (New York: Harcourt, Brace, 1960), pp. 86–99 and 131–39, provides a good summary of the work of the Fund and the Bank. See also International Bank for Reconstruction and Development, *The World Bank, IFC and IDA: Policies and Operations* (Washington: IBRD, 1962), International Monetary Fund, *The First Ten Years of the International Monetary Fund* (Washington: IMF, 1956) and *idem, Annual Report, 1964* (Washington: IMF, 1964), and Richard N. Gardner, *In Pursuit of World Order* (New York: Frederick A. Praeger, 1964), pp. 173–88.

[19] For economic cooperation through the United Nations, see Leland M. Goodrich, *The United Nations* (New York: Thomas Y. Crowell Co., 1959), pp. 262–91. Also Robert E. Asher, "Economic Cooperation Under UN Auspices," *International Organization,* Summer, 1958, pp. 288–302.

the onset of the cold war. Hopes for the establishment of an institution to stimulate the removal of trade barriers on a worldwide basis could not be realized without a change of heart in the United States Senate, for its consent to the International Trade Organization treaty was necessary. The Senate repeatedly failed to approve it, and thus this organization never came into being. Meanwhile a more modest effort supported by an impressively small organization began to fill its place, the General Agreement on Tariffs and Trade. In spite of its name, GATT is a rather formless organization with "members," not merely an agreement with "signatories." The basic GATT agreement is almost continuously being revised through very intricate simultaneous bilateral and multilateral negotiations among the members. (The "Kennedy Round" which began in 1963 is the sixth general set of negotiations among more than fifty states.) Each state bargains with all the others through GATT for tariff concessions. They also set rules for trade with each other that are intended to liberalize the interchange of goods. The most-favored-nation principle is the cornerstone. The rules are flexible, and a system has gradually been evolved to settle grievances and make recommendations regarding their application.[20] GATT also provides a convenient forum for consultation on trade problems and development of new policy, including special difficulties presented by trade in agricultural products and the trade requirements of underdeveloped countries.

All these organizations are global, not only in the problems they deal with but also because their membership is not restricted to a particular region; yet none of them has a membership as numerous as the United Nations itself, since the Communist-bloc countries almost without exception do not belong. (Czechoslovakia and Cuba joined GATT before entering the Communist bloc. Czechoslovakia was ousted from the Fund in 1954 for failure to conform to the rules.) Some of the members of the economic organizations do not belong to the UN, as for example, West Germany, South Korea, and South Vietnam. The Bank and the Fund have somewhat more than one hundred and GATT about sixty members, and with the growth of membership they have had to alter the way they function.

The work of the Bank and the Fund includes action programs as well as mediation and the making and applying of rules. GATT, which has no resources to allocate, is confined to the latter functions; at an earlier stage at least, it constituted what some have called "the world's conscience" in the field of trade. However, all these agencies depend in the last analysis upon the action of the member states. Like the technical commissions organized under ECOSOC, these agencies employ methods based on exchanging information and making analyses, setting international standards, illuminating and narrowing issues, and providing training and advisory services. Unlike a number of other kinds of UN agencies, they have functioned effectively outside the glare of public attention; this has permitted expert to deal with

[20] See Richard N. Gardner, "GATT and the U.N. Conference on Trade and Development," *International Organization,* Autumn, 1964, pp. 685–96.

expert in a relatively non-political atmosphere, informally and with the emphasis on accommodation.

The Bank and the Fund are formally but loosely tied in to the United Nations through contractual agreements regulating their relationship and are subject to some rather vaguely defined supervision by the coordinating ECOSOC, but the weight of decision-making is distinctly in them. Although the Bank and the Fund have governing boards composed of a representative from each member, the day-to-day work is supervised by executive boards of fourteen directors plus the President (Bank) or Managing Director (Fund). Voting arrangements are distinctive because they give those with the heaviest involvement a large share in a weighted vote; in other more informal but more influential ways the heavily involved members dominate the organization.[21] GATT has practically no organization at all: a very small staff (about one hundred) plus occasional conferences and committee meetings of the members. Each agency maintains special relationships with other international economic organizations having related interests, including the European Common Market and the OECD.

Like the economic agencies just discussed, the Organization for Economic Cooperation and Development has developed in pragmatic fashion and represents another kind of connection across state boundaries among national governmental officials at the operating level. It grew out of the Organization for European Economic Cooperation, set up to enable the recipients of Marshall Plan aid to cooperate for European recovery. The members having reached this goal, other tasks then became evident, most of them economic but some also political. The European Common Market was established by six of the members in 1957; it was followed by a British-led counterpart among the "Outer Seven" the European Free Trade Association (EFTA) in 1959. Rivalry between the two groups seemed to some interested observers a danger to Europan solidarity. Meanwhile, there was an enormous job to be done in helping underdeveloped countries, a task assumed on a large scale in the 1950s only by the United States. By the end of the decade the American economy was in some ways less flourishing than that of some European countries. Furthermore, the "dollar gap" had disappeared, and instead the Americans were experiencing what was to some a frightening "gold drain." Neither the United States nor Canada belonged to the OEEC, although they sent observers to many of its meetings. By 1960 a Western or Atlantic rather than purely European approach seemed desirable to tackle problems which all the countries in the larger area had in common.

Thus on American initiative a new organization, the OECD, was formed

---

[21] In recent years such advances in cooperation have taken place that a question seldom goes to a vote in the Fund [*Economist,* October 5, 1963, p. 58]. For an illuminating discussion of the political process in this agency, see Ervin P. Hexner, "The Executive Board of the I.M.F.," *International Organization,* Winter, 1964, pp. 74–96.

in 1961; it includes eighteen European countries, the United States, Canada and Japan. With a careful eye on the United States Senate, the American negotiators succeeded in persuading their potential partners to deemphasize the tariff bargaining aspects. They concentrated instead on coordinating (and increasing) aid to underdeveloped countries and on cooperating in suitable ways to build up their own economies. Nevertheless, an interest in the expansion of world trade for the benefit of all was clearly in evidence in the working out of the organization; it appears in Article I of the establishing treaty. A special advantage envisaged for the OECD was that members could combine subjects ordinarily divided in most governments and between different international agencies, such as the problem of economic growth.[22]

In deference to the non-NATO members the words "Atlantic" or "Western" were not used. The general emphasis was on the harmonizing of economic policies among highly industralized (and therefore wealthy) countries and the improvement of their help to the non-industrialized countries, a North-South rather than an East-West relationship. For certain purposes Japan, Yugoslavia, and Finland participated, and Japan eventually became a member.

Expanding on a practice already developed by OEEC, almost all the numerous committees which work on various problems of economic cooperation have come to use the confrontation technique. It is of great importance in one of these, the Development Assistance Committee (which antedates the OECD); another in which it is used is the Economic Policy Committee; and a third is the Scientific and Technical Personnel Committee. These confrontation procedures are similar to those used in the Annual Review in NATO and require inter alia an official who is responsible for formulating in his own country a particular kind of policy in the economic field at home to come face to face with his counterpart in the other member countries. Thus he must take cognizance of the ideas and suggestions (and criticisms) of the latter. In the formative stages of national policy, the decision-maker is thereby made aware of an international concern. OECD has no funds of its own for development purposes. However, a Development Center under its auspices trains officials in aspects of economic development for non-industrialized countries and undertakes research in this field. In this same area, ad hoc coordinating teams of small groups from the Development Assistance Committee investigate the needs of particular recipient countries. This Committee also illustrates how the OECD has helped to close the gap between a government's recognition of principles of developing aid and actual operating programs to implement the principles.

The exchange of information and the preparation of statistical reports (which in turn means standardization of terms and techniques for reporting)

[22] Besides the penetrating analysis of the OECD by Henry G. Aubrey already cited, see OEEC, *The Organization for Economic Cooperation and Development* (Paris: OEEC, 1960), and Richard P. Stebbins, *The United States in World Affairs, 1961* (New York, Random House, 1962), pp. 128, 135–36, and 149–52.

are other ways in which OECD carries on its work. It also has adopted a Code of Liberalization of Capital Movements. An illuminating example of its methods is "Working Party Three" on monetary policy, composed of members whose currencies are of vital significance in world markets. These officials (one is the Under Secretary of the United States Treasury) meet together at roughly six-week intervals. They exchange views on the monetary situation and learn what their counterparts are doing or intend to do in their own countries. They do this on a very informal basis, without the intention of coming to an explicit agreement between their governments.

In several formal and informal ways the OECD maintains liaison with other organizations and groups, including GATT, the EEC, and EFTA. The OECD Council may invite non-member governments or organizations to participate in its activities. Trade negotiations are only a peripheral interest in the OECD, which recognizes the primacy of GATT in this field. OECD is smaller, and its more homogeneous membership permits more freedom for discussion than can occur in the much larger, more heterogeneous organizations such as GATT and the International Monetary Fund. However, groups whose formation sprang from OECD discussions may relate their work to other agencies. Thus, the Group of Ten (representatives from the ten leading industrial countries who discuss international liquidity problems) passed some responsibilities on to the Fund in 1964. NATO had already forsworn the kinds of economic activities which the OECD is especially well fitted to perform. The OECD has stayed clear of the controversies between the EEC and the EFTA.

The supreme organ of OECD is a Council on which the member states are represented by the appropriate ministers or, as is more usual, by permanent representatives. A secretariat of about 1,200 handles the huge job of documentation for the many committee meetings which are taking place constantly; some secretariat members also work out proposals for discussion. The Secretary General usually presides at meetings of the Council and may submit proposals to it or to the subordinate organizations. Decisions and recommendations are usually taken by mutual agreement. Abstention does not invalidate such a decision, but only means that it will not apply to the abstaining member. In the committees more informal procedures operate, and reasonable exceptions are made. A distinctive feature of the OEDC is that the participants in a particular activity or decision may be a much smaller number than the whole body, consisting instead of only those members immediately concerned. No matter how the decisions are reached, their implementation remains up to the member governments. They may be legally binding, but depend in the last analysis on the psychological pressure which is presumably generated by close consultation of the responsible officials under OECD auspices.

SOME NOTES ON
BURDEN-SHARING AND
FAIR SHARES

ONE MEASURE of the value Americans put on United States participation in NATO is the "sacrifice" they are prepared to make for NATO purposes. Unfortunately, no single set of figures conveys a clear picture of even the dollar costs involved. For example, there is no widely accepted basis for deciding what part of the defense expenditures of the United States (or any other member) do or do not "serve NATO purposes." We may agree that French military expenditures in Algeria, Portuguese military expenditures in Angola, and American military expenditures in East Asia, whatever their justification, do not relate to the commitment for the defense of the NATO area as that commitment is set forth in the North Atlantic Treaty; but drawing a clear line between costs incurred for the defense of the NATO area and other NATO costs is not possible.

It is also impossible, for those who are concerned lest the United States may be contributing too much (or too little) to the common defense of the NATO area, to find a wholly objective measure of relative sacrifice. Even if one accepts the progressive income tax principle for judging what share of the burden it is "fair" for the United States to bear, he still has to decide how progressive the allocation of sacrifice ought to be.

With these caveats in mind, we may begin by noting how large were the proportions of the gross national product and of total government expenditures which the United States and various other members of NATO have allocated to all defense activities. In 1950, before the defense mobilization occasioned by the Korean War, the proportion of the United States gross national product allocated to military expenditures (5.8 percent) was lower than the corresponding figure for several NATO allies, but the proportion of total national government expenditures allocated to defense (36 percent) was the highest of the NATO members.[1] (The figure for Turkey, not yet a member, was higher.) By the next year the proportion of the United States GNP allocated to defense had risen drastically to 14.1 percent. This figure surpassed that of all other members although for many of them too the proportion of the GNP spent on defense had risen sharply.[2] After 1951 the United States figure continued to be higher than that of any other member, although it gradually declined to close to 8 percent. The comparable figures for a majority of other NATO members have fluctuated but tended to rise after the mid-1950s.[3] These are the kinds of figures often cited to indicate that the United States was bearing by far the largest share of the defense burden of the alliance (and also cited by some to suggest that the others have not been carrying their "fair" shares.

As General Norstad repeatedly pointed out before Congressional committees, the percentage of GNP allocated by a country to defense by itself very inadequately represents the level of sacrifice of that country; it does not indicate what its citizens have done without in order to spend what they have spent on defense. Secretary McNamara pointed out in 1962 that the per capita GNP of even the wealthiest European members was less than half the per capita GNP of the United States.[4]

Although one does not thereby measure the overall American contribution to promoting the common defense of the NATO area, the extent of one form of that contribution, military aid to the European members of NATO, may be expressed as a percentage of the defense expenditures made by these same states out of their own funds. In 1953, the peak year of deliveries of arms and equipment and of provision of training, the dollar costs of United States aid were about 28 percent of the European allies' own expenditures for defense in the NATO area. By 1959 this figure had declined to 7 percent, and after 1959 it dwindled further. (European defense expenditures were more than doubling in the 1950s, while the dollar level of United States military aid was fairly stable until 1960; it then began to decline.) [5] The

[1] Senate Committee on Foreign Relations, *Hearings, Mutual Defense Assistance Program for 1950,* 81st Cong., 2nd sess. (1950), p. 105, provides table. Had it been proportions of total government expenditures at all levels of government that were being compared, the figure for the United States would almost certainly not have been the highest in NATO. Many costs borne by the national governments elsewhere are in the United States assumed by the various state governments.

[2] Senate Committee on Foreign Relations and Committee on Armed Services, *Hearings, Mutual Security Act of 1951,* 82nd Cong., 1st sess. (1951), p. 185, provides table.

[3] House of Representatives Committee on Foreign Affairs, *Hearings, Foreign Assistance Act of 1962,* 87th Cong., 2nd sess. (1962), p. 134, provides table. Further figures given in *idem, Foreign Assistance Act of 1964,* 88th Cong., 2nd sess. (1964), p. 100.

[4] House of Representatives Committee on Foreign Affairs, *Hearings, Foreign Assistance Act of 1962,* 87th Cong., 2nd sess. (1962), pp. 86–87.

[5] Senate Committee on Foreign Relations, *Hearings, Mutual Security Act of 1960,* 86th Cong., 2nd sess. (1960), pp. 101–02; and Secretary of Defense, *Annual*

Comptroller of the Department of Defense has estimated that for every dollar the European allies received from the United States in the period 1949–1960 for military assistance, they themselves spent $7.70 for defense.[6]

These figures on United States military aid somewhat overstate the extent of the American supplement to the defense effort of the European allies, particularly for the West European allies and for the 1960s. The American aid figures include this country's share in the alliance's joint expenditures for infrastructure, mutual weapons development, military headquarters, and the like. With such joint expenditures excluded, the resulting figures portray more exactly the extent of direct military aid to the various European allies; such United States military aid expenditures in 1960 were about 4 percent of the defense expenditures incurred by the European allies.[7] The United States share of infrastructure costs has dropped by stages from well over 40 percent to about 30 percent.[8] For military headquarters the percentage has been less. For mutual weapons development and similar projects, where the sharing is decided item-by-item, the United States has in no case paid more than 50 percent.[9]

In the early days of the Mutual Defense Assistance Program the giant share (79 percent in 1950) went to Europe. Europe's share was sharply reduced in the mid-1950s but increased in later years as costly "modern" equipment was provided to NATO allies.[10] Thus, about half of the United States military aid for Europe in the FY 1960 budget was to improve NATO's air defense capability.[11] In 1962 Europe received about one-third of the total funds appropriated for foreign military assistance, if one includes the large allocation for aid to Greece and Turkey.[12] (The figure cited for

---

Report, July 1958 to June, 1959, p. 85; and Department of Defense, *Proposed Mutual Defense and Development Programs FY 1966* (Washington: Government Printing Office, 1965), p. 196.

[6] Senate Committee on Appropriations, *Hearings, Foreign Assistance Appropriations for 1962,* 87th Cong., 1st sess. (1961), p. 151.

[7] House of Representatives Committee on Appropriations, *Hearings, Mutual Security Appropriations for 1961,* 86th Cong., 2nd sess. (1960), pp. 481–82 and 2405–09.

[8] *New York Times,* March 1, 1961; Senate Committee on Appropriations, *Hearings, Foreign Assistance Appropriations for 1962,* 87th Cong., 1st sess. (1961), p. 460. By 1964 the United States share for infrastructure and military headquarters was $60,000,000 [House of Representatives Committee on Foreign Affairs, *Hearings, Foreign Assistance Act of 1963,* 88th Cong., 1st sess. (1963), p. 14].

[9] House of Representatives Committee on Foreign Affairs, *Hearings, Mutual Security Act of 1959,* 86th Cong., 1st sess. (1959), p. 145; House of Representatives Committee on Appropriations, *Hearings, Mutual Security Appropriations for 1961,* 86th Cong., 2nd sess. (1960), p. 2565.

[10] House of Representatives Committee on Foreign Affairs, *Hearings, Mutual Security Act of 1957,* 85th Cong., 1st sess. (1957), pp. 658 and 670, provides figures.

[11] Senate Committee on Foreign Relations, *Hearings, Mutual Security Act of 1960,* 86th Cong., 2nd sess. (1960), p. 194.

[12] House of Representatives Committee on Foreign Affairs, *Hearings, Foreign Assistance Act of 1962,* 87th Cong., 2nd sess. (1962), p. 71, provides table.

1950 does not include aid to those two countries.) If one excludes aid to Greece and Turkey, about 40 percent of the total budgeted for 1962 was to be spent on the joint expenditures described in the preceding paragraph, often referred to as "area" or "multilateral" activities which are of benefit to the whole region and alliance.[13] In succeeding years, direct military assistance to NATO allies in Western Europe almost ceased; and the two categories, aid to Greece and Turkey and "area" expenditures, account for almost all military assistance funds spent for NATO purposes.

A very different way of measuring the extent of United States military aid to Europe is to express the funds budgeted for military aid to Europe as a percentage of the total United States defense budget. For 1961, this figure, which has since declined further, was already less than one percent.[14]

For SEATO's military headquarters the United States has contributed 25 percent, and the next highest contributor, the United Kingdom, 16 percent.[15] One should note that only a little over $1 million per year has been available to the SEATO permanent organization.[16]

The United States pays for about two-thirds of the OAS regular budgets, the annual total of which is roughly $15 million, but it has also provided special contributions. Beyond a certain point the United States cannot go, despite the slender resources of the other twenty members, lest the multilateral character of the program disappear.[17]

In OECD and GATT organizational expenses are small. The effectiveness of neither organization depends upon extensive financial support. The United States contributions to OECD and GATT in 1963 were roughly $2.5 million and $200,000 respectively. (The administrative costs of the Bank and the Fund are greater, and the United States contributes several million dollars annually to each.) [18]

Various standards of ability to pay have been used in the economic organizations to describe each member's share of the costs of membership. In the OECD, for example, budget shares are based upon a scale derived from each

[13] Senate Committee on Foreign Relations, *Hearings, Foreign Assistance Act of 1962,* 87th Cong., 2nd sess. (1962), p. 270, gives figures.

[14] Senate Committee on Foreign Relations, *Hearings, International Development and Security,* 87th Cong., 1st sess. (1961), p. 687.

[15] House of Representatives Committee on Foreign Affairs, *Hearings, Mutual Security Act of 1959,* 86th Cong., 1st sess. (1959), p. 150, gives shares.

[16] George Modelski (ed.), *SEATO: Six Studies* (Melbourne: F. W. Cheshire, 1962), p. 25. The United States does make other contributions to SEATO activities of about one million dollars per year. It also contributes to the Secretariat of CENTO, although not a member [House of Representatives Committee on Foreign Affairs, *Hearings, Foreign Assistance Act of 1963,* 88th Cong., 1st sess. (1963), pp. 545–46].

[17] John C. Dreier, *The Organization of American States and the Hemisphere Crisis* (New York: Harper and Row, 1962), pp. 116–19.

[18] House of Representatives Committee on Foreign Affairs, *Hearings, Foreign Assistance Act of 1963,* 88th Cong., 1st sess. (1963), pp. 545–50, contains extensive tables of contributions to international organizations.

member's per capita GNP; the United States contributes 25 percent.[19] Equivalent formulas may be agreed upon in regional security organizations for administrative costs and infrastructure expenditures, but these costs are only a tiny fraction of the total contribution of the members to the costs of collective defense. By far the larger part is made by each member as it separately determines what it calculates that it is committed or impelled or able to spend. For this there is no agreed formula capable of objective application. The size of a member's contribution to the common defense reflects various political and social, and international and domestic factors in addition to its ability to contribute. The indispensability of the organization to the member and of the member to the organization, credit given or claimed for non-monetary types of contribution, and the competing demands on a member government by its own citizens all influence the size of the contribution actually made.

[19] House of Representatives Committee on Foreign Affairs, *Hearings, Foreign Assistance Act of 1964*, 88th Cong., 2nd sess. (1964), p. 677.

INDEX: AUTHORS

INDEX: SUBJECTS